DEEPLY INTO THE BONE

DEEPLY INTO THE BONE

RE-INVENTING RITES OF PASSAGE

Ronald L. Grimes

University of California Press

Berkeley   Los Angeles   London

Grateful acknowledgment is made for permission to reproduce the following paintings by Marc Chagall: P. 1, *Temptation* (1912). Saint Louis Art Museum. P. 15, *Pregnant Woman* (1913). Stedelijk Museum, Amsterdam (on loan from the Netherlands Institute for Cultural Heritage). P. 87, *Acrobat* (1914). Oil on brown paper mounted on canvas, 16 3/4 × 13". Albright-Knox Art Gallery, Buffalo, New York, Room of Contemporary Art Fund, 1941. P. 151, *Birthday* (1915). Oil on cardboard, 31 3/4 × 39 1/4" (80.6 × 99.7 cm). The Museum of Modern Art, New York. Acquired through the Lillie P. Bliss Bequest. Photograph © 1999 The Museum of Modern Art, New York. P. 217, *The Bird Wounded by an Arrow* (ca. 1927). Stedelijk Museum, Amsterdam. P. 285, *I and the Village* (1911). Oil on canvas, 6' 3 5/8" × 59 5/8" (192.1 × 151.4 cm). The Museum of Modern Art, New York. Mrs. Simon Guggenheim Fund. Photograph © 1999 The Museum of Modern Art, New York. P. 335, *A Wheatfield on a Summer's Afternoon* decor for *Aleko* (Scene III) (1942). Gouache, watercolor, wash, brush and pencil on paper, 15 1/4 × 22 1/2" (38.7 × 57.1 cm). The Museum of Modern Art, New York. Acquired through the Lillie P. Bliss Bequest. Photograph © 1999 The Museum of Modern Art, New York.

University of California Press
Berkeley and Los Angeles, California

University of California Press, Ltd.
London, England

First paperback printing 2002

Library of Congress Cataloging-in-Publication Data

Grimes, Ronald L., 1943–.
Deeply into the bone : re-inventing rites of passage / Ronald L. Grimes.
    p.   cm.—(Life passages)
    Includes bibliographical references and index.
    ISBN 978-0-520-23675-2 (pbk. : alk. paper)
    1. Rites and ceremonies.   2. Life change events—Religious aspects.   I. Title.   II. Series.
BL600.G745 2000
291.3'8—dc21   99-053678
                                                     Rev.

Manufactured in the United States of America

11   10   09   08   07   06
10   9   8   7   6   5   4   3

The paper used in this publication meets the minimum requirements of ANSI/NISO Z39.48-1992 (R 1997) (*Permanence of Paper*). ∞

CONTENTS

Numerous people took risks by telling candid stories about their passages. Since their identities are revealed as the book unfolds, I will not name them here, but I thank them profusely. Without their courage, this book could not have been written.

I am most appreciative of those scholars who read and commented on the manuscript that eventually became this book. Robbie Davis-Floyd, Madeline Duntley, Lawrence Hoffman, and Robert Kastenbaum helped me discern the difference between the forest and the trees. I thank Doug Abrams Arava, Jan Spauschus Johnson, Mimi Kusch, and Reed Malcolm for their finely tuned editorial work on the manuscript for this book. The students and teaching assistant in my Rites of Passage course of 1998 helped make the book more accessible.

My thanks also go to Norma E. Cantú for permission to quote from her unpublished article on *quinceañera,* to Ghada Elturk of the Boulder Public Library for her help in locating resources on the same topic, and to Harold Remus for responding to queries about rites of passage in the ancient Mediterranean world.

Wilfrid Laurier University awarded me a year as University Research Professor. I am grateful for both the time and this expression of my colleagues' confidence in my research. Without such generous support, this book would have taken a decade to write.

As always, Susan Scott's reading was finely nuanced; it enabled me to undertake the most pervasive and self-searching revisions.

Rough Passages,
Reinvented Rites

Within a few months of one another, four different women asked me if I knew of any rites they could use to celebrate menopause; an actor from Los Angeles requested some examples of birth and naming ceremonies; three students asked if I could recommend a reliable, cross-cultural book on weddings; and four film companies asked for advice on documenting rites of passage.

Not long after finding myself in this thicket of inquiries, a neighbor asked if we could talk about how her family might prepare to initiate their toddler when he reached adolescence. Having read about teenage neo-Nazis in the newspapers, she wanted to spice up his life with celebrative occasions that would make racist rallies and ceremonial hazing less attractive. Today's teenagers, she felt, are without moorings or elders capable of transmitting enduring human values to the young. I admitted that, like her, I was concerned about my children's transition into adulthood: If wise elders don't initiate adolescents, won't adolescents initiate themselves? But who, I mused, will train us uninitiated adults in the art of initiating?

Within a few months, a man who identified himself as an employee of a state legislature said he was involved in a project to introduce rites of passage in that state's public schools; was I interested in consulting on the project? I had to ponder: Would I want public school teachers initiating my school-age children? Did I have confidence that schools could do a better job than churches, synagogues, or temples have done?

Then an inquiry came from the president of a group that assists the terminally ill in ending their own lives. He said he was beset with requests for help in constructing appropriate rites for such an occasion. Some people, he remarked, considered the taking of their own lives a sacred act, but they could find no resources in traditional Christian or Jewish books of worship. Would I assist in constructing such a rite?

On another occasion a group called to ask if I knew of rites that might be adaptable for North American Buddhist children. There are, they complained, few ritual resources in the Tibetan Buddhist tradition that might be used for birth or early childhood celebrations.

Finally, one of my own brothers surprised me with an e-mail message. Had I written my own funeral—he knew I sometimes assigned such tasks to poor, unsuspecting students—and if so, could he read it? Writing his will had set Darrell to contemplating things he could no longer avoid.

What fuels this surge of interest in ritual and this anxiety over passages? Perhaps synagogues, temples, and churches have been slow to revise existing rites and create compelling new ones. Perhaps people sense the need for bodily and collective ways of making meaning. Perhaps we desire personal control of crucial moments such as birth and death, coming of age, and marrying. Perhaps religious authorities and commercial entrepreneurs such as funeral directors and wedding consultants do not know what is best for us.

Whatever the reason, the past two decades have witnessed a resurgence of interest in the construction of rites of passage. The aim of inventing or constructing rites is bold, some might say arrogant. But without constant reinvention, we court disorientation. Without rites that engage our imaginations, communities, and bodies, we lose touch with the rhythms of the human life course, just as we become temporally disoriented without seasonal and commemorative rites that recreate our connections to the natural world and the course of human history.

The question I try to answer in this book is often put to me like this: "I am planning a wedding (or some other rite of passage), but I'm not happy with the traditional ceremonies offered by mainstream religious institutions. Can you give me some ideas about what's done in other cultures or at least suggest some readings that would help?"

The professor's inclination is to deliver a minilecture: "You can't make sense of rites outside their cultural and historical milieu, and, therefore, you shouldn't go around scissoring out parts of a rite for your own private use. Rites belong in their home cultures." Even though I do believe that rites depend on context for meaning, most of us will never live in cultures other than our own. We glean what we can from books, films, and stories, all of which select, summarize, and distort. One danger is that rites encountered in such media will seem like plums for the taking, but cross-cultural learning about ritual does not have to take the form of crass imitation or wholesale importation of other people's rites.

Even though I sometimes deliver the professorial minilecture on understanding rites in their context and insist on studying practices that we cannot translate into action in our own society, I also take practical inquiries seriously. The question, then, is not whether but how inquirers can enrich their own ritual sensibility by attending to rites from places and times other than their own.

Since most of us have little choice but to imagine the rites of others, and since some of us have no rites to call our own, the words *imagining* and *inventing* appear repeatedly in this book.[1] Inventing has a more practical ring, while imagining sounds more spontaneous. When it comes to ritual, inventing is perhaps the more primary notion, since we cannot invent without imagining, but we can imagine without turning what we imagine into an invention. When we invent, we give teeth to what we imagine. Ritual, like art, is a child of imagination, but the ritual imagination requires an invention, a constantly renewed structure, on the basis of which a bodily and communal enactment is possible. Unlike some other forms of creativity, imagining ritually cannot transpire merely "in the head" but is necessarily embodied and social. Furthermore, the imaginative is not the opposite of the real. Rather, imagining is a way of transforming and renewing the real.

We sometimes think of imagining as the act of originating, as coming up with firsts, not poor duplicates. But neither imagining nor inventing is a creation out of nothing. Even if our desire is to create new rites of passage, we do so with the materials at hand, with the stuff of our cultures and traditions. Even if we radically dismember this stuff, we are still dependent upon it. Rites, unlike wheels, survive precisely by being reinvented and reimagined; there is no other option.

Reimagining ritual can be threatening to religious institutions, since, conventionally understood, imagination is about the made up, whereas religion is supposed to be about the given. Although I treat ritual traditions with respect, I challenge them—sometimes directly, sometimes indirectly—by setting an imagined ritual alongside an actual rite. By reimagining, I dance into the abyss that comfortably separates the spiritual from the social scientific, the personal from the scholarly, and the narrative from the analytical.

Although I write on ritual and teach about religion, I am often at a loss to provide quick answers to the questions people ask. Ritual studies scholars are seldom up to the task of advising people on questions of practice; answers to theoretical questions come more readily. Although I have been conducting research on ritual for over twenty-five years, it still seems pretentious to claim expertise on such an ancient and globally varied phenomenon as the rite of passage. Who can hope to become an expert on rites of passage in North America, let alone the world? My only option is to enter the fray, struggling along with others to find more insightful ways of comprehending the great human transitions and reinventing meaningful ways of ritualizing them. I mean to challenge the all-too-comfortable segregation of those who practice ritual from those who think about it.

Deeply into the Bone is about the power of rites, both traditional and invented, to facilitate or obstruct difficult passages in the course of a human life. Not every passage is a rite of passage.[2] We *undergo* passages, but we *enact* rites. Life passages are rough, fraught with spiritual potholes, even mortal dangers. Some passages we know are coming; others happen upon us. Birth, coming of age, marriage, and death are widely anticipated as precarious moments requiring rites for their successful negotiation. But there are other treacherous occasions less regularly handled by ritual means: the start of school, abortion, a serious illness, divorce, job loss, rape, menopause, and retirement. More often than not, these events, especially when they arrive unanticipated, are undergone without benefit of ritual.

Even a single rite of passage can divide a person's life into "before" and "after." An entire system of such rites organizes a life into stages. Some cultures litter the human life course with numerous rites, cairns to keep pilgrims on course; others hardly blaze the trail at all. These ceremonial occasions inscribe images into the memories of participants, and they etch values into the cornerstones of social institutions. Effective rites depend on inheriting, discovering, or inventing value-laden images that are driven deeply, by repeated practice and performance, into the marrow. The images proffered by ineffective rites remain skin-deep.

Passages can be negotiated without the benefit of rites, but in their absence, there is a greater risk of speeding through the dangerous intersections of the human life course. Having skipped over a major passage without being devastated by a major upset, we may prematurely congratulate ourselves on passing through unscathed. In the long haul, however, people often regret their failure to contemplate a birth, celebrate a marriage, mark the arrival of maturity, or enter into the throes of a death. The primary work of a rite of passage is to ensure that we attend to such events fully, which is to say, spiritually, psychologically, and socially. Unattended, a major life passage can become a yawning abyss, draining off psychic energy, engendering social confusion, and twisting the course of the life that follows it. Unattended passages become spiritual sinkholes around which hungry ghosts, those greedy personifications of unfinished business, hover.

The notion of a rite of passage depends on three key ideas: the human life course, the phases of passage, and the experience of ritual transformation. Life-cycle theorists suggest that human lives follow a relatively uniform path. A life proceeds according to a scenario, a stock plot, with enough flexibility to allow for improvisation. The path of human development is intersected by a series of turning points that divide it into predictable phases. Each turning point is both a crisis and an opportunity.

Rites used for negotiating these turns proceed through three phases: separation from the community, transition into an especially formative time and space, and reincorporation back into the community. The effect of ritual passage is to transform both the individuals who undergo them and the communities that design and perpetuate them. Rites of passage change single people into mates, children into adults, childless individuals into parents, living people into ancestors. Rites of passage are stylized and condensed actions intended to acknowledge or effect a transformation. A transformation is not just any sort of change but a momentous metamorphosis, a moment after which one is never again the same.

Classical rites-of-passage theory, first formulated by Arnold van Gennep, invokes spatial metaphors to explain how rites work. According to this theory, a rite of passage is like a domestic threshold or a frontier between two nations. Such places are "neither here nor there" but rather "betwixt and between." Just as a person moving from outside to inside a living room is met with ritualized gestures (handshaking, greeting, or hugging), so one who crosses a national boundary is subjected to passport checking and customs, the required ceremonial gestures. Since the threshold zone is a no-man's-land, it is dangerous, full of symbolic meaning, and guarded. A rite of passage is a set of symbol-laden actions by means of which one passes through a dangerous zone, negotiating it safely and memorably.

Ritual knowledge is rendered unforgettable only if it makes serious demands on individuals and communities, only if it is etched deeply into the marrow of soul and society.[3] A rite of passage is more than a mere moment in which participants get carried away emotionally, only to be returned to their original condition afterward. Witnessing a moving play, attending weekly worship, or experiencing an orgasm can transport us into reverie, but a few days later our commitment needs rekindling. Ritual practices such as daily meditation and weekly worship are responses to recurring needs. These rites move but do not transform.[4] By contrast, when effective rites of passage are enacted, they carry us from here to there in such a way that we are unable to return to square one. To enact any kind of rite is to *per*form, but to enact a rite of passage is also to *trans*form.

Effective ritual knowledge lodges in the bone, in its very marrow. This metaphor first struck me with force while in a discussion with an archaeologist. He was explaining how certain values and social practices can be inferred from ancient bone matter. An archaeologist can deduce from bone composition that the men of a particular society consumed more protein than the women. On the basis of bone size and shape, it may also be evident that in some cultures women habitually carried heavier loads than men. Certain social practices are literally inscribed in the bones. Even though we imagine bone as private, and deeply interior to the individual body, it is also socially formed.

Of course ritual is not really a something that dwells in a literal somewhere. Rites are choreographed actions; they exist in the moments of their enactment and then disappear. When effective, their traces remain—in the heart, in the memory, in the mind, in texts, in photographs, in descriptions, in social values, and in the marrow, the source of our lifeblood.

To speak of meaning as if it resides in the marrow is, of course, to speak ideally, about the way a rite of passage *should* work. As a matter of fact, rites can run shallow or become decadent. We should honor the corpses of dead rites. We can learn much by studying rites that are no longer practiced, especially if we understand why they died.

Rites do not always do what they ought to do. As a result, readers may know as many bad examples of passage as good ones. Rites can not only fail to achieve what they purport to do, they can also become a means of oppression, so we cannot afford to view them through a fuzzy, romanticized lens. If rites drive meaning to the marrow, then the criticism of rites must cut to the bone.

Deeply into the Bone is not a how-to book with step-by-step instructions on how to prepare for an impending birth or assemble a hasty funeral. I have little faith in such books. Like sex manuals, they may satisfy the curious, but the behavior they inspire is wooden. Techniques without understanding, like changed performances without changed attitudes, are more damaging than they are helpful. So my aim is to affect attitudes about ritual. This book articulates a vision and pursues an argument; it is not a value-free compilation of facts. I press readers to be both more imaginative and more critical of rites. By juggling personal accounts, local descriptions, persistent themes, and big questions, I try to lure readers into conversation: Is this how you and yours experience passage? If not, then how?

I walk the thin line that divides popular from academic writing. I take popular writing about ritual more seriously than most scholarly writers do, but I also attend to scholarly writings more seriously than do most popular writers. Popular writing can make ritual seem more wonderfully promising, more completely understood, and more immediately transparent than it really is. Scholarly writing can make ritual seem opaque or boring. I want to avoid both pitfalls by providing a thoughtful, constructive discussion.

My aim is less to convey information about rites of passage in the world's religions and cultures than it is to instigate a conversation in which readers can fruitfully reflect on their own experiences of passage. My goal is to glimpse the variety of ritual practices from such an angle that readers will pause, remember, and reimagine practices that have become staid. If this reimagining precipitates renewed energy and will for actual ritual enactment, all the better.

This book cuts across cultures and religions, and although it addresses Western, especially North American, readers, it privileges no one religion or culture. Often it considers rites that spring up between converging or conflicting traditions. Climatologists were eager to have close-ups of Saturn and Jupiter not only to study those two planets but also to comprehend more fully the earth's climate by using comparative data. We study things distant to understand better things close to home.

Because rites of passage appear around the world and concern deeply human transitions, it is easy to lapse into universal claims: "When there is a death, you should grieve"; "Everyone rejoices at a birth"; "Weddings are dramatizations of love." Universalism allows us to glibly assert that rites everywhere mean the same thing. Reductions to the lowest common denominator are an invitation to stereotyping and pilfering. The point in examining other people's rites is not to steal or even borrow them but to evoke more fruitful thinking about our own.

Seeing the damage done by universalism, scholars sometimes become cautious, restricting their attention to the particulars of a specific region, language, culture, or religious tradition. Localism, the study of the local to the exclusion of the rest of the world, implies that we cannot speak of rites of passage in general but only of specific rites: a Sephardic Jewish wedding between a specific bride and groom in a specific place on a specific day, for example. Rites of passage, after all, happen on specific dates in actual places. Rites do not happen in general but rather among discrete human beings. Rites of passage are ways of embodying meaning, and bodies are doggedly local, rooted in the entangled mess of events we like to call history or society. But the doggedly local focus is too restrictive if it renders cross-cultural or interreligious conversation impossible. If we cannot speak across the barriers of culture and tradition about realities as basic as birth and death, the lack of communication will surely destroy us. I prefer a middle course that tries to respect differences while searching for connections and continuities.

Even though comparative, or cross-cultural, methods are imperfect, we can best make sense of our own ritual dilemmas by setting them alongside those of others—people who, like ourselves, struggle to birth and die, wed and age, with a touch of grace and wisdom. A major risk in taking a global, synthetic approach is that of ripping rites out of context and falsifying them. As a hedge against this temptation, I sometimes hollow out a space in which to pursue a religion, culture, or era in greater detail than a survey would allow. I dwell on a tradition or practice in greater time depth and broader social context. Even so, readers should be warned that no single religion, culture, personality, or historical period can be fully treated in so small a space as this book.

Deeply into the Bone combines narrative with interpretation and evaluation. Each chapter includes stories told by individuals, descriptions of practices from around the world, histories of selected ritual traditions, and reflections that probe taken-for-granted assumptions about ritual. In most cases I consider rites that are either troubled or reinvented.

A commonly held view is that myths explain rites and that rites act out myths. In fact, myths usually complicate rather than explain, and few rites dramatize mythic plots. Some rites do, in fact, act out a myth, but others merely allude to a myth, and still others have no accompanying myths whatsoever. In this book I do not approach ritual by way of *ritual myths* but by calling upon *passage narratives,* accounts told by individuals who narrate their experiences of passage. There is no pretense of universality in these stories. They are idiosyncratic, selected not as representatives of specific traditions, much less of all of humanity, but as engaging stories. They reveal the disappointments and joys of ritual with less artifice and more candor than either myths or how-to and theoretical literature.

Most scholars do not pay much attention to personal narratives about ritual experience. Passage narratives are not easy to find, since the telling and recording of them is a recent and largely Western phenomenon. In addition, some theorists consider an individual's intentions, stories, and experiences irrelevant to ritual.[5] The intentions of a rite, they suggest, are stipulated, prescribed by others, so personal intentions do not matter. This presumed separation of personal intention from ritual performance, such theorists claim, is what makes ritual distinctive. If personal intentions do not matter, then neither do first-person stories about ritual experience.

Yet I believe that there is no good reason to exclude ritual narratives, especially when participants themselves tell autobiographical stories as a way of making sense of a rite.[6] It would be poor scholarship to overlook such data. Since people tell personal stories about passages, their accounts constitute a legitimate part of the meaning of the rites. Stories about passage are not mere reminiscences. Sometimes the telling and retelling become extensions of the rite itself, stretching it from the original performance in the past until it touches and transforms the present. On the one hand, narratives can render rites even more meaningful than they were in the actual moment of their performance. On the other, they can downplay a rite's original significance. A nephew's story may enhance the meaning of a favorite uncle's funeral, making it more real in the telling than it was in the acting. A divorcée, in talking with her new boyfriend, may downplay the significance of her wedding ceremony. Although the nephew's story amplifies the rite's importance and the divorcée's story diminishes it, both extend the meaning and effect of the rite beyond its brief, original enactment.

Births and initiations, like weddings and funerals, are moments of truth, but they are also moments of pretense, occasions upon which people put on their best faces. Scrubbed or painted faces can mask disagreements and power plays. Rites of passage can be rife with face-saving, posturing, and empty decorum. Things are supposed to go smoothly—no birth defects, no stained wedding garments, no arguments at funerals—but, as anyone involved with the planning of these occasions knows, there is always something going on behind the scenes. Someone is jealous of another's position in the limelight; Dad really wanted a boy; the brothers are fighting over the parental estate; a secret infidelity in an upstairs bedroom mars a "perfect" wedding. The weddings that open both *The Godfather* and *Deer Hunter,* with the violence and abuse lurking in the backgrounds of the performances, are apt illustrations of this point. Rites of passage can seem perfectly magical—but only if you keep your eyes and ears trained on what transpires center stage. Backstage, there often seethes a morass of spiritual stress and social conflict.

One redeeming feature of troubled births, dubious initiations, and awkward weddings is that they make compelling stories. Almost everyone can spin a yarn about a sullied wedding or a dreary funeral, not just because there is no such thing as a perfect wedding or a flawless funeral but also because birthing, aging, marrying, and dying lure out all the skeletons that respectable families keep stashed in their closets. Abstract descriptions of rites are desiccated. Because they lack trouble, they also lack life. Passage becomes interesting when the pageantry of ceremonial display is transparent to the human social drama that runs behind its screen.

In *Nice Families Don't,* Robert Munch, author of many fine children's books, stages the appearance of an ugly, green fart just when a "nice" family most wants it believed that the air in their house is clean and clear. The kids know—and tell—the truth. The truth is that nice families *do* blow the cover of decorum, even on sacred occasions. They fight at funerals, trivialize their adolescents' coming of age, compete at weddings, and secretly regret births. Even in nice families—*especially* in nice families—crude, embarrassing, and even tragic shadows lurk behind the squeaky-clean faces that most rites of passage call for.

Because life passages can be threatening, they beg for humor. In the county where I live, farm people do not use the phrase "rites of passage"; rather, they joke about "hatching, matching, and dispatching." They know that the most troubling occasions are also the most human and in need of levity.

To some ears, ritual *creativity* or *invention* sound like oxymoron, like "a green thought," for instance. From this point of view rites are traditional and conventional, not created or invented. It is true that *creativity,* and its partner, *imagination,* do come with some heavy baggage. These words can sound romantic and individualistic. To call people creative or imaginative is to render them godlike or childlike. But imagination is not the purview of geniuses or creativity the work of individuals disconnected from their histories and societies.

Rites are not givens; they are hand-me-downs, quilts we continue to patch. Whether we call this activity ritual creativity, ritual invention, ritualizing, ritual making, or ritual revision does not matter as much as recognizing that rites change, that they are also flowing processes, not just rigid structures or momentary events.

In my own fieldwork, I encounter two models for ritual creativity. One I call the ritual plumber's model. Something is broken—it won't flush—so you fix it. The birthday party worked last time—the kids loved the cake and candles—so don't fix it. The plumber's model of ritual creativity is practical and free of high-flown expectations. Ritual plumbers are not enamored of the rhetoric of art. They feel more comfortable with the notion of inventiveness than with the boastful-sounding idea of creativity. Someone needs a divorce rite? Well, you sit down with a couple and find out what needs doing. Then you build, borrow, or buy some scaffolding that will contain the process, and you string cord across it from here to there. You hang it with a few buckets capped with spill-proof lids, and there you have it—a crude but perfectly workable tool that will do the work of splitting up the couple forever.[7]

The other model is that of the ritual "diviner."[8] Circumspection and allusion are of the essence to this model. Yes, you want results, but you know that too conscious a fixation on them will get you the opposite—some contrived, self-conscious piece of bad poetry. So you wait, attend, contemplate, watch, see what emerges. You follow impulses like a scout sniffing the wind. You watch for a raised eyebrow, a hesitation, a sneeze that has the ring of a song. Attuned, you snatch it deftly and edit it minimally. Your aim is to find, "to divine," the right tone, which, when struck, will cause the thing (this moribund marriage we are using as an example) simply to shatter like glass or explode into dust that the breezes can carry to the four corners of the world.

The plumber's model and the diviner's model can be used to describe groups as well. Ritual plumbers are, for instance, a committee commissioned to revise a liturgy. They count the cost of making changes, and they develop tools for doing specific jobs. They consult their manuals about procedures they may have forgotten. They vote on changes. The majority rules. Thus it is that the prayer book or oral tradition or ritual text is different now than it was a decade ago.

When a group of ritual diviners meets, it has to await revelation, the moving of the spirit. Perhaps this revelation comes directly from some holy source, is mediated in trance, or is read from cast bones. However the divined rite arrives, something about the process is not completely subject to the control exercised by those who invent new rites or fix up old ones. For ritual diviners, emergent ritual is not "made," much less "made up," so diviners are circumspect, shy about the notion of inventing or revising rites.

Someone has to mop the floor after a wedding, just as someone has to climb the mountain or descend to the depths. Without both maintenance and mystery, the celebration cannot go on. These two processes can be linked to social roles—beadle and prophet, religious bureaucrat and charismatic leader—but they are also kinds of ritual work. Of course, I am speaking like a ritual plumber now: Ritual "works" or is "work." But ritual diviners know that the divine appears in ordinary guise—as a plumber or village idiot or beggar or thunder across a mountaintop. Without a serious commitment to both the nuts and bolts of ritual, and without a devotion to the mysterious breath of its life, rites of passage flounder.

To answer the most basic question, Why enact rites at all? ritual plumbers and ritual diviners have no choice but to collaborate in formulating a response: "Ritual is one of the oldest forms of human activity we know. It may have been the original multimedia performance—an archaic, unifying activity. It not only integrated storytelling, dance, and performance, but it also provided the matrix out of which other cultural activities such as art, medicine, and education gradually emerged, differentiating themselves from one another."

Today ritual helps integrate and attune life on an increasingly globalized planet. There is a growing suspicion that the so-called Western way of life has reached a precipice. In a few hundred short years it has done untold damage to the planet and to indigenous peoples. Extraordinarily long-lived cultures such as the Hopi and the !Kung have an enduring commitment to ritual. Ritual is their way of attuning themselves to one another and to the land; ritual is their means of maintaining a sustainable culture. "Their" ritual practices may, in the long run, be more practical than "our" practicality. Psychologists and anthropologists are suggesting that the "spiritual technology" of ritual has survival value for the human species as well as beneficial ecological consequences.[9] If we do not birth and die ritually, we will do so technologically, inscribing technocratic values in our very bones. Technology without ritual (or worse, technology *as* ritual) easily degenerates into knowledge without respect. And knowledge without respect is a formula for planetary annihilation. It matters greatly not only *that* we birth and die but *how* we birth and die.

CHAPTER I

Celebrating New Life,
Ritually Nurturing the Young

When people want to marry, they plan a wedding. A ceremony for an adolescent coming of age is called an initiation. When someone dies, the community says good-bye with a funeral. But when a mother gives birth, what do we call the accompanying rite? There is no word in English for a ceremony that might mark the event. Our only choice is the generic term *birth rite*. The absence of a more specific term should warn us: Birth is the least ritualized of the great human transitions. If the literature on the topic is any indication, then births are less often and less elaborately ritualized than coming of age, marrying, or dying. It is something of a cruel irony that the "curse" of death receives more ritual attention than the "gift" of life.

Birth is a *passage* of utmost human importance, but a birth is not necessarily a *rite* of passage. When we fail to wrap newborn children and their newborn parents in a blanket of powerful symbols, clichéd images soon fill the void: She's bearing down, having been ordered to push. The camera, located just beyond her feet, captures her grimacing face; her knees are spread apart and draped discreetly with a pale green sheet. We are not privy to the action below; that's private. Only the medical priesthood is authorized to peer into the holy of holies. The husband keeps his distance. In deference to the physician, the camera now shifts slightly. The doctor, usually male, edges into the picture. A nurse, always female, hovers in the background, the father peering out from behind her. One more groan, a final breath-holding pause, then the telltale cry, as the camera cuts to the doctor, now lifting up a perfectly formed child like a trophy. The mother breaks into tears of joy as the doctor hands her the baby. The new mother gazes lovingly at her husband, having produced a wonderful gift for him. For a brief moment the child *belongs to* her, but it is *for* him. Shortly both will have to give up control of the child, as the nurse spirits it away down the hall. Mom needs her rest, and Dad has to return to work, where his coworkers will congratulate him with slaps on the back, perhaps even a cigar.

If we do not have birth rites, we certainly have ritualized birth scenes. We know how they are supposed to go; they follow a prescribed order so sacred that it permits only minor variations. Our expectations of a successful birth are generic and heavily scripted. The script is so deeply inscribed that it seems to be no script at all. The choreography of birth seems so natural that a birth rite would disrupt the real, which is to say, the biomedical, work of birth.

Myriel Ekamp's brief story illustrates the point:

> At the birth of my second son, Colin, my doctor asked if he might say a prayer of blessing for our child and of thanksgiving for his safe delivery. My husband and I were taken aback. We had not expected this conjunction of science and religion in a twentieth-century hospital. We said yes, and the doctor spoke a brief prayer aloud.
>
> I have come over the years to attach increasing significance to that doctor's simple ritual. For no logical reason and certainly through no particular manifestation of Colin's character, I have come to regard Colin in my heart as the "child who is blessed," rather like some reluctant prophet in scripture. . . .
>
> This story is the only story I have that celebrates my giving birth as a sacred event in its own right. It is the only story I have for Colin that locates him, however remotely, in a sacred landscape. There are few events which evoke . . . "the ache of existence" more than the birth of a child.[10]

The doctor in this narrative surprises us. Initially cast in Myriel's mind as a scientist, he uncharacteristically performs a priestly or pastoral act. By itself, neither the medical nor the religious action is unorthodox. Doctors, after all, may pray—though not in spaces defined as scientific sanctuaries. The doctor violates a professional taboo that would keep scientific work pure, untainted by ritual. It is permissible to pray and fine to doctor, as long as you separate the two actions, performing them in two different places. Differentiating medicine and ritual into discretely cordoned-off sectors is a primary tenet of the dominant Western worldview. In this view prayer is not a legitimate medical procedure any more than the behavior of physicians is ritualistic.

Fortunately, the doctor's transgression is cushioned by his permission asking as well as by the birthing mother's religious commitments. Her expectations differ from his, but her values do not. Even though the doctor's praying and blessing constitute a kind of guerrilla rite that surprises her, Myriel does not feel violated. In fact, she later experiences the doctor's superimposed actions as a gift. A mere liturgical fragment, the prayer continues its attitude-shaping work long after its utterance has ended. His small act has big consequences: Colin becomes a blessed child. Although the doctor's action has an effect, it is culturally anomalous, out of place. In the sterilized atmosphere of this sanctuary of technology, overt ritual acts would seem to defy rather than to complement the space. Importing ritual to the birth room makes about as much sense as offering ceremonial apologies to animals used in laboratory experiments or practicing Tai Chi during coffee breaks at a Ford plant. The rhythms and sensibilities of religious liturgy do not harmonize well with those of industry and technology.

Someone once said to me, "The birth event is so self-evidently sacred that it needs no rite to sanctify it," but the sacrality of events usually attracts rather than repels ritual attention. Birth narratives, especially in contemporary North America, rarely make the sacrality of birth a major theme. Even in home-birth narratives, in which spirituality might emerge without entering into obvious conflict with scientific medicine, ritual is seldom important to the kind of spirituality expressed in these stories.[11]

A friend once jokingly remarked, "After giving birth, mothers are too tired for ritual activity." She was right, but being tired does not prevent participation in initiations, funerals, or weddings. So, however true it is that giving birth takes an enormous amount of time and energy, this fact alone does not account for the scarcity of birth rites in the industrialized West. There are periods before and after a birth when rites could be performed. A birth rite does not have to coincide immediately with the birth event; funerals, after all, never coincide with deaths.

Of course, there is the practical problem that technologically driven hospital birth is so thick with required medical procedures that there is little time for ritual ones. Wherever Western biomedicine is imported, it displaces nonmedical birth practices, including ritual ones. The issue is not the practical one of insufficient time but that ritual occupies only a tenuous place in our worldview, and when it appears to be in conflict with supposedly scientific procedures, ritual must yield to science.

An anthropologist once suggested to me that because of high infant mortality rates (in every century before the present one), tribes and villages were reluctant to spend ritual resources until they were sure a child was going to reach maturity. This is a speculative way of accounting for the sparsity of birth rites, and although there may be some truth to it, more research is needed to demonstrate that truth. One reason to doubt this explanation is that it presupposes a kind of pragmatically driven, cost-benefit analysis that is typical of only a very recent phase in Western history. I suspect that many ritual traditions would continue even in the face of clear economic evidence that the results of rites are not worth the time and energy that people invest in them.

The same anthropologist offered another possibility, namely, that in some societies, a newborn is not regarded as a person. People are made, not born—constructed by social recognition rather than by biological gestation alone. Social recognition of personhood, he said, is conferred by naming or initiation ceremonies rather than by birth rites. It is probably true that as one's standing in the community increases, so does the ritual attention that one receives. Such increased attention is evident in funerals for royalty, for example. It is certainly the case that in some societies humanity is ritually conferred rather than automatic, that personhood is not a mere matter of being born or undergoing biological maturation. However, the dead, who are in the process of becoming ghosts or ancestors, are not quite people either, and they often garner elaborate and sustained ritual attention. So the question, Why does the birth event receive so little ritual attention? remains.

Another possible answer is this: Since birthing is woman's work, and, historically, the work of women has been undervalued, perhaps it should be no surprise that birth is underritualized. If the adult male is construed as the normative human being, it follows that females and children will fail to measure up. Not measuring up, they receive fewer of a society's resources, including its ritual ones. I suspect that if men gave birth, birth rites would be cross-culturally widespread and elaborate.

Both in the West and East, in Christianity and Hinduism, for instance, so-called second, or initiatory, birth is considered more important than first, or biological, birth. This fact may explain the high expenditure of ritual resources on initiation and the stinginess regarding birth. Who benefits from considering biological birth as inferior to spiritual rebirth? Typically, men do, since they become the guardians of initiatory rebirth. We should be wary of ripping ritual rebirth out of the soil of actual childbirth, because the second birth gets its life from actual birth.

Why are birth rites so absent? Could it be that they are so entangled with other cultural processes—medical, customary, and folkloric—that it is difficult or even impossible to distinguish ritual from other kinds of activity? The problem, then, would not be the absence of birth rites but the blindness imposed by our definition of ritual. According to this view, birth is not underritualized; it simply appears under labels other than that of ritual, for example, baby showers, baptisms, and namings. It is true that there are celebrations, birthdays, for example, that mark, but do not coincide with, the event of birth, so the full range of childhood celebrations needs to be identified and studied more carefully. But even when we take into account birthdays and other rites for children, it still seems to me that birth in Europe and North America is not as highly ritualized as weddings or funerals, and that it is not as highly ritualized as initiations are in most other places.

Then again, perhaps it is not birth *rites* that are absent but *descriptions* of birth rites. Birth rites are not only scarce in hospitals and religious institutions, they have also been almost invisible in scholarship as well. Early-twentieth-century ethnographies, the majority written by men, were little concerned with "the first passage." Either the ethnographers did not consider the topic important, or they were denied access to the event. Beginning in the 1970s, under the influence of feminist scholars, birth became a topic in its own right. Works such as Brigitte Jordan's *Birth in Four Cultures* and Sheila Kitzinger's *Women as Mothers: How They See Themselves in Different Cultures* facilitated a comparative study of birth in its folk as well as its biomedical forms. Now a growing body of literature, a mix of scholarly and popular writing, continues to emerge.

Unfortunately, little of it attends to birth ritual. Most contemporary research focuses on either the physiological or the political aspects of birth. Current social scientific research concentrates on such topics as the control of birth, power in decision making, alternative birthing styles, and resistance to biomedical technology. Ritual is seldom taken into account, even by writers studying ritually saturated cultures. Even though the comparatively recent entry of women into ethnographic fieldwork may account for the sparsity of literature on birth (as compared to the other passages), it does not explain the scant attention paid to the ritual aspects of birth. Perhaps contemporary anthropologists do not focus on ritual, or maybe birth rites themselves are rare, small-scale, or too sequestered to be noticed. Although future scholarship may change this impression, the literature does seem to imply that not only are birth rites underdescribed and understudied, they are also less often celebrated and less fully elaborated than the other major rites of passage.

Pulling up My Skin for Laces

Perhaps the problem that I have described with birth ritual has nothing to do with the nature of birth itself or with the way it has been studied but with our understanding of ritual. This view is espoused by Robbie Davis-Floyd, one of the leaders in the movement to put birth on our conceptual map and one of the few scholars to think about it ritually. She urges us to notice what is traditional, even ritualistic, about Western hospital birth.

This is what Elise Pearsal, one of the women in Davis-Floyd's study of American birth, had to say about her experience:

Well, they marched me down the hall to labor and delivery, and I mean, it was—watching these big double doors swing open, it was like walking through the gates of hell. . . .

And then some orderly came at me with a long hook and broke my waters. Apparently, they said, that would help. And I didn't know. I just didn't know. Well, that for me was one of the worst moments of the whole experience. It was like all my hopes and dreams of how it was going to be sort of floated out with the waters. I'll never forget that. It was just an awful feeling. Warm and sad, it was like tears flowing out, you know? And I couldn't walk, I couldn't do anything. I was stuck, you know? By that time, I was totally humiliated. I was incapable of—and then some orderly came in with those electrodes to stick in the baby's scalp—I looked up and saw him come at me with it between my knees. Skip and I both screamed at him that we didn't want that. He looked kind of shocked and went away. That's the one thing we managed to avoid. And I'm proud of that, because it would have hurt my baby. At least I managed to protect her from having that horrible thing screwed into her scalp.

Then the doctor, who was at church, sent word that I would have to have a Cesarean. By then, that sounded like a great idea—Skip and I agreed we would do that. At *least,* we thought, it will get us out of here. We just gave up—we knew we couldn't do it anymore. So they gave me another paracervical, and we all just waited for the doctor to come. And it wore off, and he still didn't come. So I had a whole 'nother hour of contractions, waiting for him, and that was bad, because there was no reason to try anymore.

Then they wheeled me down the hall—I still remember the feel of the wind in my face and impressions of everything passing me by upside down. They did the Cesarean, and it felt like somebody stepping on my stomach with a boot and pulling up my skin for laces. And I was cold, so cold. And my mouth was dry, but they wouldn't give me any ice chips. I begged for ice chips, and they said no. And the anesthesiologist tried to strap my hands down, but I wouldn't let him. That was too much. I still had some dignity left, and I would not let them take it away completely. And so when they handed me the baby, I could hold her right up by the neck. And she was beautiful. She looked just like a little monkey, but she was beautiful. I knew right away that she was mine, completely and totally my baby. . . .

When I was relating to the baby, I was totally happy—I was thrilled with her. But all the rest of the time, I felt so sad—like—gray around the edges. Just sad and gray. And I couldn't really put my finger on why. And ashamed. I felt so ashamed of myself for screaming, and for not being able to do it . . . and then when I realized that I probably hadn't even needed a Cesarean, I started to realize that I felt raped, and violated somehow, in some really fundamental way. And then I got angry.[12]

Waves of emotion course through Elise's birth story, drawing us into her shame and anger, making us want to fight or flee. But Elise herself keeps returning to her experience, as one does to a trauma, first trying to justify it, then trying to understand it. In a part of the story not told here, she compares her birth experience with that of a friend who underwent protracted labor but did not resort to a Cesarean. This comparison made her feel shame. Eventually, by comparing her experience to others' and by reading, Elise worked through her shame to anger and then from anger to understanding and critique.

Readers may not consider this an account of a ritualized birth, even though Elsie's reference to the double doors as the gates of hell evokes Dante's descent and its mythic framework. Her experience of a Cesarean delivery also suggests the story of Persephone's rape. And the conclusion might also remind one of the Callisto myth, a story about initiation by rape.[13] But the mythic allusions, intended or not, are not enough to lead most of us to consider hospital birth as anything but a technical, scientific procedure. By dictionary definitions of ritual, a Cesarean section is not a ritual enactment.

In *Birth As an American Rite of Passage*, Robbie Davis-Floyd studies the birth experiences of one hundred American women. Her argument, that hospital birth is a technocratic rite, is provocative. Hospital birthing procedures, she says, are not merely *like* ritual, they *are* ritual.[14] Contrary to those who claim that we have no birth rites, Davis-Floyd argues that we have a very powerful one. The procedures of hospital delivery, she says, are not merely scientific but also symbolic, rendering birth one of the most powerful ritual acts in contemporary Western culture. Because of their redundancy, rhythm, intensity, and cognitive impact, birth procedures are rites that inscribe the values of a technological culture into the bodies of birthing women and their newborns. "By making the naturally transformative process of birth into a cultural rite of passage for the mother," says Davis-Floyd, "a society can take advantage of her extreme openness to ensure that she will be imprinted with its most basic notions."[15]

In reflecting on Elise's story, Davis-Floyd shows how one cognitive matrix, either holistic or natural, can be overwhelmed by a technocratic one. A belief in the sufficiency of nature can be displaced by a ritual message proclaiming the supremacy of technology. Technocracy is a system of hierarchical values that, by the strength of its metaphors, construes the body as a machine and doctors as technicians. In this worldview, the birth process is akin to a factory production. Because defects are supposedly inherent in the female body-machine, at any moment something can go wrong and need "fixing."

The mother is acted on in assembly-line fashion. From the moment she is rolled down the hall in a wheelchair, then hooked up to the electronic fetal monitor, to the moment she is told to push, a mother is the object of ritual actions that stamp messages deeply into her psyche by way of her body—very intimate and vulnerable parts of it.

Davis-Floyd does not believe that women are merely passive recipients of these actions. She maintains that they often actively choose a medicalized birth to gain a sense of control over what they perceive as a potentially dangerous and out-of-control process. Even so, such a birthing system exerts pressures that curb a birthing mother's ability to perform autonomously, argues Davis-Floyd.

"I felt I was in a drama, a play, and that everyone else knew their lines. I was like a last-minute replacement actor who had not seen the script beforehand or had the time to memorize my lines. I was forced to improvise and made to feel foolish—as if I were missing my cues and getting my lines wrong."[16] This confession by a friend recalls Carol Laderman's comment: "American women are delivered by obstetricians; Malay women give birth."[17] A birthing mother in a North American hospital, unlike her Malay counterpart, is not the lead actor or director of a cultural drama. Rather, she plays the role of an underprepared understudy. Or worse, she becomes a ritual object, the recipient of symbolic manipulations on a clock-driven assembly line supervised by technical wizards. A good birth is one that produces a healthy baby, not necessarily one characterized by a good birthing experience.

Davis-Floyd studies the bewildering array of obstetrical procedures, making explicit the ritual purposes and symbolic messages she believes are encoded in them: Women's bodies are inherently defective; women's bodies are like machines; babies are products; doctors are technicians, and so on. She identifies the psychological effects as well: Women learn to distrust their own instincts, to submit to authority, and to suppress questions. She also marshals evidence that some features of technological birth, such as the lithotomy position (lying on the back with legs open), internal electronic fetal heart monitoring, and excessive episiotomy (surgical widening of the vaginal opening) rates are demonstrably unnecessary or of questionable medical value. Yet medical personnel continue to advocate them even in the face of evidence that they are unnecessary or even harmful. What appear to be scientific procedures are really rituals maintained because medical personnel are habituated to believe their performance will hedge danger and death.

Neither the women who choose to birth in the hospital nor the personnel who work there are to be condemned. After all, 98 percent of American women give birth in hospitals and only 2 percent at home.[18] The target of criticism should not be people but rather a social system and the messages its procedures convey despite people's good intentions. The point is not that technologically managed births are bad, since they are sometimes necessary and sometimes joyful. Rather, the point is to show that birth should not be treated like a kind of illness and to expose the values and meanings of hospital procedures so that patients and parents can question them.

The hospital is not a neutral environment that can be used equally well for technocratic ritualization, on the one hand, and for liturgical celebration on the other. Since the hospital environment is designed specifically to be conducive to technocratic ritual, one has to counter-ritualize, that is, ritualize *against* the dominant symbols of the institution in order to celebrate.

Since we are not used to thinking of the actions of obstetricians and nurses as ritualistic, then what exactly does Davis-Floyd mean by "ritual"? She answers explicitly: "A *ritual* is a patterned, repetitive, and symbolic enactment of a cultural belief or value; its primary purpose is transformation."[19] Whereas the medical profession prefers to define birth biologically and technologically, Davis-Floyd emphasizes its cultural and symbolic dimensions. In doing so, she renders birth less familiar and more akin to the way we have learned to think about the rites of other societies. What Davis-Floyd does with birth in American culture is not very different from what anthropologists do with life-cycle transitions in other cultures: She reads between the lines to infer preconscious, unintended meanings. She pits implied meanings against those verbally espoused by medical personnel, and she considers the psychological effects of procedures, not just the intentions of doctors and nurses. Although Davis-Floyd speaks of birth procedures as "sending symbolic messages," she is clear that these "messages" are not optional "reading" for a mother's leisure time. Rather, the meanings are performed, inscribed in a woman's flesh and psyche; thus, episiotomies and Cesareans appear no less ritualistic than tribal circumcisions and clitoridectomies.

Students in my courses usually polarize when they read *Birth As an American Rite of Passage*. One faction argues that the so-called ritual of hospital birth is purely in the eye of the beholder. "You can't call medical procedures either ritualistic or symbolic unless the people performing them say they are," the anthropology majors argue. "Besides," chime in the philosophy students, "the meanings Davis-Floyd attributes to actions in the hospital are unverifiable. How would she know if those *were not* the meanings of those acts?"

Another group of students is quite moved by Davis-Floyd's perspective. They are not sure it matters whether, by her definition, *most* human activities are seen as ritualistic. This group consists largely, but not exclusively, of religious studies students and of women, some of them anticipating marriage and childbirth. One year this second faction included a young male doctor. He was so struck by the argument that hospital procedures constituted ritual that he declared he was changing some of his practices so they would be less humiliating to birthing mothers.

There is truth in both responses. Although Davis-Floyd's definition of ritual is by no means idiosyncratic—there are reputable definitions as broad as hers—her use of it is provocative.[20] The metaphoric move of construing certain acts as ritual affords a perspective from which criticism is possible. Gaining such a perspective is crucial, since the words and procedures of doctors in Western societies are treated as more sacred than those of clergy. By *sacred* I mean "less open to question, more likely to be regarded as utterly true." Diagnoses have incantatory force. They are often delivered and received as true simply by virtue of being uttered. To think of them as ritual utterances threatens to deprive them of scientific sanctity.

Nevertheless, as helpful as I find Davis-Floyd's perspective, I also stumble over her definition of ritual. According to her definition, what would not be ritual? Attending school, going to work, housecleaning, driving, delivering the mail, and playing basketball could all be construed as rituals. Even taking out the garbage is *repetitive* (Tuesday mornings before 8:00 A.M.), *patterned* (from countertop to under the sink, to bins behind the garage, to street curb—always the same order), *symbolic* of primary Western values (cleanliness, orderliness), and *transformative* (of the landscape). Do we really want to define garbage removal as ritual? I am taking Davis-Floyd's definition to absurd lengths to make the point that nothing in her definition (as distinct from her intention) prevents one from regarding anything and everything as ritual. Her definition leaves us not knowing what to exclude.

Who considers hospital birth ritual? Medical personnel by in large do not, nor do most mothers. Davis-Floyd herself sees obstetrical procedures as ritual. Sometimes the persuasive force of her argument convinces parents and medical practitioners that she is indeed correct. Her argument depends on the metaphor of hospital birth *as* ritual. The metaphor is powerful, and we need to consider it seriously without taking it literally.

Although I have no objection to seeing any activity "as" ritual, it seems to me that housecleaning and hospital birth are not ritualistic in the same way as a Hindu *puja* or Catholic mass is ritual. The difference is not between the irreligious and the religious but between the unintentional and socially unrecognized nature of hospital "ritual," on the one hand, and the intentional, socially recognized nature of temple and church rites on the other. Generally, priests think they are engaged in ritual; generally, physicians deny that they are. So Davis-Floyd is really implying that medical personnel are *unconsciously* performing rites. The difference between conscious and unconscious ritual is subtle but important. Consider this scene:

The focal point of the shrine is a box or chest built into the wall. In this chest are kept the many charms and magical potions without which no native believes he could live. These preparations are secured from a variety of specialized practitioners. The most powerful of these are the medicine men, whose assistance must be rewarded with substantial gifts. However, the medicine men do not provide the curative potions for their clients, but decide what the ingredients should be and then write them down in an ancient and secret language. The writing is understood only by the medicine men and by the herbalists who, for another gift, provide the required charm. . . .

In the hierarchy of magical practitioners, and below the medicine men in prestige, are specialists whose designation is best translated "holy-mouth-men." The Nacirema have an almost pathological horror of and fascination with the mouth, the condition of which is believed to have supernatural influence on all social relationships. Were it not for the rituals of the mouth, they believe that their teeth would fall out, their gums bleed, their jaws shrink, their friends desert them, and their lovers reject them. They also believe that a strong relationship exists between oral and moral characteristics. For example, there is a ritual ablution of the mouth for children which is supposed to improve their moral fiber.

The daily body ritual performed by everyone includes a mouth-rite. Despite the fact that these people are so punctilious about care of the mouth, this rite involves a practice which strikes the uninitiated stranger as revolting. It was reported to me that the ritual consists of inserting a small bundle of hog hairs into the mouth, along with certain magical powders, and then moving the bundle in a highly formalized series of gestures.[21]

This is an excerpt from a wonderfully ironic article called "Body Ritual among the Nacirema." It appeared in *American Anthropologist*, a scholarly journal. Readers with a keen eye may have noticed that Nacirema is "American" spelled backward. Those with even sharper vision may have seen through the description to discover the act of toothbrushing behind it. By referring to bristles as hog hairs, dentists as holy-mouth-men, medical procedures as magical gestures, and medical Latin as an ancient and secret language, Horace Miner lets us see a familiar household routine as ritual. By using the rhetoric of ritual, he renders the familiar strange and the in-house exotic. The effect of the article is twofold. First, the description helps us notice the ritualistic qualities of activities close to home; thus it makes "us" seem more like "them." But the article also warns us that we should be less ready to read as ritual everything we do not understand about another culture.

More is at stake in Miner's article and Davis-Floyd's book than trivial comparisons: Toothbrushing is *like* ritual; giving birth is *like* ritual. We should not let Miner's humor cause us to miss the essential point, namely, that Americans, who like to think of themselves as beyond ritual, are as ritualistic as any other group. He shows that ordinary human actions are characterized by certain qualities that we associate with ritual: repetition, stylization, and the use of special places, times, and objects.

No cultural consensus considers hospital birth, toothbrushing, TV watching, and housecleaning as ritual. Even though few would say these activities *are* ritual, many are capable of seeing them *as* ritual. Ritual, like beauty, is not only "out there" but also in the eye of the beholder. In fact, effectively cultivating a ritual sensibility depends in part on learning to see the ritualization that suffuses ordinary human interaction.

Following Davis-Floyd, I am willing to think of hospital birth *as* ritual provided we signal the metaphoric move we are making by the use of a special term such as *ritualization* rather than *rite*. We need a fuzzy term, one with soft, permeable, even vague boundaries,[22] but we also need a clearer one with hard boundaries. The soft version I call "ritualization"; the hard version, "rite." In performance theory it is common to distinguish *social drama* (the soft, messy stuff of everyday *activity*) from *stage drama* (the more sharply focused, fictional presentations of *acting*). What happens on stage is a transformation and condensation of what happens at home or in the street. In a similar fashion, the unformed, shapeless stuff out of which rites emerge is ritualization, activity that is not culturally defined as ritual but that someone could interpret as if it were.

The presence of one or two qualities such as repetition and symbolization does not make something a rite. A rite emerges from a ritualization process only when a group enhances or amplifies these qualities to the point at which a definitional threshold is crossed. The difference between ritualization and rites may not always be absolutely clear, but it is too important to overlook. Whereas the notion of ritualization invokes metaphor—one "sees" such and such an activity (hospital birth, for instance) "as" ritual—rites of various types are "there." A group consensus recognizes them. As I use it, the term *rite* denotes specific enactments located in concrete times and places. Often they can be named: *puja* (Hindu worship), *bas mitzvah* (the Jewish puberty rite for girls), *kālacakra* (a Tibetan rite of empowerment). The term *rite*, then, refers to a set of actions intentionally practiced and widely recognized by members of a group. Rites are differentiated, even segregated, from ordinary behavior. Often they are classified as "other" than ordinary experience and assigned a place apart from such activities.[23]

In sum, conventional ritual theory demarcated human actions into two distinct kinds: ritualistic (nonutilitarian, expressive) action and nonritualistic (utilitarian, means-end oriented) behavior. Davis-Floyd has countered this overly simplistic split by emphasizing the continuity, rather than the discontinuity, of ritualistic and ordinary acts. Although I doubt that she intends to, her approach implies that every human activity is ritual, that there is no meaningful difference between ritual and nonritual. I have proposed a middle, or transition, category, a limbo zone called ritualization, in which activities are tacitly ritualistic.

A final note about ritual terminology: I use the word *ritualizing* to denote the activity of deliberately cultivating or inventing rites. Ritualizing is more conscious and intentional than ritualization. A family that invents a ceremony to mark a birth is ritualizing. Unlike rites, ritualizing does not typically garner broad social support; it seems too innovative, dangerously creative, and insufficiently traditional. So deliberate ritualizing happens in the margins and is alternately stigmatized and romanticized. Since ritualizing implies the invention of a tradition, it can feel contradictory, because traditions are not supposed to be inventable. Whereas rites depend on institutions and traditions, ritualizing, at least in the European American West, appeals to intuition and imagination. However, when sustained, ritualizing may eventuate in rites, with their own attendant institutions and power struggles.

You Have a Compass within You

While some in the West are worrying about the absence of ritual in birth, elsewhere in the world people are concerned about the disappearance of birth rites, and they are sometimes in conflict with those who consider the persistence of rites a problem. Traditional people, although they may have richer ritual traditions, are no less troubled in their handling of birth than we are. Indigenous people struggle with the problem of clashing religious beliefs and changed social configurations.

The largely rural state of Trengganu is on the east coast of peninsular Malaysia.[24] Because of its piety and traditionalism, the area is sometimes referred to as "the land of believers." The Malays who live there are officially Muslim, but their religion also includes indigenous spirits as well as characters from Hindu shadow plays.

In the village of Merchang, a girl does not become a woman in what Westerners imagine to be the usual way, that is, by undergoing an initiation at the onset of menstruation. No rites mark her transition. Socially, she becomes a woman only by marrying and then giving birth.

Each month, the story goes, blood from the heart drips down through the uterus. Although Jin Tanah, or "earth spirit," loves the sweet blood of parturition, he detests the stench of menstrual blood. So even though a girl is considered taboo during menstruation, no rites are necessary to protect her, because the spirits will keep their distance. During menstruation, a girl cannot engage in daily prayer. The restriction is but one among many of the consequences of Eve's curse, which followed her defiant act of ingesting the poisonous forbidden fruit.

In Merchang, girls are typically married by fifteen and pregnant by sixteen. Malays know well enough that babies are the issue of intercourse, but prenatal development in their part of the world takes a more circuitous route than it does in the West. Fathers become "pregnant," but in their brains. After forty days the child is thrust into the mother's womb. The child inherits its rationality and self-control from the father, its emotions from the mother. In the womb no child is alone; the placenta is its sibling.

In the seventh month of a woman's first pregnancy, the midwife, known as a *bidan,* enacts a ceremony called "rocking the abdomen."[25] The *bidan* rocks the pregnant woman, who is lying down, back and forth using colored cloths tied around her belly. Each rhythmic turn releases her from a spiritual danger. A uterus-shaped coconut is wrapped with a knotted cord and rolled across her distended belly. The expectant mother unties the knots, anticipating a child's successful negotiation of the umbilical cord as it makes its way down the tortuous birth canal.

Later, after birthing, a mother is bathed in lime juice and water to decrease her spiritual heat. The event is not a purely physical one, and the lime juice is not merely a poor substitute for commercially perfumed bath oil. The concoction cools the spirit. In addition, the new mother is presented with yellow rice to enhance her life force and red hard-boiled eggs to signify her successful birthing.

Currently the Malaysian Office of Religious Affairs disapproves of such birth practices, so many of them are rapidly disappearing. Rural Malays who use traditional midwives retain what they consider the crucial traditional elements, although mothers make the trade-offs they feel they must make, substituting Muslim prayers for indigenous ones. Earlier in the twentieth century, prospective fathers, like mothers-to-be, were required to observe ceremonial restrictions: no hair cutting, sitting on the doorstep, or harming living creatures. If a father-to-be shot an animal through the eye, his child would be blind. If a father pulled the leg off a dead animal, his child might be missing a limb. If a thoughtless father sat on a doorstep, he risked blocking the birth canal. Since these things *might* happen, fathers should take precautions.

Badi, evil spirits that reside in human corpses and wild animals, are drawn to anything teeming with life. *Hantu,* disembodied spirits, lurk about pregnant women. "It was the curiosity of the archangel Gabriel that created these spirits. God entrusted the Breath of Life into Gabriel's hands and ordered him to place it near Adam's nostrils so that his still lifeless body might be animated. Gabriel opened his hands before reaching his destination, and the Breath of Life escaped. Having no body to receive it, the Breath became hantu, the disembodied older siblings of humankind. Like all siblings, hantu are sometimes beset with feelings of envy toward their younger brothers, the children of Adam, since humans are beings of the light while spirits must live forever in darkness. And like human siblings, they occasionally find ways to even the score."[26]

There are deformed, bloodsucking demons too. Although female, they are the opposite of what a good Malay mother should be. These demons, like humans, are beset with gaping holes and driven by a craving to fill them. So they threaten the unborn and newly arrived. These demons gobble up fetuses, slurp mothers' milk, and barricade the birth canal.

The midwife, although she performs the necessary physical tasks, also enacts ritual ones. She purifies the atmosphere with incantations: "Hey, I know the reason for your origins. / Listen well to my commands, / For if you do not, I swear I will curse you. / Fly away, become dust, become wind. / My teacher has taught me to be effective. / My teacher is effective through the holy words / There is no God but Allah and Muhammad is His Prophet."[27] The midwife sings as she scatters to the four cardinal points rice, salt, turmeric—substances lush with symbolic meaning, loaded with affect, replete with protective power. Not only are evil powers dispelled, but good ones such as the *bidandari,* the seven celestial midwives, are called to assist.

Ritual activity increases as birthing troubles multiply. When the birth process veers beyond the capabilities of the attending midwife, the *bomoh,* an indigenous practitioner, arrives to perform ceremonies. During the painful and protracted work of a young mother laboring with her first child, this *bomoh* chants the creation story, links it to the process of human conception, and addresses the unborn child:

In the name of God. First of all I want to put a secret in its proper place. . . .
When the Light of Faith had just begun, when the Divine Pen had begun to in-

scribe all that was written in the Book of Faith into the Hadith [Muslim sacred traditions], explaining Heaven and Earth, then came three utterances. The first Utterance became iron, the second Utterance became the Breath of Life, the third Utterance became semen. The semen swelled and glistened like a white sail and became foam. . . . First it was the Sea of Practice, second the Sea of Experience, third the Sea of Thought, fourth the Sea of Reason, fifth the Sea of Coitus, sixth the Sea of Tiredness, seventh the Sea of Patience, eighth the Sea of Foam. The foam was carried by the wind, tossed by the waves, by the seven rolling waves, by the groundswell. Where will the foam land . . . ?

Gabriel himself thrust it into the father's brain for forty days. Its name was Light of Allah. It fell to his eyes. Light of Lights. It fell to his chest. True Sultan, happy center of the world. It fell to his big toe, King Phallus is his name. . . .

Then you fall into your mother's womb, in your mother's womb nine months, ten days. The first month you are called Dot. The second month Light of Beginning. The third month Light of the Soul. The fourth month Light of the Countenance. The fifth month Light of the Womb. The sixth month Abdullah the Slow. The seventh month bow to the right, bow to the left. Bow to the right, you are a son. Bow to the left, you are a daughter. The eighth month Light of Birth. The ninth month your outline and measure can be seen. . . .

You carry the twenty attributes of Muhammad. You know your mother's body. You open your eyes and utter three prayers. The first utterance lifts the soul to the breast. The second utterance [lifts] the Breath of Life to the breast. The third utterance lifts the vital force. May all your feelings be good. You let yourself breathe in the five vital forces as you wave your arms thrice. You have a compass within you from the day you first stand."[28]

If there is disharmony between a *bomoh* and birthing mother, the mother can call another ritual specialist as a replacement. The mother, not the midwife or ritual specialist, is the primary agent—up to a point. A Malay parturient mother is vigorously discouraged from giving vocal expression to pain. If she is having difficulty in labor, it may be that she has deviated from her demure role, so her husband is instructed to step across her supine body three times. If it is suspected that she has strayed sexually, she may be asked to drink water into which her husband has dipped his penis. Both actions reestablish the proper hierarchy of male over female, allowing her to birth with ease and grace.

After birth, the baby's father buries the placenta under a palm tree and offers prayers for the dead. Since the placenta is the baby's elder sibling, a brief funerary gesture is only fitting. Sometimes the umbilical cord is ground up and small bits of it put in the older siblings' food. The act contributes to family harmony by undermining the premises of sibling rivalry. After all, the part of the new sibling that resides in the belly of the older siblings would not want to beat up on itself.

The Malay medical establishment disapproves of traditional midwifery. The government regards the procedures enacted by the *bidan* and *bomoh* as dangerous and their rites and beliefs as superstitious, so it trains its own biomedically oriented midwives. They sometimes work alongside, but often displace, traditional midwives and ritual specialists. Villagers complain that the government midwives are not always available and that they do not stay for the entire birth process. And they lack ritual competence, the vocabulary of dramatic symbolic acts. But country people know the government midwives are licensed. They also know that government midwives can sterilize scissors to avoid infections, give enemas to avoid the defecation precipitated by hard pushing, and call on ambulances or access state facilities.

Thus, as is the case globally, ritually saturated indigenous birth traditions in rural Malaysia are being displaced by biomedicine, most of it Western in origin and sensibility. It would seem that almost everywhere birth science is displacing birth ritual. Laderman, the medical anthropologist who taped and translated the *bomoh*'s incantation and provided the ethnography on which my description is based, is not romantic about Malay birth. She worries about unsterilized utensils and dietary taboos, but in the last analysis, when she compares the American way of birth to the Malay way, her conclusion is that the American system renders women passive and has a tendency to transform doctors into lead actors.[29]

Laderman is unwilling to consign Malay birth rites to the rubbish bin of superstition. She employs the language and ideas of Western psychology. Protective rites and chants, she says, reassure birthing mothers. Symbolic acts not only provide an alternative focus to the pain, they also empower a mother by identifying the creativity of birth with the creation of the universe. The rites honor her power and help contain her fear. Laderman cites studies showing that fear and other psychological factors can provoke uterine inertia, a slowdown or full stop in labor. She concludes that rites have an effect, but that they work psychologically rather than magically.[30] They modify psychological, therefore physiological and even biochemical, processes such as endorphin production. Endorphins are the body's way of masking pain and inducing euphoria.

Laderman's psychobiological explanation, though hardly the kind a *bomoh* would propose, facilitates a tentative accommodation between two otherwise mutually exclusive worldviews, one indigenous and ritualistic, the other Western and scientific. In my view, if no middle path is found or created between birth rites and biomedicine, indigenous ritual traditions are more likely to suffer the crash fatally. Ritual is an endangered species of action. It will not suffer well or for long the heavy tread of medicalization.

The European American world has historically distinguished what something *does* from what it *means*. It has commissioned religion, philosophy, language, and the arts to be custodians of meaning, while assigning biology, chemistry, and physics jurisdiction over efficacy. But this division of labor does considerable damage to the healing arts. As placebo research has demonstrated, what a pill *means* determines, at least in part, what it can *do*. Sugar pills can cure, or curses kill, if I am convinced of their efficacy. The right words, hurled in a ritual curse, can lead to death, if my consciousness has been formed by a culture in which curses are seriously delivered or seriously received. In short, ritual gestures deeply embraced have concrete physiological results.

Conversely, medicines can be made less effective if they are administered in a way that deprives them of meaning. So we should ask of our own biomedical birthing system, What happens when birth transpires in sterile, meaning-deprived environments? I am not suggesting that government midwives and Westernized hospitals are meaningless, only that the meanings they incarnate are desiccated rather than saturated. They lack the ability to compel the spirits or to evoke the imaginations of birthing mothers and fathers.

We in the European American West have little experience with birth rites. For us, ritual is an activity of the sanctuary, not the delivery room. We can only imagine birth rites as traditional and outdated activities that science, in fact, *ought* to displace. The problem with equating ritual and tradition and then divorcing both from birth is that such a move results in a stark polarization between effectiveness and meaning, science and ritual. The split makes us overlook the efficacious knowledge enshrined in traditions and blinds us to the traditional facets of science as a social institution. Science, after all, can be as intractable and resistant to change as religion can.

For the past two centuries we have worried more about the damage done by tradition than about the destruction wrought by science. Until recently, science has been all promise and tradition, mainly a threat. Our fear of tradition and ritual, those partners in crime, is probably at no time more intense than at birth, the origin of our species, the means of continuing our names and gene pools. What we fear about traditional cultures and practices is well summarized by the Malay proverb, "Let the children die, but do not let traditions die."[31] As a matter of fact, Malays do not take their own proverb literally. They are as fierce in the defense of their children's lives as we are, but we imagine them as slaves to tradition. We fear compelling traditions, so we, with our mortality and morbidity statistics, not only defend our children from traditional birth, we also presume to protect traditional people from themselves and their rites. But is it any different to be enslaved to technology and science?

Half the truth is that we fear traditional, ritualized birth and are happy to see incantations traded for sterile scissors. The other half is that we can hardly resist the romance of "natural" birth. The power of the *bomoh*'s incantation is irresistible. We hear it as deeply moving poetry, since it addresses the query that every parent wants to hurl at the ear of the universe, Will my new baby find its way through the jungle of this world?

It is hard not to envy a birthing system in which one's spiritual needs are attended to as fully as one's physical needs. We may not believe literally that a child's life course proceeds from the archangel Gabriel to Dad's brain, resting forty days there before passing on to the mother, who then does her part. Even so, the imagery makes profound, if obviously male, sense. If we borrow, we must borrow thoughtfully, not mindlessly, since we do not borrow as "true believers."

But is believing what Malays do with these images? In the urban, educated West we have a tendency to literalize other people's myths and rites, even though we read our own symbolically. Their birth ways, we speculate, are not science, maybe not even ritual; rather, they are magic, or worse, superstition. At best, we admit their ways to the category of custom. But attaching any of these labels is a gesture of dismissal, our own kind of verbal magic that with the wave of a hand declares, "For others' use only."

Whether we "believe" incantations or not, it is hard to deny the power of the *bomoh*'s images and our lack of them at crucial moments such as conception, birth, and the beginning of a child's education. The Malay ritualist wraps a laboring woman in the narrative of creation, sacralizes the procreative act, and speaks encouraging words to the child, whom she carries but a moment longer and then no more. We, the technologically adept, have no such gifts to offer.

Like most people I want the best of both worlds. I imagine coupling the technology of Western biomedicine with the spirituality, poetry, and imagery of ritual. I would like to scissor out the ritual and leave behind the poor health practices, superstitions, and local customs. But what is it I would like to scissor out? Which parts are the ritual ones? The *bomoh*'s chant is obviously ritualistic; it encapsulates a creation myth. But the causal sequences (if you sit in a doorway, you block the birth canal) seem to me superstitious, since I do not hold such beliefs. But is this assumed superstition an adequate reason for rejecting birth chants? Can we successfully appropriate the "poetry" of one tradition and reject the "bad science" of another? Can we so easily escape our own skins and so readily take over another tradition's ritual practices?

The more I ponder the Malay birthing system with an eye to reimagining my own, the fewer answers and the more questions I have. What are we to make of the father's burying the placenta and addressing the dead? What do the dead have to do with birth? Is this thicket of practices really ritual or local custom? Is it the outcome of deep insight or the chaff of mere habit? And what about having to suffer the humiliation of drinking from a cup into which your husband has stuck his penis (especially since Malay women say they find oral sex humiliating)? Is such an act primal wisdom or ritual humiliation? It seems impossible to separate ritual actions from other activities. And even if we could identify and excise the ritual parts, we probably would not always like what we ended up with.

In the final analysis, the project of reimagining birth, and doing so by contemplating the rites and symbols of other cultures, can only succeed if the aim is something other than wholesale expropriation. The aim, I believe, must be to reimagine our own practices and our own past and to do so in a way that borrows, not the symbols of others, but their imaginative courage. In this way perhaps we can achieve a perspective capable of making the all too familiar a little stranger.

Children Are Not Born but Made

Every culture has its own way of producing young. However natural birth may seem, it is also cultural. A birth is actively shaped, its style and tenor marked by the time and place in which it occurs. Children are not only born, they are made. A birth event is inevitably, though selectively, expressive of the culture of a particular time and place. There is no such thing as a pristine space into which a child may be born free of society's hand. Even when individuals resist the values of their elders, thus choosing to act counterculturally, they still do so in ways characteristic of, or possible in, a particular time and place. However much we may succeed in producing germ-, technology-, or city-free birth, no one succeeds in having a birth that is culture free. Although genes determine births in inescapable ways, so do societies. Babies may escape this or that culture, but not culture itself. Even so-called natural births are cultural events.

The human body is not an inert object. It is carried, "worn," decorated, ignored, experienced. Not only is our exterior—our skin, hair, eyes, teeth, and so on—enculturated, but so is our interior. How deeply we breathe, how we habitually feel about ourselves, where we sense our center to be, how we imagine, feed, and care for a fetus in the uterus—all these are shaped by the histories behind us and the societies around us.

Even a birth surrounded by nature, far from cities, buildings, and high-tech medicine is inscribed with the values of a culture, not simply those of the birthing mother. "It was their custom," Ben Black Elk said of traditional Lakota women, "to find a wide open place out on the prairie, where one could look out on the great hoop of the horizon and see in all directions. The mothers in giving birth felt the need to have a full view of the open horizon."[32]

Birth is also inextricably embedded in time. History tattoos its values on the newborn as well as on those gathered around it. In one era babies are awaited; they come in due time. In another, they are dragged out, more or less on schedule, by the use of labor induction and forceps. In one decade mothers are given drugs that induce "twilight sleep." In another, mothers anticipate conscious birth. At one time, babies are given immediately to mothers. At another, they are whisked away to sterile quarters for feeding by nurses.

Even within a single culture, there can be significant, even dramatic, changes in birthing practices across time. Birth practices come and go, sometimes for better, sometimes for worse. Obstetrical practices, even the most stubbornly scientific ones, are fashion and fad driven. So we attain the most enlightening perspective when we consider specific births in actual contexts.

In 1973 Mary Crow Dog, a Lakota woman later known as Mary Brave Bird, stood at a historic nexus. Caught in a cross fire, both literally and metaphorically, she was about to give birth. She found herself unable to embrace traditional Lakota birth but also unwilling to assent to the standard hospital scenario. The place is Wounded Knee during the confrontation between the American Indian Movement (AIM) and the FBI.

I was determined not to go to the hospital. I did not want a white doctor looking at me down there. I wanted no white doctor to touch me. Always in my mind was how they had sterilized my sister and how they had let her baby die. My baby was going to live. I was going to have it in the old Indian manner—well, old, but not too old. In the real ancient tradition our women stuck a waist-high cottonwood stick right in the center of the tipi. Squatting, holding on to that stick, they would drop the baby onto a square of soft, tanned deer hide. They themselves cut the umbilical cord and put puffball powder on the baby's navel. Sometimes a woman friend was squatting behind them, pressing down on their stomach, or working the baby down with some sort of belt. They would rub the baby down with water and sweet grass and then wipe it clean with buffalo grease. I did not think I was quite that hardy or traditional to do it exactly in that way. And where would I have gotten buffalo grease?

. . .

I should have found a *winkte,* that is a gay person, to give my baby a secret name. Winktes were believed to always live to a great old age. If they gave the newborn such a hidden name, not the one everybody would know him by, then the winkte's longevity would rub off on the little one. Such a winkte name was always funnily obscene, like for instance Che Maza, meaning Iron Prick, and you had to pay the name-giver well for it. Well, I had no money and how was I going to find a winkte at Wounded Knee. I could not very well go to every warrior and ask him, "Are you by any chance gay?"

. . .

I did not always have lofty thoughts about traditional birth giving on my mind during the last week before I went into labor. More often I was preoccupied with much more earthly things such as getting safely to the toilet. Being in my ninth month I had to urinate frequently. The women had cleaned out a garage and with the help of some men made it into a four-way ladies' room. It was really weird. You always met a number of girls lined up, waiting their turn. Seeing my big belly they usually let me go ahead. Sometimes tracers were all around us like lightning bugs as the bullets kicked up the dust at our feet. Somehow or other this shooting did not seem real.

. . .

Monday, just as the morning star came out, my water broke and I went down to the sweat lodge to pray. I wanted to go into the sweat but Black Elk would not let me. Maybe there was a taboo against my participating, just as a menstruating woman is not allowed to take part in a ceremony. I was disap-

pointed. I did not feel that the fact that my water had burst had made me ritually unclean. As I walked away from the vapor hut, for the third time, I heard
that ghostly cry and lamenting of a woman and child coming out of the massacre ravine [site of the Wounded Knee massacre in the late nineteenth cen-
tury]. Others had heard it too. I felt that the spirits were all around me.

. . .

I had no injections, or knockout medicine, just water. I gave birth inside a
trailer house. As I said, I had wanted to deliver inside the tipi but that would
have been risking all our lives. Well, my labor lasted until 2:45 P.M. and then it
went zip, just like that.

A couple of hours before Pedro was born a cow gave birth to a calf. The
old-style Sioux are proverbial gamblers and they had been betting which
would come in first, the cow or me. And the cow had beaten me by a length.

When the baby was born I could hear the people outside. They had all
come except the security manning the bunkers, and when they heard my little
boy's first tiny cry all the women gave the high-pitched, trembling brave-heart
yell. I looked out the window and I could see them, women and men standing
there with their fists raised in the air, and I really thought then that I had accomplished something for my people. And that felt very, very good, like a
warmth spreading over me.

. . .

All those tough guys were weeping. And then my girl friends came in, taking turns holding the baby. Grandma Wawasik went to the window and held
up the baby and a great cheer went up. They were beating the big drum and
singing the AIM song.

. . .

They brought in the pipe and we prayed with it, prayed for my little boy
whom I named Pedro. I am glad I did because this way Pedro Bissonette's
name is living on. And right away after my son was born he lifted up his little,
soft head and so I knew that I had a strong child, because they don't do that
until they are two weeks old. And the macho Sioux men said, "For sure, that's
a warrior." As I looked at him I knew that I was entering a new phase of my
life and that things would not, could not ever be the same again.[33]

Rites of passage often represent a compromise between religious traditions, on the one hand, and bodily or political exigencies on the other.
Births happen in taxis, weddings by shotgun, and funerals on the battlefield. The timing of Pedro's emergence is both fortunate and unfortunate.
The standoff heightens the drama and importance of his birth, but the
conflict also endangers mother and child. Pinned down by FBI rifle fire

and refusing to leave, AIM members, along with supporters such as Mary, are cut off from their traditions. She cannot give birth in a tipi, and even if she could, she is ambivalent about the "old, old" ways. Even so, the intensity of the time heightens the value of traditions. Having been alienated from many Lakota traditions, Mary Crow Dog is now busy learning, absorbing some of them for the first time. Although critical of the macho strutting of some of the men, she is moved by their joyous weeping and rejoices when they remark that the newborn Pedro is a warrior.

Because birth is cultural and historical, it is also political, inextricably bound up with the exercise of power. Certain parties take charge of birth. Some are given access to the birthing circle, while others are excluded. For instance, since Mary is in the first stages of delivery, she is excluded from the sweat lodge and is irritated, seeing no good reason for the exclusion.

Because of the politics of birth, some voices are heeded while others are silenced or ignored. One person's opinions are construed as counting more than another's. Birth is not only courted and celebrated but also contested. The contestation of a birth can be downplayed or hidden, but competition for attention and resources is inevitable. At every birth there is a struggle for control, even when the aim of gaining control is that of giving it up. To whom does Pedro belong? Mary? Leonard Crow Dog? (He and Mary are not married.) The state (if Mary and Leonard both go to jail)? The Lakota people? The grandmothers?

Even though mothers and children are agents, that is, capable of action, they are also objects of action, recipients of aggression and ritualistic manipulation. To deny or obscure the politics of birth is to disempower those most fundamentally implicated. Birth rites typically encode or display fundamental assumptions about who has and does not have power and how those who have it should use it.

The politics of birth does not preclude the presence of either affection or cooperation. Whatever competition and jealousy may have separated the women at Wounded Knee, in Mary's story these women consolidate. But even when cooperation defines the basic ethos of a birth, a larger politics frames and constrains the actions of everyone involved, even those in charge. However much a doctor or midwife might choose to trust a mother or father, the law nevertheless may hold one party responsible. There are legal constraints and social limitations that bear upon the will to trust and cooperate.

Birth is not only the moment of biological emergence, it is also a complex biological and social process, so it would be a mistake to focus too

exclusively on the moment of delivery itself. Although we conventionally speak of birth as an event, it really sprawls across historical time and
social space. Birth can involve several institutions and their subcultures:
homes, hospitals, birthing centers, religious institutions, the media, the
advertising industry, neighborhoods, kinship groups, and women's
groups. Socially, the making of a child takes longer than twenty-four
hours of labor or nine months of pregnancy. Even considered biologically, there is no single instant that constitutes birth, since conception
and gestation precede delivery, and physiological afterbirth and then
child care follow it. These biological events are wrapped in cultural processes, making the event "thicker" and longer than the simple term *birth
rite* would lead us to believe. Birth rites are embedded in *passage systems*, which is to say, assumptions (both shared and contested) about the
life course, rites for negotiating this obstacle-laden course, and social
arrangements for enacting and perpetuating these rites.

It is a Western habit to subdivide flowing processes into discrete
phases and a convention to divide the birth process into three such
phases: prenatal, natal, and postnatal. But the occasions upon which
people actually enact rites are more varied and interesting than any be-
fore-during-and-after scheme would make it seem. These are some of
the activities that people across the world choose to ritualize:

- birth-control practices
- conception and fertility practices
- pregnancy beliefs and taboos
- birth education, both the informal absorption of birth lore and the
  formal, or ceremonial, transmission of knowledge about birth
- protective actions during pregnancy, at birth, and after birth
- ceremonies for miscarriage, stillbirth, abortion, and infanticide
- gender-preference practices (frequently to ensure the birth of a male)
- divination aimed at determining the gender of a fetus or the life
  course of a newborn
- the construction of sacred or special sites such as birthing huts
- couvade (male labor symptoms)
- delivery procedures, for instance, cleansing, purifying, and dramatizing or stylizing breathing and posture
- acts of deference and demeanor that undergird hierarchies of expertise in birth knowledge

- bonding behavior—between parent and child, child and others
- practices regarding the onset of lactation and the termination of nursing
- expressions of caregiving such as assisting in birth, sending cards, visiting, doing chores
- consultation of ritual practitioners such as priests or shamans
- telling or reading birth-related narratives, such as personal birth stories or myths about mother goddesses
- postbirth seclusion practices, eating selected foods, "lying-in" (being confined)
- emerging from confinement
- naming, blessing, and welcoming children
- parent-recognition ceremonies and gestures
- status-declaration rites, for instance, in recognition of a royal heir
- community celebrations, feasts
- ceremonial gift giving
- body-marking rites, for example, circumcision
- "first" celebrations, for instance, first solid food, first haircut, first step, first word
- birthdays
- ceremonies of incorporation into a family, ethnic group, or religion
- early childhood education rites such as learning the alphabet, beginning study, entering school

This long list of possibilities may seem to contradict the claim that birth receives comparatively little ritual attention. But living traditions vary greatly in the degree to which they actualize the ritual possibilities of birth and early childhood. Few of these moments are actually ritualized in a given tradition. Several may be rolled into one. A single rite could recognize parents, facilitate the exchange of gifts, celebrate motherhood, and incorporate children into the community. The list above pulls apart strands that would normally be braided together. Many actions are insufficiently formalized or differentiated to warrant calling them rites; they are more accurately regarded as *ritualized gestures.*

In some societies, a complex series of ceremonies links conception and pregnancy with delivery and early childhood. In others, there may be a single rite or none at all. The !Kung of the African Kalahari Desert have no formal birth rites, although a celebration sometimes follows a birth. The only birth or childhood rite is that of first haircutting.[34] There are no birth specialists such as midwives, and !Kung women, although sometimes accompanied by a female relative, aspire to birthing alone.[35]

By contrast, the Tikopia of the Solomon Islands in Melanesia once had a dozen birth rites, three preceding and nine following delivery. Even so, there were no rites to ward off miscarriage and none for conferring personal names or weaning. Men, even brothers, were sometimes present at a birth. In addition, there were men's as well as women's rites after birth. Postnatal rites immediately following childbirth were short; longer, more formal ones followed later. Some of the more formal rites were performed only for first births, suggesting that they were more about creating kinship ties or socializing new parents into their roles than about greeting newborn children.

Although occasioned by birth, numerous Tikopia childhood ceremonies were neither birth nor child centered. Instead, these rites ensured that a child, upon becoming an adult, would be able to engage in productive economic activity. Although just born, one boy was both given these orders and invested with these wishes: "Jump on your enormous stool / To go and grate coconut to make a pudding for us / We are hungry / . . . May the fish observe your hook / Light be your line / . . . Light be your eyes for the sea-snail / Create an orchard for yourself from the reef."[36]

Despite their strong desire for children and the rich ceremonial culture surrounding birth and childhood, traditional Tikopia attached no stigma to infanticide. As a result of Christian missionary pressure, food shortages, and the time demands of wage labor and education, many traditional birth rites, including infanticide, are no longer practiced.

In most birthing systems the degree of ritual elaboration falls between the ritual profusion of the Tikopia and the ritual sparsity of the !Kung. Javanese religion, consisting of Muslim, Hindu, and indigenous elements, has four major birth-related feasts called *slametans*, one at seven months of pregnancy, one at birth, one five days after birth, and a final feast seven months after birth.[37] The *slametan* is a general, all-purpose ritual form that is adapted to a variety of occasions, suggesting that it is not necessary to have a different rite for each major turn in the life cycle.

The Yoruba of southwestern Nigeria have two birth rites, "stepping into the world" and "knowing the head." In the first, a diviner uses palm nuts to discern a seven-day-old baby's name and its future impact on the family. The second, performed before the child is three months old, divines the child's "inner head," his personality. As one Yoruba named Ọṣitọla puts it, "He is a new man. Nobody knows him. He is still coming from heaven. We don't know what he is doing here. Until we know what the child is doing here, we can't treat him like ourselves. We treat him like a stranger who has not been used to this place. Until he is used to this place, he can't have the knowledge [that a full person would have]."[38]

When a Muslim child is born, the *shahādah* is whispered into its right, then left, ear. A child hears the declaration that all Muslims are supposed to hear five times a day: "I bear witness that there is no God but Allah and that Muhammad is his prophet." The first word that a newborn child hears, then, is the name of God. In effect, a child is being readied to respond to the call for prayer. Seven days later the child is named in a ceremony called *aqīqah*. Traditionally, the name includes *abd,* "slave of," plus one of the "beautiful" names of Allah. In effect, every child is named "slave of God." The naming rite usually includes an elaborate feast, in which sheep or other food animals ("two for a boy, one for a girl") are slaughtered and gifts are given to the poor.

After a Sikh birth, gifts are given, doors decorated, and mothers secluded. After thirteen days the mother has a ceremonial bath and discards her old clothes. Parents go to a *gurdwara,* a Sikh place of worship, to be given the initial letter of the child's name. The letter of the alphabet is picked at random from Sikh scriptures. Traditionally, a ceremonially prepared sugar-and-water nectar is placed in the baby's mouth with a miniature ritual sword. *Chhati,* celebrated when a boy is five weeks old, is a feast organized by the paternal family, and *lohrdi* is a seasonal celebration in January for families into which boys have been born; there is singing, a bonfire, and gift giving.

These are only a few, briefly sketched examples of the rites in various birth systems. Many so-called birth rites precede birth by several months. These ceremonies tend to be protective, preventive, or divinatory, conjuring protective forces and energies. Throughout most of human history, infant mortality rates have been high. Birthing, for both mother and child, is a time of ultimate vulnerability, and prebirth rites anticipate difficulty, diagnose the social, spiritual, and psychological dangers that might threaten newborns, and then ward them off with symbols of easy, successful birth.

Some postbirth ritual actions, such as circumcisions, are better understood as preinitiations, preliminary inductions into a family, tradition, or gender. These rites are less about averting danger than they are about establishing social legitimacy and group membership. They make one visibly a Jew or Muslim or woman or Christian or Brahmin. Naming rites are often classified by scholars as birth rites, but naming is less about birth than it is about establishing identity, working out the balance between an individual and the group into which he or she is born.

The meanings enacted in a birth rite are not autonomous but deeply embedded in institutions and traditions of meaning. Because of this tangle of connections, it is not always easy to separate a rite from custom, folklore, or medical procedure. Distinguishing these domains can be useful, but only if we recognize that the consequences and determinants of birth may lie not only outside the rite but outside the birth itself. A mother may not be able to support all her children and thus may choose to abort rather than ritually celebrate a pregnancy. Her reasons may be neither biological nor ritualistic but purely economic. Birth rites, like all rites of passage, are not magnificently elevated and insulated occasions; they are gestures swelling up out of a sea of relationships into a momentary performative event.

Male Mothering

Birth rites are conditioned by imaginative as well as political and cultural factors. In couvade, the performance of "male labor," these factors converge. In most societies fathers are excluded or absent from the birth event itself. They are bit players waiting in the wings. In a few societies, fathers are essential but secondary players who assist mothers and midwives in the birth process. In our culture, doctors often displace both mothers and fathers as central actors. After the event, however, the power of mothers over their children, especially boys, is sometimes curbed by the paternal claims of men, even though mothers typically spend more time with children. Cross-culturally considered, it is rare for men, including fathers, to be active participants in birth.

Couvade seems to be an exception. From the French word *couver,* "to brood or hatch," couvade is the male practice of displaying pregnancy symptoms, of miming labor or other actions of birthing women. In some instances, the display is ritualized; in others, it is not.

In North America a small percentage of men, 10 percent, according to some sources,[39] develop pregnancy symptoms. Expectant fathers put on weight around their bellies or experience frequent nighttime urination, back pains, morning nausea, and cravings for special foods. Some even feel pains while their wives are in labor. Medically, this condition is known as the *couvade syndrome;* it is not quite a rite, although it is ritual-like.

In a few non-Western cultures, men are required to observe restrictions similar to those that bear on their expectant wives. Men may be confined during a lying-in period after birth or be required to refrain from intercourse and abstain from certain foods. But neither unconscious acting out nor moral and religious taboo is quite the same as an explicit couvade rite.

Several explanations of couvade have been proposed. A late-nineteenth-century explanation was that men who practiced it were henpecked, bullied by their wives into superstitious behavior. By participating in their wives' labors, husbands were forced to share the pain. But this interpretation is pure guesswork; there is no evidence that men interpreted their actions in this way.

The preferred contemporary interpretation of couvade is that it is a ritualized expression of sympathy between a father and a mother or a father and a child. Since the father himself cannot bear a child or suffer labor pains, he joins in the only way he can: dramatically, ritually. In an enormously attractive description, Nor Hall espouses this "soft belly condition of the Buddha." She writes, "The father needs not to go about business as usual, needs not to get things done, but rather to leave work undone, to brood rather than be busy. . . . To be brooded over is to be completely covered by an extraordinary concentration of warmth that waits for the slightest stirring in the depths. It is a gathering of energy that is nonforceful even though it has purpose. Its purpose is not to penetrate—which is unusual for the spirit regarded as masculine—but to bring forth. . . . Brood force is as intense as the storming God and as soft as the underbelly of a hen. It is very heavy, but will not break an egg."[40]

However much we may prefer this empathetic interpretation, it is not usually espoused by those who practice couvade. Their explanations are magical, not psychological. Hall's view is not a summary of what tribal practitioners do, or even what they say they are doing, but an evocation of what Westerners *aspire to be* doing. When Hall says that the tribal father stays in bed with the baby, becoming the child's nurse so the mother can go back to her work, she ignores instances in which a mother not only has to nurse a child but also nurture the child's father.[41] Hall's portrait is of an aspiration not a fact. She is describing *imagined ritual* rather than enacted rites.[42]

A less idealized explanation is that couvade is a father's way of upstaging a mother. Envious of his partner's power to give birth, and feeling competitive at seeing mother and child at center stage, he calls attention to himself: "Look at me. I can do that. I hurt too." Practitioners seldom, if ever, admit to such a motive. But when a birthing mother is burdened by having to tend to the needs of a "birthing" father, it is hard to deny the plausibility of such a view, especially if couvade is engaged in *after* birth rather than during pregnancy and labor. A variant of this politicized view is that couvade is simply a dramatic way of establishing paternity, a way of saying to society at large, "Look at me! I am the dad. Don't forget, I fathered this child."

An explanation commonly offered by practitioners is that a father, like a mother, can endanger the life of a child by not observing restrictions. The Waiwai of Brazil consider the soul of the newborn child weak, not yet fully attached to the child itself, so the soul wanders around, vulnerable to spiritual danger.[43] However loosely connected to the child itself, a newborn Waiwai soul is thoroughly entwined with the souls of the parents. So whatever affects them can also affect the child. Therefore, the father, not just the mother, has to behave cautiously, observing restrictions.

It is impossible to say what the "real" meaning of couvade is, since the data are too sparse to warrant reliable judgments and because indigenous interpretations differ considerably from Western psychological ones. Although the topic was the object of much writing and speculation in the early part of the twentieth century, it is not well documented; accounts are brief and dated. So couvade may be a ritual fantasy rather than a rite.

The meaning of couvade differs depending on whether it coincides with or follows pregnancy and labor, and on whether it manifests itself as a symptom or as a rite. In any case, both motives, empathetic participation and petulant competition, are widespread experiences of men during their wives' pregnancies and births. So whatever couvade may mean elsewhere, in North America both impulses require recognition—if not in ritual then in imagination. Whatever rites we imagine or enact, they should attend to both the altruistic and exploitative possibilities of simulated labor. Hall's empathetic version of couvade is worth contemplating, provided we also critique the manipulative version. Couvade illustrates not just that birth is contested and imagined but that it is contested *because* it is imagined, and imagined *because* contested. In short, the ritualizing of birth is influenced by myths and by powerful, controlling images.

In some myths, the world is created by copulation rather than by verbal command. ("Come close, dear" makes more intuitive sense than "Let there be. . . . ") The coming together of two divine people, at once separate and identical, is an almost universal metaphor for mystical experience, the indwelling of human and divine principles. But soon the two who have become one become two again. However much the rhetoric of lovemaking, weddings, and mysticism may cast two people as one, when a couple gives birth, this mystical oneness is often torn into two pieces, leaving in its wake a man who has to go back to work and a woman who has another mouth to feed. The unity is real, but so is the duality.

As we contemplate birth's ritual possibilities, we inevitably must ask, Who is this birth rite for? One possible answer is, The rite is for the protection of a child. Another is, The rite is for society at large; it facilitates a child's entry into membership. Another is, The rite protects and encourages the mother, then recognizes and celebrates her centrality in the creation of life. A fourth possible answer is, The rite *appears to be* for mothers and children, but is *really* for fathers, doctors, the patriarchy in general.

A few feminist and Marxist writers assert that birth rites are really about the determination of paternity and descent lines. Rites are ways for men to control women's bodies and to co-opt their reproductive labor. Karen Paige and Jeffery Paige argue the baldest version of this theory: "Reproductive rituals . . . are attempts to gain political advantage in conflicts over women and children rather than mechanisms for satisfying the psychological needs of individuals or for symbolically reducing social conflict and tension. Reproductive rituals are motivated by self-interest; their sentimental and religious symbolism merely cloaks their true objectives."[44]

This Marxist interpretation flatly contradicts Hall's Jungian view. For Paige and Paige, reproductive rites are a form of psychological warfare. Men use them to monitor the loyalty of their kin as well as to assert their rights over a woman's "reproductive capital."[45] Theories of birth and ritual are as politicized as birthing itself. Cross-culturally and historically considered, it is all too obvious that men often assert jural rights over the newly born. But the perspective espoused by Paige and

Paige is reductionistic, displacing every other facet of birth with the political dimension. But the politics of ritual do not preclude its very real
psychological, religious, and imaginative aspects. Religion and psychology are not mere cover-ups for politics but real domains in themselves.
The importance of a hard-hitting Marxist view is that it keeps us from
indulging in clichéd sentiments about birth. The danger of sentimental-
izing is not that we will express too much emotion but that we risk substituting superficial feelings for recognizing the complex negotiations
surrounding birth and birth rites.

Begreasing and Bespewing Poor Infants

We gain perspective not only by peering across oceans at other cultures
but also by gazing back through centuries. Like ethnographic approaches to ritual, historical ones put us in contact with the rich soil in
which rites grow. A global look at rites of passage necessarily trims
away much of the context, the root ball that grounds and feeds rites
that spring up out of it. To counteract this distortion, we should consider at least one instance of birth ritual in a more thickly textured way.
Considered in sufficient historical depth, an all-too-familiar rite can appear strange or provocative. Too often we study history in order to justify or explain current practices, but another reason is to stretch our capacity for imagining ritually. Lifting a rite out of the past with the hope
that it will grow in the present usually fails. Nevertheless, our sense of
what is ritually possible can be enhanced by momentarily suspending
our own practical questions for the sake of immersing ourselves in the
ritual sensibility of another time.

Baptism suffers the double contempt of being too familiar and too
frequently interpreted without benefit of its history. If there is a Christian birth rite, the most obvious candidate is baptism. Baptism is the
only rite of passage universally recognized as a sacrament by Christians. Holy Communion, the other rite universally attributed the high
status of sacrament, is a rite of worship, not a rite of passage. Weddings
and funerals do not have the same status as baptism, because, although
they are rites of passage, they do not hold the rank of sacrament for all
Christians.

The rite of baptism was not, and is not, always for infants. In ancient
Judaism, from which early Christianity borrowed its ceremonial bath,
baptism was a phase in the rite of conversion. Sometimes called "pros-

elyte baptism," it accompanied circumcision, the definitive liturgical act undergone by an adult male in converting to Judaism; it was an optional, not a central, action.

There is little doubt that early Christian baptism was adult baptism by immersion. Infant baptism by sprinkling or pouring was a later development. When the early Christians began proselytizing, they, like the Jews, used baptism to mark the conversion of adults from their old traditions to their newly adopted one. But unlike Jews, Christians made baptism into a core liturgy, allowing it to replace circumcision. For Christians only "circumcision of the heart" was required. Circumcision went from being a ritual practice to being a metaphor. The Christian view was that the act of baptism, augmented by Jesus' blood sacrifice, relieved Christians of the necessity to cut the penis, spilling token drops.

Early Christian baptism, then, initiated a neophyte into salvation and group membership. All converts, whether children or adults, were baptized into Christian community, belief, and practice. This rite of Christian initiation was preceded by a long period of teaching, nurturing, and testing called catechesis. Initiates, known as catechumens, were excluded from the central worship rite, the Eucharist, until they had been educated, baptized, and fully admitted to Christian life during the Easter vigil.

Conducted at sunrise and undergone in the nude, early Christian baptism was a dramatic and powerful experience. Conceived as a mystical death and resurrection, it was followed immediately by the granting of a major ceremonial privilege, participation in the communion liturgy. Since an initiate's first communion coincided with Easter, the most important Christian holy day, the impact could be overwhelming.

As Christianity gained a foothold in Europe, fewer church members converted from non-Christian religions, and more came from Christian families. The assumed baptismal subject was no longer an adult stranger, a former pagan or Jew, but a child of Christian parents.[46] So baptism gradually evolved from being an initiation rite to being a birth rite—of sorts. I hedge, because infant baptism, even though it followed closely on the heels of birth, was spatially and ritually cordoned off from birth itself. Although some babies were baptized at home, there was constant pressure to locate the rite in ecclesiastical rather than domestic space. Enacted in a church within eight days of birth, the rite was kept free of the blood and pain considered the privileged domain, and distinctive curse, of women. Throughout the Middle Ages infant baptism was less about welcoming a child, praising the bravery of mothers, or educating parents than it was about making church members and setting new souls on the path leading to the kingdom of God.

Illustrated in this brief example is an important principle: A rite may change types. Baptism migrated from being an initiation rite to being a birth rite. This shift created a problem, since it left a gap in the Christian ritual system. Originally, baptism was, among other things, a ceremonial guarantee of participation in communion, but Holy Communion assumed a kind of knowledge that no infant could possibly possess. What would now ensure that communicants were aware of the significance of their actions?

The short answer? Confirmation. But confirmation did not yet exist as a rite; it had to be invented, constructed out of materials at hand. Originally, confirmation was merely a phase in the baptism rite. Later it split off to become a ceremony for adolescents, a ritual process to ensure that they were prepared for communion, that, religiously speaking, they were adults. Since rebaptism would constitute a public admission that infant baptism did not suffice, Christians instead constructed a ceremony that reaffirmed the actions performed on a child's behalf at baptism by godparents. Thus, confirmation became Christianity's "maturity rite," an initiation into ceremonial adulthood.

For centuries, confirmation has been liturgically problematic and theologically suspect, not to mention experienced as ineffectual and anticlimactic. In fact, by the Middle Ages Christians even took communion *before* being confirmed. Uninitiated, they still had access to the holiest rite of all. So confirmation gradually lost, or never quite realized, its reason for being. In the twentieth century, this failure led some Christian groups to look at ethnographic data with a eye to constructing "real" initiation rites modeled after tribal ones in which adolescents demonstrate or attain maturation by undergoing hardship.[47]

Rites usually come into being with effort and under the pressure of controversy. Their inheritors and inventors intend them to serve well, but if badly conceived or poorly executed, rites can do more harm than good. Rites, even whole ritual systems, can go into decline. They do not spring into being full-blown and healthy. Some die in their infancy, some in adolescence. A few make it to old age and become venerable. Others, regrettably, hang on well beyond their years.

So far we have considered baptism's evolution from an initiation to a birth rite. Now we turn to a particular moment in its complex history, one in which some Christians decided to refrain from infant baptism altogether. In Tudor and Stuart England (1509–1714), baptism, for both better and worse, mattered.[48] Because of the various reformations (German, Swiss, Dutch, and English) and subsequent civil unrest in England, what one believed, said, and did ritually in response to a birth were of considerable consequence.

In the English Christianity of the period, there were two birth-related rites, each followed by a social celebration. Infant baptism was enacted a few days after birth, and the churching of women, never considered a sacrament, concluded the sequestered month after a woman gave birth.

At the time, the air was thick with controversy. Some Anglicans wanted to retain an elaborate infant baptism ceremony, eliminating only what were considered its more obviously "Romish" elements such as making the sign of the cross and using elaborately decorated fonts. Puritans, however, preferred to reduce the rite to its bare essentials, the application of water and the recitation of a simple formula: "I baptize thee in the name of the Father, and of the Son, and of the Holy Ghost." All else was "outward form, mere ceremony." The more radical Puritans would have done away with infant baptism altogether and the most radical with all rites, period.

James Calfhill, a Protestant writing in the 1560s, regarded the "crosses and ashes, water and salt, oil and cream, boughs and bones, sticks and stones" used by the priests in baptism as the paraphernalia of witchcraft. He criticized his less Protestant brethren for "not sticking to the ceremonies of the received fathers, having chosen rather, of their own fantastical and idle brain, to use crossing and conjuring, begreasing and bespewing of the poor infants in baptism." He had had enough of ritualized spitting and anointing, of "conjuration, consecration, or insufflation." He detested the creeping elaboration of the baptism rite—the introduction of honey, milk, wine, oil, salt, spittle, and tapers.[49] Puritans argued that baptisms were not baths, literal or magical; they were signs of a divine inward cleansing of the soul, nothing more, nothing less. The inner movement, not the outward ritual act, was considered essential. Protestants who wanted to peel away the ceremonial accretions and get to liturgical bedrock had an array of labels for rites they disliked: superstition, magic, popish acts, spell making, conjuring, sometimes even ceremony. In any case, ritual was worth fighting for. Or against.

Hotly debated questions concerned birthing parents: Was it inward faith or the external performance of the rite of baptism that saved souls? Were unbaptized babies damned? Should they be given Christian burials? What did the rite of baptism really accomplish? Did it merely admit one to the Christian community, or did it also ensure salvation? These questions were of concern not just to priests and theologians but to parents who were theologically, biblically, and ritually "literate."

The baptism of newborns, especially before 1640, was religiously and socially obligatory. The early Christian practice of postponing baptism so it would coincide with Easter was no longer in force, so unless there were extenuating circumstances surrounding a birth, baptism was mandated to occur without delay on the Sunday or holy day after delivery. Theologically considered, the rite resolved the newborn's ambiguous status—a baby was incapable of committing a sin but was nevertheless tainted by original sin. There were penalties, stiff ones, for clergy or parents who did not promptly baptize the children in their care. In the few rare instances in which Protestant parents refused infant baptism, their children were taken from them and forcibly baptized. Dissenting Puritan William Drewett of Gloucester and his wife declared in 1576 that they would disown their child if it were polluted by forced infant baptism. The bias against a particular version of the rite could be as strong as that for or against ritual itself.

The baptism rite of this period served two functions. It was a mystical transformation (although factions argued whether or not it was a guarantee of salvation) and a rite of passage into community membership (although not into full membership). The rite enshrined a great deal of ambiguity. It cleansed, but children seemed little in need of ritual cleansing. It also admitted into membership, but not completely.

The rhetoric of the Tudor and Stuart Christian baptism ceremony was replete with aquatic symbolism—not only the Jordan of Jesus' baptism but the flood and the Red Sea as well. Although the rite itself did not make the connection explicit, baptismal water was easy to associate with amniotic fluids, the "liquor" in which the unborn swam. With only a bit of interpretive imagination, baptism could serve as a birth rite whether theologians and clergy intended it that way or not.

If we step back from the rite of infant baptism, viewing it in tandem with an actual birth, the quick change of trajectory is stunning. The newly born was required to be reborn. Barely a week dry, a child was reintroduced to the waters of birth, only now they were pure, sanctified. Unlike first birth, second birth required no blood. That had been spilled already, by Christ and by the mother of the child.

For the Anglicans at that time, baptism both transformed and incorporated a child so decisively that a second baptism into adulthood was unnecessary. On the continent, radical religious reformers contemptuous of infant baptism because of its lack of biblical support insisted that adults be baptized again, hence their name, Anabaptists. By insisting on the inefficacy of infant baptism, Anabaptists effectively eliminated Christian birth rites.

The English rite of infant baptism was not only mystical, effecting (but not determining) the divine economy of salvation, but also social. It was the public initiation and naming of a Christian, hence the unofficial title, christening. Parents had little to do in the ceremony itself. In fact, mothers, by convention still "abed," were often not present at all. Godparents, also called witnesses and sureties, presented the child and, when asked, offered its name. The rite addressed the child directly, but since a newborn child is unable to answer on its own accord, the godparents replied instead: Yes, this child will forsake the devil. Godparents were interrogated as stand-ins, proxies for the child.

Some godparents were only fictive kin; others were blood relatives. In any case, the rite established relationships that could be either lasting and significant or merely perfunctory. Infant baptism not only admitted a child to a community but also expanded the definition of a family, solidifying ties among relatives, friends, and allies. In adolescence or adulthood a godchild might call upon a godparent for spiritual counsel (the officially intended purpose) but also for financial aid or other, less spiritual kinds of assistance. Godparents were expected to behave as "avuncular benefactors" even though many did not.[50] The conventional gift from a godparent to a godchild was a silver spoon, hence the saying "a silver spoon in the mouth."

Infant baptism sometimes established namesake relations as well as godparent relations. A parent might honor a relative, friend, or member of the royal house by conferring that person's name on the baptized child. To lend a name or to be asked to serve as godparent was an honor. For parents, it was a social coup to have the right person agree to sponsor a child. Choosing godparents displayed parents' power to garner influence and tug on the lines of power. Many threads of social debt and credit were knotted together by the ceremony.

After the liturgical portion of the rite, a christening party followed, replete with sexual banter celebrating male prowess and female fecundity. Lubricated with alcohol, the celebration provided a context for exploiting the social and political dimensions of childbirth.

After 1604 only "lawful ministers" could baptize, but before that time laypeople had been authorized to perform the rite if the situation were dire and it appeared a child might die. The usual layperson to enact the emergency version of the rite was a midwife. She straddled life and death, mediating the chasm that separated the birthing place from sacred space. Later in the birth process, she sometimes stood, holding the child, to be recognized along with the godparents.

But the male clergy worried about midwives and even constructed a rite for "survivors" of their baptisms. The ceremony included the demeaning formula, "If thou be not baptized already, I baptize thee."[51] The baptismal rite was so powerful that clergy did not want to risk having an invalid version performed by a mere midwife, but neither did they want to risk repeating it inadvertently on the same person.

Churching and Gossiping

The second major rite in the Tudor-Stuart birthing system of England was the *churching of women,* also known as the thanksgiving and the purification. According to the liturgical texts, the ceremony was a thanksgiving celebration for safe deliverance, but some contemporary feminist scholars see the rite as a tacit declaration of the impurity of the parturient female body. In their view churching was a ceremonial cleansing of the pollution of birth, a way of treating birthing mothers as if they were taboo. But the text of the English rite makes no overt mention of purification in the way it does of thanksgiving. Before churching, a parturient woman was, according to the folklore of the day, "green," but the term meant unwell rather than polluted. There is little doubt that the patriarchy feared and wanted to control birth, but there is evidence that women experienced churching more as an occasion for coming out than as a ritual humiliation forced upon them by men. Churching was an occasion for the public reemergence of a mother following the more sequestered, female-only folk ritualizing that surrounded birth itself.

Consistent with their state, whether virginal or penitent, churching women traditionally wore white veils. But many Protestants considered the practice too Catholic or too Jewish—not only a remnant of Mosaic and Levitical law but a "papish superstition." They preferred to think of the ceremony as a thanksgiving, in which case a woman coming to church was less a penitent than a celebrant. Considerable controversy surrounded the wearing or not wearing of veils. The practice is now regarded variously—as a virginal and bridal sign, as a shelter and enclosure, as protection for one in a contaminated state, as a symbol of penitence, as a token of submission to superiors, as a sign of reverence before God, as a mere expression of modesty.

Like the Malay birthing system, the English one was in a process of rapid change. In both traditions birth rites are permeated, prefaced, and concluded by the protocols of midwifery, folk medicine, and camaraderie among women. Though not recorded, these protocols were nevertheless real, even if we have less documentation about them. If there were no liturgical rites in the birth room, there was certainly ritualizing. Theologically, baptism was a "remedy" for birth, because sin was implicit in being conceived and emerging human. But these views, however important to the sanctuary, were not completely determinative in the birth room. In the birth room, there were the remedies—"kitchen physic" (home remedies), herbs, and incantations.

Midwives were not beyond using Latin incantations to facilitate birth: "O infans, sive vivus, sive mortuus, exi foras, qui Christus te vocat ad lucem" ("O infant, whether living or dead, come forth because Christ calls you to the light").[52] "Teeming" (pregnant) women were often advised to wear amulets or, if Catholic, to petition the saints. From the distance of the twentieth century, it is difficult to know whether such usage was inventive domestic ritualizing, customary behavior, or ritual magic.

The church, however, was less worried about the bleeding of the boundaries between liturgy and ritualizing than it was about lapsing into superstition or witchery. Clergy were concerned about midwives and their practices, lest they lapse from orthopraxy, "right practice." So visiting bishops formally and ceremonially queried midwives. But these inquisitions were sporadic and unsystematic. Nervous about violating the privacy and sanctity of the birth room, clergy tried to supervise—from a distance, since they acknowledged that birth was woman's domain.

The social fest that followed the liturgical portion of churching was known as *the gossiping*. There was plenty of alcohol, and therefore gossip, hence our association with the term today. The festivity was very much like the social events that followed infant baptisms, weddings, and funerals. The occasion was a time for men and women alike to meet, talk, eat, drink, and celebrate.

Important to a woman's recovery and restoration was not only social reincorporation but sexual reintegration as well. Churching and gossiping marked the resumption of sexual relations between husband and wife. A gossiping could even become an occasion for giving vent to male fantasies: "All Rites well ended, with fair Auspice come / (As to the breaking of a Bride-cake) home: / Where ceremonious Hymen shall for thee / Provide a second Epithalamie. / She who keeps chastely to her husband's side / Is not for one, but every night his Bride: / And stealing still with love, and fear to Bed. / Brings him not one, but many a Maidenhead."[53] In this man's view, churching and gossiping transformed a woman and restored her virginity. Symbolically, not only has she lost nothing by giving birth, she has also gained hymens to lose in the future. The flower, once bloomed, may now be repicked again and again.

Appropriate Craziness, Extravagant Praise

Many of the rites considered in this book endure but a moment. Since we access them by way of observers' descriptions and participants' narratives, our attention is usually on a ritual event rather than on a ritual tradition. However, I have just sketched a long process, two hundred years in the life of Christian baptism. Histories of ritual traditions are not only sources of information, they are also repositories of the collective human imagination that can rekindle imaginations and instigate ritual revisions or reinventions.

What can we possibly learn from such an example, now that the world is no longer divided between "papists" and the puritanical, now that churchgoers appear impatient with debates over the fine points of theology and liturgy? One obvious factor in the Tudor-Stuart period is that of dissension. First, Protestants split off from Catholics then subdivided among themselves. Participants disagreed about what was central and peripheral. They argued about the meanings of actions and debated their relative importance. Our example illustrates that ritual traditions are neither uniform nor unchanging. Rites can undergo not only revision but revolution. Whole ceremonies can appear, disappear, or change their functions. Rites emerge and then fall into disuse. Whole ritual sensibilities can shift within a few generations. In long-standing ritual traditions there are enormous possibilities for both ritual creativity and ritual loss.

Although we may not want to advocate the reinstatement of "be-greasing and bespewing" or believe that unbaptized infants are lost, paying lavish ritual attention to the newborn may be a wise move for other reasons. Although we resist the notion that a parturient mother needs ritual purification, a rite welcoming her back from her perilous journeys and reactivating her social network could be genuinely help-ful. And why not have a celebration in the church basement, where jok-ing about female fecundity and male prowess are the order of the day rather than out of bounds?

After the Reformation, infant baptism lost what little tenuous con-nection it had with the actual childbirth process, and the churching rite eventually died out altogether. The slow process of taming baptism left many Western Christians bereft of a birth rite and without a compelling initiation rite. Before Vatican II, infant baptism, particularly the Protes-tant variant of it, had become innocuous, so bland that undergoing it implied not only automatic church membership but ethnic or national membership as well: "Was I baptized? Sure, I am Italian, aren't I?" Sub-stitute "English" or "Irish" or any of several other nationalities.

Infant baptism is no longer widely regarded as a prerequisite for sal-vation. The Catholic version of the rite has somewhat more weight than the Protestant one, but it is no guarantee of salvation either. The Or-thodox variant retains more of baptism's rich archaic tactility, but in North America even Orthodox infant baptism is becoming optional to new parents. Although denominational officials still disagree about the theology of infant baptism, the day of abusive name calling, physical at-tacks on baptismal fonts, and ceremonial disruption of christening rites has passed. The ritualistic and theological differences no longer make much difference—at least to nontheologians. So if either baptism or churching is to have any meaning, that meaning will have to derive from something other than the threat of social ostracism or loss of sal-vation.

In this post-Reformation era, denominations that baptize infants are trying to redefine and renew the rite. Catholic parents now have access to ritual texts that contain brief blessings for conceiving a child, sup-porting the mother during pregnancy and near the time of birth, reas-suring parents before childbirth, bringing a child into the home, confer-ring a mother's blessing of the child when nursing or feeding, and assisting parents after a miscarriage.[54]

Some Protestants and Catholics hope to use infant baptism not merely to make church members or to save souls but to enhance the value of children and to ensure their care. Newborns are threatened not only by poverty, inherited drug abuse, and abortion but also by dysfunctional and increasingly isolated families. We can no longer assume the permanence of the nuclear, much less the extended, family. The shared culture and religious rhetoric of Tudor and Stuart England that enabled communication, even across great class differences, cannot be assumed in mobile and multicultural North America. So pastoral theologians, hoping to forge a stronger link between nature and faith, birth room and congregation, now speak of a "domestic church," expressing their desire to avoid a tug of war between family ritualizing and ecclesiastical liturgy.[55]

Christian theologians Herbert Anderson and Edward Foley claim that for Christians "[baptismal] water is thicker than blood."[56] In other words, spiritual "kinship" in Christ is stronger than biological kinship. There is little doubt that in other times and places the godparent-godchild relation was deeply formative. But in contemporary North America, their claim seems largely an aspiration rather than an achievement or a fact. Here, baptism seldom has the power to make or sustain community, although it may supplement or enhance it. However weakened kinship ties may be in today's world, the blood of kinship is still thicker than the water of liturgy.

Even if infant baptism expresses no more than a devout hope, it is still one of the few ritual moments in which Christians, however nominally, attend to the spiritual needs of infants and parents. At the very least, the rite's language and gestures aim specifically at cultivating a hospitable environment for the newly born and keeping alive some recognition of the basic human paradox, namely, that the first step on the human journey is a step toward death. If pastoral theologians like Foley and Anderson are not only serious but also successful in calling for "appropriate craziness" at the moment of birth and for "extravagant praise" of a child's uniqueness, parents may, in fact, find the distance between birth room and sanctuary not so great after all.[57]

Cosmic Fetuses and Bundle Babies

By considering historic Christian baptism, we are already on the verge of reimagining birth and birth rites. Aspiring to create bonds stronger than those of kinship, wondering if fecundity and virility might be celebrated in church basements, and reveling in the sensuality of early baptism are implicitly creative and critical acts capable of precipitating profound changes in actual ritual practice.

But we are not used to thinking of ritual in this way. Popular parlance implies an opposition between ritual and imagination: Ritual is supposed to be about conserving the past, while imagination is said to create the future. Imagination is mythologized as a kind of radar enabling visionaries to divine the path that lies ahead, or it is a kind of secular magic that artists use to conjure new and exciting realities. If art and artists are assigned the job of keeping an eye on the future, then ritual and ritualists are left with the task of being guardians of the past.

I take issue with this view. Ritual is not simply the culmination of memory; it also requires imagination. Even when a rite commemorates the past—somehow transporting participants back into mythic time or transposing the mythic origins into the present—imagination constructs the bridge. Ritualizing is an imaginatively suffused act.

But rites do not thrive in a vacuum. They change as cultural values and worldviews change. If they do not, they lose their relevance and die. To live, rites and the traditions they mediate need constant revision. A living rite at once connects with tradition and is attuned to significant shifts in fundamental values and basic, orienting images. *Birth rites* only make sense in the context of *birth systems,* that is, the institutions, personnel, images, and knowledge that a culture or tradition has about birth. Birth rites grow out of birth practices and birth imagery.

In the late 1960s Dr. Michel Odent of the Centre Hospitalier Général de Pithiviers in France pioneered a method of birthing under water. At about the same time others pioneered a form of therapy called "primal scream," and still others developed a form of deep breathing that claimed to precipitate prenatal or birth memories. All these methods were premised on the notion that birth is a trauma for the child. Whereas therapists worked with adults to heal them from the trauma of birth, Odent wanted to ease the birth process itself, making the transition less abrupt. Since a fetus gestates in a safe, warm, watery place suffused with low light, Odent replicated this environment in the form of a birthing pool, where a newborn, assisted by gravity, could emerge from a mother assisted by the water's buoyancy.

Though not developed for ritual reasons so much as for practical and psychological ones, this birthing practice had enormous ritual possibilities, since water is so widespread a symbol in the world's mythology. Here, we might say, is a baptism at the very moment of birth. The practice was not widely taken up in either Europe or North America, even though it attracted a small, devoted following. This ritual-like way of birthing remains marginal in both Europe and North America, but photographs of water birth provided compelling visual images that inspired those wanting to pursue alternative birthing strategies.

Another example of a cultural moment with implications for birthing ritual occurred in 1965. The Swedish photographer Lennart Nilsson published *A Child Is Born,* a book of photographs documenting the conception and gestation process. In the same year *Life* magazine popularized the photos. Then in 1990, when the abortion issue had a high profile, Nilsson published a second series, these in lush, highly manipulated color. Though photographic, they were hardly scientific or documentary, and they were employed by antiabortion advocates in their arguments against pro-choice proponents. One scholar observed, "Both series of photos, but particularly the later ones, are made to suggest the abstract, cosmological import of the creation of life. Through incredible magnification, the brightly colored images of swirls and folds, and the planet-like fertilized egg, are made to look like images of outer space—conception on a grand scale. The images present the fetus-as-miracle, as the wonder of Man [sic], far beyond the mundane scale of a simple, ordinary, female body."[58]

The film *2001: A Space Odyssey* concluded by superimposing on planet Earth a fetal image, much like Nilsson's "eggs." Later, *Close Encounters of the Third Kind* popularized a nonthreatening, fetal-like space alien. Ann Kaplan argues that the 1980s and 90s witnessed the transformation of the fetus from a part of the mother's body into a subject acting in its own right. It even became a cosmic entity, a perfected being.

With the fetus imagined as a complete, even perfected, human, toy manufacturers could then create My Bundle Baby, a doll in a womblike pouch that could be tied around a child's waist, or the Mommy-to-Be doll, which contained a baby (not a fetus) inside. However much these dolls may live up to their manufacturers' claim that they teach nurturing and the skills of motherhood, they also erase the differences between fetuses and children. Whereas the Tudor-Stuart debate was over baptism's capacity or incapacity to ensure salvation, the contemporary Western debate is about the definition of personhood. Birth rites necessarily imply such definitions and therefore are not likely to escape controversy.

Having to ponder dolls may tempt us to segregate ritual from popular culture lest we pollute sacred liturgies with the fluff of fads and the manipulations of marketing strategies. But popular imagery conditions the way people respond to traditional symbols, so we cannot afford to ignore the interface. Strongly delivered images, even transient ones, press reality to assume their shape. Whether we like it or not, birth rites compete with toys in erasing or creating lines between categories of being: fetus/child, mother/woman, father/man. The strength of rites, especially liturgical or religious ones is that they characteristically endure, but they typically adapt to cultural change slowly, and this is their weakness. A strength of commercially produced symbols is their capacity for rapid change, but this rapidity is also a weakness that signals opportunistic motives.

Rites both use and inculcate symbols. Birth, with its rites, is not just a process we imagine *about* but an event we imagine *with*. Birth provides one of the most fundamental images of creativity. We use it to signal great cosmological leaps. Near the end of the film *2001*, a cosmic fetus appears, symbolizing the evolutionary transformation precipitated by an encounter with intelligent life on another planet.

Birth symbolizes both "the" creation and human creativity. It is one of the most universal metaphors for positive and significant transformation; we speak not only of reborn selves but also of the births of nations. So the first task of a reinvented birth rite would be to enshrine the most powerful birth images we can recall or imagine. A rite fails if its basic symbols are trite or clichéd. For a birth rite, either traditional or newly invented, to be effective, it needs to accomplish many tasks:

- helping pregnant mothers sense the importance of their work
- cultivating safe deliveries without offering false, or "magical," hope
- drawing fathers or partners and other family members more deeply into the bonding power of the birthing event
- encouraging parents to assume responsibility without overburdening them
- integrating newborns into traditions deeper than the present and communities larger than nuclear families
- fostering a sense of the preciousness of a human life
- cultivating appreciation for an individual's uniqueness

However we imagine birth, we should do it in a way that enhances our ability to respect the process and weather the bodily and social changes it necessarily involves. Sugarcoating birth with fantasy or pounding it with technology are not likely to help us do either.

Kneeling on the Earth

Technocratic values exercise enormous pressure, so it should be no surprise that only 2 percent of North American women give birth at home. Home births are usually attended by midwives, and statistics show that infant mortality rates are lowest in countries such as Sweden and the Netherlands, where midwives, not doctors, are considered the normal birthing experts. Despite the statistics, in North America it is widely held that a mother who births at home jeopardizes her baby's life, but could birthing in a hospital jeopardize a baby's spirituality?[59]

Although it is possible to experience fulfilling births in hospitals, most of these institutions are inhospitable environments for felicitous rites. The project of reimagining birth requires a more congenial place where it can be fully explored. The home can be one such space:

Today is Thursday, May 17, five days after the birth. . . . Still wearing my purple sweatsuit, I check my profile when I pass by a mirror, expecting to see my belly fully collapsed and tucked flat inside my pants. The other day I felt so grungy. I just want to be beautiful again, I thought to myself. Beautiful instead of efficient, instead of organized, sitting still, resplendent with Being. In my mind's eye I glimpse my new mothering self—hair loose, thick and glossy in a shimmering aura of calm, impassive as the Mona Lisa.

I tell people I feel like a holy person. I don't think they know what I mean. They nod and say, yes, spacey, yes, tired, still euphoric, disconnected from your body. But I mean, holy—a part of me fully dilated, reemerging slowly and reluctantly, from a state of grace. Dilated, still open, the soul's eye, seeing. The lips of the soul parted way back, effaced, disappearing behind the corners of the mouth of the body, birthing.

Saturday, May 12
2:30 A.M.

A powerful contraction yanks me awake, strikes sudden and hard, like a temple gong, in the center of my being. The cervix opening. No mistaking the sensation. I clamber out of bed, grope for undershirt and nightgown, and slip into the bathroom. Cold marble floor, night-light on. Sensations like those of my first labor with Cailleah: cramping, emptying, shivering. Could be labor; could be just rehearsal. Have to wait a while before I'm sure. I sit on the toilet erect, quiet, shaking. I hear Ron sniff; he's awake. Moments later, his voice, low and clear, drops into the cool stillness of the bathroom. Should we call the midwife? he asks. Let's wait, I say. Not for long, though. I hear him on the phone already, so I wash, brush, and ready myself. Now I am clean, awake, prepared, resigned. We move downstairs. The contractions come quickly. Ron times them at two to three minutes apart, each lasting forty-five seconds. I put on some music, liquid piano solos, then steal into the little bathroom off the kitchen. Cold toilet seat, cold wood floor, night-light only.

3:30 A.M.

Mary and Grace arrive. Grace first. Then Mary calls Martha, her backup, and soon she arrives as well. I hear their voices, low and muffled, friendly, busy in the kitchen and living room, setting everything in order. During my first labor I'd forgotten to tell everyone where all the birth supplies were, so people kept coming into the bathroom and asking me simple questions I couldn't answer, like, Where are the towels and the wash basin? and, What did you do with the ground sheet? This time I had put all the items together in an obvious place and left notes instructing everyone about everything. They leave me to my work. I am relieved. Alone.

Like a nocturnal animal poised in the dark, I sit silent and focused, listening, staring at the smudges on the wall. I concentrate on opening, breathing deeply through each contraction. The Virgin stands to my left, feeding me flowers. The womb opens to feed on them—small purplish-blue petals that calm me, that nourish the baby for the journey ahead. I picture my womb as a lotus blossom, gradually roused from its steady sleep into full flower. Birth, birth, I hear myself repeat the word as I breathe out, eyes closed, legs apart, my hands and mouth loose, my body a star in the night.

Between contractions, coming thick and fast, I stand and shake loose my hands and feet. "Do your hands tingle?" Mary asks, then Grace again later. "No. I'm trying to normalize between contractions," I say, "trying to keep the blood circulating." With each contraction I enter a dream space, a void between the worlds. And between waves I crave ordinariness: light, movement, sounds, laughter. These keep me tethered and calm. I must give birth on the earth, not in this twilight sphere.

At some point the waters break. There's very little blood, mostly water. Lots of it, running down my legs again and again, surprising me each time.

"The water's nice and clear," Mary notes. By now I'm hot and sweating. My hair is damp. It clings to my gown. Please bring me a cold, wet cloth. Ron hands me a musty blue washcloth. It feels wonderful. I'm thirsty. Cold water. Juice. "Is it okay to keep drinking?" I ask. Yes, and keep peeing too, they say. I stay on the toilet not because of the blood or water but because there my limbs open. I feel relaxed, contained, and safe. Perched on the red horse blanket outside the bathroom sits Ron. Ready.

I feel the shift suddenly. The contractions have changed. They're not about opening any more. The urge to push begins. I tell Mary. She says, yes, that's because your waters have broken. I head into the living room. The rest migrate there as well. I strip off my nightgown, but I don't feel ready to push the baby out. I need to make a transition of some sort, yet I don't know what that is. I feel exposed and retreat to the bathroom. Everyone wonders at this reversal; so do I. I ask Ron to press down on my lower back. The pressure feels good. Grace comes and sits outside the door. She asks if she can massage my feet. Her touch is like Ron's—steady, firm, gentle. But I lurch back onto the toilet when a contraction overtakes me. The waves are stronger now, and I hear myself whimper as the breath escapes my mouth. I am tired. I want to sleep between contractions. They won't let me. I want to lie down.

Outside the bathroom, kneeling on all fours like a mare, I lay my head on the red horse blanket and close my eyes for a moment's rest. The cold night air seeps through the doorway. I pull my hair down around me. Then I'm up and rocking slowly, back and forth on hands and knees, through each siege. My hair falls over my face. Heavy, long and dark, it keeps me warm. The veil that hides and protects, I fold it back and feel luxurious, sexual, primal. My strength is in my hair, I think to myself.

Now and then I worry that I won't be able to hold up long at this pace. "How am I doing?" I ask. I need something from them: words? wakefulness? assurance? These people are my hands and feet. I reach out to feel them, groping for a tether. Stretching and shaking out my limbs, I look to the warm, tea-filled bodies in the kitchen for help. I need reassurance. I already know what they think. What I need is something else. They think I'm doing splendidly. I'm not writhing or disoriented. I don't cry out. The baby's heartbeat is steady. We are fine. "She's the expert. She should show your prenatal class how it's done," Mary says to Martha. Pulling on a pair of white translucent gloves, Mary checks me. It's the only time she does so during the entire labor. "Oh, the head's just this far (she indicates a space the size of a bread morsel) from crowning. How's your urge to push?"

"It comes and goes," I say, nothing more.

I slip back inside the bathroom. The clock chimes every half hour; I try not to think of the time. This state, these contractions, last a long, long while. The labor seems timeless, relentless. Is everything okay but just slow? Am I doing all I need to do? This position feels the best, but does it slow me down? I'm tired. Just tired, that's all. Will Cailleah be awake before the baby is born? At this pace will I make it through until morning?

Eventually, we move back into the living room; I forget why. I think Ron suggests we try it. They've turned the music off. First the piano, then the Indian flute music, played over and over. Better to have it quiet now, one soloist. Daylight filters through the south window, where the succulents hang like sentinels. Grace sits to my left, her back resting on the wall. I haven't seen much of her since the foot rub. Now I see that she's been keeping vigil. Realizing my back is toward her, I try to turn slightly, so I can see her, acknowledge her.

But like the plants, I turn and yield to the light. On all fours again, I look down, noticing the sheet laid out beneath us is studded with large daisies crowned with slender, green leaves. I turn to tell Grace that the sheet she brought for the birth is wonderful—the glad white daisies will soon to be bathed in blood. How apt. I look toward the toy box and see that Ron has assembled the birth objects: the casting made of his hands, moccasins, the name doll made from a gnarled tree limb, the temple bell. He is to my right, kneeling. Mary sits on the arm of the couch, Martha, in the rocker. I turn and ask if Mary wants to do anything, like take my blood pressure. No, she says, calmly. You're doing fine. I laugh and say, well, this is less eventful than a prenatal checkup. We all laugh. I feel good, normal. Happy. Working. The sun rises.

I am on my knees, palms to the floor, legs spread wide apart. Surrounded but alone. The Virgin is gone. Now there is only sky, wide, achingly blue New Mexico sky. The room is perfectly still. Contractions come, and I breathe like a desert creature into the sky. It greets me with strength. I feel myself expanding, becoming as wide and bright and glorious as the horizon. I drink in the brilliant blue and rise to greet it, arching forward through the tight, clenching ache. A desert animal rising to greet the sun. Hands and vulva seek the floor. My head arcs upward, seeking sky, its brilliance and clarity high above a small, dark creature kneeling on the earth.

6:00 A.M.

I crawl from my desert niche over toward the couch, where I reach out for someone to hang onto. Grace moves to my left, Ron to my right. They are equal, well balanced, fresh help as I crouch into sudden readiness and sudden helplessness. Squatting position. Utterly vulnerable, I hang between them, gripping their necks and shoulders, then bear down, focusing on my lower belly, trying still to breathe, breathe the baby out. No pushing, please, no straining, no cracking open like a great begonia tuber as in Cailleah's birth. Mary leans into me, firm and gentle, with hot compresses. The wet heat feels good, drawing the sharp stinging back into the folds of the cloth. Martha fetches the hand mirror so we can look down to see the wet, dark head crowning. Watching the crowning, seeing what I'm feeling, suddenly strengthens me. It's all getting very hard now. I can't keep this up for long. The pressure is enormous, the work immense. The stinging, searing line of being I've become is now utterly dependent on others: these two to hold me up, this one to catch the baby, and this one to be born in his own good time.

6:30 A.M.

I feel a sudden, intense shift in sensation as another's body escapes mine; it leaps out in one amphibious flip. A boy, large, round, and dark. Bryn, naturally.[60]

Not long after Bryn's birth, Susan, my wife, said she felt she had crossed a line beyond which there was no turning back. Even though she was already an adult and had given birth before, this time she had traversed a frontier, dividing her life into before and after. Although this was her second child, not her first, Susan organized a postpartum rite. Whereas the "home-birth prep party," which preceded Bryn's birth by a month, had been occasioned by anticipatory anxiety, the postpartum rite was about letting go of an old way of life. The rite was a response to what Susan experienced as revelation; the birth had exposed her mode of being in the world. Not that she intended to keep on having babies, but that the work of this birth was a metaphor for the person she most fundamentally was: one who creates by following the rise and fall of underlying rhythms, one who delivers *without pushing*.

In our marriage the births of our two children have been the occasions for our most searching inquiries into the nature of ritual and spirituality. Neighbors and colleagues would not have recognized anything that Susan and I did as a birth rite. There was no proper name for the collection of activities; we did not even use the generic term *birth rite*. There was no shower, no birth announcement, no baptism, no circumcision, no formal naming ceremony. Despite the absence of named rites, the births of both our children *felt* ritualized, making it is easy to understand why someone might consider pregnancy and birth a "natural initiation process."[61]

For both Susan and me, giving and receiving birth exercised adult-making, as well as mother- and father-making, power. The birth felt like a rite of passage not only because we actively greeted it, by engaging in special actions (meditation and tea making, for instance) and putting objects (for example, diapers and dolls bearing potential names of our child) in specially prepared places, but also because it required risk, provoked anxiety, gathered community, led to the contemplation of perennial human questions, precipitated a protracted period that put us betwixt and between worlds, elicited celebratory responses, and fundamentally changed our lives.

Susan's account is shot through with metaphors, memories, and dream images that contribute to the ritual sense of the event.[62] The metaphors are not literary flourishes but images recalled from the experience itself. The world she creates in the story is in some sense other— on the edge of myth, fantasy, vision—even though it is replete with earthy things: the toilet, blood, sweat, body parts. The desert and the Virgin are present in ordinary rooms.

For the two of us these images and events represented glimpses of other realities we have seldom encountered. But, Susan admits, telling her birth story shut down more conversations than it opened up. When the flower-feeding Virgin appears to a non-Catholic in the bathroom and a New Mexico desert shows up in a living room in southern Ontario, what is a listener to think? Does this woman really think she's a mare? (Does the angel Gabriel really deposit a child in a man's brain?)

A major difficulty with giving birth in North America is that there is no adequate language for it or for other spiritually significant events. Experiences that require metaphor are too often heard as either literal and therefore delusional or as merely poetic. The existing language of birth tends to force such a choice. Not only are we ignorant about how to respond ritually, we are also not taught how to speak of the spirituality of an event. The language of how-to books on birth is either biomedical or psychological. Before the twentieth century, birth was not even considered a proper subject of conversation.[63] If birth is hardly a topic at all, it should not be surprising that it is seldom the topic of spiritual reflection or ritual action.

Despite the plenitude of research on altered states of consciousness, "birthing consciousness" is not a category that appears on lists of possible states of consciousness. Dreaming, reverie, meditation, and other altered states are, it would seem, higher states than birthing consciousness. Even though an occasional researcher compares birthing with shamanic and mystical states or speaks of the sacredness of birth, little has been done to compare birth consciousness with that of traditional mind-altering practices such as vision quests and trance dances.[64]

Birth consciousness has profound spiritual possibilities that are ritually underexplored in the European American West. Here, births are more commonly greeted in a language and attitude that are means-end oriented. Despite the depths of emotion experienced during birth, we do not easily connect birth with ritual. Our understanding of ritual is too stubbornly associated with flat affect. With few exceptions, birth space and ritual space are imagined as opposites.

Despite the surreal qualities of Susan's journal entries, the living room remains the living room; hers is no shamanic journey to some nether region. But neither does the birth transpire in medical space. Conventionally, hospital rooms and bedrooms are the proper places for birth. In Susan's story, both are displaced in favor of two other places, neither of which is usually considered a ritual space and both of which are made special by what transpires in them. Bathrooms, usually private, and living rooms, orderly and on display, are not ritual sites. But in Susan's experience, and mine as well, birth thickened ordinary acts into liturgical gestures, charged nearby objects until they vibrated like icons, and saturated the place where we live—so much so that the living room tingles even today, many years after the event. Ordinary spaces became pregnant with meaning—the metaphor could hardly be more apt. So this birth, like the one two years before, became sacred, holy. Where space is made sacred, it is difficult *not* to think of the activity in it as ritualistic. I am convinced that one has to work overtime to strip birth of its inherent holiness. *The holy—that about which one wishes to remain steadfastly silent and about which one cannot stop talking.* Susan and I are circumspect about speaking of our children's births as holy or sacred. Experiencing a birth is like entering and awakening from a dream in a culture in which dreams are never recounted over breakfast. In the end, daytime consciousness leads us to forget rather than to integrate the wisdom of the night.

Our two children, unmistakably present at their own births, were in some sense absent as well. They do not remember their births (although Cailleah, Bryn's sister, is tempted to think she does). Susan and I are determined not to forget. So it *feels* to the kids as if they remember their births, since they have heard the stories often, since they can point to and dance on the spot in the living room where they first touched down on earth. At home, retelling the stories of our children's emergence renders birth special, but at school, home births are regarded as weird, so our children grow silent when their friends tease them or when the public-health nurse cheerfully announces, "Now you have all been to hospitals—on the day you were born! Which hospital were you born in?"

Susan's is not a typical North American home-birth story, even when compared with those written by women who have chosen home births or were inspired by Ina May Gaskin's *Spiritual Midwifery*. On a Web site dedicated to the posting of home-birth stories, few sound a sustained spiritual note or describe birth in religious language.[65] However much Susan and I felt the births of our two kids to be holy and the activities surrounding them ritualistic, our experience is not the norm. It fails to conform to the working definitions of either religion or ritual. A typical reaction goes something like this: "Yes, we can tell that you feel strongly about the births of your children. So why not say that their births were very emotional events, but not that they were religious or spiritual or ritualistic ones?"

The trouble with reimagining birth rites is closely linked to the difficulty of redefining religion, spirituality, and ritual. If we think of religion as belief in or worship of God, or if we take ritual to be the collective repetition of traditional actions, birth will seem bereft of both religious significance and ritual form. But if we consider religion to be the way humans value most comprehensively and intensively, and if we regard ritual as the enactment of our most generative gestures and most grounded postures, birth is a moment fraught with religious significance and ritual possibility.[66]

There is a growing tendency to distinguish sharply between religion and spirituality: Religion is institutional, traditional, and perhaps even moribund, while spirituality is personal, spontaneous, and alive. The current notion of spirituality allows one to espouse a religiosity not identified with the Christian mainstream. One cannot take out membership in spirituality, since it is not denominational, but one can be "deeply into it."

Until recently, spirituality and ritual were also construed as opposites: Ritual was physical, exterior, superficial, and institutional, while spirituality was metaphysical, interior, deep, and personal. In both scholarly and popular usage, ritual still connotes things religious, collective, repetitive, and traditional. But for a growing minority ritual is becoming a tool of exploration and a means of pursuing personal spirituality.

The Western tendency to split things apart and set them in opposition has plagued all three ideas. We need interlocking, rather than polarized, conceptions of religion, spirituality, and ritual. By *ritual* I mean *sequences of ordinary action rendered special by virtue of their conden-*

sation, elevation, or stylization. By *spirituality* I intend *practiced attentiveness aimed at nurturing a sense of the interdependence of all beings sacred and all things ordinary.* And by *religion* I mean *spirituality sustained as a tradition or organized into an institution.* Defined this way, religion, spirituality, and ritual are neither mere synonyms nor archenemies. In these definitions the social is not cast as the opponent of the personal; the sacred is not split off from the profane; and spirituality is not the opposite of either religion or ritual.

A Birth Well Attended

The ability to invent meaningful rites depends to a large degree on our ability to attend, to be fully and unreservedly present. Ritual is not just a way of acting, it is also a kind of awareness, a form of consciousness. Even without benefit of ceremony, birth itself has the power to bond people, etch the human body, and engender hope at an almost cellular level. Birth marks the maternal body. However stringent the dieting and dedicated the exercise that may follow childbirth, a mother's body is forever different. The event renders her and the newborn permeable. And those who attend—fathers, partners, friends, relatives—if they are attuned, are not mere assistants but supporting actors. For a few precious hours or days, those close to the birth event are in a position to soak up whatever meanings course through the blood and suffuse the air. Ritualizing the event is the best way to ensure that the meanings absorbed are those that represent our most profound aspirations.

We human beings are symbol-driven animals, acting not only on the basis of what things *are* or *do* but what they *mean.* Symbols are tools with which we discover, construct, and communicate meaning. Since of all human activities rites are among the most thickly clotted with symbols, we should be deeply concerned if they are absent from birth. Most of us were not greeted with birth rites. We dropped into a ritual vacuum. Even so-called birthdays look forward to growing up rather than backward to being born. Birthdays are less about the day of birth than they are about the lapse of another year.

Whatever human beings may *add to* birth ritually, the most important action is that of attending, which is to say, contemplating, absorbing, and yielding. Shortly after the birth of his son, Doug Abrams Arava wrote a letter that anticipated the day when his son, Jesse, could read it for himself. It concludes this way:

I could now see your small head covered with hair making its way through the birth canal, but my heart would sink after each contraction as you would move back inside. Like the tug-of-war with the sea that I had experienced while netting fish in Brazil, we would have to move with the rhythms of nature, sinking back to pull (or in this case push) forward. Nature does not move in straight lines or with uninterrupted progress, I now understand, but in waves and in cycles. I moved down in front of Rachel to prepare to catch you. As you began to crown, I bent down and kissed the top of your head. I must have been trembling, but all I can remember now was the incredible excitement and anticipation I felt as you pushed your way out. Great tears of joy were streaming down my face. The plates on your head had squeezed together to make it out of the tight opening, and your head was long. Finally, your face popped out and your head fell into my hands. Then your shoulders. I held you under your arms and pulled the rest of your slippery body out of the birth canal and onto your mother's chest. There you rested. At your first cry, we sang *shirat ha'asabim* [song of the grass] to you just as we had sung it each night before going to sleep while you were in the womb. You looked at us and were calmed. When your cord stopped pulsating, I cut it and said the *shekianu* blessing ["Blessed are You, our God, King of the universe, Who has kept us alive, sustained us, and brought us to this season"].[67] I took you in my arms as Rachel and the midwives delivered the placenta, the body fruit that had nourished you for nine months. You and I stared into each other's eyes, yours filled with brightness and wonder, mine with the greatest joy I have ever known. I remember thinking how grateful I was to be your father.[68]

These impassioned words are not a description of "the" Jewish rite of passage designed to recognize the spiritual importance of birth, because, in fact, Judaism has no ceremony appropriate to the actual moment of birth. Nor do Christianity and Buddhism. Even so, it is hard to deny the appropriateness of breaking into song when a child clears its mother's body or of uttering a blessing when the umbilical cord is severed. We are not taken aback, since this is a Jewish father at home rather than a physician in a hospital or a rabbi officiating at a ceremony.

But if this is not "the" Jewish birth rite, is it really a rite at all? Can rites be short and improvised and still have their intended effect? Don't rites need to be long and traditional? Do brief gestures such as praying, singing, and blessing constitute rites of passage? Theorists say rites of passage transform. No one doubts that a birth transforms a mother or a family, but would anyone claim that a prayer, song, or blessing transforms? Aren't they simply ancillary responses to the transformation already wrought by ordinary biological means? For those swept up in such powerful occasions it makes little difference whether such actions transform or acknowledge transformation, whether they conform or do not conform to formal definitions of ritual. What matters is that they integrate people into rhythms larger than themselves.

Doug and Rachel (the birthing mother as well as a physician) knew that after the birth of a son the officially expected rite of passage was *brit milah*, circumcision, a rite performed on the eighth day after a boy's birth (unless doing so would endanger his health). Although the two parents had doubts about doing it, they carried out this traditional ceremony. Doug wrote,

Tomorrow after taking your foreskin, we will give you a name. Why must we take away in order to give? What is not complete, whole, about your perfect little body? God, I hope in this act we do not take from you your innocence, shattering the peace we have known during this week after your birth, in a barbaric, holy blood sacrifice, that will make you a member of our tribe and enter you into a covenant with our people and God, your source.[69]

There is a line in the *brit milah* that makes some parents shudder. It says, "I saw you wallowing in your own blood." In North American Judaism, these words are often not translated. In fact, they are sometimes dropped altogether from the rite. But the rite itself is not dropped. Despite their ambivalence about circumcision, Doug and Rachel had their son circumcised. Attached to the script for the service were several explanations of its importance and meaning. One of them included a quotation attributed to Leopold Zunz: "To abrogate circumcision . . . is suicide, not reform." The traditional rite is not easily dispensed with, and it can precipitate agonizing questions.

Later, Doug and Rachel, who are Reconstructionist Jews, carried out a second cutting rite, *upsheeran*, ordinarily an Hasidic practice. Among Hasidic Jews, a young boy's hair is not cut. He is allowed to become wild, at least symbolically. He romps androgynously outside the pale of civilization. But at age three, his locks are shorn. Just as circumcision symbolically separates Jesse from maternal containment and sets him to orbiting in the world of males, so *upsheeran* separates him from babyhood and moves him into childhood.

In the Aravas' series of ritual decisions we glimpse a family doing what a growing number of contemporary families are choosing to do.

At the moment of birth, Doug and Rachel improvise; at circumcision they honor their tradition; and at first haircutting, they borrow. They cobble together out of the materials at hand a nurturing symbolic environment for their newborn child.

Nurturing Ritual Sensibilities

Since the next chapter is about initiation into adulthood, we will soon leap across a decade and a half of the most formative years in a person's life. Between a baby's emergence and the onset of maturation at adolescence, one's ritual sensibility is fundamentally shaped by being either nurtured or ignored. So it makes little sense to let the rites of childhood fall between the cracks simply because the standard scenario leaps from birth ritual to coming-of-age ritual.

Even though kids may be cast as bit-part players, decorating wedding processions, for example, most ritual actors are assumed to be adult members of a society. At birth a child is either the object or occasion of ritual; rites are done for or around the child. Even though newborns cannot be primary ritual actors, they immediately begin the task of learning to be ritually competent or incompetent. The task of developing a ritual sensibility proceeds most effectively when a child is born into a world already reverberating with the sounds of celebration.

Defining, conceptualizing, and reimagining may be largely adult activities, but absorbing a gestural and symbolic vocabulary starts at birth or even during gestation (since fetuses respond to light, sound, and tactile stimulation). It is, then, a great mistake to shield children from passage—to hustle them away from the fluids and odors of birth or protect them from the disturbing sounds of death.

Fancying ourselves as having outgrown an enchanted world in which magic was possible, we adults suppose birth rites are for the mother and family, not for the child, who, after all, does not understand the words. And, in our supposedly disenchanted, technocratic world, birth rites are not aimed at demons either, for there are no such forces threatening a child's life. We are certain that birth rites, even when they appear to be aimed at determining the sex or fate of newborns or at deterring flesh-hungry demons, are *really* about encouraging parents. Adult rites are taken to be mere psychological devices or esthetic flourishes, not cosmic acts; they only affect beliefs, not the way things really are.

In a child's world, however, the boundaries between mother and child or the living and the dead are less sharply drawn. One of the most persistent features of Western ritual and art is the attempt to reconnect domains that Western adulthood has taught us to sever. By observing and interacting ritually with children we can learn a great deal about what it takes to develop a ritual sensibility. With encouragement and example, children can become adept ritual makers.[70]

Psychologist Erik Erikson maintains that humans develop ritual skills in the same way they develop moral or intellectual ones—in stages more or less uniform and predictable.[71] The first ritual teacher, Erikson suggests, is the mother. She cultivates a ritual sensibility whether or not the word is in her vocabulary and whether or not she intends to. Later, a child's family, school teachers, and peers also become ritual instructors, even if unwitting ones.

Between a newborn and its mother there transpires what Erikson calls a "greeting ceremonial." A daughter signals Mom that she's now awake and hungry. Mom bends over the crib, smiles, touches, coos. Daughter momentarily stops crying and looks toward Mom's face. She picks up Daughter, cuddling, sniffing, checking. Then she tips Daughter gently into an almost horizontal position, the baby's head cradled in Mom's arms, baby's little muzzle now searching out the breast.

And so it goes. Watched for several days, the whole scene, though it may display minor variations, could not be more predictable if it were choreographed. The interaction, though not governed by rubrics in anybody's book of rites, is highly ritualized. Even the abusive or neglectful versions are. And thus Mom nurtures a sense of the numinous, of a powerful sustaining presence. The capacity to experience numinosity is the most basic of all ritual sensibilities in the Eriksonian scheme. It makes no difference whether Mom has seen, likes, or remembers paintings of the Madonna and child, the interaction is sacred; it reaches the core of one's being. The sense of the numinous arises from what Erikson calls the mutuality of recognition. Recognized by a hallowed, sustaining presence, a child recognizes that presence in return. The infant's separateness is transcended in the same act that confirms his or her distinctiveness.

This is only the first stage in developing ritual competence. Besides the numinous phase, there are five others—judicial, dramatic, formal, ideological, and generational—each layered atop the previous one. If an earlier stage is ill formed, later ones will be deficient, and the muscle of ritual competence will atrophy from lack of exercise. Remedial action will be needed.

To sketch out the rest of the developmental scenario: From parents and family our proverbial daughter will absorb judicial skills, learning to discriminate between good and evil. Ritualizing, however culturally varied, requires this ability.

By playing, the maiden will practice dramatic elaboration of normal interactions. She will mask and perform herself as beings she is not: wolves, princesses, dragons, goddesses, and other mythological entities. She will generate imaginary plots and tinker with climactic endings. What is ritual if not dramatic?

As she reaches school age, the daughter, on whom all hopes ride, will learn about forms, social and otherwise. She will take account, with or without enthusiasm, of rules that govern formalities. She will learn to care for details and construct order, for of such are rites made.

Then, if her learning is not disrupted or impeded, the adolescent daughter will discover the power of ideas and irreversible commitments—yet another requirement of ritual systems.

Finally, when the daughter becomes a woman, she will glimpse her own mortality and have to face the necessity for transmitting her own skills and knowledge to others. And how will she do so if not ritually? Generational competence requires that she honor her connectedness with preceding and succeeding generations.

Schematically outlined, this is the developmental process of learning to act ritually, as Erikson constructs it. It may be that the developmental pattern he outlines has ethnocentric and gender-specific dimensions. It may be that the scheme is a form of academic mythmaking, storytelling rather than science. But stories are crucial, and a story about the slow development of ritual skill across time is one we in the West very much need. I agree with Erikson's basic claim, that the human capacity for ritual is sculpted, slowly and in stages, out of the raw stuff that nature provides. Ritual ought not to be done unto children but with them.

The Dove Still Travels with Me

Because of the technocratic nature of hospitals, attempts at early ritualizing *with* rather than *at* or *for* children may be more successful if begun later, after the birth event. An obvious occasion would be that of welcoming or naming both those newly born and those recently adopted.

The artists who comprise Welfare State International in Ulverston,

England, are sometimes called "engineers of the imagination." From 1972 to the present, this collective, directed by John Fox and Sue Gill, has not only been producing large-scale civic celebrations replete with pyrotechnics, good humor, mind-boggling images, and barbed social and environmental critique; it has also been facilitating rites of passage. Welfare State associates have managed weddings, taught workshops on funeral making and assisted people in planning child-naming ceremonies. Unlike commercial wedding planners and professional funeral directors, their aim is to empower ordinary people by encouraging them and equipping them with techniques for creating rites. Unlike much New Age ritualizing in North America, Welfare State ceremonies are not pilfered from native traditions, and they are not fad ridden or deliberately confrontational. The rites are creative but down-to-earth. *Engineers of the Imagination: The Welfare State Handbook* and *The Dead Good Funerals Book* are among the few how-to books that I recommend.[72]

In the former, Lois Lambert, a Welfare State associate, tells of this naming ceremony:

On Easter . . . six families and their guests gathered to celebrate the naming of seven children in the grounds of Duncombe Park in North Yorkshire. As we collected ourselves under the high cupola of the Tuscan Temple, many of us still strangers to each other, we looked forward to the day with a mixture of feelings. Some of us had been involved in the preparations during the previous week; building a giant of earth and stone in the woods, making and rehearsing a shadow play, erecting a huge bird whose wings spanned a wide avenue, whitewashing the old orangery where the feast was to be held, and cooking the pig which would be served at it. Some of us knew the order of events. All of us welcomed the chance to dedicate our children in front of friends and strangers, a gesture of hope and blessing, protection too, in the face of the terrors of our present world. . . .

Our child, Richard, who was to be named . . . was a lad of eight, and we had chosen him for our son when he was four months old. So this ceremony of dedication was especially important to my husband David and myself, since we had not been present at his birth. . . . We wondered how Richard, old enough to play a conscious role in his naming ceremony, would handle the day.

. . . We had driven together to Duncombe Park, and as we stood under the dome waiting for everyone to gather, there was a sense of being outside the usual boundaries of time. It had been a steep climb to reach this spot from the cars, and at the top there was an unexpected landscape that was at once natural and artificial. A wide grass walk opened out in front of us, bordered by unkempt woods on one side and tidy rows of evergreens on the other—a long vista with a Greek Temple at its end, toward which we walked slowly chatting to those we knew and also to one or two we didn't. The children played around us, excited by the space, and with us also was a great grandmother of ninety-two, who had come to take part in the naming of her great-grandson George. . . .

Three musicians awaited us at the Greek Temple and led us toward a tented space where we were to be shown a shadow play. With them, carried on his father's back, was six-month-old Hannes, also to be named that day, who jumped up and down in his papoose trying to grasp the bird's nest in his mother's hat as she played the saxophone. The family had come from Holland and already there was a sense in which we all felt that we were on a journey together, having come from very different directions. This feeling was reinforced by the shadow play in the darkened tent, where we were all brought together in a small space for the first completely directed moment. It was the story of Gilgamesh and his search for Eternal Youth; he finds it, but loses it to a serpent who finds it tasty, changes his skin and vanishes in thick grey swamps forever. So Gilgamesh lost Eternal Youth but found the salt of Life sweeter and danced with Death in Joy and Pain and Wonder.

For most of us this was our first experience of a shadow play and the moving images on the white screen lit by flaming torches had a subtle effect on us as a group; the tent seemed like a portal to another world where rare and magical things could happen. Jamie explained that we were now embarking on the next stage of our journey—a Quest through the elements. Now, for the first time, we entered an area that was not tamed or landscaped. Having climbed with some difficulty up into the woods which bordered the tent, we had not gone very deep into the woods when we found ourselves approaching a tree which spread its branches to form a dome, under which creatures of all sizes and shapes had grown naturally out of wood and moss had been gathered together and placed in a forest of jagged perspex pieces. Above them the trees suddenly became a spring and all the branches came alive with streams of water.

Boris [who had planned the day] had written a short dedication for this space, which Jamie delivered like a familiar fireside story: "Noah dropped his telescope among the old certificates in the cupboard / And muddied his boots on the new found land / But the eager angels still rode the surf / And the speckled dew, like fishes' eyes / Flashed beneath the indifferent stars; / Rain washed the diamond roads / and flowers sang the pungent breeze. /

When the new morning rain had come / and gone again by dinner time, / Noah smiled in his cup and replanted the / everlasting vine."

Some went forward and cupped water in their hands to drink or washed their baby's hands or face; others seemed to decide that this was after all a space to dream in. No one told us what to do as we listened to the water cascading down from the branches of the tree, and at this stage I sensed an uncertainty as to what, if anything, was required of us.

Now we followed the musicians to a huge recumbent giant built of earth and stone, with a smoking pit of a stomach. Here there was no such uncertainty; taut fishing rods, one for each child, reached into his smouldering belly and one by one the parents pulled out a paper gift; a winged ship, a lighthouse, a dove. Richard and four-year-old Kylie Stark were able to do their own fishing, but they needed parental help with the heavy twelve-foot rods, and there was laughter and supportive cheers as each child struggled to free the gift from the giant man.

Here too there was a story for us: "There is a land of men—base-metal in their groins, / Where no mortal treads. Upon their shoulders / Perfection flutters like a silver bird. / The shadow of hunting does not stain their pure breath. / Sometimes this God-fired jungle flames with newer life: / Phantom tigers tremble on the brink of dark pools / Which reflect the lolling eye of greater heavens."

From the earth man we wound our way through the trees to a cleared circle where stood a kiln about four feet high and three feet in diameter, built of twigs and bundles of straw to form a delicate criss-cross pattern. It was topped with a nest. . . . As we approached, the kiln was fired, and as the flames licked the nest each family was given a brightly painted egg of paper and sawdust and invited to place it in the nest. "Come back later and see what hatches," we were told. "Burning apples fall from orchards where not even God has been / And from the sawdust egg the terracotta of our hearts / Wings forth and beats the sullen air anew."

Water, earth, and fire; we went on our way with a sense of having set something in motion. We soon found ourselves in a high wide avenue across which stretched the wings of a huge white bird. Here we took our children forward, and holding them high in our arms we made the declaration of names: "Richard Soyinka Lambert / May you dance in your visions / May you sing your dancing visions to the world." Our hearts were full as we watched each child held high and heard the names echo in that space of air: "Hall George Daedalus Vanbrugh Howarth / Kylie Ann Stark / Hannes Antonius Van Raay / Bryony Stroud Watson / Katherine Bronia Witts / Thomas

Christopher Llewellyn Witts / May their names sing as long as these brave trees / May their lives echo on in the stars / May our love give them help as they travel alone / May our prayers hold their hand as they fly."

As each name rang out a rocket exploded into the sky. Each stage of this gentle journey seemed to have been preparing us for this moment. "In the company of those we love / Of friends who warm us / And strangers who augment our little world / We name our children."

[Then follow a grand feast, a treasure hunt for the children and finally, the concluding action, the liberation of doves. Lois Lambert concludes:] We parted from each other having travelled together through territory that we do not often negotiate in our society, which packages and parcels out our experiences for us so that we lose touch with all that is profound or disturbing in our lives. We had confirmed and celebrated our shared humanity, making a public declaration of our love, our hopes for our children. There had been nothing strange or mystical about the day, we had not been seeking for a powerful magic in which to lose ourselves. All day there had been plenty of time to talk, to explain, to experience each focused moment in our own time. . . . Nothing had been too much trouble for this celebration and every element of it had been prepared with care for this afternoon alone—the decorations in the orangery, the shadow play, the images and spaces in the woods, even the two chemical toilets which we had of necessity to erect in the woods, had been made as magnificent as possible, with white drapes, foliage and flowers.[73]

Although the telling of this rite is straightforward, the power of its imagery is considerable. Even without the assistance of photographs and videos to capture the sights, sounds, and colors, the prose evokes the wonder of the event. The poetry is integral to the rite, not merely something added to it. The poetry lies in the way places and objects are crafted as well as in the way the poems themselves are written. It is not uncommon for poetry to be included in rites of passage, especially weddings, but it is rare that the rhythm, the actions, and the structure of the places are as poetic as the poetry. Consequently, poetry laid into Western rites of passage tends to dangle, calling attention to itself. We in the contemporary West tend to segregate poetry and ritual into separate domains, the one literary, the other religious. When poetry does make its way into ritual, the temptation is to use poetic means to levitate participants into realms precious and supposedly profound. This way of trying to unite poetry and ritual often fails or embarrasses participants.

In Lois's account, the poetry is not severed from outdoor chemical toilets, from huffing and puffing up hills, from the prose of explaining what this action or that thing means. Like buildings in which air ducts and electrical wiring are left as a visible part of the decor, this rite's bones are sticking out. Rather than violating the aesthetic, they are made an integral part of the ritualizing. There is no mystification of power and no pseudomagical conjuration. But magic there is—the magic of the everyday made special by the concentration of human energies and affections.

Celebrated on Easter, this naming ceremony co-opts the sacrality of the season, but it refuses to be shackled either by the Christian liturgical calendar or by conventional uses of the Bible. Biblical characters appear, but burning apples fall from orchards where not even God has been. God is not omnipresent or all-powerful. Noah and God are cast in uncharacteristic roles played in spaces decidedly pagan or secular. There is no sense that the children should make way for patriarchs or that their naming celebration should be transmuted into worship.

The age range of the children is considerable, and the rite is not driven by a rigid sense of timing that would insist that naming must coincide with birth or necessarily occur at a specific age. So the social and ritual structures are loose, and the ideology that rationalizes the actions is downplayed. We are never told *why* these children are being named. Likely they already have names, and some have been using them for quite some time. Never mind; this is an occasion upon which the children's lives become centers of sustained, collective, celebrative, adult attention. Who could ask for more? If the named children were too young to remember the events, the chances are that the adults will both recollect and retell the story, and the story will then do some of the work of spiritual formation.

Kylie Stark was three years old when this ceremony was performed. In 1998, as a twenty-two-year-old arts professional, she recollected the event this way:

I remember nothing of the poetry or the stories, and few of the images. My overall impressions are emotional—excitement, confusion, a feeling of expectation. I remember the surroundings, the lush green woods and the tree which wept, but the two most vivid images are of doves. At home I have a small clay dove which I picked out from the kiln at some point in the ceremony. The dove has traveled around the world with me in a backpack; it travels with me to this very day. At the time, I was delighted to be given a present. As I grew older, I endowed it with mystical powers due to the unusual circumstances from whence it came. Now it is a physical confirmation that the day actually existed. The most specific memory I have from the actual ceremony is of being given a live dove to release to the winds. I distinctly remember the thrill of holding the bird, the excitement of letting it go, and watching it fly away, followed swiftly by disappointment that it had gone forever.

When people asked about the naming ceremony, I often replied, blithely and without thinking much, that I had to walk through fire and water and let go of a dove. It was only when I traveled to Bali and witnessed the cultural importance of ritual in all aspects of life there that I really began to question and to think about what the naming ceremony actually meant to me. It was a celebration of new life and a way of welcoming children into the natural world. It brought together people who were not committed to the beliefs of a particular religion, and it enabled them to "christen" their children. Obviously, a celebration can be done in many ways, but the basic ideas of fire, air, and water, along with the dove as a representation of freedom, give the ceremony a sense of cohesion and simplicity without the need for ritualized movements or incantations. I'm sure I have idealized the experience, forgotten the cold wind and sense of uncertainty and misdirection. Perhaps I have even invented some aspects of it, but the ideas and feelings behind the naming ceremony remain, for me, brilliant and beautiful.[74]

Although Kylie was young when this naming ceremony took place, it continues to form her. The celebration's work is accomplished not only by way of memories, which she admits are vague, but by means of a treasured object, the dove. Kylie's sense of herself is also shaped by stories of the celebration as told to her by adult witnesses. Memories, objects, and stories were formative, but it took a cross-cultural experience in Bali to evoke her reflections on the meaning of the naming rite. Does it matter if she has "invented" some aspects of the rite? I don't think so. In fact, evoking inventions is something rites ought to do.

Kylie's testimony suggests that we should never assume a child is too young for ritualizing. Some aspects of a rite may make their way into the marrow by being remembered, but others, long forgotten, may nurture attitudes that suffuse an entire life, weathering the transition between generations. Learning to ritualize is like learning a language. Such learning works best when it begins fresh out of the womb, the limbs still flexible, the brain still permeable.

Reinventing Birth Rites

It was obvious that when the artists of Welfare State International designed a naming celebration, they were inventing a rite. Likewise, Kylie Stark's recollections were a reinvention of sorts, a reconstruction based on hazy, though compelling, memories. Elise Pearsal's account of a horrific hospital birth and Susan Scott's story of an almost beatific home birth were examples of reimagined ritual processes. But we were being no less imaginative when we followed Robbie Davis-Floyd in construing hospital birth as ritual or when we empathetically entered into the ethnographic and historical reconstructions of Malay and Tudor birth. Although we are not likely to transpose the Malay or Tudor data into new, Western ritual inventions, we imagined ourselves into other people's shoes.

But where does all this reinventing, storytelling, and reconstructing leave us? What should we do or not do about ritualizing birth? If we are dads, should we imitate Doug Abrams Arava's wonder at his son's birth? If we are doctors, ought we interject prayers and blessings over the newborn, as Myriel Ekamp's doctor did? If we are Indians, should we reenact Mary Crow Dog's embattled birth? Would anyone seriously argue that we should reinstate the Tudor practice of churching women or that, Western men, like Malay husbands, ought to insist that wives drink penis-stirred water to symbolize their submission?

The impulse to imitate or import rites is alluring unless we envision the possible outrageous results of doing so. If we imagine the results vividly, then the opposite temptation arises: to play it safe, regarding rites of passage as an interesting fantasy not to be acted upon.

Neither ploy will suffice, the one that would reduce us to slavish imitation and crass importation of other people's ways or the other that would restrict us to mere wishful thinking. It is more fruitful to ask what sort of process the ritualizing of birth and early childhood might take. A ritual plumber's account could include steps such as these:

- attending
- imagining
- studying
- inventing
- improvising
- evaluating
- reinventing

The most basic requirement is that one attend carefully and fully to the birth event itself, noticing its nuances and details as a poet notices a thing of beauty or as a monk studies, chants, and prays a sacred verse. I am not talking about sentimental rehearsal of the generalized feelings of exultation at a recollected birth but about the contemplative, non-judgmental following of the course of pregnancy, birth, and early childhood. We need to pay this kind of attention not just at the moment of birth but during its preparation and aftermath, attending not only to the physiology of birth, but also to the reconstellation of relationships and to the stories that birth engenders. Effective ritualizing begins with an attitude that is respectful and receptive, one that is as free of judgments and agendas as possible. Ritualizing not grounded in primary bodily rhythms and rudimentary social configurations violates the event rather than enhances it. So from the gradual swell of the belly to the first day at kindergarten, the primary ritual actors should be taking note, because the most compelling symbols and images are already there, in our own homes and backyards. (Having put it this way, the ritual plumber begins to sounds strangely like the diviner of rites.)

Well attended, births are extremely evocative of imagining. We not only ritualize and think about birth, but we think *with* it. After all, we sometimes speak of initiations and deaths as births of a sort. The acts of giving and receiving a birth set dreams and imaginings into motion, and these can become basic sources of ritual construction.

Then there is reading and studying about the birth rites of other people or our own people in other times. The trouble with *starting* here is that we may introject ideas and images, consume them without digesting them. Out of touch with our births and our own imaginings, we risk substituting someone else's rites that have little or no connection with our actual lives. Such images and ideas are heteronomous, imposed artificially from the outside. But if we have attended and imagined birth well, we are less likely to become either enamored of or horrified at the rites available to us in the literature. In fact, we may find our own ability to think, plan, and act ritually enhanced.

Having done some homework, it is possible to begin the work of ritual construction. Perhaps the notion of construction itself is grandiose, too evocative of tall buildings and well-paid architects. Even the idea of invention can be intimidating if we believe it involves making something from nothing. Perhaps a better way to conceive of ritualizing is as cutting and pasting. Ritual making is a skill as complex and difficult as any art, so we need practice. But first it is necessary to give ourselves permission to engage in it in a way that is admittedly elementary. The structure for a birth rite can be as ordinary as greeting, as practical as name giving, as much fun as feasting, or as simple as a time of silence.

Although it is easiest to experiment on the basis of some plan, outline, or script, I find it rewarding to experiment and improvise first, then to write a script based on what emerges. If people simply have the intention to ritualize an event, and if they allow themselves to feel awkward or self-conscious, it is my experience that appropriate actions will present themselves. Well attuned, people can sometimes discover exactly what words or gestures a transitional moment calls for. But an atmosphere conducive to making mistakes, feeling awkward, and venturing the untried is a prerequisite.

Improvising invites evaluation. Few of us want to be burdened with judgmental comments during the throes of passage, but *after* an enactment, ritual evaluation can become as normal as planning. Reinvention and criticism require each other. Attentive observation, imaginative improvisation, and honest evaluation constitute a cycle. However peculiar such a process might seem in other parts of the world, it is based on activities that we in the West employ when handling occasions we deem important.

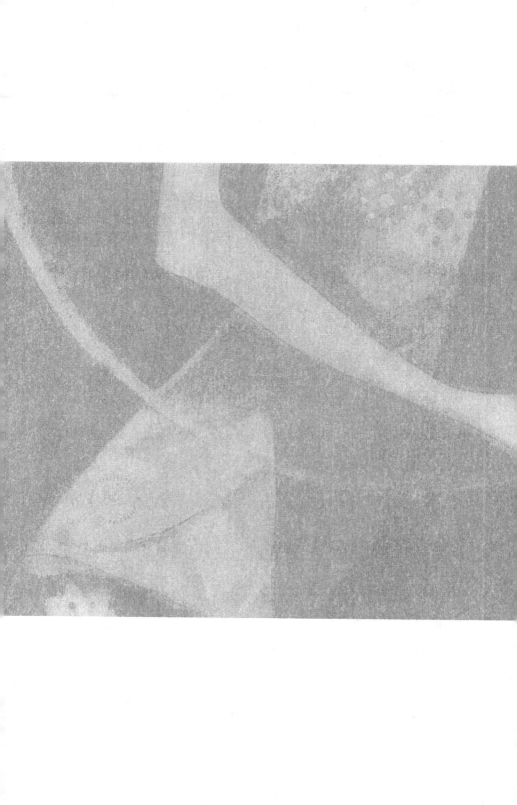

CHAPTER 2

Coming of Age,
Joining Up

As she approached ten, my daughter Cailleah wanted to have her ears pierced. "It's too early," I protested to Susan. "I'm not ready for her adolescence yet. I wasn't even ready for mine, and that was forty years ago."

Our daughter was beginning to blossom, wanting a room of her own, and starting to lock the bathroom door. Not that I had any objection to ear piercing. The act itself is harmless enough. That little flap at the bottom of the ear isn't good for much else. But when I said, "Okay, okay, but why not wait, and then you can get your nose pierced, and an eyebrow if you like, and maybe your belly button too," she was not sure whether to laugh or get mad. She was still young enough that belly buttons were funny.

"D-a-a-a-d," she exclaimed in that tone girls use with their fathers.

I tried another ploy: "How's this? Let's say you wait until you're thirteen or, better still, when you get your period. Mom thinks that would be the best time."

"I want it now."

"Your period?" I said, baiting her.

"No! That's not what I meant."

"I'm teasing. But think about it. Ear piercing would be something special. It would mark a *real* occasion."

"Well, would you want to celebrate *that?*"

"What?"

"You know what."

"Well, uh, sure. Why not? Girls in traditional societies do it then. Boys don't have any red flags to signal them when it's time. Girls do. That's when they can begin to have babies."

I wanted Cailleah's ear piercing to signal not only a substantial bodily change but also to mark the assumption of a greater degree of responsibility for her actions. I hoped to choreograph her ear piercing so that it would coincide with the onset of menstruation. The twin set of symbols would connect her to the paradoxes of life in the adult world. The one act, ear piercing, would be ritually controlled; the other, the onset of menstruation, would not and could not be. The one action would be public; the other, private. Both would be irrevocable.

But Cailleah had her own opinions. "I am not everybody else," she announced. "Besides, this is not one of those, what do you call 'em, traditional societies. And, sure, well, like, you really think I'm going to start having babies at thirteen? I don't want to have babies at all. Or even get married. Like, I don't even want to be a teenager. Don't you get it, Dad? I just want to have my ears pierced. The other girls, lots of 'em, got it done when they were, like, three or six."

"You're not other girls, remember?"

However much I wanted to feel victorious in the skirmish, I knew I hadn't won. To tell the truth, I'd be sad if I had. I knew the issue would cycle again and again.

Ultimately, Cailleah will win. She must. And I must help her; she's my daughter and I am her father. Secretly, I admire her tenacity in discussions, her persistence in pursuing goals. But I teased and tugged at her, knowing she would need arguing skills later in life. So in one sense I was initiating her already—but without an initiation rite. Initiating goes on all the time.

At about the same time as the ear-piercing dilemma, our son, Bryn, had just started playing soccer. On the day his team was in the process of losing its third game in a row, it was pouring rain. Bryn was hot and sweating, then cold and shivering. Suddenly, he was crying, his hand badly bruised under a pair of flailing cleats. Did he want to come off the field? No, he would finish the game. When it ended, he was crying less from the pain of his injury than from the humiliation of yet another defeat. Trying to comfort him, Susan offered him hot chocolate and a dose of mythologizing: "It was an ordeal, Bryn—like Odysseus."

She was right. We could see Bryn turning a corner in his young life. Intended or not, once the game was wrapped in a bandage of myth, it became an incidental initiation. Initiation goes on all the time.

But I am left wondering whether incidental and perpetual initiation is enough. Shouldn't there be something more definitive and intentional—first for our daughter, then for our son?

Parents all want the same thing: for our kids to grow up well. But the young have their own agendas—to be one of the girls, or boys. Pierced ears are a symbol of control over one's own body and a token of connection to peers, perhaps also a way of declaring independence from parents. What kind of violence would we have committed if we had seized the occasion and forcibly made a large-scale ceremony of it? What kind of violence did we commit by opting for diffuse ritualization instead of a discrete rite?

And why the fuss? Aren't my son and daughter already assuming increased levels of responsibility for their actions? Is there really a neat dividing line between one stage of life and another? Isn't a puberty rite based on the emergence of physical characteristics or on reaching a particular age just a social fiction? Even if we had convinced Cailleah to wait for ear piercing until the onset of menstruation, would combining two forms of bloodletting into a ritual act be any more than a contrivance—perhaps sensible in a tribal world but quixotic in a pluralistic and mobile urban world? Would we have succeeded in creating a distinct before and after? And who are we after all—two uninitiated adults, mere parents—to resist one of the great forces of contemporary culture, peer pressure? We can lay claim to no single religious tradition that will help us do the job, but wouldn't an invented initiation be self-conscious and awkward? What would we be initiating Cailleah and Bryn into?

As a high school freshman, I was "initiated"—now I would say abused—with oak paddles wielded by upperclassmen. Off campus, guys had contests breaking them over our rear ends. On campus, they forced us to carry their books and polish their shoes. These and other acts of groveling were meant to humiliate us in front of our girlfriends. Dad, vaguely sympathetic with my complaints, offered the thin comfort of stories about his initiation into the university. He'd been forced, he boasted, to swallow raw liver dipped in castor oil. The meat was tied to a string and, once downed, it was yanked back up by guffawing upperclassmen. Dad's initiators, like mine, had neither the authority nor the wisdom one customarily attributes to elders.

So the question remains, What people or institutions are qualified to initiate? In some societies one has little or no choice; initiation is required. Running away is not an option, since such an action would amount to self-exile. In the pluralistic and mobile sectors of the West, however, initiations, even in tightly knit communities, are optional. An individual can protest or move away. Because personal autonomy is so highly and unquestioningly valued, ritual structures are questionable and ritual authorities suspect. That we can question implies that we can choose, and that we can choose means we can also reject. Our problem is not that we are subjected to initiations we would rather flee, but that we know so few authentic and compelling rites.

Initiation as a Global Problem

The *Encyclopedia of World Problems and Human Potential* declares the current lack of rites of passage an urgent global problem: "The absence of rites of passage leads to a serious breakdown in the process of maturing as a person. Young people are unable to participate in society in a creative manner because societal structures no longer consider it their responsibility to intentionally establish the necessary marks of passing from one age-related social role to another, such as: child to youth, youth to adult, adult to elder. The result is that society has no clear expectation of how people should participate in these roles and therefore individuals do not know what is required by society."[75]

In the absence of *rites* of passage major transitions become *ritualized*. Bereft of the explicit framing of rites, unconscious and unintentional activities displace conscious and intentional ones, often with deadly consequences. In her novel *The Women of Brewster Place*, Gloria Naylor paints a picture of unconscious initiatory behavior in bold and disconcerting strokes. In the neighborhood of Brewster Place elders do not initiate the young. Peers "initiate" one another, with rape and homicide as the outcome. A group of young black men, whose behavior is highly ritualized, encounters a lesbian woman:

These young men always moved in a pack, or never without two or three. They needed the others continually near to verify their existence. When they stood with their black skin, ninth grade diplomas and fifty word vocabularies in front of the mirror that the world had erected and saw nothing, those other pairs of tight jeans, suede sneakers, and tinted sunglasses imaged nearby proved that they were alive—they move through the streets insuring that they could at least be heard, if not seen, by blasting their portable cassette players and talking loudly. They continually surnamed each other man and clutched at their crotches readying the equipment they deemed necessary to be summoned at any moment. . . .

Bound by the last building on Brewster and Brickwall, they reigned in that unlit alley linked, dwarfed warrior-kings. Both with the appendages of power, circumcised by a guillotine, and baptized with the stream from a million non-reflective mirrors, these young men wouldn't be called upon to fight a war in a far-off land, point a finger to move a nation, or stick a pole into the moon—and they knew it. They only had that three-hundred-foot alley to serve them as a stateroom, armored tank and executioner's chamber. So Lorraine found herself, on her knees, surrounded by the most dangerous species in existence—human males with an erection to validate in a world that was only six feet wide.[76]

The young men's behavior is not reducible to their poverty or skin color. It is also a consequence of ritual deprivation. William Golding's classic novel *Lord of the Flies* illustrates a similar dilemma among a group of white English choirboys marooned on an island. Modeled on some of Golding's own students, they polarize, tribalize, and ritualize. By the time of their rescue, two of them lie dead.

In *Symbolic Wounds* Bruno Bettelheim paints a provocative portrait of a small group of emotionally disturbed children whom he studied in Chicago. He maintains that the only difference between these four children and normal children is the degree to which normal ones hide, and disturbed ones display, their ritualistic tendencies. In a section entitled "A Spontaneous 'Initiation Rite,' " Bettelheim describes some disturbing scenes: a girl who wishes she were a boy and loudly announces her "dripping period"; a girl who feels she is both male and female and wants to cut her finger to make it bleed; a girl who squeezes water balloons between her legs so she can urinate like a boy; a girl who pulls at her vulva to make it a penis; a girl who hates her clitoris; a boy who feels cheated at not having a vagina; a boy who wishes he had both male and female parts; a boy who declares his rectum a vagina; and boys who wish to tear off breasts and rip out vaginas.

Bettelheim's treatment becomes an origin myth that accounts for the spontaneous rise of initiatory activities. Since I read Bettelheim's work as myth (a story expressing fundamental values), let me present it as a story rather than an argument:

Once upon a forgotten time in a faraway place there was a tribe. The women of this tribe were tough. Not only were these women powerful by virtue of their birthing, they were also the inventors of ritual. Originally, there was only one ritual. This primal ceremony was a fertility rite. It celebrated the birth of all things: people, seasons, seeds, animals, and growing things wild and domestic. There was no coercion in the ceremony. No one was forced to participate. Doing so would have violated the women's sense of the interconnectedness of all things. However, participation weighed on the men's minds, reminding them of the obvious: They were not the givers of life. Their role in the production of humankind was incidental.

After one of the festivals some of the men became fed up. They decided to separate and have their own kind of ceremony, one in which they could celebrate their own kind of power. This joint effort of the menfolk was necessary for their ego development. The rite was instigated to master two commonly shared problems: their inability to create new life and the lack of clear demarcations between phases of their lives. They needed the ceremony in order to define (and thus reinvent) their own manhood. Unlike women, who cannot escape the certainty of their womanhood, men before this time could never be sure of their manhood. The results of this collective male effort they called "initiation."

After the invention of initiation, men, like women, could give birth—only men did not birth mortal bodies, mere helpless babes. Instead, they gave "real" birth, "second" birth, to men and the human spirit. These primal men took their sons away from their mothers and "cooked" them into men. They laid hands on the boys' penises, sliced them around, longways, and underneath. Teaching them to bleed, the primal elder males conferred on these ancient adolescent boys the power to bleed and give birth.

All these procedures were secret. The men knew they had to protect their newfound knowledge. Their best kept secret was this: Men's power is a fiction, a cultural invention, a ritual construction. This is still the best kept open secret in the world.

Eventually, male-dominated initiation supplanted female-inspired fertility celebration as the model tribal rite. No longer was there a single, holistic ceremony. Today we mourn its loss. Ever since that day, we have been longing for an all-inclusive "rite of rites."

Bettelheim observed behavior resembling the actions of tribal initiation. He regarded the actions as spontaneous, therefore as evidence that we are all "primitive." He explained these acts as originating in the envy males feel for females' ability to give birth. Bettelheim's story, although it is an academic myth, is not entirely fanciful. In some Melanesian societies elders describe the genital surgery they perform on boys as making them "menstruate."[77] As an explanation, Bettelheim's account is less than adequate, but as a story, it is worthy of contemplation because of the critical questions it poses regarding male ambivalence and violence toward females. It is also worth considering the possibility that initiatory activity arises whether or not we want it to and whether or not it is supervised by elders.

The modern family emerged when the nuclear family began displacing the extended family. But some say that we are witnessing a further transformation into a postmodern, postnuclear, family. One writer observes, "As the post-modern family rushes down upon us, parents are losing their role as educators. The task passes instead to the peers."[78]

Initiation in Western society often takes this postmodern, peer-driven form—adolescents initiating adolescents, sometimes compulsively, unconsciously, and violently. Such initiations, detached from family and community, are practices that may be substitutes for traditional initiation conducted by elders who represent a lineage.

In addition to the scourge of violence among peers, there is the conundrum of diffuseness. Although in the West there is passage into adulthood, there are few, if any, explicit, effective rites of passage to demarcate them. Certainly, there is no nation- or culturewide initiation, only a motley array of activities such as beginning menstruation, getting a driver's license, reaching drinking age, graduating, moving away from the parental home, or earning an income. Among a growing number of young people, initiation into adulthood is experienced as a vague and uncertain process, not well focused by an identifiable rite of passage. Because of the West's cult of youth, disdain for the elderly, and indifference toward ancestors, there are few initiatory occasions during which the young can receive the spiritual wisdom of generations. Would-be apprentices are bereft of elders. Young seekers look for the wise old guardians of myth but relate to actual old people with indifference or contempt. The young dream of being mentored by elders but treat the elderly as obstacles to career development and self-fulfillment.

The Reality of My Own Body

The global problem is not simply that our young lack compelling initiations but that many of the existing rites are dysfunctional. Even traditions with explicit initiations are in trouble. Since religious and ethnic groups seldom publicize their most disturbing troubles, fiction is sometimes more revealing than journalistic or ethnographic description.

Ozzie Freedman is being prepared for his bar mitzvah, but he asks too many questions of Rabbi Binder. Binder is neither receptive nor encouraging. He does not listen well, and he stifles questions about God's role in a plane crash at La Guardia airport as well as about the divinity of Jesus. When the frustrated rabbi, with a flick of his irritated hand, sets Ozzie's nose to bleeding, the teenager flees to the synagogue roof:

If one should compare the light of day to the life of man: sunrise to birth; sunset—the dropping down over the edge—to death; then as Ozzie Freedman wiggled through the trapdoor of the synagogue roof, his feet kicking backwards bronco-style at Rabbi Binder's outstretched arms—at that moment the day was fifty years old. As a rule, fifty or fifty-five reflects accurately the age of late afternoons in November, for it is in that month, during those hours, that one's awareness of light seems no longer a matter of seeing, but of hearing: light begins clicking away. In fact, as Ozzie locked shut the trapdoor in the rabbi's face, the sharp click of the bolt into the lock might momentarily have been mistaken for the sound of the heavier gray that had just throbbed through the sky.

With all his weight Ozzie kneeled on the locked door; any instant he was certain that Rabbi Binder's shoulder would fling it open, splintering the wood into shrapnel and catapulting his body into the sky. But the door did not move and below him he heard only the rumble of feet, first loud then dim, like thunder rolling away.

A question shot through his brain. "Can this be *me?*" For a thirteen-year-old who had just labeled his religious leader a bastard, twice, it was not an improper question. Louder and louder the question came to him—"Is it me? Is it me?"—until he discovered himself no longer kneeling, but racing crazily toward the edge of the roof, his eyes crying, his throat screaming, and his arms flying everywhichway as though not his own.

"It is me? Is it me Me Me Me Me! It has to be me—but is it!"

It is the question a thief must ask himself the night he jimmies open his first window, and it is said to be the question with which bridegrooms quiz themselves before the altar.[79]

Philip Roth's short story "The Conversion of the Jews" exposes a dark side of the initiatory process known as the bar mitzvah. Roth hints at the failure of the rite, one in which elders are no longer wise and in which initiates are defiant rather than respectful. In Roth's story, initiation has become merely a way of exercising social control, a use Ozzie resists. Ozzie *Freed*man wants be "free" of Rabbi Binder, who "binds" him. Initiation, as Roth portrays it, has degenerated into a battle between rabbinical evasion and student rebelliousness.

The is-it-me question is central to the initiatory process, but here it isolates the would-be initiate rather than enhancing his sense of participation in a community and history. Instead of experiencing a felt connection to an elder, Ozzie's threshold crossing shuts a trap door behind him. As the narrator reflects on the situation, Ozzie is not a kid about to become a man but a kid overshadowed by the specter of becoming an old man. Initiation should "make him a man" not an old man in the late afternoon of the November of his life.

The main reason for having rites of passage is to enable mindful attendance to events that might otherwise pass us by. Rabbi Binder attends to neither Ozzie nor his questions. My guess is that the rabbi could have declined to answer the question if only he had attended to Ozzie himself.

Attending is not something only individuals do. It is something institutions and traditions do—or don't do. As we discovered while investigating birth rites, Christian confirmation came into being when baptism ceased to be an initiation rite restricted to adults. But confirmation, as we saw, has a checkered history, and, as Vivian Hansen's story suggests, questions continue to arise about its effectiveness in initiating adolescents:

I was confirmed when I was fourteen. I prepared for the ceremony, studied the meanings behind the faith, and memorized the creeds. The ritual was long practiced and well rehearsed. The accouterments were perfect; the special effects assumed a mystical importance. This was a Christian rite of passage.

I studied the rituals of the church every Thursday night for two years. Those years were formative. My breasts grew, my body made curves around my frame, and I tried to make sense of the present and future. I menstruated every thirty days, cried every twenty-one. No ritual existed to explain this cycle. Christ had no vagina. He bled only when he was nailed to the Cross. His suffering was final and redemptive, while mine was chronic and apparently meaningless. . . .

I was to be confirmed on April 21. My period arrived on April 19th along with its pain and fatigue and the introspection required by my imminent religious rite of passage. All day that Friday I hurt, my cramps rolling in waves over my abdomen. I prayed. I wept. I suffered. Outside, springtime emerged from the cold, unyielding ground, but the blooming crocuses, bluebells, and fragrant daffodils did not help my disposition or my physical, mental, and spiritual pain. I knew only the presence of my own body and the overwhelming power of its emerging force.

My brother teased me mercilessly when he found out that I was menstruating: "How are you going to walk up the aisle? All that blood will leak right through. Everybody will see it and laugh, especially the boys." I shrieked in frustration, mortified by the callous mockery I would get from the congregation.

My mother found me that night, weeping beside my bed for no apparent reason.

"Girl, what's the matter?"

"I don't know where Jesus is. I try to talk to him, but he's out of reach. I want to take communion on Sunday, but I want to be with him first." She had nothing to say. How could she know, after all, where they had laid him?

I resolved nothing. Saturday was spent bleeding and musing over the echoes of my brother's vulgar comments. Sweat dripped from my brow, and I took frequent baths to rid myself of the filth. I hoped to stem the tide of blood, tears, and misery.

Nothing helped. I showed up at the church in a short white lacy dress and walked down the aisle, the bleeding bride of Christ. I felt my brother's eyes upon my back. I felt as crucified as if the crowds had, in reality, nailed me. I knelt at the altar, ready to be transformed, to experience the power of communion.

"The Body of Christ, given for you." I felt the biscuit melt in my mouth, drying and searing my tongue.

"The Blood of Christ, shed for you." The red fluid merged with the host, helping me to swallow the body.

All I could think of was the mortifying fear that my own blood would show and efface the ceremony, erasing the perfection.

The ritual over, I sneaked into the bathroom, assuring myself that I had padded all the shameful parts. No blood showed. The ceremony was complete. My endometrium was concealed, the rite of passage completed.

My confirmation happened just that once. I have pictures of my white virgin self, my smooth and supple young body smiling into a camera lens. That girl is triumphant, because her menstrual pad worked when it should have. I suffered through the rites and performed my religious commitments, but they required me to exclude the reality of my own body.[80]

Vivian's story illustrates another kind of initiatory trouble, rarification, the detachment of a rite from its physiological roots. In much of the European- and Christian-influenced West, not only are rites of passage out of synch with social and biological rhythms, but contradictory messages are structured into the rites themselves. The result is a double bind, a message received spiritually and biologically that says, in effect, "Do this. Don't do this. And don't speak about the contradiction between the two messages." In telling the story, Vivian slices through the double bind. She articulates the contradiction between being urged ritually to embrace the redemptive qualities of blood while, at the same time, having her own most persistent relation with blood, menstruation, liturgically denied. A religion of incarnation—one that declares that God became flesh and that hopes for the resurrection of the body—conveys the tacit message, "Flesh and blood are suspect. Let flesh and its desires not be mentioned; let blood and its stains be hidden."

One evening, after I had finished a public lecture in which I read Vivian's story aloud, a man remarked, "You were pretty hard on institutional religion, weren't you?" I admitted that I was. He then told me that his church provided mentors and had a ceremony for thirteen-year-olds. He said it was a party at which adolescents were presented with a Bible. I replied that his church was doing more than many others. A party, a gift, and a relationship are not negligible, but they are only beginnings, paltry offerings alongside traditional initiations. Parties mark but do not transform.

In theory, initiation rites effect an irreversible transformation from an old state to a new one. An initiation into adulthood is supposed to make a girl into a woman or a boy into a man. Saying that initiation transforms is not entirely incorrect, but it does blur the line between the ideal and the real. What rites *really do* may differ from what they *are said to do*. Ritualists and theorists too readily offer glorified accounts or abstracted descriptions rather than candid accounts of actual ritual experience. Like all idealizations, such portrayals of ritual are selective in what they report. Seldom do participants describe flawed initiations. Instead, they tender general summaries abstracted from actual occasions and real personalities. When specific rites and ritual actors are talked about, the best examples are selected. So either way, abstracted or specific, ritual accounts tend to hide blemishes and ignore flaws. Rites of passage, both in theory and practice, depend heavily on posed group portraits. Rites are a people's way of putting itself on display, and such portraits are never objective or neutral; they are touched up, airbrushed. We paint or perform them so they will present us in the best light, even if it is artificial.

There is a tendency, perpetuated by theorists and do-it-yourself ritualists alike, to exaggerate the degree of transformation that occurs in initiation. Declaring boys men or girls women does not necessarily make them so, as is evident in Vincent Crapanzano's description of a circumcision rite conducted near Meknes, Morocco:

The boy is carried by his mother to the room where the operation is to take place. A crowd of women, including the prostitute, and men, surrounding the women gather in front of the house. The mother—or some other female relative or a midwife—stands in front of the door. Her left foot is in a bowl of water which contains a piece of iron; in her left hand she holds a mirror into which she stares; in her right hand she holds a white flag. The iron is said to draw the pain from the scissors, ultimately from the wound, to the bowl where it is cooled down by the water. The mother stares into the mirror to prevent herself—and the boy—from crying; the flag represents the flag of Ali [the Prophet Mohammed's son-in law], of Islam. Mother and son are for the moment symbolically equated.

The operation itself is a simple affair. The boy is held by an older man, preferably but not necessarily his paternal uncle, and is told to look up at a tiny bird. The barber pulls the foreskin up, slips some sheep dung in between the foreskin and the glans, and then with a single cut of a scissors, he snips off the foreskin. The dung is said to protect the glans from nicking. The penis is then plunged into a broken egg to which a little rabbit dung and henna have been added. This is said to cool the wound down and aid in healing.

As soon as the foreskin is clipped, a signal is given to the musicians who are waiting with the villagers in front of the house. They begin to play the circumcision music; women begin to dance. The boy is swaddled as an infant in a cloth; heat is said to hasten healing. He is placed on his mother's naked back—or the back of another woman—in such a way that his bleeding penis presses against her. His mother dances along with other women until he stops crying. Then he is put to bed. In some ceremonies at this time women give him candies and other tidbits. He is fed a hard boiled egg and gravy when he wakes up—to give him strength. His mother cares for the wound until it has healed. She sprinkles it with powdered henna. His father returns after he falls asleep.[81]

In this rite Moroccan boys are not transposed from the spatial and cultural domain of mothers and children to that of men, although without this rite, they will be unable to make that move later. Like bat mitzvah for Jewish girls or *quinceañera* for Hispanic girls, this circumcision rite for Muslim boys is a necessary but insufficient condition for passage into adulthood. The rite returns the boy, still a child, to his mother. After all, he is typically between three and seven years of age. Although he is declared a man, ironically, his "manhood" is wounded. The rite of passage is less a passage than the anticipation of one, and its trajectory is circular, not linear. The boy is given a dramatic preview of manhood, but his movement into it, although ultimately facilitated, is, for the present, postponed. What this rite actually does is different from what scholars have taught us that initiations do.

Jewish bar and bat mitzvahs are conventionally spoken of as rites of passage and as initiations, but are they really? One team of researchers suggests that these rites are not initiations because their purview is only religious.[82] These rites, they say, admit a child to the study of the Torah, but they are not tickets to the status of full adult. A child, they contend, is not made an adult simply by beginning to assume a bit of moral and religious responsibility for her or his actions. It is important to understand that ritual adulthood and social adulthood may not coincide and that neither is necessarily identical with biological adulthood, which is to say, puberty.

Initiation, then, presents a thicket of problems. First, there is the predicament of its absence, disappearance, or invisibility in Western industrial societies. The diffuseness of initiatory impulses can precipitate a menacing and unconscious form of self- or peer-initiation. Second, even in traditions with initiation rites, intergenerational antagonism may displace intergenerational bonding. In addition, traditional rites themselves can become so ethereal that they fail to connect with the bodily realities and spiritual needs of those who undergo them. Finally, there is the problem of dissonance: Initiations may not do what either theorists or practitioners claim they do.

Patterns of Initiation

The lack of explicit or compelling initiation ceremonies in the West, coupled with the possibility of initiatory failure or abuse, precipitates basic questions: What is initiation? What kinds are there? What does initiation accomplish? How do initiation rites work?

The answers that many give, both inside and outside academe, are indebted to Mircea Eliade and Arnold van Gennep. Eliade, the most influential historian of religions in the twentieth century, declared that initiation evokes a revelation of the sacred and that it is the primary means of making us fully human. Even though initiation rites are sometimes subject to political manipulation and neurotic distortion, they rise above the fray of everyday life. In his words, initiation is "metacultural and transhistorical."[83] If Eliade is right, then we risk our children's humanity if we fail to initiate them.

Eliade believed initiation to be most fully developed among people he labeled primitive or archaic, those living in small-scale, nonindustrial societies. But he also considered initiation universal, arising even in the complex societies spawned by "modern man." In the contemporary West, Eliade believed, initiation appears less often in ritual performances than it does in dreams and nostalgia for spiritual renewal, so he bemoaned the loss of fully ritualistic initiation. At the same time, he also anticipated its inevitable reappearance. The conviction that the industrialized West has lost traditional initiation rites but that they spontaneously reemerge is largely a result of Eliade's, and C. G. Jung's, influence.[84]

Despite his contention that initiation is timeless, Eliade knew that initiation changed across the long sweep of history. Early initiations were collective; modern ones, individualistic. Early initiations were more ritualized; contemporary ones were more likely to be merely thought or imagined rather than acted out. As a result of the historical process, certain "survivals," bits and pieces of rites, were left behind from bygone days. One finds initiatory survivals in the literary quest for the holy grail. Throughout the course of Western history initiation has become less conscious, less explicit, less fully embodied. In dreams, fantasies, psychotherapy, and the arts, we stumble unwittingly through initiatory patterns.

Eliade conceived of initiation as a mystical death and resurrection, a spiritual rebirth. In his view, initiations use a dramatic structure, replete with staging and spectacle, to facilitate "acts of rupture" in which initiates are "killed." Ritually forced to "die" to some old state, they ritually reenter the womb, thereby returning to the mythic origin of the cosmos, the source of power capable of renewing them. The process has three moments—dying, returning to the generative origins of the cosmos, and being reborn. Following this pattern, initiates achieve a new state of being. Not only are they remade, but the initiating elders and other members of the entire community are rejuvenated as well.

Now, several years after Mircea Eliade's death, it is difficult to defend his conviction that initiation rites rise above the nitty-gritty of time and transcend the differences among cultures. His claims that they are *the* means of ensuring our humanity, that they guarantee a revelation of the sacred, and that death and rebirth are always the dominant themes of initiation must be questioned. Eliade's views once seemed like incontrovertible facts, but now they are read by most scholars as academic mythmaking. Because his ideas are popularly invoked to justify and structure initiatory experiments, they function like myths. Even though Eliade's generalizations are based less on actual initiations and more on an idealized vision of what initiation might be, people act them out, thereby paying them homage.

Romanticized conceptions of initiation imply that those who do not initiate are inhuman. But do we really want to make such a claim? Muslims, for example, do not initiate anyone except converts. If a child is born to Muslim parents, raised in a Muslim family, and taught the Qu'ran from an early age, Muslims see no need for an initiation rite.[85] Initiating goes on all the time. Do we really want to suggest that continual spiritual nurture and sustained religious education are less humanizing than definitive, one-time initiation rites?

Besides blurring the differences between idealized and actual initiations, Eliade left us with another complication: an overinflation of the category itself. In popular speech, initiation connotes entry into adulthood, but Eliade and others who follow him include two other kinds of initiation—not only into adulthood but also into secret societies and religious vocations. These two forms are not rooted in the life cycle.

Even if we focus only on initiation into adulthood, we would not solve a basic conceptual problem, that of determining when adulthood arrives. Cultures vary in their ways of carving up the life cycle. Many do not separate childhood from adolescence, adolescence from adulthood, or adulthood from old age. And even among groups that distinguish adolescence from adulthood, not all use age as their cue to begin initiating. Initiation rites do not cluster around a supposedly obvious age: twelve, eighteen, or twenty-one. Since coming of age is a gradual process, there is no universally "obvious" time at which to celebrate it. Some so-called initiations happen at three; others, at eighteen. But does anyone really think a toddler "initiated" at three is an adult? Is the circumcision of a seven-year-old boy a late birth rite or an early initiation rite? Confusion is created by imprecision in the idea of initiation itself. Even if we were to classify circumcision at seven as a birth or childhood rite, initiation at twelve is hardly the same as initiation at eighteen or twenty-one. Our expectations of the age sets are different; those in the first set are just entering adolescence; those in the second range are just entering adulthood.

Besides the impossibility of setting a definitive age range for initiation, there is the conundrum of gender difference. Some initiations, especially for women, may be simply the first phase of, or a prerequisite for, marriage.[86] In some societies initiation-marriage is a single unit considered incomplete until the establishment of a household or the birth of a first child.

Not only are initiations sometimes indistinct from birth or marriage rites, they also may extend across long periods of time and involve several grades, or degrees. Among the Sambia of Papua New Guinea a man is not fully a man until he reaches the sixth degree of initiation and has two children.[87]

Because the term *initiation* is overloaded, I find it useful to distinguish: *rites of childhood* that follow birth but precede entry into adolescence, *adolescent initiations* that facilitate an exit from childhood and entry into adolescence, and *adult initiations* that negotiate an exit from adolescence and an entry into early adulthood.[88] These divisions are necessarily provisional, since they do not reflect every society's way of dividing up the life course.

It is common not only to segment the life cycle into several *stages* and to distinguish several *types* of initiation but also to assume that rites of passage transpire in *phases*. In fact, these phases are virtually definitive of the notion of rites of passage. *Rites de passage* is the French title of a classic text published in 1909 by Arnold van Gennep and translated into English in 1960. Had van Gennep not coined the idea, we would not be considering births, initiations, weddings, and funerals as the same kind of ritual, because these types are not always classified together by practitioners.

Van Gennep's theory of passage is based on the obvious fact of change. At every moment we are shedding cells, thinking newly configured thoughts, dreaming new dreams. Cars rust, building timbers rot, governments topple, minds change, and people grow old. Van Gennep grappled with such change metaphorically, as if it were a movement through space. In his view, a person passes through a series of relatively static, clearly defined positions, which he called *statuses*. At junctures between these positions are *pivots,* at which one's life trajectory veers, changing direction. These turning points are moments of intense energy and danger, and ritual is the primary means of safely navigating the rapids.

Van Gennep's theory rests on an analogy: Social "movement," that is, a change in status, is akin to a bodily movement through space. This change in status is like journeying across an international border or walking through a doorway. A frontier divides two countries, and the threshold of a portal separates inside from outside. In both instances a midpoint separates two zones, or moments, thus becoming a zone or

Separation → Transition → Incorporation

(preliminal) → liminal → (postliminal)

Figure 1. Arnold van Gennep's
Threefold Scheme

moment in its own right. The result is the threefold scheme depicted in
figure 1.

Drawing on the Latin root for threshold (*limen*), van Gennep calls
these zones *preliminal, liminal,* and *postliminal*—before the threshold,
on the threshold, and after the threshold. Naming the three in this way
calls attention to the central phase, liminality. Van Gennep also called
the three moments *separation, transition,* and *incorporation.* This second way of naming them makes them sound more like phases in a process than places on a map, and it calls attention to their dynamic, rather
than to their static, or spatial, qualities.[89] Although van Gennep believed that every rite of passage passes through all three phases, he
thought different kinds of rites emphasize different moments. Funerals
emphasize separation; births and weddings, incorporation; and initiations, transition.[90]

When we speak of rites of *passage,* we are implicitly invoking the
spatial metaphor. The image is that of a person passing between two
adjacent places. The most easily comprehensible and widely assumed
example is that of male initiation. Young boys are (1) taken from a village and their mothers (separation); (2) sequestered in some cordoned-
off place, where they suffer ordeals as initiates and receive sacred
knowledge (transition); and (3) finally returned, now men, to their village in order to assume the role of adult (incorporation).

Today the model is considered biased, a distortion of the trajectory
of women's lives and the structures of their initiations.[91] One theorist,
for example, suggests that women's initiations follow another pattern,
that of enclosure, metamorphosis, and emergence.[92] Women, it seems,
are less likely to be sequestered in the bush than to be enclosed in a circumscribed domestic space.

In some of van Gennep's examples, social passage is not only *like* ter-
ritorial passage but requires it, literally. If a boy does not go to the
bush, he cannot return a man. In other examples it does not seem that
van Gennep believed that separation is necessarily geographical; it may
be purely symbolic. Thus, his fundamental point is not so much that

Separation (dying) → Transition (return to origins) → Incorporation (being reborn)

Figure 2. The Equation of van Gennep's and Eliade's Patterns

one must go away to make a change but that a rite of passage is a phased process of transition making, a "movement" from one social "space" to another: from girl to woman, boy to man, layperson to clergy, outsider to insider. In van Gennep's view, rites of passage are the primary means of effecting these transitions. I think, however, that he made a serious mistake by making initiation the model for the other rites of passage and by letting male initiations serve as the model for all initiations.

It is commonly assumed that initiation rites display a pattern shared throughout great expanses of time and across the vast array of the world's traditions. This belief is largely the result of van Gennep's and Eliade's influence. In Western popular culture the schemes articulated by van Gennep and Eliade are often equated (see fig. 2). The pattern that Joseph Campbell "discovered" (I would say invented) in the so-called myth of the hero—separation / initiation / return—is sometimes added as a third layer. In this superimposed form, the pattern has become a formula used by groups to prescribe actual ritual practice. This three-phased scheme has become a formula in how-to manuals. Even in rare instances where more, or other, phases are recommended, the influence of Eliade and van Gennep, along with Jung and Campbell, is prevalent. For example, one author proposes these ten steps for creating initiation rites: preparation of a sacred space; removal of initiates from ordinary space; preliminary instruction by elders; symbolic death and disorientation of the initiates; ordeals; instruction in the wisdom and the mysteries; symbolic reconstruction; community festivity; thanksgiving; and finally, return to ordinary life as a responsible adult.[93]

This outline is stamped out using the templates forged by Eliade and van Gennep. Having escaped the confines of scholarship, these notions are now yoked together and saddled with the task of ushering adolescents into adulthood.

The elaboration of three phases into ten steps would appear to nuance initiation beyond a mere beginning-middle-end structure. But if we look at descriptions of actual rites, rather than abstract summaries of patterns and phases, we find that there is more to initiation than either three phases or ten steps. Here are some of the elements that appear in initiations from various cultures:

- being taught by mentors, spiritual parents, or elders
- showing respect, displaying subservience or obedience, being humiliated or intimidated
- undergoing strategic deceptions, surprises perpetrated by elders
- learning sacred, sexual, or cultural knowledge
- becoming acquainted with sacred objects
- being allowed access to secrets; gaining access to previously off-limits areas
- experiencing disenchantment in the face of revelations
- having to keep secrets from those who are younger or uninitiated
- being separated or secluded
- overcoming pain and fear
- fasting, making sacrifices
- observing food, sexual, and other behavioral taboos
- being hazed, subjected to painful or unpleasant treatment
- regressing, returning temporarily to childlike states
- experiencing distortion of one's sense of time, space, causality, and identity
- having values questioned or even destroyed and then reconstituted on some other basis
- strongly identifying with a gender or age cohort; being differentiated from the other sex and from other kinds of people (sometimes regarded as not fully human if not initiated)
- assuming new responsibilities; giving up dependencies
- having one's status elevated; passing through initiatory levels or degrees
- imagining, envisioning, dreaming, praying
- mastering difficult tasks
- keeping vigils, sleep deprivation
- body marking such as genital operations and tattoos
- dramatizing, acting out, performing, using masks and costumes
- receiving a new name
- giving and receiving gifts

- partaking in celebratory meals and other kinds of festivity
- being received, incorporated, welcomed by elders, a community, or a cohort
- telling stories about initiatory experience
- becoming an initiating elder

This incomplete list is only a reminder of initiation's complexity and a warning against oversimplification into memorable patterns. The items on the list are widespread, but not necessarily universal, elements of initiation rites. The usefulness of schemes like those of van Gennep and Eliade is their simplicity and perhaps their usefulness in organizing rites or writing articles about ritual. But the value of a "parts list" is that it reminds us of initiation's diversity. Today scholars consider the patterns articulated by van Gennep and Eliade to have been imposed rather than discovered in the texts they studied. In short, *invented* patterns, treated as if they were *discovered,* came to be *prescribed* as if they were laws determining how rites should be structured. There is nothing wrong with either inventing or prescribing, provided we know what we are doing.

Questioning Eliade and van Gennep reminds us that theories are no more God given than rites. Just as we use theories to question rites, we should also use rites to question theories. We should be suspicious of threefold sequences, since they too obviously reflect the Western intellectual habit of preferring threes—the doctrine of the Trinity (Father, Son, Holy Ghost), the idea of dialectic (thesis, antithesis, synthesis), and the generic narrative (beginning, middle, end).

Initiation around the World

The slipperiness of abstract and supposedly universal patterns may leave us wishing for reliable facts about initiation. "The facts" about initiation come in two forms. The *ethnographic* form arises from burrowing deeply into the soil of a single culture and studying its rites as expressions of a specific people. The *comparative* form is cross-cultural, sometimes statistical, and presumably scientific. The comparative data depend on the ethnographic data. Since it is impossible for a researcher to observe the world's initiation rites, the actual object of large-scale comparative studies is normally a set of texts, representative samples of ethnographic descriptions. Much of this literature is catalogued and classified in the Human Relations Area Files (HRAF). Studies based on these files typically consider data from a variety of geographical areas representative of different kinds of societies. Summarizing key findings in such studies can help orient us to initiations, but it also reveals the limitations of this kind of research.[94]

The global research on initiation distinguishes biological puberty from social adolescence. Puberty is signaled by the appearance of physiological changes such as menarche in girls or the deepening of the voice, onset of ejaculation, or appearance of facial hair in boys. According to the available data, the median age range of menarche is fourteen, with adolescence ending two years later. For boys, puberty begins at sixteen, with adolescence typically concluding two to four years later.[95] Even though puberty is a biological fact, its onset is partly determined by social and cultural conditions. An exact age for puberty is not permanently fixed by nature. The age of first menses in the industrialized West has steadily declined. Since the age of first marriage continues to increase, the result is a protracted adolescence in many of these societies.

Social adolescence is even more variable than physiological puberty. Most, but not all, societies recognize adolescence as a stage, and many mark passage into or out of it ritually. Roughly half the world's societies have initiations for one or both sexes. However, this statistic does not mean that half the world's population initiates, since the societies sampled in the HRAF are mostly small-scale. Initiations are more likely to be found in simply organized societies and less likely in bureaucratic, industrial, and large-scale societies. Also, initiation rites tend to decline in societies in which gender as a principle of social organization is downplayed, and they appear with more frequency in Africa, the Pacific, and the indigenous Americas than in East Eurasia and Mediterranean regions.

Roughly 40 percent of societies sampled in one study had initiations for males, and 58 percent had them for females.[96] Societies in which women contribute more significantly to production are more likely to have initiations—for boys as well as for girls. Slightly more than half the societies sampled initiate only one sex, and the number of societies initiating only girls is double the number of those that initiate only boys. Societies that initiate both sexes are statistically more frequent among societies in the middle range of economic and social complexity.

Boys are most typically initiated in groups when they reach a certain age. Girls are more often initiated singly, when they begin to menstruate. Consequently, male initiations emphasize same-sex bonding to a greater degree than female initiations do. Because of the collective nature of boys' rites, they occur less frequently. Boys' ceremonies tend to be more public, last longer, and exhibit higher levels of dramatization. They are more likely to have large community feasts and to elicit highly displayed emotional responses.

Having to perform ritual feats is more characteristic of male than of female initiations. Female initiations are more likely to require a girl to observe restrictions, whereas male rites are more likely to require a demonstration of skills or an exhibition of prowess. The focus of boys' rites tends to be on assuming responsibility, the focus of girls' rites, on fertility and sexuality—in short, on men's productive role and women's procreative role.

If we set this broad-stroke global portrait alongside Western initiatory aspirations, an interesting set of tensions appears. It is conventionally held in North America that a major aim of initiation rites is to make adults. But since some cultures lack the notion of a generic adult, it may be a more accurate generalization to say that traditional initiations make men and women. It is rare that initiations for boys and girls are held together. The Hopi practice of doing so is exceptional. The aim of many traditional initiations is to ingrain clear images of manhood and womanhood. The primary intention may be less to create responsible adult citizens and more to define proper male and female roles, making it easier to enforce rules regarding the display of gender. Boys learn to be hard and withhold tears, girls, to be expressive, nurturing, or submissive.

Among certain groups in Melanesia, initiations are said to dismantle identities that were originally androgynous, male-female, in order to create single-sex people capable of reproducing in relationship with each other.[97] In other words, many initiations in traditional, small-scale societies do not produce men or women, much less generic adults, but rather potential fathers and mothers. The global data emphasize strongly gendered identity formation and reveal fundamental differences between ceremonies for females and males, whereas North Americans experiment with initiating boys and girls together. Many societies do not initiate both sexes, much less together.

The global data cannot tell us what we should do. At best, they can only suggest possibilities and probabilities. The move from descriptive data to prescriptive scenario is not automatic or easy. But scholars have attempted it, and it is easier to see the fantastic nature of such leaps in studies that are dated. For example, one empirical study concludes (supposedly on the basis of its data, little of which is American) that what American society needs is to increase the authority of its fathers. The authors suggest that forcing young boys to move away from home would probably be more effective than an initiation rite for breaking the overdependence of sons and mothers and for forging a substitute bond between sons and adult males. Defining the mother-son bond as the problem and father-son bonding as the goal is, I think, the outcome of the authors' Freudian theory, not an obvious inference from the data. The authors conclude with an astounding recommendation. They say that instead of undergoing a formal initiation rite, males should be drafted by the Selective Service into the military at an earlier age so they can be "exposed to the authority of responsible adult males."[98] This sort of reasoning illustrates how statistical studies of initiation can be as fanciful as any work of fiction.[99]

From this brief discussion of the global data, we can see what sorts of questions the data have been made to answer. Obviously missing are practical and evaluative questions that contemporary readers pose: Are traditional rites of passage effective? Should we be enacting them or inventing our own? Were our ancestors more ritually adept than we? How do diffuse educational practices compare in effectiveness with ritually structured transitions? Are societies that initiate adolescents into adulthood mentally healthier and socially more dynamic than societies that do not? How important is initiation to the formation of personal and social identity? These are some of the recurring questions that reporters, parents, filmmakers, and students ask about initiation, but the ethnographic and statistical writings on initiation do not answer them well.

Those who would study worldwide ritual practices to lay a solid foundation for either the understanding or the reinvention of rites have little choice but to question the solidity of that foundation. The Western idea of initiation, whether in its scholarly or its popular guise, is a construction, a product not just of research and description but also of interpreting and imagining. However close social science hovers to the quotidian realities of human existence, it has its own way of soaring into the stratosphere and rendering the real fantastic. Social scientists, like the rest of us, are motivated not just by facts but also by images, traditions of interpretation, moral commitments, and biases.

Initiatory Fantasy

If there is a global crisis concerning initiation, it is not merely that such rites are disappearing or difficult to find. It is that the void is filled with less desirable activities such as unconscious or peer-group ritualization. Another substitute is initiatory fantasy.

In small-scale societies dominated by a single tradition, it is possible for elders to initiate on the basis of their own ritual experience: As initiated, so initiate. By contrast, in disaffiliated sectors of the West, ritual fantasy, rather than ritual experience, often determines practice. Wedding photos in brides' magazines, initiation scenarios in movies, and birth or death scenes on television can shape the desire for passage and condition actual ritual performances.

The fantasy of initiation, more than the memory of it, can shape how people act when they attempt to conceptualize or ritualize passage into adulthood. How we think of initiation is influenced as much by advertising, novels, film, and television as it is by how our parents and grandparents experienced it or how scholars theorize about it. In large-scale, highly mobile societies, initiatory fantasy may even become a primary ritual substitute.

By *fantasy* I mean a particular way of imagining—one that is self-preoccupied and projective. When we *project,* we displace our own qualities, both good and bad, onto others. We locate "out there" what is really "in here." When we project, we perceive others in our own image.

When Western tourists observe other people's initiation rites, debunking them as "primitive" or praising them as "mystical," they are displacing their own primitive or mystical qualities. "Others" are primitive, therefore inferior to "us." "They" are "mystical," therefore superior to us. Projection is compensatory, growing out of what we lack, what we are unable to own, or own up to. Because it is a way of avoiding responsibility, projection destroys the possibility of authentic cross-cultural interaction and interreligious communication. When a group *fantasizes* its initiations, it should expect trouble.

Comparatively speaking, Western industrial societies spend less time and energy on rites than do people living in more traditional, small-scale societies and less than Asian, Middle Eastern, and African peoples.[100] In an increasingly deritualized environment an initiatory dilemma arises. One might frame it as a brief set of questions: Do we

North Americans, as diverse as we are, initiate? If so, do we do it well? If not, should we? If so, how should we imagine and construct initiation rites? And who is this "we" who should do the constructing?

A black South African psychologist was less circumspect in commenting on the Western initiatory dilemma: "You whites do not initiate," he said. "You have various religious events—confirmations, I think you call them, and things like that. But you do not initiate your boys, and that is why you have so many boy-men. That is your shame."[101]

People experimenting with reinvented initiation rites summarize the dilemma something like this: "There are few initiations into adulthood in Western countries. The ones that remain are ineffective or limited to small, relatively traditional, fairly closed groups. Since a solid sense of adult identity is essential to the health of both our society and the planet, the ritual indifference and disability of industrialized, so-called first-world nations is destructive. In the absence of specific initiation rites, diffuse ritualization, peer initiation, and unconscious self-initiation occur. All three substitutes lead to distorted self-images, violence, and lack of vocational direction. Thus, we are urgently in need of renewed initiation rites."

Among many disaffiliated North Americans of European descent there is a growing hunger for compelling ritual experience, especially initiation with its apparent promise of adult identity and spiritual competence. Among people who hold such a longing, initiation does not require solidarity with the ancestors or increased social responsibility; it is rather a means of personal growth and self-enhancement.

The European American world is known for its aversion to ritual, a distaste cultivated by periodic waves of iconoclasm ("image breaking"), the Protestant reformations, Puritan antiritualism, and American utilitarian pragmatism. Because of this heritage, a half-conscious hunger for ritual drives many to stalking the rites of other times and places in the hope of "finding," "discovering," or "borrowing" them. This desire may express deep spiritual longing, or it may be a fad, but it is persistent.

The Western longing for initiation is often characterized by a lack of knowledge about actual rites and by naïveté about the way ritual really works. In workshops and retreats ritualizing often takes the form of experimentation and invention, both characterized by a high degree of self-consciousness and a roving eclecticism. Clashes begin arising when the building blocks of experimental ritualizing are expropriated from "other" traditions and "other" religions with little sensitivity to the ethical issues involved. This experimental ethos is no longer confined to so-called countercultural groups; it affects middle-class neighborhoods and mainline denominations as well.

Rites of passage are only one among many kinds of ritual, and initiation is just one of the rites of passage. Even so, initiation exercises an inordinate influence in North American fantasy life. No other kind of ritual provides such a provocative window on the imagination of the European American West. Not only has initiation played a privileged role in ritual theory, it also dwells at the heart of an enormous amount of popular fantasy, literature, drama, and film.[102]

Two psychologists of religion, Robert Moore and Doug Gillette, claim that without initiation into adulthood, men become less than human. Uninitiated males, they argue, are more likely than initiated men to abuse both the environment and their neighbors, particularly women.[103] Perhaps they are right. But what is the answer they propose? Remythologizing and new rites based on these recovered myths. Movies, claim Moore and Gillette, are the contemporary equivalent of myths, stories that enshrine sacredly held values. A movie they strongly recommend is *The Emerald Forest*. Briefly, the story is this: An engineer is building dams in South America. His son, Tommy, the film's hero, is kidnapped by a band of natives. Eventually, the boy, who comes to be known as Tomé, lives among a group of "good" Indians, the Invisible People. Now, several years later, he is an adolescent on the verge of manhood. He is coming of age, ready for a man-making initiation rite. Meanwhile his father, half crazed by the loss of his son and pursued by the Fierce People, the dark-skinned, "bad" Indians, is crashing noisily through the jungle spraying everything that moves with a bullet-spitting machine gun. Will he find his son? Will his son become a man? These are the two questions that drive the plot. The ritual drama of Tommy's initiation is framed by the social drama of his father's rampage through the jungle.

In a depiction of initiation that is rife with clichéd Indian dancing and other stereotypes of native behavior, Tommy undergoes initiatory torture. Dying as a child, he is born a man. Awaiting him is a native girl with round, naked breasts. Blond, well tanned, and muscled, Tommy soars like an eagle. Assisted by hallucinogens, he envisions the sacred stones, source of the Invisible People's life. He alone retrieves them.

In the forest he encounters the dark-skinned Fierce People, who are bearing down on his father intending to killing him. At first father and son do not recognize each other; too many years have passed. But eventually, beneath a roaring waterfall, they do. In the end, the white boy not only recovers the source of the Invisible People's lives, he also saves his father from death and wins the admiration of a bare-breasted girl as well. Such is white male initiatory fantasy in the West.

Moore and Gillette consider *The Emerald Forest* a compelling example of initiation ritual, one that leads to "calm, serene maturity."[104] The two authors treat the movie with deference, raising no questions about its rampant ethnocentrism. They do not question its values or criticize its images, and they uncritically accept the fantasy of initiation as if it were a proper template for ritual enactment.

Unlike births, weddings, or funerals, tribal initiations are often made objects of expropriation. Rites can be spiritual booty taken in colonialist conflict. Moore and Gillette say they "feast on the diversity in the transition rites of the different peoples."[105] Their feast is a table laden with clichés and stereotypes.

We North Americans do not "borrow" other kinds of ritual to the same extent that we cannibalize other cultures' initiations. We do not borrow native funerals or mourning practices. Instead, we take vision quests and ordeals. Inaccurate depictions of tribal initiations have a long history. These highly selective, distorted portraits contribute to exploitative interactions. For this reason, unselfcritical presentations of initiation rites feed the Western initiatory neurosis by simultaneously denigrating and romanticizing people living in small-scale, traditional societies. Such people are depicted as more primitive and stupider or as more mystical and wiser than we. In either case, they are not quite human.

David Oldfield, author of a program called *The Journey*, conducts adolescent initiations using guided imagery and basing his activities on the heroic journey as described by Joseph Campbell. The basic medium of the program is mythic narrative. One version of the program consists of forty hours, much of it guided imagery proceeding through stages named "The Call to Adventure," "Finding One's Path," "The Heart of the Labyrinth," "The Wood Between the Worlds," and finally "The Ceremony of Passage."[106]

"In modern America," Oldfield observes, "there are no formal rites through which young people can express the yearnings of soul that usher them from childhood into adulthood. We do not honor the inward journey of adolescence with vision quests, like the indigenous people of North America, or help the young cultivate the wisdom of their dreams, as did the ancient Greeks." As a result, Oldfield thinks adolescents have lost touch with themselves. In his view, "What matters to the soul is authenticity: Is this me, my path, my life, or am I acting out someone else's fantasy of me?" Initiating, says Oldfield, "is tremendously important—not only to the individual being and her family but to the renewal of the life of the community, the nation, and the planet." Exuberantly, he declares, "The soul of the young can renew us all."[107]

Things ancient and tribal are set in opposition to things modern. "They" have initiations; "we" do not. We are "multicultural"; they are singular: "the" indigenous people. Oldfield takes no account of diversity in initiation practices—of societies that do not initiate, of groups that initiate women rather than men, of groups whose initiations we would likely consider abusive. He melts a multiplicity of nations into one. Crucial to Oldfield's initiatory fantasy is the individualist value that underlies his view of authentic ritual. For him, initiatory authenticity consists of figuring out *my* direction. And *my* direction is interior rather than exterior. *My* way arises from psychic, as opposed to communal or traditional, sources. Individualism is not merely a belief in the value of individuals; it sets individual and community in opposition and then ranks individuality higher.

In search of meaningful rites, many find themselves trapped between institutionalism and individualism. On the one hand, rites of passage proffered by long-standing traditions and organizations can seem moralistic and verbose, out of touch with current needs and sensibilities. On the other, the self-deceptions and skin-deep insights of ritual entrepreneurs and do-it-yourself manuals can be both embarrassingly naive and self-deceptive. In view of these alternatives, we have little choice but to assume an attitude that is wary and questioning of reinvented as well as of traditional rites.

Key to Oldfield's vision are these elements: an interior "journey" not located in actual space; ritualizing enacted primarily in words (in some versions, on a tape recorder); a plot driven by a hero (who, except for helpers, is largely alone); actions measured by a self-focused definition of authenticity.

Neither Oldfield nor Moore and Gillette intend to isolate participants from their geographical environments, encourage overdependence on the technology of media, provoke antisocial behavior, or cultivate self-preoccupation. But their approaches unwittingly cultivate these values, and the good intentions of authors and workshop leaders do not by themselves prevent these outcomes. As much as I sympathize with the contemporary North American desire for initiation, I believe the desire is deadly if left unexamined.

Much of what is imagined about initiation is derived not from the study of ritual texts, much less from observed ritual performances, but rather from mythic texts.[108] This point is basic but often overlooked: A myth is not a ritual. A myth is a story—usually told, sometimes read, occasionally transposed into a script and performed. A rite is a performance—typically enacted, almost never told. It makes sense to ask if there is a connection between a particular mythic story and a specific ritual enactment. But it flies in the face of what we know about myths and rites to assume this connection, and worse to assume that we can deduce initiation rites from heroic myths. There is no evidence that the plots of myths generally mirror the structures of corresponding rites.

Even though there is, for instance, a connection between the story of the Last Supper and the rite of the Roman Catholic mass, no one would be foolish enough to suppose that Peter and Judas must show up in the mass just because they appear as characters in the biblical story. Inversely, no one would think it possible to infer the singing of hymns, the wearing of robes, and the use of flat wafers from the narrative of the Last Supper. You cannot infer initiatory practices from a myth, or mythic characters from initiatory scenarios. Even in instances in which we can be certain there is a connection between the initiatory myth and ritual, we cannot make direct, inferential leaps. It makes little sense, then, to treat the plot of the so-called heroic pattern popularized by Joseph Campbell as a model for constructing initiatory rites of passage. These patterns are at an even greater remove from ritual than myths are, since patterns are generic summaries, mere abstractions. Initiation is not a kind of acted-out adventure story; it is the forging of a bond between generations. Bonds forged in adventure stories only last the length of the story.

Another difficulty with myth-based initiatory fantasy is that it is ahistorical. Fantasy construes initiation as a timeless, unchanging, singular, universal structure. But good studies of initiation show how drastically a traditional initiation rite may change in a short time.[109] If the fact of historical ritual change were absorbed into popular initiatory fantasy, the stereotypes of initiation would collapse.

The Improved Order of Red Men

Initiatory fantasy has a long history in the West. The West may lack a culture- or nationwide ceremony that conducts adolescents into adulthood, but we do not lack initiations into group membership. These kinds of rites are widely practiced, even though they may not be labeled initiations. There is no good reason why an occasion has to *be called* initiation in order to *be* initiation. One should look for initiation under other names: orientation, promotion, conversion, confirmation, ordination, and so on. Sororities, fraternities, civic organizations, religious organizations, educational organizations, sports groups, ethnic groups, native groups, and even some businesses enact rites—some secret, some public—that are initiatory. Such occasions either start (that is, "initiate") a process, or they mark degrees of advancement through the ranks.

In addition to looking for contemporary initiations under other names, we should also be aware of their presence in history, since some periods have been heavily ritualized. In the latter half of the nineteenth century, Victorian America was replete with remarkable examples of actually performed initiatory fantasy. The Improved Order of Red Men, founded in 1834, was not an organization of Indians but rather of white males organized into "tribes."[110] Although the order no longer exists, many other Indian hobbyist groups filled the void after its demise. Today groups of "wanna-bes," non-Native people who perform quasi-Indian ceremonies, still thrive in both Europe and North America.[111]

The Improved Order of Red Men was originally a drinking society for working-class men. Oddly enough, it later became a temperance group. Between 1850 and 1900 the Improved Order defined its primary work as that of creating effective rituals, but many of its experimental scripts failed to receive general approval. By 1865 the organization was virtually dead. However, in 1868 the Grand Lodge began offering cash prizes for ritual scripts. One script was so effective that the lodge's membership leaped dramatically. Having invented a new adoption degree, the order was soon initiating ten thousand new members a year. In 1900 it could boast 350,000 members and an annual income of over a million dollars.[112]

Even though First Nations people were still in the process of being subdued and forcibly confined to reserves, small groups of white people were busily undergoing what Lewis Henry Morgan, founder of the Order of the Iroquois, called "inindianation" [sic].[113] Members of the Improved Order of Red Men were not concerned about the actual deaths being visited upon aboriginal people, but they were fascinated with symbolic deaths. The theme dominated their adoption degree rite, as described here by Mark C. Carnes:

> Teach us the trail we must follow while we live in this forest, and when it is Thy will that we shall cross the river of death, take us to Thyself, where Thy council fire of love and glory burneth forever in righteousness.

Then the council fire was kindled; in the preparation room the candidate— a "paleface"—removed his shirt and shoes and put on moccasins. A Scout rapped at the "inner wicket" and motioned for the candidate to follow. They padded silently around the lodge room, avoiding a group of Indians who were sleeping at the far end. Then the Scout tripped over one of the Indians. The awakened Indian shouted, "Spies! Traitors in our Camp!" and the group captured the candidate; the Scout escaped. The Indian hunters conferred around a fire.

> *First Brave:* This paleface is of a hated nation: let us put him to the torture!
> *Second Brave:* He is a squaw, and cannot bear the torture!
> *Third Brave:* He fears a Warrior's death!
> *Fourth Brave:* Let us burn him at the stake!

The initiated was informed of this decision.

The braves and the candidate proceeded to the opposite end of the lodge and were led to a tepee. Just after they were admitted, another Indian rushed at the candidate with an uplifted knife, only to be intercepted by a hunter who assured him that the paleface would soon be tortured. "Then let us proceed, paleface," the hunter said, "and unless some Chief interposes, you perish at the stake. Why do you tempt your fate? or is it your wish to become a Red Man?" The candidate was prompted to answer yes. The hunter warned: "Know, then, that Red Men are men without fear, and none but such can be adopted by our Tribe." After more questions the hunter demanded proof of the candidate's courage.

The initiate was bound to the stake, and the hunters were told to prepare their scalping knives and war clubs. The Indians commenced a scalp dance and started to light a fire. Another Indian summoned the Prophet from his tent. But the Prophet halted the execution and berated the hunters for their impulsiveness, noting that the candidate had proven his courage. He added that the family of Red Men were dedicated to their "brothers," the "children of the forest." However, he warned the paleface that the final decision on his adoption rested with the Sachem. The Prophet gave the candidate an eagle's feather . . . as proof of his courage.

After more speeches and a pledge of secrecy, the candidate was led to another tepee in the far corner of the lodge. As he approached, the Sachem threw open the flap and upbraided his guards for sleeping on duty, thereby allowing a paleface to come into his presence. The warriors did not immediately respond, and the Sachem started to throw a tomahawk at the initiate. One of the hunters then grasped the Sachem's arm. "No, Sachem, no! Thy children when on duty never sleep!" The hunter added that the initiate had passed the ordeal and had been endorsed by the Prophet. He produced the eagle's feather as proof. The sachem, realizing his error, tossed his tomahawk aside, shook hands with the candidate, and welcomed him to the order.[114]

This hour-long rite, only part of which is described here, was invented in Baltimore by a committee and inspired by a book, Lewis Henry Morgan's *League of the Iroquois*. However implausible it may seem to speak about "creative" ritual or the "invention" of tradition, rites have been designed by committee or constructed by imitation. So-called New Age ritualizing is not new.

From a contemporary vantage point it is difficult not to wince at the rite. King James English is pilfered for clichés that are spewed from the mouths of pseudo-Indians. The tenor is that of a poorly written and performed Christmas pageant, but one in which adolescents rather than children play the parts. The rite casts grown men as brave children petitioning both the sachem and the prophet as fathers, who in turn address the Great Spirit as father. The "paternal redundancy" of the rite is striking.[115] These are not "wild savages" but business associates, neighbors, and townspeople, performing themselves into the role of motherless brothers, the offspring of a hierarchically arranged set of fathers. Their canoe paddling, war, bravery, and death are purely allegorical. Their Indian identity and spiritual authority are not only invented but self-conferred. Viewed from within the confines of the order, the authority is earned, but from the viewpoint of those whose dominant symbols are being appropriated, they are specious. Today, such a rite would evoke outrage from native communities. The Victorian versions coincided with protracted assaults on native people and their territories; there was little time and no occasion for voicing indigenous criticism. But today's New Age versions are subject to an increasingly angry and resistant counterattack.

Historians estimate that in 1896 between 28 and 40 percent of all American males were members of fraternal organizations.[116] How was it possible for so many to take such rites seriously? What was their function for the millions who were initiated? The usual answer is fraternity, a sense of solidarity among middle-class Protestant men uncompromised by the presence of others—women and Indians but also uninitiated men.[117] Members were able to make business contacts and maintain a web of social connections.

As Carnes notes, these factors may explain why men joined social clubs and business and professional organizations but not why they joined organizations whose only stated purpose was ritual and whose rites were so time-consuming that they inhibited extensive fraternization and networking.[118] Organizations such as the Improved Order of Red Men and the Knights of Pythias were not community service clubs like the Kiwanis or Lions Clubs of today. When twentieth-century Masons wanted more time to socialize or serve the community, they eliminated or curtailed the rites. As strange as it may seem to us, ritual itself was the motivation for joining. In groups like the Red Men, initiation into degrees was the staple of regular meetings. These rites were not one-time affairs like college fraternity initiations, which happen once a year. There were multiple degrees of initiation. In the case of the Red Men they were adoption, hunter, warrior, and chief.

Carnes's own answer to the question, Why did so many ritualize? is gender specific. It is that young men found in the rites solace and psychological guidance for negotiating the troubling passage into manhood. In undergoing the symbolic journeys and ritual deaths, he says, young men who were regarded as not quite masculine could be reborn fully masculine; they could feel themselves to be men. Fraternal man-making rites were an alternative to a "feminized Protestantism."[119] This was a transformation that the churches' ritual systems did not offer.

In Protestant North America there is a long history not only of inventing rites but also of complaining about the diversion of money and time into "ritual babble." Eventually, there emerged groups such as the Shriners, who were dedicated to recreation rather than to ritual, to mocking what they considered the ceremonial pretensions of established ritual groups. By the 1920s and 1930s the rites seemed ridiculous rather than profound. But criticism and strangeness did not by themselves lead to a decline of the ritual orders, nor did the demise come about because of secularism and rationalism. Rather, they began to wane as the membership aged and young men ceased to attend. Carnes claims that attendance dropped because the early twentieth century witnessed a decrease in mothers' involvement in the lives of their children, coupled with an increase in the involvement of fathers. Fathers and sons were, he implies, less distant, thus there was less need of ritual to mediate the distance.[120] In short, the rites were out of step with the changing social structures and thus the psychological requirements of those who might have been drawn into fraternal order membership.

Betwixt and Between

To expose the pretensions and ethical insensitivity of reinvented initiations or to criticize the distortions wrought by theory is not to say that we should avoid imagining and theorizing altogether. Reimagining is essential on both a theoretical and a practical level. A new theoretical vision of ritual began to emerge in the 1960s and 1970s in the prolific writings of Victor Turner, who was largely responsible for a radical reconception of ritual. He stood conventional ritual theory on its head. For him, ritual was not the guardian of the status quo or a means of garnering social consensus, as it had been previously under the influence of the French sociologist Emile Durkheim. Rather, ritual became deeply subversive and creative. By the time of his death in 1983, Turner had become the major theorist of ritual in the twentieth century. Like van Gennep and Eliade, Turner exercised considerable influence not just on ritual theory but also on popular ritual practice. His work was too far-reaching and original for us to treat him as a mere student or successor of van Gennep. Nevertheless, he developed certain images and ideas that continued the trajectory begun by van Gennep.

The most widely read of Turner's works, *The Ritual Process*, was published in 1969. In Turner's imagination, liminality is not just a phase in an initiation rite but any betwixt and between "space" in which cultural and ritual creativity are incubated. For Turner, it is specifically the middle, or liminal, phase that enables ritual to do the work of transformation. In his view all genuine ritual is transformative. Ritual that merely confirms the status quo rather than transforming it he called ceremony. In Turner's vision, ritual is a hotbed of cultural creativity; and its work is to evoke creativity and change, not to buttress the status quo.

Turner was concerned that rites of passage seemed to have their proper matrix in small-scale societies. He remarked, "*Rites de passage* are found in all societies but tend to reach their maximal expression in small-scale, relatively stable and cyclical societies, where change is bound up with biological and meteorological rhythms and recurrences rather than with technological innovations."[121] Nevertheless, Turner was ambivalent about leaving those rites behind as if they were irrelevant to large-scale societies. Although he admitted that rites of passage achieve fullest expression outside societies such as ours, Turner retained his interest in rites of passage, making them the model for understanding how ritual in general works. He not only treated one rite of passage, initiation, as the quintessential rite of passage, he also regarded one of its phases, liminality, as definitive of ritual. In Turner's writings liminality became even more autonomous than it had been in van Gennep's. Liminality was not only an important dynamic of ritual, it was also a value, if not a virtue. Liminality had moral and religious worth. It was the generative, creative principle of ritual in particular and culture in general.

For Durkheim ritual had been an agent of bonding, a kind of social glue. But for Turner the new image of ritual was that of a generator or matrix. In Turner's theory—perhaps more accurately, in his vision—*ritual* is subversive, the opposite of *ceremony,* the staunch conservator of culture and guardian of the status quo. Ceremony may be the glue of society, but ritual is its mother.

Turner was convinced that a powerful but temporary kind of community emerges during liminal moments in ritual. He referred to it as *communitas* and regarded it as the *fons et origo* ("fountainhead and origin") of social structure. The generative effects of liminality, then, are not limited to artistic or ritualistic creativity; they include new and adaptive social forms as well.

Turner was deeply interested in rites of passage, especially the inversions and ludic, or playlike, recombinations appearing in them. For him liminality constituted a zone of creativity, because it is a crucible in which culture is reduced to its fundamental elements, its "alphabet." This reduction facilitates their playful recombination in novel or fantastic patterns. Turner referred to these elements in a variety of ways, as archetypes, first principles, and building blocks.[122] The whole set comprises a template, ultimate measure, or paradigm.[123] In Turner's own words, "Put a man's head on a lion's body and you think about the human head in the abstract. Perhaps it becomes for you, as a member of a given culture and with appropriate guidance, an emblem of chieftain-ship. . . . There could be less encouragement to reflect on heads and headship if that same head were firmly ensconced on its familiar, its all to familiar, human body. . . . Liminality here breaks, as it were, the cake of custom and enfranchises speculation. . . . Liminality is the realm of primitive hypothesis."[124]

Turner's theories are now being subjected to critique for distorting the patterns of women's initiation and for failing to explain the rites of societies outside Africa, where he conducted his most sustained re-search. But Turner unshackled the Western scholarly imagination, which had been able to conceive of ritual only in terms of its more staid features. In addition, he crossed the near-sacred line between theory and practice. Not only did he engage in "performance ethnography," an experimental form of pedagogy much indebted to both ritual and the-ater, he was also initiated by the Ndembu of Zambia. He not only stud-ied them; he studied *with* them.

Like the research of Victor Turner, mine has not been "pure." Both my fieldwork and theory continue to be influenced by participation as well as by observation, by experimental and cross-cultural ritualizing. One story illustrates the troublesome aspects of working in this way. My official infant baptism consisted of a few proper drops of water on my head. I know the event happened, because I have a piece of paper certifying that it did. My parents seldom talked about it, except to say that, yes, it had been done so I should not worry. I cannot remember my confirmation at age twelve, although I know it too was performed. Nei-ther rite continues to form me, if either ever did.

But in 1980 I underwent what one could call a "cross-cultural bap-tism" that gave me pause. I was invited by Jerzy Grotowski, director of the Polish Theater Laboratory, to join an international group in some ritual experiments.[125] I was assigned to a group led by Haitians who were both Vodun practitioners and artists.

Late one afternoon, after strenuous physical and spiritual exercise in the mud and rain, we approached a gurgling stream in the forest. We crept up on a waterfall, as if it were a deer who might flee from our in-trusion. The waterfall was hardly magnificent. It was ordinary, not much taller than we. The Haitians—some of them wrinkled with age, others tawny and adolescent—led us, one by one, beneath the chilly cascade of water. Some stripped off their clothes. Others remained dressed. Nothing could have been simpler. There were no words, only hands carefully offered, skin and bone bracing skin and bone against the threat of slippery stone. The shock of the water, the gasping that punctuated our week-long silence, the remarkable gentleness of our teachers—all this drove something deeply into the bone. What that something was I could not name then, nor can I name it now.

I return to that moment, reimagining it, bathing in it. In that cold, watery moment I felt I understood baptism for the first time. But "baptism" had arrived too late, and it hurried me away from, not toward, the church. Later, I would read accounts of early Christian initiation with great sadness and longing. I had not known that ancient baptisms were conducted at sunrise or that candidates entered the water naked. Even now, when I no longer desire entry into the church, I imagine that I am standing, shivering and naked among the sleepyheaded candidates. Their faces flush; mine does too. For a moment I am one of them, embarrassed, red faced, newborn, though old and bearded. Ah, how messy, how wonderful, this initiatory birth-and-water stuff.

My Afro-Caribbean-Polish "baptism" lodged itself in the bone but left me stranded. Though sensuous and meaningful, it led into no enduring community, since the community was temporary, ending when the project finished. In this respect my experience is typical of others who experiment with ritual. I know of many people initiated on weekend retreats who end up beached like whales unable to flop back into the deep waters. In my view this is the most intractable dilemma facing reinventors of rites.

So the task of reinventing initiation requires not only the construction of ritual (both practically and theoretically), it also requires the reconstitution of community. We need to rethink initiation's relationship to community. Traditional initiations are done by elders, and initiates are incorporated into their own communities. In today's world we are faced not only with fantasized, unconscious, and peer initiations but also with cross-cultural ones such as Turner's induction by the Ndembu or Karen Brown's initiation into Vodun.[126] Like the numerous wilderness-experience initiations that have sprung up in North America, these are initiations that do not eventuate in ongoing community. But if we believe that rites reflect their social circumstances, then what else should we expect of rites enacted in a religiously pluralistic, highly mobile world? It is common to hear both clergy and scholars denying that peer initiations, cross-cultural initiations, and initiations without community are not real rites. But excluding such practices by definition

does not make them go away. These made-up, nontraditional, acultural
rites enacted in momentary communities may not be perfect or last a
lifetime, but they are real, and their way of coupling powerful gestures
with intercultural cooperation and communal transience does reflect
the world we live in.

Debt Payments, Whippings, and Washings

Theoretical formulations, statistical studies, initiatory fantasies, and
cross-cultural ritual experiments all have their own way of going far
afield. They need to be supplemented by the study of detailed ethnographies. Fearing distortions that beset grand cross-cultural generalizations, many contemporary anthropologists and historians restrict themselves to writing locally focused ethnographies or histories. These are
better grounded, although they often contain what lay readers may
consider the "boring" details of a rite. Such descriptions are thickly
textured on the premise that rites only make sense in their home environments. Unlike global surveys based on representative samples,
ethnographies are based on months, sometimes years, of participant
observation.[127] In a similar way, histories of rites not only provide rich
descriptions but also allow one to see rites responding to social pressures and changing across time and circumstance.[128]

Ethnographic descriptions of initiation rites are not easy to find. The
secrecy of some initiations has kept observers out or imposed speech
prohibitions on participants. Another reason for the lack of detailed accounts is that participants themselves may not have complete knowledge of an initiation rite. Their knowledge is sometimes specific to their
limited roles in the initiatory process. In some traditions no single individual has complete knowledge of any rite. To have this much knowledge of a treasured resource would be to have too much power.

The data are also skewed by a lack of scholarly constancy in gathering it, constructing theories, and working out definitional disputes. In
the early part of the twentieth century, initiation was a central topic in
the anthropological discourse on religion, but in the latter half, it was
largely ignored by anthropologists, psychologists, and religious-studies
scholars. This marginalization of the topic has left both the definition
and the conception of initiation in disarray. Scholars argue, for instance, whether ritual inductions of individuals, rather than groups
(usually called cohorts or age cohorts), count as initiations. Excluding

the induction of individuals would mean that most women's rites would not count as initiations. A second example of the kind of trouble arising from lack of sustained theorizing is that there is no consensus on whether a diffuse array of activities such as smoking, attending rock concerts, getting a driver's license, becoming sexually active, and leaving home amounts to initiation.

With researchers debating such basic definitional and conceptual issues, few are willing to conduct extensive cross-cultural studies or to make global statements. The most reliable materials on initiation, then, are detailed descriptions of single ritual performances, specific initiatory traditions, and region- or gender-focused studies of rites.

In Papua New Guinea a *narandauwa* is "a woman whom people come and look at."[129] The term *naranduawa* also refers to the rite itself, which begins when a young Yangoru woman begins to menstruate. In earlier times *naranduawa* was only the first phase of a ceremony that was much more complex. Today, only this single phase is practiced. Upon menstruating for the first time, the girl—we will call her Tambwi—becomes the object of heightened community attention. Her status is publicly proclaimed, and since her flow is regarded as polluting, she is secluded. Her head is shaved, and she is subjected to whipping and required to fast. Her parents, too, are polluted, "since their blood is in her," so they are put in seclusion as well. If she had lived in earlier times, Tambwi would have undergone scarification of the breasts and belly.

Besides being deprived of ordinary interpersonal contact and subjected to unpleasant treatment, Tambwi is also the object of special care and attention. She is washed by her mother and looked after by her brother. On the fourth day of her seclusion, she is bathed in scented steam and honored with songs. On the fifth, she is decorated in finery and seated on a palm-flower sheath, where she receives gifts from a prestigious, ritually pure female relative. The relative wipes the sweat of her own armpit across the girl's breast and then offers her palm for the girl to lick. In this way, Tambwi ingests wifely virtues. After ceremonial debts are paid to the ancestral shades, her mother's brothers, and the maternal kin, as well as to those who looked after the girl's parents in seclusion, the initiate formally breaks her fast.

Tambwi's emergence is gradual. On one evening she is ritually washed and her body rubbed with special shrubs and shoots. On another, she burns her hut and initiation skirts and then heads to the river to celebrate with young adults. Likely Tambwi is relieved that young

Yangoru Boiken women are no longer subjected to the ordeal of brambles and stinging nettles that greeted initiates in the old days.

The rite concludes about a month after it began, near the time of her second period. Tambwi dives through the legs of her father, who is standing in a river. She seizes ginger root with her teeth from between his feet. Then she bakes fish to distribute to children. Finally, after consuming a bit of meat and a twist of *ningi* plant, she is free to eat what she wishes.

Paul Roscoe, who describes Yangoru women's initiation, says that the debt payments, whippings, and washings are thought to lift a girl's menstrual pollution—but not completely.[130] Assuming she marries, Tambwi and her husband will not become adults until they have their first child. And their purification will not be complete until their children are initiated. Among the Yangoru initiation is only an entry into a first initiatory grade; the second and third grades of initiation are entered by undergoing first-intercourse and first-birth rites. These continue the process of purification and of conferring female and male strength, since males, like females, are polluted, require ritual seclusion, undergo whipping, and make payments to ancestors and relatives. So maturation, whether female or male, does not happen in a single moment, as we in the West sometimes surmise is the case among other peoples. Transformation does not depend on a single rite but on a protracted series of rites.

Unlike the fantasies, films, statistics, and theories of initiation, this description, as short and generic as it is, pulls us up short. We notice how unpleasant initiation can be, how much time and how many resources it uses, how foreign its values and imagery, how little it resembles heroic adventure, how impossible it would be to reduce it to three phases, how hard it would be to locate the rite at a single transition point in a life cycle, and how difficult it would be to distinguish it from other passages such as marriage.

Bartering a Traditional Celebration

Perhaps it seems we have painted ourselves into a corner. Some say initiation is a global problem. On the one hand, if initiation rites are absent, the young become disoriented. On the other, if such rites are present in traditional forms, they are dysfunctional or dissonant. But if we set to imagining initiation, we lapse into self-indulgent fantasy or induction without community. If we turn to the classical theorists for help, they disappoint us. And if we seek refuge in the facts, they evade our questions or themselves degenerate into fantasies. If we have recourse to ethnographies, they seem so culture specific that there is little hope of exporting them for our use. What is left to do?

We have little choice but to consider actual initiation rites in which participants are actively adapting to changes closer to home. Actual rites are local and specific, usually more ordinary and less dramatic than much of the popular literature would lead us to believe. Real initiation rites are characterized by boredom, spending money, family squabbles, and lots of tedious labor.

Quinceañera is celebrated among Hispanics both in the United States and in Mexico for fifteen-year-old girls.[131] It is both a coming-of-age celebration and, in the urban American Midwest, a way of establishing cultural distinctiveness in the face of the homogenizing pressures exerted by a non-Hispanic majority. There is speculation that the rite is a mixture of Spanish courtly ritual, Aztec initiation, and Sephardic Jewish ceremonies (since sixteenth-century *conversos* settled in northern Mexico). But there is no compelling historical evidence that this coming-out celebration is a synthesis of these traditions, since most accounts of *quinceañera* date from the 1920s to the present.

In an earlier time, when women married at a younger age, the celebration may have announced a girl's availability for marriage. Today, the rite is less an announcement of marital availability than it is an exit from childhood and a first step into adulthood. *Quinceañera* resembles a debutante ball. Much of the fiesta consists of dancing and eating in community centers or, in the past, homes. The festivities are usually preceded by solemnities such as a mass in a Roman Catholic church. *Quinceañera*, then, has religious dimensions not typical of debutante balls. Although the celebration is scheduled to fall on or near a girl's fifteenth birthday, it is sometimes made to coincide with confirmation— perhaps an implicit recognition that the church's rite does not accomplish all that needs doing at this major transition in a young woman's life. Usually only one girl undergoes the rite, but in places where the demand is high or there are few priests, only one *quinceañera* per year may be celebrated for a cohort of fifteen-year-olds.

Since the rite is usually rehearsed and videotaped, and much attention is focused on dress, the ceremony can seem like a wedding, so priests work to eliminate the matrimonial overtones. Dresses, usually white for Chicanas and pink or pastel for other Latinas, are formal, "grown up," signaling a girl's maturity. There are other signs as well that the rite has sexual—not only social and religious—implications. Makeup and high heels, for instance, are not only permitted but considered appropriate. Before mass, the honoree receives a gold medal, usually of the Virgin of Guadalupe, along with an adult-sized rosary and an adult edition of the Bible or missal. The costs of these and other items necessary for the ceremony (such as musicians, a sound system, church rental, flowers, decorations, limousine, food, cake, video documentation, photo albums, and champagne for toasts) are sometimes underwritten by *madrinas* and *padrinos,* female and male sponsors.

At the beginning of a *quinceañera* mass there is a ceremonial entry. The honoree is accompanied by her attendants, called *damas* (ladies) and *chamberlains* (their escorts), as well as by the girl's family and godparents. All are formally dressed and sit at the front of the church, where honoree and attendants are addressed in a special homily. Sometimes the girl renews her baptismal vows or is ceremonially blessed by her parents.

As with many weddings and funerals, the liturgical rite is followed by socializing and feasting. The beginning of the reception is formal but flexible, so elements of contemporary culture are regularly patched into it.

Norma Cantú, who both underwent and studied *quinceañera,* describes the entry as performed in the border town of Laredo, Texas:

At the beginning of the formal Quinceañera presentation, the procession—made up of the honoree, her parents, her court of honor and her sponsors, called padrinos and madrinas—files into the hall. The music group, which in Laredo tends to be a Tejano or conjunto group, plays a "marcha" while the master of ceremonies announces the names of the participants and their parents. In the cases where the godparents participate in the procession they too are introduced. At the very end, the emcee announces the honoree and her parents who enter and take positions of honor. The first song, selected by the honoree and her parents, is usually a waltz, which she dances with her father. Then, if appropriate, with her grandfather(s). It used to be "Sobre las Olas"; now it is more likely to be "A Ritmo de Bals" that the honoree dances with her father. Immediately after ending the "first dance," with her chamberlain, she, along with the group, dances a choreographed piece; the chamberlain and the damas and their escorts join in. In Selina Reyes' 1994 quinceañera, the order was inverted. The whole group danced the first dance, a choreographed piece, to the music of "A Ritmo de Bals." She then danced with her father to a Whitney Houston song, "I'll Always Love You," tears streaming down her cheeks, as she was overcome with emotion. As in many other occasions, such as weddings, her presentation became a truly bilingual and bicultural event. At most quinceañera celebrations, at the conclusion of the special dance presentation, the rest of the invited guests join in the dancing. Then they partake of a meal, almost always it is traditional fiesta food—pollo en mole, fritada de cabrito, or tamales. For my fiesta, my uncle brought three cabritos [kid goats] which my grandmother cooked en fritada [in a stew] and asado [broiled] along with the huge cazuelas [clay pot] of rice and beans and enough tortillas to feed our family for a month. Food is an important element in the reception and has undergone some of the most dramatic changes. Whereas thirty years ago fiestas such as baptisms, weddings and quinceañera required mole, cabrito, pozole, tamales, depending on the season and the occasion, today's celebrations seem to require only that there be a meal and a cake. We must note one of the most significant changes: a change from these traditional celebratory foods to whatever the caterer offers—steak, a cold-plate buffet, or even a Mexican buffet with enchiladas and tostadas, foods that would have been deemed too ordinary for a fiesta. The choice of music for the dance—conjunto, country, pop, rock, tejano—may also shift and change from one generation to another. At my older cousins' fiestas and at my own, the music came from a record player and consisted mostly of boleros by Chelo Silva and other regional singers. The live music, when it was affordable in the fifties and sixties, was provided by local groups such as Los Hermanos Valdez, Beto Silva, or the Valenciano Brothers or groups such as the Royal Jesters. Sound systems such as Pobrezza and Elvira's Sound System provide a mix of anything from pop music to cumbias to rancheras and tejano to conjunto; live music can be a rock group or even a punk band instead of the more common tejano or tropical group. The change signals a cultural preference that signifies the postmodern scheme of a culture that turns on two axes: that of South Texas and Northern Mexico and [that of] various planes of social class. In this border culture everything goes, all is bartered, even traditional celebrations.[132]

Even though Laredo, Texas, is closer than Papua New Guinea, Norma's description reminds us how utterly rooted in language, region, time, and culture rites of passage are. If we are privy to this tradition, our mouths will water at the mere mention of mole, and our feet will search for rhythms, but if we are outsiders, the description may seem opaque rather than obvious.

Not only does our response to Norma's description signal distance from or proximity to the tradition she is describing, it also implicitly calls into question major theories of passage. For instance, the celebration does not have the three van Gennepian phases, preliminal, liminal, and postliminal. It has two major phases, religious and social, each containing several subphases. A more detailed account, one that included preparation and an aftermath, would likely require us to admit even more phases. We would have to *impose* a threefold structure on *quinceañera* to make it conform to the theory.

And would we, following Eliade, find in this rite the death and rebirth of an initiate? Hardly, since the only death and rebirth motif is the one embedded in the mass. Christ may have died and been reborn, but these fifteen-year-old girls do not die symbolically or otherwise. Would we claim that the ceremony transforms girls into women? Not likely, since the changes described seem incremental rather than monumental. And would members of the community consider a girl inhuman if she chose not to undergo the rite? I doubt it.

Of course, we could relabel *quinceañera*, calling it a birthday party or a celebration instead of an initiation, but that would distort, maybe even demean, it. *Quinceañera*, like bat mitzvah, is an initiation, but not one that fits the classical pattern, which was based largely on Australian Aboriginal male practices.

Quinceañera is refreshing for its recognizable, human ordinariness. The church has to be paid. Girls fret over what to wear. Parents worry about how much fancy dresses and gold medals cost. Someone has to figure out which band people will like best. The rite does not sound like an initiation—at least not in the way we have been taught to imagine or theorize about initiations. There are no seclusions, masks, transmissions of mystical knowledge, or trials in the wilderness. But other features of initiation are present: deferring to elders, receiving gifts, absorbing instruction, and relinquishing dependencies. At best, then, theories and schemes, definitions and charts, are preliminary devices, makeshift maps not to be confused with the territory they supposedly depict.

Initiatory Wonder

I have been talking like a ritual plumber, asking whether and how initiations work. I called upon Norma Cantú's account of *quinceañera* because it exposes the workings of a rite without mystifying them. I see nothing wrong with treating a rite as a means for inculcating virtues or as a device to keep adolescents from becoming delinquents, but if we think of rites only in this way, we miss something essential: their capacity to evoke wonder. Wonder is an attitude different from the means-end reasoning we employ when treating ritual as a tool. It is awe over the fact that something *is* or that all things are interconnected. Wonder is not about usefulness but about being and being together. It is what happens when the senses and spirit are engaged so that ritualists see things anew, as if for the first time, or when they experience a felt connection between one domain of human existence and another.

Medieval German and French Jews marked the transition from home to school with a delicious rite, which, when well imagined, can set us to wondering:

At age five or six, a Jewish boy living in medieval Germany or France might begin his formal schooling by participating in a special ritual initiation ceremony. Early on the morning of the spring festival of Shavuot (Pentecost), someone wraps him in a coat or *talit* (prayer shawl) and carries him from his house to the teacher. The boy is seated on the teacher's lap, and the teacher shows him a tablet on which the Hebrew alphabet has been written. The teacher reads the letters first forwards, then backwards, and finally in symmetrically paired combinations, and he encourages the boy to repeat each sequence aloud. The teacher smears honey over the letters on the tablet and tells the child to lick it off.

Cakes on which biblical verses have been written are brought in. They must be baked by virgins from flour, honey, oil, and milk. Next come shelled hard-boiled eggs on which more verses have been inscribed. The teacher reads the words written on the cakes and eggs, and the boy imitates what he hears and then eats them both.

The teacher next asks the child to recite an incantation ordering *Potah*, the prince of forgetfulness, to go far away and not block the boy's heart (*lev*, i.e., mind). The teacher also instructs the boy to sway back and forth when studying and to sing his lessons out loud.

As a reward, the child gets to eat fruit, nuts, and other delicacies. At the conclusion of the rite, the teacher leads the boy down to the riverbank and tells him that his future study of Torah, like the rushing water in the river will never end. Doing all these acts, we are told, will "expand the (child's) heart."[133]

Even though adults put boys through this rite, the adult teacher acts in concert with the child. The rite's importance is heightened by having it coincide with a seasonal celebration, the festival of Shavuot, which recollects the giving of the Torah to Moses.[134] The beginning student sits on the teacher's lap; the relationship is tactile as well as auditory. The student's first taste of learning has actual flavor. His initial, formal encounter with words has body, density. Rich with gustatory resonance, how could such words not nourish? The student does not have to sit at a desk. What joy! He sways back and forth and sings his lessons—all with his teacher's approval. What child would not come home wonderstruck?

This Ashkenazic school initiation rite was displaced by bar mitzvah, a less sensual ceremony. One reason for its displacement was pressure from Christians, who had begun fantasizing that Jews were ceremonially desecrating the host in mock communions. In the face of Christian ritual fantasy, the Jewish practice of eating morsels bearing verses of scripture became too dangerous.[135] But imagine the consequences of retrieving or reinventing a beginning school rite inspired by this practice. Our schools would have a difficult time living up to the promises implicit in the ceremony.

Today's school teachers use positive reinforcement. They do more than hand out smiley-face stickers. They devise elaborate systems for rewarding achievement. They espouse playing-can-be-fun ideologies and foster learning from peers. But school systems, even religiously sponsored ones, are largely ignorant of the power of ritual, except the ceremonial sort used at assemblies or employed to establish hierarchies and maintain order.[136] Instead of elevating learning to the level of ritual celebration, schools use ceremonies as tools for social control or reduce them to the level of empty play.

Younger children are less worried than adults about the distinctions among play, ritual, work, and drama. But unless adults go beyond instructing children about ritual to teaching them ritually, children's mastery of ritual skills will atrophy. The trouble is that even if kids do master the language of ritual, there are few places in which to "speak" it. So it is essential that we create "sanctuaries," safe "nests," where ritualized play and ritual experiment are possible.

I have been critical of the initiation practices of Western religious institutions, but on occasion they do, in fact, succeed in evoking wonder and mobilizing youthful enthusiasm. Rites of passage are ways of marking events with exclamation points, highlighting a moment of personal and social change as worthy of collective attention.[137] Miriam Ashkin Stanton recollects such an occasion:

My bat mitzvah was absolutely indescribable! It was the best day of my life since my birth! I feel so fresh, new, and changed. I'm on a spiritual high! Something about me is different. I stand taller; I feel so uplifted—as if I can do anything I choose! I've grown not just years but centuries in my religion, my courage, and my confidence. I have seen that I can accomplish a seemingly impossible goal. I feel as though this weekend was the best dream of my life. I had imagined my bat mitzvah so many times, and suddenly it has happened. I feel so sweet and new, as if a spring has showered my soul. I am so light and happy. There is no way to describe all my feelings—only that I am a new person, and it feels wonderful, majestic!

The ceremony was overwhelming. When I first stood up in front of all the people, I thought I could never go through with it. "Scared stiff" isn't the right way to describe my feelings; I was "scared shaking." It was terrifying. I began the service as if in a dream. I heard myself reading and singing, felt myself standing in front of my loved ones. I looked at the blur of faces, everyone smiling and proud. My eyes closed for just a second, and I could feel myself let go. I suddenly knew that I was ready. My courage grew.

I was called up for the Torah service, and my voice held a new strength. A warm feeling rose inside me, and I had to share it with my audience. Suddenly I was proud, not only of myself and my accomplishments, but of my parents, my brother, and my friends for going before me. I was proud of every person witnessing this transformation, and I was filled with admiration for all Jews—for living their religion, their spirituality. I stood taller, and I felt myself grow stronger. Suddenly, I knew I was leading this community, this family of mine. My voice, my spirit, was growing, reaching out to their souls. I felt tears in my eyes; a bond was beginning to grow between me, Jews, my community, my beloved rabbi, family, and everyone important in my life. I was a link in the chain of centuries that I couldn't begin to imagine.

I was passed the Torah and felt my lips sing and chant; I heard my voice as if it were outside of me. I took the Torah, the Torah I held my very first day of religious school, the Torah I have undressed so many times, the Torah that has been a part of my childhood. I began to walk around the sanctuary with it in my arms. Memories flowed through me. I used to carry the scroll around the sanctuary, imagining my bat mitzvah, and then, suddenly it was the same moment years later. I was a little girl and at the same time a new young adult. I felt a refreshing separation from the world, and yet a strengthening connection.

Then, with my prayer shawl around my shoulders, I began to chant. My voice swelled through my entire body. It was ethereal, surrounding me. The minor keys filled my heart—so mysterious and fulfilling. A feeling of airy happiness filled me.

I finished. The audience was a blur of tear-stained faces. I read through the Haftarah in a trance. My speech came . . . I read loudly, knowing how much I had waited for the moment to share it with everyone. I read my Midrash and was proud that I had tried something unique. My thoughts on Judaism and my bat mitzvah were all so perfect for me.

I radiated my thank-you to Myra—Myra, my wonderful rabbi, teacher, and friend, an inspiration throughout my life. I admire and respect her, because she has helped me learn who I am. She has forced me to question myself and my thoughts. She has inspired me to defend my beliefs and opinions. I thanked her from the bottom of my heart, because I wanted her to know how much she has changed my life. Myra is one of the heroines of my childhood.

I finished the service in an unearthly dream. I have never believed in God as a character who can change my life without my consent. But I have always believed in spirituality and belief. My bat mitzvah filled me with a presence of something loving, refreshing, and hopeful. I feel that it brought my soul out of me, for all the world to see. It made me a prouder and stronger person. I have never been so fulfilled, joyful, relieved, and uplifted in all my life. Special moments are short, but they last a long time. My bat mitzvah was my moment—one I will never forget as long as I live.[138]

The enthusiasm of Miriam's story is infectious. She is not cut off from her tradition, resentful of her parents and brother, or alienated from the religious leadership of her congregation. In the face of this narrative, it would seem alarmist to declare that initiation in the European American West is stagnant, imprisoned in fantasy and nostalgia or apathy and recalcitrant traditionalism. Testimony like hers reminds us that Western religious institutions can sometimes mount effective rites of passage. But Miriam is an exceptional young woman, and her rabbi an exceptionally nurturing and adaptive teacher, so I suspect that Miriam's joy and commitment are atypical.

In any case, this particular bat mitzvah, a simple rite as initiations go, made its mark on those present. The ceremony was worth the effort of a busy teenager to prepare, undergo, and record her impressions of it. Writing is one way she can ensure that the event will not die in the doing. Miriam's narrative provides a glimpse of a rite, scarcely older than the century we live in, but the ceremony evokes in her a sense of history that exceeds a mere century. However adolescent her emotions, and however certain adults may be that aging erodes the human capacity to achieve Miriam's multiple, wonder-suffused exclamation points, one can hardly deny the value of celebrating character-forming events that engender in youthful lives a felt connection with other parts of humanity.

To admit the hyperbolic qualities of Miriam's recollection is not to deny or override other more mundane dimensions of the rite that may go unreported in her account. That she declares her connections with Jews everywhere and announces pride in her brother is not to claim that she knows all Jews or to deny that she argues with her brother. And however true it would be to point out that the story is self-focused, adults have to ask themselves: In the throes of adolescence, where else should one focus?

Even though I have taken issue with Eliade, Miriam's account seems an apt illustration of his claim that initiation enables people to attain the status of full human beings. Without initiation rites, he says, people cannot achieve the higher, which is to say, spiritual, mode of being. "Initiation represents one of the most significant spiritual phenomena in the history of humanity," he wrote. "It is through initiation that men attain the status of human beings."[139] Miriam's story is apt testimony that girls, no less than men, have the capacity to become fully human.

Initiatory Disenchantment

Although it may sound contradictory to say so, reinventing initiation requires not only the evocation of wonder but also the willingness of elders to disenchant initiates. Initiatory enchantment is not the same as the ritual alienation that Vivian Hansen experienced. Ritual alienation arises from unwitting double binds within a rite, but initiatory disenchantment is strategic rather than accidental. When Hopi boys and girls are initiated, they are flogged. The disenchantment of learning that the masked dancers known as kachinas are their relatives dressed up in masks and costumes is more devastating than the whipping. Helen Sekaquaptewa tells of her experience:

Little children are told that the kachinas are magic and come from their home in the San Francisco peaks to take part in the various ceremonials. . . . When the day came for Kachinvaki [a rite enacted in February in connection with Powamu, sometimes called the Bean Dance], my mother dressed me in freshly washed clothes. First she wrapped an old belt around my waist, next to my skin. It went around two or three times and I wondered at the time why the two belts?

. . . The kachinas came in fast and were fierce-looking things. They stood by the fireplace. The first child in line, if it is a boy, has on only a blanket, which his sponsor removes, and he stands in the nude. The godfather takes hold of the hands of the boy and pulls him over in front of the whippers and lifts the arms of the boy above his head, while he receives four hard lashes. If the godfather sees fit, he may pull the boy away and put out his own leg and take one or two lashes for his godson.

It goes fast, with much crying. When a whip gets limp a new one—four yucca branches—is taken. The whippers take turns with the lash, while the mother whipper urges them on, mostly with the boys, saying, "Whip him hard. He is naughty. Don't be lenient with him. . . . "

If a little girl is wearing a shawl, her godfather takes it off, takes hold of her hands and leads her over to get whipped, as he holds her hands above her head. I knew then why my mother put two belts on me. The four lashes were given around the waist and it didn't hurt much. The tips of yucca did give a little sting. . . .

The final event is an all-night dance where the kachinas come and dance; all wear costumes, but some do not wear masks. Other masks are lined up on a shelf, and during the evening all remove their masks so that children see that it is men and not magic. . . .

It was quite an ordeal for me. When I went back to my home I wished I didn't know that a kachina was a man with a costume and a mask, when all the time I had thought they were real magic.[140]

One of the most revealing features of Helen's story is that she is more disturbed by the revelation of the kachinas' identity than by the whipping.[141] The disenchanting revelation bites more deeply than the token flogging. The short-run effect of her people's deception is disappointment. Like other Hopis who have undergone this initiation, she feels angry and betrayed. But in the long run most Hopis give up a childlike faith based on an either/or dichotomy: *Either* those performers are my relatives *or* they are kachinas. In place of their naïveté, Hopis develop an adult spirituality founded on one of the most widespread and fundamental religious paradoxes: Sacred people, like sacred objects, are both ordinary and sacred. Hopis learn that revelation is not only a divine given but also a human construction. While the short-term tactical consequences are negative, the long-term strategic ones are constructive.

To be effective, reinvented initiations must be able simultaneously to evoke wonder and to provoke disenchantment. Just as it is easy to confuse disenchantment with alienation, so it is easy to confuse wonder with mystification. Mystification has both destructive and banal forms. The Nuremberg rallies are an extreme example of destructive ceremonial mystification, and Cecil B. DeMille's *The Ten Commandments* is a banal one. Whereas wonder is about the revelation and celebration of being or being connected, mystification is about transcending ordinariness and overcoming enemies. Mystification hides the powers that be— behind a cloud or a flag, for example—for the sake of manipulating people to do or feel what the mystifying powers would like. Disenchantment, with its unmasking tendencies, goes hand in hand with wonder; mystification does not.

He Emerged as One of Them

The reinvention of initiation requires an ability to sustain a connection between the sacred and the humorous as well as the wondrous and demystified. The initiation of sacred clowns among the Tewa Pueblos of New Mexico is striking, although seldom described by insiders or witnessed by outsiders. Alfonso Ortiz, both an anthropologist and a Tewa Pueblo Indian, has described the ritual process undergone by a friend.[142] Linky was sixteen when he first began to have dreams about spiritual matters that he did not understand. Later, he found an object carved from stone, which was interpreted by a medicine man as having to do with sacred clowning. The medicine man, who queried Linky thoroughly, purified him with smoke waved across his body with eagles' wings.

Pueblo clowns, though different from European American clowns, sometimes wear makeup and outlandish clothes and commit outrageous acts. But they do so in concert with sacred ceremonies, not as part of a carnival or circus. In addition to mocking, inverting the usual hierarchies, and sexual or scatological teasing, they also help control crowds and reassemble torn costumes. In short, they combine the functions that European and North American cultures assign variously to priests, clowns, police officers, and backstage workers in theater. Being a sacred Pueblo clown is a high calling, not a menial or perfunctory job, and the position is for life. When initiated, a clown becomes a Made Person, which is to say, he is ceremonially remade in the image of the ancestors. Since, as clown, one becomes forever different, families weep, both with happiness and sadness.

The training is intense. In Linky's case, it extended over a two-year period. Since the initiation process requires one to attend virtually all ceremonies during the time of training, an initiate has to leave work whenever it is required. Jobs are often lost by clowns in training.

The dreams did not stop, and soon others signs appeared. Linky heard a voice and saw a mysterious three-foot tall Kossa, a clown painted with horizontal black-and-white stripes. Linky told his family, who again consulted the medicine man. This time the consultation was explicitly ritualistic, and the whole society of curers was present. Linky and his father brought a tobacco offering and addressed the senior medicine man in the appropriate way.

The conclusion drawn by the medicine men was that Linky was being called to join their society. He was encouraged to take four days to consider the matter in discussion with his family and relatives on both sides. Almost a hundred people had gathered by the time the decision was announced that Linky would, in fact, accept the calling. After further questioning and much weeping, Linky began his training, knowing that a change of mind would result in his complete exclusion from Pueblo ceremonial life. Now his relationship with others began to be characterized by deference, circumspection, and distance. Finding Linky, his friend, now much more reserved, Ortiz reflects, "As he walked away I had the feeling that, in a very important sense, I had said goodbye to him forever. We, as scholars, emphasize and understand well that aspect of rites of passage which enables individuals or even whole groups of people to pass over into new statuses and roles, but we do not pay much attention to what is left in the wake of such movement for those who knew the individual before he became, as in the present instance, a priest."[143]

For two years Linky accumulated gifts to give, acquired costumes and paints, secured sacred stones, collected food for the final rite, and prepared his *lake bowl*, a sacred ritual object in which priests would ritually recreate the primordial lake from which Pueblo people emerged in the beginning. Linky was instructed in chants, rites, and sacred stories. He was purged by a ceremonial sucking of foreign objects from his body. His family too was ritually cleansed.

Linky and the other clowns started things off by trooping into the village plaza in two rows, with Linky in the middle, singing and dancing in somber formation. During this period of dancing the clowns sang their own special songs of power, the same ones they sing the evening of each winter solstice, and the atmosphere on the plaza was electric. There was an outward celebration on the part of Linky's relatives, with the women throwing out basketsful of food-stuffs and other useful articles to the audience at large. This kind of mass give-away is expected of relatives during the initiation of a Made Person. Despite this outward display of festivity and celebration, there was also an atmo-sphere of apprehension, and some of the same relatives who were conduct-ing give-aways were also quietly weeping. The audience watching the pro-ceedings was not as large as one might expect for a ritual occasion of this importance, and those who were present on the plaza huddled close to the house walls, near their own doors if possible. They only ventured out near the center of the plaza briefly to retrieve goods when they were being thrown. Other people watched the proceedings from inside their houses.

We begin to understand the reasons for this ambivalence to the atmo-sphere of the plaza through the next sequence of activities. Just as suddenly as they trooped onto the plaza the clowns stopped and sat Linky down on a bed of ashes. Because the other clowns shielded him from full view during the dance we did not see that Linky was also dressed in a filthy, tattered breech cloth, and he wore on his shoulders an equally tattered piece of gunny sack for a cape. We also perceived that he lacked the horned leather skull cap with corn husk tips. Once they settled Linky cross-legged on his bed of ashes, two of the older clowns immediately excused themselves, saying they were going off to "Chihuahua" in Mexico. The remaining clowns gathered around Linky and began to taunt and insult him in the most humiliating manner imaginable. Nothing about his life before this vow was beyond their commentary and de-rision. Every so often they would pause and sing the following little ditty: "This is the one we have made up to look like an owl, behold him" (repeated sev-eral times). Throughout all of this, even when the line of spectators along the walls broke into guffaws of laughter at some especially telling barb aimed at Linky or some member of his immediate family, Linky himself remained im-passive. Being steeped in the comparative literature on clowns, initiations, and rites of passage in general, I could not help but gain the impression that, if the clowns were not deliberately attempting to erase Linky's prior identities and loyalties, at least they were rendering these prior identifications and loyalties impotent to influence Linky as a clown. I shall return to this point presently.

My musings were interrupted by the sudden reappearance of the two clowns who had earlier departed for Chihuahua. They carried a large, ter-raced bowl containing a mixture of urine and feces. This they passed to Linky, who downed large drafts of the liquid, smacked his lips, and proclaimed it was good. This final act of humiliation—yea, degradation, in our terms—was necessary, for this is the way a clown begins to exert control over waste, in order to turn it to better use in curing and other activities. Linky knew this demonstration was expected of him, and he was prepared, for all the while he was consuming the waste the other clowns never let up on their insults and taunts.

Suddenly it was over, or at least I thought it was over. The last moments with Linky on the ash pile were moments of such solemnity for the audience that I could not imagine what the clowns could possibly do for an encore. Well, the mood of the prayerful solemnity settled over the clowns as well, one of the most rapid turn-abouts in mood I have ever witnessed. Linky's ceremonial father, the clown who had been charged with presiding over his symbolic rebirth, came forward with a new leather skull cap which he had made for Linky, and he placed this slowly and affectionately on Linky's head, making sure it fitted. Linky then got up, joined the others, and listened as the chief clown addressed all present in a brief welcoming prayer for Linky. Linky was now one of them. He had devoted literally hundreds of hours to religious work during the preceding two years; he had undergone fasting and other deprivations for the four days prior to this afternoon; he had undergone almost unbelievable taunts and insults in full public view; and he had drunk filth with gusto. In brief, Linky had taken everything—every insult and humiliation—that the clowns had to offer, and now he emerged as one of them.[144]

How striking are the differences between the two society initiations that we have considered, this one and the one enacted by the Improved Order of Red Men. There are some obvious similarities between the "adoption" rite of the Improved Order of Red Men and the initiation of a sacred Pueblo clown. In both rites there is secrecy, a substantial time commitment, a pronounced boundary between insiders and outsiders, and the transmission of lore from elders. But superficial similarities are misleading, so it is imperative to notice the contrasts between the two initiations. The rites of the Red Men are new, contrived, self-conscious, and in certain respects plagiarized; those of the Pueblo are traditional and have evolved over a much longer period of time. Those of the Red Men are comical by virtue of their seriousness; those of the Pueblo are sacred by virtue of the seriousness with which they take humor.

Even though I have no desire to romanticize Pueblos rites, I have no hesitation in criticizing the rites of the Improved Order and admiring the Pueblo ones. The initiation of Pueblo clowns is situated differently in its culture. The history is different as well. Pueblo clowning is not dependent for its dominant symbols on the subjugation of another people. In fact, economic subjugation threatens the ritual tradition of clowning, because initiates like Linky, especially if they work off the reservation, are in perpetual danger of losing their jobs. Initiates into the adoption degree were well-to-do, middle-class entrepreneurs. Initiates who become Pueblo clowns are, according to Ortiz, typically gentle and yielding; they are without hard-and-fast male egos, people with little investment in competition or aggression, boys who are willing to work at tasks usually performed by girls.[145] The difference between a climactic moment fraught with ritual aggrandizement (the Red Men) and one that culminates in ceremonial humiliation (the Pueblos) is considerable. It is true that Pueblo clowns sometimes evoke terror as well as humor. They sometimes break windows, snatch things, demand attention, gobble food, pinch rear ends, indulge in profanity, and provoke general pandemonium. However, their lives are seriously circumscribed outside the context of ceremony. Their initiations do not constitute authorization to exploit relationships for the sake of business deals.

In the film *Dance Me Outside* there is a hilarious scene in which four Indian boys put a white man through a parodied initiation rite. They con him into running around naked while they keep their clothes on. They dress him up in a stereotypical Plains bonnet without letting him see the American Airlines logo on it. They grant him a power animal and a new name, not ever revealing that their ritual tease is a ploy to distract him while his wife is being impregnated by a childhood sweetheart, an Indian fresh out of jail. By the end of the late-night ordeal, one of the boys develops a bit of affection for the poor guy. After all, although he has made a fool of himself, he threw himself wholeheartedly into the ceremony.

For different reasons both natives and nonnatives are uncomfortable with this scene, but it does point to something important. Even though the film is largely about Indians and is a critique of nonnative desires to imitate native initiations, the author of the story on which it is based is a white man, W. P. Kinsella. Nonnatives deceive themselves unless they are brutally honest, willing to subject initiatory desires to cross-cultural critique and able to laugh at themselves.

Reinventing Initiation Rites

Rites, especially initiations, present opportunities for exploitation as well as for maturation. As Barbara Myerhoff put it, "In ritual, we incorporate the gods into our bodies, return to Paradise, and with high righteousness destroy our fellows."[146] What she says is even more true of initiation rites than of other rites of passage. The project of reinventing initiation thrusts us into a snake's nest of ethical issues, making it the most difficult of the passages to responsibly reinvent. Currently, Westerners are "borrowing" far more initiations than funerals, weddings, or birth rites, but do we have the right to "borrow"? In my view, only with explicit consent. Currently, the envied ritual goods are vision quests and sweat lodges. In 1980 the Traditional Elders Circle of the Northern Cheyenne issued a declaration against carrying and using sacred objects such as pipes. Addressed to "people who use spiritual ceremonies with non-Indian people for profit," it declared quasi-Indian ceremonies "questionable, meaningless, and hurtful."

In 1984 the Southwest chapter of the American Indian Movement held a leadership conference that passed a resolution labeling the expropriation of Indian ceremonies (for instance, the use of sweat lodges, vision quests, and sacred pipes) a "direct attack and theft." It also condemned certain named individuals (such as Brooke Medicine Eagle, Wallace Black Elk, and Sun Bear and his "tribe") and criticized specific organizations such as Vision Quest, Inc. The declaration threatened to "take care of" those abusing sacred ceremonies.[147]

Another document, even more widely circulated, criticizes those who would lay hands on native rites. The Declaration of War Against Exploiters of Lakota Spirituality complains, "Whereas for too long we have suffered the unspeakable indignity of having our most precious Lakota ceremonies and spiritual practices desecrated, mocked and abused by non-Indian 'wannabes,' hucksters, cultists, commercial profiteers and self-styled 'New Age shamans' and their followers; and whereas with horror and outrage we see this disgraceful expropriation of our sacred Lakota traditions has reached epidemic proportions in urban areas throughout the country . . . , we hereby and henceforth declare war against all persons who persist in exploiting, abusing and misrepresenting the sacred traditions and spiritual practices of our Lakota, Dakota and Nakota people."[148]

After at least a decade and a half of trenchant criticism, it is disheartening to see how much initiatory exploitation continues.[149]

Another ethical issue that hangs like a dark cloud over initiations, both traditional and invented, is that of power and abuse. Some initiations resemble cults. Or more accurately, many cults depend on initiatory processes. We must ask ourselves: Do adults have the right to inflict pain on children and adolescents? To engage in deception or intimidation? To put initiates' lives at risk? In the West there are moral and legal codes that militate against such practices, so we cannot afford to idealize or romanticize initiation in the process of reinventing it.

I am wary of reinvented initiations in a way that I am not of new birth, marriage, or death rites. There is little reason to fear initiations such as the bat mitzvah that Miriam Stanton underwent or the *quinceañera* that Norma Cantú described. Celebrations like these are modest, proffering no claim that they are "making" women. Instead, they celebrate transitions. They do not depend on the dismantling of an identity and the reconstruction of a new one. They are not shrouded in secrecy or dependent upon ordeals, risks, and demonstrations—all of which are more typical of boys' than girls' initiations.

I resist pseudo-Indian initiations and heavy-handed rites that require unquestioning surrender to ritual leaders, but I have little confidence that mainstream schools, families, or religious institutions alone can perform the task of initiating. School teachers may be well qualified to socialize but not to initiate. Unlike tribal elders, parents in nuclear families loom too large in their children's lives to be effective mentors. And religious institutions too often resemble Vivian Hansen's church in its stubborn refusal to incorporate bodily realities into rites for adolescents.

I reject the sexism and cultural imperialism of the heroic model propounded by Joseph Campbell and find the Jungian tendency toward purely interiorized initiations precious and disembodied. Ethnocentric images in heroic films like *Emerald Forest* or books like *Hero with a Thousand Faces* do enormous damage.

I am, however, impressed by the initiatory sophistication of Hopis and Pueblos. Perhaps I could even imagine ways of incorporating ceremonial clowning and ritual disenchantment into mainstream institutions. Still, I refuse to import rites and cannot imagine who would tolerate someone whipping children or dumping feces on them to instruct them in humility.

All these doubts and caveats threaten to reduce one to a state of paralysis. But each time I decide it is safer to do nothing, I hear the Ozzie Freedmans of this word heading for the roof top and threatening to jump. I glimpse the young men of Brewster Street stalking yet another woman.

African American Rites of Passage

African-centered rites of passage are among the most serious, sustained, and socially grounded of North American experiments with initiation. Since the mid-1980s a number of African American organizations have adopted an explicit rites-of-passage program. One of the best known is the National Rites of Passage Institute (NROPI) in Cleveland, Ohio.[150] Paul Hill, Jr., founder of the NROPI, is a social worker and president of the East End Neighborhood House. He espouses an African-centered worldview, which draws on the cosmologies and ritual practices of a number of African peoples, including the Akan of Ghana and the Yoruba of Dahomey.[151] Since Hill is quite aware that he and his associates are not literally replicating what happens, or has happened, in Africa, he speaks of their recovery of African tradition as taking "a step forward into the past."[152]

African-centeredness does not imply slavishly looking to Africa for models but rather cultivating a sensibility that shares certain features typical of African worldviews: perceiving the universe as alive; emphasizing the unity of all things; attributing spirit, therefore value, to nature; honoring elders; and relating ritually to both nature and society.[153]

Hill believes that African-centered rites of passage are essential for the survival of African Americans as a people. Rites are a way of resisting the lure of the American Dream. Whereas the American Dream separates individuals from their families, communities, and, ultimately, the world, an African-centered paradigm rooted in rites of passage connects individuals with communal and cosmic resources.

Hill aspires to reconnect the life cycle with the seasonal cycle, the remaking of human beings with the regeneration of time. A crucial link between the two kinds of ritual are the *Nguzo Saba,* the seven principles celebrated during Kwanza, the African American cultural celebration that began in 1966 and now occurs every December. These moral principles include: unity, self-determination, collective work and responsibility, cooperative economics, purpose, creativity, and faith. The institute recently added an eighth principle, respect. In effect, these are the virtues instilled by the educational-ritualistic process.

The National Rites of Passage Institute has directly initiated five hundred youth. Another ten thousand have been initiated by adults trained by the institute. In the five years between 1993 and 1998 the institute provided long-term training for 746 adults and short-term training for another 178. Recently, the institute was invited to start rites-of-passage programs for selected public schools in both Cleveland and Youngstown as well as in the Grafton Medium Security Facility of the Ohio prison system. Currently, the institute coordinates a process called Passages for children between six and eleven and one named Journey for twelve- to eighteen-year-olds. The boys are called Simba Wachanga (young lions); the girls are called Malaika (angels). Rites-of-passage programs may be either freestanding or sponsored by organizations such as neighborhood associations, schools, and religious institutions.[154]

The program for boys takes from two to four hours a week and lasts from one to three years; it is both educational and ritualistic. Key elements include separation from routines; being taught by elders and expressing respect for them; experience with nature; peer cooperation; instruction (in sexual, financial, hygienic, spiritual, and political matters); self-defense; community service; tests of courage and character; extensive use of symbols, special names, special language, and special dress; and a formal culmination rite that facilitates a transition into young adulthood.

The ceremony itself is preceded by candle lighting and a procession in colorful African costume. Candidates are addressed by one or more parent, sometimes by a peer as well. Then an elder charges the candidate formally, "Therefore, I _____ , charge you _____ before God, your parents, friends and even our illustrious departed forebears, to continue in the highest and best traditions already set before you. Never be content with mediocrity or the achievements of the distant or recent past. Always maintain the pioneer spirit in whatever vocation you choose for yourself. Finally, respect yourself; hold your friendships in sacred trust; never abandon your family, for it is still the basis of true community; never neglect your spiritual life."[155]

Then, as drums roll, the candidate drinks these elements from the kikombe cup: salt, representing wisdom; vinegar, representing difficulties; honey, representing every good thing in life. As candidates are anointed with olive oil, they are given a meaningful ancestral name. Finally, a prayer of passage asks God for the conferral of spiritual energy and the wisdom to know right from wrong.

Paul Hill is impassioned in his declaration that "the African American male's lifelines to masculinity are systematically severed." The result is that "nobody ever officially tells him when he has attained manhood and there is generally too little to signify or certify it concretely. There is no ceremony or ritual . . . to usher the African American male into proper manhood."[156]

Hill says that adults are not born but made.[157] They do not develop automatically and naturally but are constructed ritually, actively, and culturally. He is convinced that identity, community, history, spirituality, and the environment are all at stake in the decision to initiate, or not to initiate, adolescents into adulthood.

Hill compares traditional African initiation rites with what he takes to be its Western equivalent: institutionalized education. For African Americans, Western education is miseducation, education away from themselves and toward the production of "Afro-Saxons." His comparison takes the form of a set of polarized contrasts: "The old rites were religious; the new rites are usually secular. The old rites ran by sun and seasonal time (outdoor and active); the new rites operate by clock and calendar (usually sedentary and pursued behind closed doors). The old rites centered on concrete experiences; the new rites rely heavily on words and abstractions. The old rites provided physical risks and danger; the new rites substitute organized sports, which combine moderate challenge and minimal risk. The old rites were dramatic, intense, forceful, and fast; the new rites are slow, strung out, and often vague about ultimate destination. The old rites engendered awe; the new rites commonly produce detachment and boredom. The old rites typically gave a sense of vital participation in the historical unfolding of the culture as a whole; the new rites are often only creating holding areas where youths are held in isolation from the larger cultural reality rather than allowed to experience it. The old rites resulted in an immediate and unmistakable status change; the new rites provide no such direct deliverance into adult roles and status. The old rites were over at a determined place and at a determined time, witnessed by the community as a whole; the new rites can go on indefinitely and be severed (dropping out and being pushed out), perhaps never resulting in general community recognition. The old rites were in the hands of caring and concerned adults who had the interests of the youths at heart. The new rites are frequently monitored by uncaring employees whose purpose for being involved is related to their own financial condition (a shift in locus of control from the family to the state)."[158]

Hill not only draws on the myth and ritual of Africa, but he is also indebted to certain non-African, scholarly constructs, notably van Gennep's threefold pattern and Turner's idea of liminality. Hill says of van Gennep that he "was able to ascertain the existence of numerous principles, beliefs and practices which constituted the African paradigm for living."[159]

One could take exception with some of Hill's generalizations. For instance, it seems obvious to me that van Gennep's scheme and theory are European, perhaps even Christian, at their root, and that the tripartite scheme persists because it is convenient, not because it is African centered or even correct. In addition, there are African traditions that do not initiate in so ideal a fashion as the ones Hill contrasts with Western education. And there are Western schools and teachers who both care and are capable of incubating ritual activity. But these are minor quibbles. Van Gennep's scheme, regardless of its origins, can be useful for organizing rites, and it is certainly true that the mainstream educational establishment generally eschews initiatory responsibilities.

NROPI is now facing the real difficulties of initiation—those generated not by failure or fantasy but by success. One problem created by any initiation is that of unintentionally creating outsiders. Another difficulty is that of unwittingly authorizing exploitative uses of the training. In a recent issue of *The Drum,* the institute's newsletter, Jefferson Jones, an institute initiate, cautions his compatriots, "Participating in a Rites of Passage does not make us any better than those who have: Not gone through it, Went through it after us, or Have gone through it with another program. Rites is not a degree program that certifies us as 'African,' 'African-centered,' or 'africentric.' Rites of Passage is a 101 Course. It gives us a reminder, a taste of what it is to be a part of a real community. And, because it does not give us any cultural authority, we must catch those times when our thoughts or actions reflect a, 'I went through Rites of Passage so I know what is right' attitude."[160]

These days many people are inventing rites, but not many are successfully sustaining intergenerational groups, and few are engaging in ongoing evaluation and criticism of their own practices. It is a sign of initiatory health that NROPI does so. Leaders and trainees are not only risking the construction of alternative rites, but they are also committed to their long-term refinement and development. In addition, initiates are required to contribute their services to a community, so their initiation is not merely about personal enrichment. The institute's rites are rooted in real communities. They do not merely float atop the high tide of armchair fantasy, indulge in weekend community, or cash in on the workshop circuit. The National Rites of Passage Institute demonstrates that reinvented rites of passage can, in fact, be effective in North America.

CHAPTER 3

Divining Mates,
Making Kin

n the absence of nationwide rites of initiation, weddings in North America, as in Europe, are *the* rites of passage. Weddings not only make kin and mark the beginning of a new family, they also indirectly serve an initiatory function. A wedding is "the most important day of your life," the manuals declare, flying defiantly in the face of divorce statistics. Through birth we pass unable to remember our emergence into daylight. And upon stumbling into the darkness of death, there may be no self to recollect the ceremonial occasion. But in marrying, we are active agents capable of recollecting and even designing the occasion. If we are typical, we do not ritually mark the births of our children, and we turn over the funerals of our elders to professionals, but when we marry, we anticipate the event, help plan it, and remember it afterward with the help of photographs and videotapes.

When Hollywood movies want to reassure audiences with a happy ending, they marshal a victory or conjure a wedding. If not a victory in a literal battle, then in a metaphoric battle. If not an actual wedding, then the promise of one: "boy gets girl," "the woman gets her man." Weddings are saddled with expectations that in other parts of the world are loaded onto the backs of initiation rites: becoming a real woman, becoming a real man, becoming a responsible adult. Despite their graduations, students in my classes believe they lack explicit initiation, so for them a wedding is often experienced as their first ceremonially marked transition across a major life-cycle threshold. Perhaps it will be the *only* rite of passage in their lifetime that they can look forward to, help design, and fully remember.

The imaginative weight of nuptial fantasy is enormous. Some of us flee it, but most do not or cannot. Although we do not all marry, we are all affected by the expectation that we should. Marrying, on time, heterosexually, in a white gown or tux is "normal," regardless of whether most people actually marry in this way.

A wedding is the single ritual performance upon which we in the

West spend the largest amounts of time, energy, and money. The imaginative, intellectual, and social resources invested in weddings are matched by no other rite of passage. Even though death is inevitable and marriage is optional, the wealth of the wedding industry far exceeds that of the death industry. We complain about the high cost of dying, but between 1990 and 1995 Americans spent an average of 3,742 dollars per funeral. Compared to the high cost of marrying in dreamed-of matrimonial style, this is a small amount. The average cost of a wedding in the same period was between 19,000 and 22,750 dollars.[161] Despite the difference in cost, wedding planners do not suffer the widespread stigmatization that funeral directors do.

Since we die only once but can marry several times, there is perhaps a greater risk of matrimonial exploitation than of funerary gouging. We begrudge expenditures on funerals in a way we do not resent money spent on weddings. It seems that money spent on a funeral either goes up in smoke or is dumped into a dark hole, but a wedding is, by convention, "seen and loved by all." A wedding is an event long anticipated and then celebrated with considerable abandon.

The 1960s were supposed to have changed the ways women and men relate to one another. But despite the images of free love, laid-back weddings, and egalitarian relations between males and females, the most marked shift upward in wedding expenditure was in the 1960s. In 1949 to 1950 the average family spent 9 percent of its yearly income on weddings. Between 1990 and 1995 it was spending 48 to 58 percent of a year's income.[162]

Although common-law marriages, like civil wedding ceremonies, are now acceptable, three-fourths of American weddings are still "religious," that is, held in churches, synagogues, or temples and presided over by clergy.[163] The traditional wedding rite still wields enormous power despite the presumed secularism of Western society. It would be tempting to conclude that we are returning to traditional weddings, if it were not so obvious that much of the tradition to which we are "returning" is recent and invented. For instance, the diamond engagement ring, now a traditional, if not required, item in today's wedding scenario, is a recent innovation.

"A diamond is forever." N. W. Ayer, who coined the maxim, fabricated a "history" that laid hold of the American imagination with the force of myth. He made diamond engagement rings appear to have deep historical roots. He did so in an imaginatively compelling advertising campaign to sell diamonds for De Beers, the world's largest diamond cartel.[164] The traditional wedding is as much the product of marketing as it is of religion.

Selling and consuming are inseparable from North American ways of courting and marrying, even though in our wedding fantasies we stash the commercial dimensions of marrying backstage. In North America the relation between advertising and ritual is integral, not accidental. The two cultural activities are so entangled that some consider advertising itself a secular ritual.[165] Wedding rites influence advertising, and advertising profoundly influences weddings. Together, marrying and commerce not only shape the ways women and men relate to one another, they also help define the nature of the American family. A new family experiences itself as real to the extent that it can afford to enact the ceremonies that advertising has taught us to fantasize.

Ritual traffics in images and is forced to compete with commercial and media-spawned images. There is a teacher in Saskatchewan who leads first-graders in a unit on weddings. Already the children, most of them never having been to a wedding, know exactly what you need: cake, people, a flower girl, a photographer, rings, a wedding dress, and, of course, a janitor to clean up the mess. . . . [166]

Images *for* weddings (such as one finds in brides' magazines) exert as much influence as images *from* weddings (photographs, for example). The wedding manuals of religious denominations, like the imaginations of children, have no choice but to compete with commercial wedding imagery. In the experience of participants, whether adults or children, images from both sources bleed together. So it is necessary to understand the process that connects ritual to both the arts and the advertising industry.

Because images bleed and meld, the actual meaning of a rite is not identical with the idealized rhetoric of wedding-planning books or the ecclesiastical rhetoric of theological documents. Real meaning is forged in the heat generated by the inconsistent, even contradictory, messages that people receive about how to birth, age, marry, and die. Because religious symbols cannot be kept pure of commercial and cinematic meanings, it is important to consider the relation of the spiritual and artistic to the commercial and political. The tensions in this interface are a persistent feature of contemporary life in the urbanized West, and they are not easy to negotiate.

Before its performance, one's wedding day is the object of sustained fantasy. Wedding fantasy, fed on the fat of media images and advertising, begins when we are young, especially if we are girls (as even a cur-

sory survey of Barbie's wardrobe makes obvious). Feminism notwithstanding, marriage is still approached with great anticipation and
touted as the ceremonial apex of female life. Birth, too, is considered
important in defining womanhood, but birth elicits meager, not lavish,
ceremony.

Money is a sacred symbol in Western nations. A revered object, its
use signals ultimate values, and its veneration crosscuts all divisions of
gender, ethnicity, religion, and class. Whereas in the nineteenth century,
money was deemed a crass, inappropriate gift for a newly married
couple, it has become one of the preferred wedding gifts.[167] It may be
that flooding weddings with money and making them occasions for
conspicuous consumption is an act of *de*sacralization, but it is just as
cogent to interpret such heavy investment as our way of sacralizing activities we deem important, since money is an icon.

Why the heavy ritual and financial investment in weddings? There
are many possible reasons. One is simply that advertising has been effective in selling the public on the need for its goods and services. Another reason for the ceremonial elaboration is a feeling, only partly conscious, that the greater the work that needs doing, the more the
ceremonial outlay needed to accomplish the task. A prospective bride
admitted her anxieties and expressed her hopes this way: "Divorce
scares me very much, and I guess I am secretly hoping that if the ceremony is good enough and strong enough and wonderful enough, it will
mean that 'magically' we will never have to get a divorce."[168] Unfortunately, there seems to be no correlation between the degree of a wedding's opulence and the rate of divorce.[169]

A "white" wedding, the model assumed in brides' magazines, is supposedly all-American. Its icon, the bride in her long white gown, is so
central that discovering the "right" gown is sometimes experienced as
an hierophany, a revelation of the sacred.[170] But even if the white wedding's exported American form is imitated the world over, the origins of
this ceremonial tradition are royal and British, not popular and American.

In 1840 Queen Victoria married her cousin Prince Albert.[171] Although she was not the first to wear a white satin dress, her fashions
and the structure of her ceremony were widely appropriated, not just in
the United Kingdom but throughout North America. Queen Victoria's
wedding to Prince Albert provided the model for what was to become
proper in etiquette books. By the 1870s the remaining major elements
of white weddings had emerged, and by the 1890s the model had be-

come the single, standard one. The canonical list of elements varied slightly from etiquette book to etiquette book, but among the prominent requirements were a white gown and veil, processing down a middle aisle, a bride given away by her father, a ceremony held in a church and presided over by clergy, a set of bridesmaids, a best man, a multi-tiered white cake, a tossed bridal bouquet, and a private honeymoon. The white-wedding tradition, no older than the mid nineteenth century, has not changed much structurally, although it continues, like a great downhill-rolling snowball, to accumulate other elements such as the catered sit-down meal, a live band, a stretch limousine, and so on.

Wedding Preparation, Wedding Aftermath

When speaking precisely, we distinguish a wedding (the rite) from a marriage (the legal and spiritual state engendered by it). A wedding may last hours, or sometimes only a few minutes. But a marriage, at least among the persevering, endures for decades. You can wed in a moment, but marrying, for better or worse, takes years.

Although we are able to differentiate a wedding from a marriage, we also collapse the distinction. "Oh, I got married last week," someone says to a friend. "Will you marry us?" a prospective groom asks the priest. Would that a priest had such magical abilities! Perhaps we can be forgiven the confusion, since, after all, ancient Greeks, those near-mythical ancestors of European culture, used the term *gamos* to mean not only wedding and marriage but also the sexual act.[172]

Newspaper announcements regularly reduce weddings to what are considered its essentials. By using the phrase "saying (or exchanging) vows" as a synonym for "wedding," they shrink it to verbal promises. The practice is echoed by cinematic clichés that reduce weddings to the repetition of vows followed by the pronouncement that a couple is now husband and wife.

When I ask young people of marrying age what they consider the heart of a wedding, they too point to the vows or, occasionally, the reception. The choice depends on whether they think I am inquiring about the weighty ceremonial part of the occasion or its social heart.

Wedding rites comprise not only the intense, public moments of concentrated performance, they also reach out into the great pool of social space. Like all rites of passage, they have two tendencies, centripetal and centrifugal. On the one hand, they generate a whirlpool that pulls everything and everyone toward a tiny center with barely visible dimensions. In a moment with no more duration than the blinking of an eye, we say "I do" and presto, it is done. Uttered, the words perform the deed; they do not merely refer to it. Before this moment one was single, after it, coupled.

On the other hand, effective rites of passage exert centrifugal force; they ripple outward toward the dim past, perhaps brushing the sleeve of an ancestor or touching the countenance of some benevolent god. They also eddy toward the future, binding it with a Hercules knot of symbols.

Both the preparation and aftermath of a wedding are ritualized, patterned like filings dancing around a magnet, pulled into orbit by the force of ceremony and celebration. If we consider ritual only the momentary and concentrated action in a set-aside place, we overlook the more diffuse wake of its ritualization.

Ask yourself what the cost of a wedding is. Before you can calculate it, you have to decide whether the honeymoon is part of the wedding. Then, as you set to adding up the figures, you bump into other questions: Are buying furniture and moving in together part of the cost of a wedding? Or only of the marriage? Are the engagement ring and rehearsal dinner wedding expenses? What about the cost of deodorant or hotel bills for distant relatives? Then there's the money spent on dating. Is that a wedding cost?

The sheer social and economic breadth of a wedding, as illustrated by the exercise of trying to calculate its cost, is enormous. However marketing strategists may calculate the costs of weddings, it is important, ritually considered, not to sever wedding rites too cleanly from their ritualized "before" and "after." If we do, we fundamentally misconstrue their meanings and consequences.

Before a wedding, dating, though not a rite, is laden with do's and don'ts. Unwritten, the rules are nevertheless binding. Not ceremonially stylized in the same way as nineteenth-century courtship (when a boy "called upon" a girl or requested her "hand" in marriage from her father), dating remains fraught with considerations of form and style, the substance of ritual. How should a guy . . . ? What should a girl say when . . . ? Hormones and social expectations conspire to drive adolescent behavior in remarkably ritual-like ways.

Even after a wedding, there are ritualistic ripples like honeymoons and wedding anniversaries. The purpose of honeymoons is supposed to be that of affording relaxed time for sexual exploration. But shipping a man and woman off to some exotic place sequestered from the prying gaze of relatives wraps a couple in a silken cocoon of isolation. The original purpose of travel together after a wedding was to visit distant relatives, deepening connections with friends and community. But in either its Victorian or contemporary guise, a honeymoon unfolds on the basis of a choreography, a set of expected moves. Not as formal as the wedding march down the aisle, the scenario nevertheless consists of expected, prescribed steps.

Some etiquette books even prescribe proper honeymoon behavior, but even when they do not, or when couples reject the prescribed ways of these books, there are instructive myths that prospective brides and grooms glean from peers and seniors. Brides and grooms learn how to behave on a honeymoon, how to perform wedding-night sex as if it were spontaneous rather than rehearsed. Even in a day when virginity is no longer a safe presumption, one cannot escape the social expectation that a newly married man and woman are supposed to get away, experiment, and enjoy each other's company.

As the expectation to perform in accordance with custom increases, so does ritualization. The wedding process, then, is not a mere moment, the exchange of vows, or even the entire wedding ceremony. On the contrary, the nuptial process reaches all the way back to childhood doll play and forward to other rites, the fiftieth wedding anniversary or the legal ceremony of divorce. Rites of passage typically reach out and overlap with other rites of passage.

To recognize that weddings are processes is not to deny that they are events too. They are focused, performative events. Although some of us try to minimize the extent to which we are caught up in performative obligations, we do not entirely escape them in weddings. In the act of wedding, a couple is watched—perhaps with sadness, perhaps with envy—but always they are on display. Everybody is on stage. The potential for embarrassment is great. Fearing exposure, we typically rehearse our weddings. If we did not, we would likely be coached on the spot, as happens in contemporary Japanese weddings.

Wedding performance is the tiny tip of a hulking iceberg. Beneath the performance floats the social drama, the desire-driven conflicts and longings of human beings busy wending their way through the maze of the life course. The poignancy of weddings arises from the tension between what is displayed on the polished, rehearsed surface and what is riding just below it.

In the film *Unveiled*, we follow three mother-daughter pairs preparing for their weddings.[173] In the next-to-last scene of this documentary, Sabrina and Shari, mother and daughter, are writing thank-you cards. The mother's manipulation and the daughter's icy alienation are palpable. The mother says she prefers her son's warm emotionality to her daughter's coolness, her "blond wasp" behavior. At the same time, the mother, a therapist, declares in what is unmistakably her professional therapist's voice, "I accept you totally." The daughter coldly ignores her mother's outpouring of emotion and instead lays down the law: Mom is not to call her every other day after the wedding. The emotional shards and social debris of the occasion are palpable.

In the final scene, Shari, the bride, makes a brief reception speech thanking her mother, Sabrina. After the daughter presents her mother with a bouquet, the camera follows Sabrina to her table, letting us see her hands trembling as she weeps.

If we had been guests, we might have thought, "Oh, how sweet." If we had been distant acquaintances of the mother or daughter, we might have considered Shari's presentation a generous act of public reconciliation. But we, the film's viewers, have been "omniscient" viewers. We've been privy to the backstage area. We know how thoroughly mother and daughter antagonized each other during the wedding preparations. So if we are moved by the gesture, we are also forced to be suspicious of it. For us, the drama of the gift-giving ceremony is not contained *within* the formal gift-giving act itself. Rather, it transpires *between* the gift-giving ceremony and ordinary, backstage life. The tension between the public face presented in the reception performance and the more private faces displayed while writing thank-you notes gives the film energy and the rite meaning.[174]

The Purity of an Angel, the Sweat of a Human

The tug-of-war between center-stage performance and backstage drama is pronounced in the swirl that surrounds brides. As Shaun Poisson-Fast makes vivid and tangible, a bride, as a sacred icon, evokes ambivalence:

I am always nervous when I talk to the bride. I usually only talk to her during the reception. A quick hug and congratulations in the greeting line is the extent of my communication with her at the ceremony. Even at the reception, I avoid lengthy communication with her. I do, however, attempt to talk to her at least once, mainly out of obligation. By the time I get the courage to approach her, it is well into the evening and she is a different bride from the one who marched down the aisle. She is usually hot and sweaty. She is a contradiction of images. She is decorated in her heavenly white gown, yet she is drenched in earthly perspiration. She exudes the purity of an angel, yet glistens in the sweat of human activity: dancing, eating, drinking, and moving banquet tables. I hug her, hoping that my hands touch clean lace or satin, and not the wet skin of her back, the exposed skin of the bride that both attracts and repels me.

There are many reasons for my nervousness around brides. One is that I am afraid I am taking time away from important meetings that could be taking place between the bride and other people. A queen cannot spend much time with any one of her subjects. She must be shared equally with everyone. She should sit in a carriage and wave to the masses in a non-discriminating manner. Personal audiences with her should be brief and anonymous.

My nervousness around brides also has something to do with sexual guilt and anxiety. Brides are beautiful (especially before they undermine their perfect image by sweating). Perhaps it is the white dress with its fine fabrics and provocative lace. Perhaps it is the careful attention which is given to the bride's hair and skin. In any case, my physical attraction to her carries enormous guilt. At my sister's wedding, the guilt came from the taboo of incest. How dare I see my sister as sexy, especially at her wedding? At my sister-in-law's wedding, the guilt may have been related to the thought of betraying my brother. How dare I see my brother's new wife in a sexual way, especially on their wedding day? Perhaps the guilt comes from having sexual feelings for the bride, a symbol of virginity. How dare I contaminate the purity and goodness of a virgin bride with my unclean and corrupting sexual thoughts?[175]

Shaun does not need to be told that the archetypes to which he pays homage are also stereotypes waiting to be shattered. He grasps the paradox of sweat on a china-doll bride who is not only virgin, queen, and angel but also human—all too human. However much the humanity of sweat repulses, it also attracts, because it tells the suppressed half of the truth. The other half-truth, the performed one, is that weddings are beautiful and happy occasions. Shaun's feelings are like those most of us feel in the presence of people rendered holy by ritual means. Ambivalence is at the heart of the sacred.

Couples sometimes ask, "Whose wedding is this anyway?" Shaun's account is testimony that weddings do not belong only to brides and grooms but to all who attend, watch, and fantasize. Audiences carry away more than leftover white cake. A wedding, however mindless or however profound, is food for thought, fantasy fodder, a template for action. The drama of a wedding continues long after its performance is finished.

If we had been at the weddings to which Shaun alludes, we would have witnessed him behaving respectably, in accord with the decorum that such occasions demand. The drama is mostly inside his head. Weddings reside in the human imaginations as surely as they do in liturgical books and ritual spaces. But the drama of weddings is also social, between people. When Shaun faced his own wedding, the drama was no longer merely interior but social. With the same dry wit and playful iconoclasm, he wrote:

We are still working on the wedding, which is in July. We seem to agree on most of the important parts. However, other elements have required some degree of compromise. I agreed to have it in a church if she agreed to have traditional koto drums. I agreed to being served by caterers if she agreed that bride and groom would help clean up afterward. I agreed to have clergy present as long as they don't get in God's way. She agreed to have a candle ceremony, as long as everyone gets a candle. She agreed to have a hand-washing ceremony, as long as we could take our time. I agreed to write our own vows, as long as I could use the word "sexy" in mine.

Since many of us consider sex and love the essence of marriage, we would not likely recognize ourselves in a reputable social-scientific definition that regards marriage as "a social contract which (1) provides for the legitimization of any children that might be born to the relationship, (2) establishes new jural relations (affinality), and (3) is publicly proclaimed by a customary act as that particular relationship."[176]

The first two criteria are legal; the third one is ceremonial. We understand that marriage is a legal act and that it creates a "jural" unit, to which the various signed and sealed documents testify. And most know well enough that a "customary act," a rite of some sort, is socially expected. But in the popular imagination these are secondary side effects or expedient means, not primary aims. To put it crassly, the scholarly definition omits everything that most of us consider essential: love, sex, beauty, fidelity. Although many contemporaries no longer hold that a wedding is a prerequisite for sex, most would, I believe, declare that a definition of marriage that omits the primacy of passionate love somehow misses what is essential to their aspirations. In scholarly literature love is *never* what weddings are about. In popular literature weddings are *only* about love.

Contemporary Western weddings are seldom about creating alliances between two families. A wedding is not about establishing lineages from which progeny spring to perpetuate the family name. It is not about exchanging or redistributing community wealth. And it is not about performing one's duty to family, nation, or tradition. Historically and comparatively considered, however, these are dominant motives for marrying, but many North Americans eschew them all as conscious aims.

Wedding intentions are permeated by imagery and myth. Unlike initiation, the fantasizing of which is often a substitute for action, matrimonial fantasy has overt behavioral consequences. A wedding is *the* public performance of romantic love, a virtue that, despite its pagan origins, most people consider quintessentially Western and Christian. Weddings are supposed to be celebrations of romantic love, the natural conclusion to individualized mate choice. First comes the passive moment: One "falls" in love. Then comes the active moment: One chooses this person rather than some other person. Then follows a series of smaller personal choices that constitute the wedding and its aftermath: what kind of wedding to have, whom to put on the guest list, what music to use, where to go on the honeymoon, where to live. Falling in love happens in the sacred space of the heart, but weddings happen in geographical space. The ceremony ratifies the interior, heartfelt, mythic feeling of being swept off your feet.

Psychologists and sociologists may consider the unconscious or social reasons for having a wedding to be the real ones, but lovers know that love is the real reason. Love is the motive enshrined in wedding texts and advocated by prospective brides and grooms. All other reasons—security, friendship, economic solidarity, family making—have their place, but they are secondary in importance. We are horrified at the thought of arranged weddings partly because they appear to contravene the primacy of romantic love.

If a Western wedding is a ceremony for sanctifying romantic love, then the concomitant aesthetic is "beauty." Funerals are not supposed to be beautiful—comforting, maybe. Births are not beautiful—moving, perhaps. But weddings, whether simple or ornate, traditional or alternative, should be emotionally and ceremonially beautiful.

Matrimonial beauty is largely visual. Weddings may be beautiful in all sorts of ways—beautiful to hear, even to smell or taste—but they must be wondrous scenes to behold. A wedding is a performance, and the omnipresence of cameras testifies to this fact. Although weddings typically involve stories, music, food, and much else, they are events to be witnessed and experienced with the eyes, hence the importance of dress, decoration, color, and movement. The photogenic nature of weddings is one of their key values, because what one is supposed to remember in times of trouble is the wedding scene, the ceremonial performance of true love lavishly appreciated by witnesses. This scene, though contrived and rehearsed, must appear natural and spontaneous, not staged.

Besides romantic love and natural beauty, a third wedding virtue is fidelity. Weddings are for forging indissoluble bonds. Whatever the odds, fidelity remains a dominant matrimonial aim. French cultural historian Denis de Rougemont points out the contradiction between two opposed models, that of passionate love and that of marital fidelity. These two impulses have different cultural and historical roots, but North Americans continue aspiring to marriages that include both romantic passion and fidelity as a sacred trust. Religiously affiliated or not, we continue to prefer marriages in churches or other religious edifices. Our preference suggests that weddings sacralize something, and that that something is the indissoluble bond of freely chosen love.

Reaching through the Veil

Dwelling on wedding stereotypes and their attendant virtues can pump up these abstractions until they assume more reality than they should. Big summaries tend to ignore the small but real historical changes and regional variations that characterize actual weddings. However well nuptial aspirations and fantasy illustrate collective values, actual weddings also imply critiques of these values. Deborah Laake tells a story about the Mormon endowment, a prewedding rite that, though American, may sound foreign, but it illustrates what happens when the "magic" of ritual is thrown into question:

For as long as I could remember, the Mesa Temple had been the focus of my most unbridled imaginings, a presence so grand it could not be dwarfed by twenty acres of lush lawn. My parents had traveled all the way from Florida to be married in this temple. . . . But until my wedding day, the interior of the temple itself had been forbidden to me. I understood nothing of its exquisite sacraments. Although the most significant rituals of Mormonism go on within its temples, and although the Book of Mormon itself warns against secrecies in religion, the temple ceremonies are nonetheless top secret outside temple walls, lest their sacred strangeness be ridiculed and defiled by nonbelievers.

. . . I was going to receive my "endowments." (Monty had received his own years before, when he'd left for his mission.) These are sacred ordinances and promises that make a person eligible for the highest heaven, and Mormons partake of them on their own behalf during their first visit to the temple. In the years to come, I would be expected to run through the same ceremony again and again as a proxy for dead ancestors. . . . Taking out my "endowments," in addition to being a very serious business, was a prerequisite to the marriage ceremony. . . .

In a moment, my temple worker glided in, and her face was the one I expected. It was also very kind. "This is your special day, dear," she said. Her gentle hands darted beneath my sheet to bless the parts of my body. There must have been a basin in our cubicle, because when she touched me her fingers were wet. She intoned, "I wash you that you may be clean from the blood and sins of your generation." She touched my head ("that your brain may work clearly"), my ears ("that they may hear the word of the Lord"), my mouth and lips, my arms, my breast and "vitals," my loins ("that you may be fruitful in propagating of a goodly seed"), my legs and feet. Her chanting and her cool fingers were both song and dance, and I was caught up, calmed. When she was finished the first round she began again, replacing the water with oil from a dropper that anointed me head to toe. I was tingling with significance now, the magic of unknown things. Finally the temple worker leaned to my ear to whisper my "new name": Sarah.

. . . We filed quietly into the cavernous Creation Room, where huge and staid murals depicting the creation of the earth loomed above the pews. The paintings were brilliantly colored, and against these frescoes of horizons and meadows and peacefully grazing beasts the chapel full of white-suited worshipers shifted and stirred like a field of daisies. . . .

When instructed to do so, I tied on almost unconsciously my own green apron, a symbol of the fig leaves that had first clothed Adam and Eve. (The ceremonial use of aprons is . . . [a] similarity between the Mormon and Mason rituals.)

. . . The "penalties" to be extracted for revealing the new maneuvers [the rites she is learning] were by now much harder to get through. My stomach flip-flopped as, in unison with my brethren, I acted out cutting out my heart, then a strong slash low on the abdomen to disembowel myself. I didn't understand whether I was promising to submit to death at the hands of someone wielding the switchblade of justice or whether I would be expected to take my own life if I found myself blurting temple secrets. . . .

I was relieved to be distracted at last by the parting of the curtains. Behind the stage, the drapes disappeared and revealed what seemed to be a very long bed sheet suspended from the ceiling. It had deep slits cut into it that were about the same height as an average man—slits that matched the markings of the temple garments except that they were much longer and larger.

I saw Monty then because he was also looking for me and grinning as though something important was coming—perhaps something that would make these rococo temple rites make sense. As I moved with the others toward the bed sheet, we were told that it symbolized the veil that separates this life from the next. A handful of male temple workers had taken their place on the other side of it and thrust their arms through the slits, and one by one the audience members were reaching their own arms through to embrace the workers they couldn't see, who in their positions in the "afterlife" represented God. When my turn came, the routine altered a little: The person who took his place on the other side of the veil was Monty. It was he who would usher me into heaven. It always happened this way for brides, who unlike the men had made their temple covenants not to God but to their own husbands.

This embrace through the veil was by far the most intimate thing Monty and I had ever done together; our furtive groping sessions could not compare with it. In fact, the idea of sharing the secrets that join the dimensions with a man to whom I'd never been able to tell the deepest secrets of my heart made me shy as I approached the veil. Coaxed into it by another one of those kindly female temple workers, who had appeared to stand beside me, I slipped my arms beneath Monty's and then around him. I moved in close so that through the sheet our bodies were touching as though we were dancing.

The temple worker now asked that we touch at the "five points of fellowship": foot to foot, knee to knee, breast to breast, hand to back, and mouth to ear.

And then, when Monty made the Sign of the Nail into my hand and asked me to identify this "token" and its "penalty," I realized disbelievingly that this was a test. The actions that were going to guarantee my entrance at the gates would have nothing to do with love or charity or the other teachings of Christ that I'd been raised to believe God valued. In fact, I hadn't heard a single one of those words spoken today, the most primary day of religious instruction in my entire life.

No, I was going to burst into heaven on the basis of mumbo jumbo. God must never have gotten past that carefree period of mortal development when he'd formed a club with little pals and refused to let them into the tree fort without a password. The mysteries of the world were fraternity rituals. A wild, bewildered giggle was forming in my throat. . . .

I reviewed with him all the "tokens" and "penalties" I'd just learned, and I came to know at last the purpose of my "new name" when Monty asked me to reveal it to him. "Sarah," I said directly into his ear. It was the secret, magic password that would identify me to Monty at death so that he could pull me through to the other side. Without Monty, I learned in that moment, I wasn't going to get into heaven at all. That's how the system worked for women, although I would never know Monty's "new name." Apparently God himself ushered in the men.[177]

Although there is seldom unanimity on any religious belief, historically Mormons have held that God himself went through the endowment rites and that couples married by means of this liturgical act "become as gods," continuing to have children throughout eternity.[178] No one can accuse Mormons of being ritually flat or theologically shy. One has to admire the theological boldness and bodily seriousness of the Mormon endowments rite. Deborah's body is anointed twice over—once with water, then with oil. The scene is tactile, kinesthetic, visual, and auditory. This "sacred strangeness" fires the senses. The outcome is—or is supposed to be—not merely a bride ready for the actual marriage rite but a bride whose ultimate destiny is ceremonially assured. Having returned liturgically to Eden, the place of the primal fall from grace, bride and groom participate in a cosmic drama that sets straight the path to heaven. Deborah will now enter eternity—on her husband's arm, of course. Sealing, celestial marriage, creates a unit that will weather death. A Mormon marriage is not only made *in* heaven, it is made *for* heaven. Husband and wife here are husband and wife there.

Deborah's story is an act of defiance. According to her tradition, she should not have published this account much less criticized the rite, since it is supposed to be secret. The story is not a dispassionate report, much less an official representation of the ceremony by the Church of Jesus Christ of Latter-Day Saints, popularly known as the Mormon Church. In the portrait Deborah paints, only a small portion of which is presented here, she holds center stage. "I'd wondered if I would ever again be so completely the center of attention" she confesses.[179] Because she recounts the occasion with the benefit of hindsight, her story is shot through with hints of its eventual outcome. Deborah is marrying a man she does not love and whom she will ultimately divorce. Not drawn to Monty, she says, but to orgasm, she wishes she were marrying someone whom she, rather than God, had chosen. She says nothing about the implied equation of God with orgasm or the tension between these two ways of accounting for her choice. In effect, she suggests she had little choice.

For some readers this premarital ceremony may seem as bizarre as any performed on a foreign continent or in the ancient past. Its atmosphere is one we more commonly associate with initiation than with marriage. The bride receives a new name, Sarah, and is sworn to secrecy. Violation of that secrecy is threatened with disembowelment and a slit throat. Although Latter-Day Saints may not interpret these threats any more literally than Catholics do drinking blood and eating flesh, the imagery is still stunning for Deborah.

The Mormon endowment rite is not only shrouded with mystery and "magic," it is also, Deborah says, her most important moment of religious instruction. It is a revelation. As in most European American weddings, this is "her day," but this ceremony is neither rehearsed nor familiar. Hollywood weddings have not prepared her. She has not attended friends' prenuptials that resemble these. She has not seen this kind of wedding preparation idealized in brides' magazines. Occasionally, non-Mormon brides are put through a minor round of premarriage counseling by their rabbis or priests, but nothing like these premarital endowment rites.

Mormon brides not only marry, thereby gaining salvation; they also conduct proxy rites on behalf of others. If Deborah remains in the tradition, she will perform rites on behalf of the dead. So this ceremony does not merely anticipate or illustrate marriage, nor does it merely express warm sentiments. It effects—at least in intention and imagination—ripple through this world and into the next. The ceremony brings salvation not only to participants who enact it but to people long departed.

Despite its metaphysical seriousness, the ceremony is "mumbo jumbo" to Deborah; its impact is psychologically, ethically, and religiously questionable. For her, it does not eventuate in an eternal bond or even lead to honeymoon bliss. On her wedding night, no longer protected by the fig leaf of ceremony, Deborah's marriage is consummated by a graceless act of coupling. Her account of the awkward and sad act of first sex is written so as to reflect what she considers the adolescent ritual drama of the endowment ceremony. The sexual disaster of the honeymoon is hitched to a theological travesty: The God implied by the ceremony, Deborah suggests, has the personality of a kid, some self-acclaimed president of a neighborhood club.

Deborah's judgment is harsh; she feels betrayed and abused. Telling the story is an attempt not only at criticism but also at rectification, perhaps even revenge. It matters little to her that most Mormon wives have not violated the ceremonial pledge to secrecy or publicly denounced the rite as adolescent.

Although the Mormon Church has not officially said so, it likely made a difference that these rites were criticized by Laake and others, since the endowment has now been changed. However true it may be that the changes were inspired by divine revelation, such revelation only appeared on the ecclesiastical horizon after critics, especially women, argued with considerable force that the rite was demeaning and anachronistic.

In 1990 the Mormons modified parts of the rite, but, since the rite continues to be officially secret, the church has offered only general confirmation that it revised the ceremony. Previously, it had been regarded as sacred and therefore above the whims of history and the reach of critics. The church has not publicized details about the new ritual script or offered a rationale for making the changes, but the reports indicate that now women no longer vow obedience to their husbands, but rather to God; the gruesome punishments for failing to keep the ceremony secret have been muted; and a dramatic caricature of non-Mormon preachers has been dropped.

Because of the history of the Church of Jesus Christ of Latter-Day Saints, religion scholars have typically regarded the denomination and its marriage practices, especially its early embrace of polygamy, as marginal to mainstream American religion. But more recently, some have argued that the Mormon Church is the quintessentially American denomination. Not only are Mormons, once feared as seditious, now known for their intense patriotism, but the Mormon Church is the largest Christian tradition to have originated on American soil. Other large Christian denominations are European imports.

Critical wedding stories are hard to find, since it is a strong narrative convention to tell them as stories with happy, upbeat endings. In many ways Deborah's account is an inversion of American matrimonial fantasy permeated with hyperbole and caricatured images: a consecrated male and female touching their "points of fellowship," two heavenly bodies grappling through a slit sheet. Nevertheless, the Mormon Church's view is utterly American in its high opinion of marriage and its casting of participants in the roles of bigger-than-life characters.

Despite decades of psychotherapeutic debunking of fairy-tale images and feminist critiques of marital arrangements, they continue to inform wedding fantasy. Even if individual brides consciously and vehemently reject these images, they continue to sell wedding dresses, diamonds, and magazines. In intention, as in myth, American marriages are still "forever." The Mormon rite projects this aspiration to the cosmic level. Mainstream American fantasy does not typically follow marriages into heaven or back to Eden, but it does declare "forever" in the face of its two enemies, divorce and death.

The ritual subordination of wives to husbands, still overt in this version of the Mormon endowment rite, is being muted or erased in many North American ceremonies; the vow of wifely obedience is all but extinct. But the idea that a wedding mystically bonds a husband and wife for eternity is still strong (even though Jesus is reputed to have declared that there is no marriage in heaven). The language of American weddings mutes the contractual dimension of marriage that would construe it as a matter of mutual agreement, emphasizing instead the eternality of true love.

Like a Horse and Carriage?

In all known cultures people marry—a striking fact, since marriage lacks the biological inevitability of the other major passages. Although it *may* be a human instinct to copulate, marrying is not a genetic imperative. Societies do not always consider mating and marriage concomitant acts; the one does not necessarily imply the other. People have children without marrying, and they marry without having children.

People *choose* to marry. If the groom and bride do not choose, then their parents or guardians choose for them. But we do not choose to be born, to age, or to die. No one escapes these processes, but marriage can be avoided. In most of the world, throughout most of human history, brides and grooms have not chosen each other. The best estimate is that in only 18 percent of societies have males chosen their mates; in 13 percent of societies females have chosen theirs.[180] In the rest, someone else has done the choosing. Whereas the parents of young animals apparently do not choose mates for their offspring, most human beings have had their mates chosen for them, usually by parents. So it is not just the wedding rite that is cultural. Marriage, the very aim of weddings, is cultural. So it is remarkable that marriage, a cultural choice, appears in every culture we know despite the fact that not all individuals marry.

American weddings vary enormously in the degree to which they are ritualized. The same is true around the world, sometimes even within a single society or group. Some traditions distinguish the required legal or religious core of a rite from its folkloric elaboration, although it is not always obvious which parts of a wedding are lore and which are legal or religious requirements. Cultural lore is often allowed to shrink, expand, or change according to circumstances.

All that is legally and religiously required to constitute a Sikh wedding in India, for instance, are four clockwise circumambulations by a bride and groom of the sacred text Guru Granth, while the four verses of the wedding hymn "Lavan" are chanted. No sacred space, such as a *gurdwara*, is required; neither are vows or kisses or signed documents. But in actual practice, Sikh weddings are usually elaborated beyond the required acts and adapted to the countries where they are performed.[181]

The only legal requirement for a Japanese wedding is its being recorded at the registry office, but the *san-san-kudo,* rounds of sake sipping, are popularly regarded as the core gesture in the Shinto ceremony, which itself is usually embedded in an elaborate, more complex rite.

Among the widespread actions that societies have used as standalone gestures formally constituting a marriage are:

- moving in together; setting up a household separate from the parents
- making a public procession or passage from one household to another
- feasting; interfamily or community meals
- presenting or exchanging gifts
- verbally expressing consent or agreement
- agreeing in the presence of witnesses, sacred objects, or sacred places
- signing or sealing a legal document, for instance, a license or wedding contract
- engaging in sexual intercourse
- having a baby
- producing a male child

Such actions have been used singly and in combination to constitute weddings. Westerners usually consider a wedding finished once its four conventional phases (engagement, ceremony, reception, honeymoon) are over, but the last two items on the list above illustrate how some groups regard giving birth as a final phase of marriage rather than as the beginning of an entirely new phase.

The task of a wedding is to make a marriage, but defining marriage cross-culturally is difficult. Even in North America, defining marriage as, say, "the ritually performed, socially and legally recognized union of a man and a woman" fails. Women marry each other; so do men. Not all marriages use rites, and, although the legal or moral status of same-sex marriages is currently debated, their social reality cannot be denied.

Some of our forebears used to believe that the couple who fell in love, and for that reason chose to marry, represented a singular achievement of Western culture. The romance- and choice-based wedding suggested that "we" were at the top of an evolutionary ladder. "Our" rites were more highly evolved than "theirs." Conjugality, which is to say, "coupledom," was not merely a fact but a value, implying that the West was more enlightened than the rest of the world. Our supposed superiority consisted of freeing the heterosexual couple from the tyranny of the larger community. All other social and emotional arrangements were inferior.

At the end of the second millennium, however, romantic love, the couple, the nuclear family, and the white wedding are all in question. High divorce rates are plaguing industrialized countries. The West is no longer confident that its way is the only way. If one considers either the sweep of Western history or the breadth of cross-cultural practice, marriages predicated on romantic love, relatively unrestrained mate choice, and the nuclear family are rare and not demonstrably better than other types of marriages.

Until recently, only the elite could aspire to such marriages. The view that love and marriage go together in some obvious way, "like a horse and carriage," is historically anomalous as is romantic longing for one's wedding day and married life. Only in the Western imagination does fantasy end so regularly with a boy-meets-girl scene that culminates in a wedding. More typical is a young couple embedded in a larger, wiser social network that it cannot, and ought not, escape. Throughout history marriage has existed for all sorts of reasons, love being only one of them.

Conjugal love and weddings choreographed to dramatize it are so familiar that they seem natural, but even as late as the seventeenth century in Europe the scenario was not taken for granted. Private romantic love was considered subversive. Only in the late nineteenth century did conjugality—the dream of a heterosexual bond that is exclusive, permanent, personal, and private—become respectable, and even then it was confined largely to educated classes.[182] So our belief that weddings are necessarily personal and private rather than public and political not only ignores the realities of married life but is also cross-culturally deviant and historically inaccurate.

The Most Splendid Couple in All of Japan

Nuptial ingenuity and adaptation are nowhere more evident than in Japan. Before World War II, Japanese weddings were conducted in homes. Among ordinary rural people marriage ceremonies were regionally diverse and fairly informal. Both ceremonies and the place of couple's residence were adapted to the circumstances. A bride might not fully move into her husband's home until a child had been born; meanwhile, she resided in her parental home. The central act performed by a bride and groom was *san-san-kudo,* three ceremonial rounds of sake, three sips in each round. This gesture, a seal of marriage, was originally performed on the basis of medieval samurai codes of etiquette. Without the samurai ethic, it continues to be regarded as the distinctive Japanese matrimonial act.

For the first time in 1900 and partly in response to the inclusion of religious elements in the weddings of European heads of state, the wedding of the Japanese crown prince included a religious phase in a Shinto shrine. This imperial wedding, admired and emulated by ordinary people, became a major source of traditional Japanese marriage rites, much in the same way that the wedding of Queen Victoria and Prince Albert became the model for North American white weddings. Traditional weddings in Japan and North America are not as old as they are popularly believed to be.

The Civil Code of 1948, which was pressed upon the Japanese by Allied occupation forces, disenfranchised the *ie,* the hierarchically organized household. The code declared individual autonomy, guaranteeing a person's right to choose a marriage partner. Senior heads of households could no longer coerce a match against a participant's will. "Love marriages" began to appear alongside arranged marriages, which used the services of matchmakers who set up meetings, either formal or fictively accidental, between a prospective bride and groom.

In contemporary Japan parental approval is still important though not an absolute or legal prerequisite. About a third of Japanese marriages involve arranging. As one's age increases, so do the pressures to use go-betweens. The once-important labels, *ren'ai* ("love marriage") and *miai* ("arranged introduction"), are becoming less meaningful, since Japanese regularly temper love interests with considerations of social appropriateness. Both matchmaking and personal attraction may figure into final decisions. One may have several *miai* before deciding on an appropriate mate, so both consultation and choice determine the outcome.

An oversimplified Western view is that Japanese weddings changed as a result of Westernization, but there were other factors as well such as demographic changes in Japan itself. Urbanization, with its dependence upon small apartments and its creation of nongeographically based communities, rendered the rural home wedding all but impossible. So eventually parlor and hotel weddings seemed not only more practical but also more desirable. Since Shinto shrines charge fees, and a few of them have their own wedding halls, the distinction between commercial and religious weddings has become less than clear-cut.

With growing urbanization individual families rather than communities began to bear the escalating cost of weddings, so *gojokai*, mutual-aid societies, were formed in the late 1940s—at first to help members save money for funeral services. By the 1950s and 1960s, *gojokai* began to offer wedding services as well. Today, the usual wedding sites are neither homes nor temples but wedding parlors, hotels, restaurants, and public halls.

Although they promote saving money for weddings, most Japanese wedding parlors are no longer mutual-aid societies but competitive businesses. Their aim is not that of assisting people who cannot afford a wedding but of profiting on the delivery of a product to those who can. No longer as intimate as the term *parlor* might suggest, "palaces" such as the Kobe Princess Palace and the White Crane Palace are large-scale business operations. In the 1982–83 wedding season, White Crane performed over seven hundred weddings.[183] The Kobe Princess Palace houses not only a Shinto chapel, six banquet halls, and a kitchen, but also waiting rooms, consulting rooms, showcases for food and jewelry, a beauty shop, a photography studio, a honeymoon-planning corner, a boutique for traditional Japanese clothing, and one for

Western and party clothing as well.[184] In effect, Japanese wedding institutions are wedding malls whose sense of the palatial borrows from Disney (one shop, for instance, is called the Cinderella Beauty Parlor). The only facility an envious Westerner might imagine adding would be a well-staffed marriage counseling center.

By the early 1990s, 80 to 85 percent of Japanese weddings were being performed in commercial establishments—30 percent in wedding parlors, 40 percent in hotels, and 10 percent in other commercial facilities.[185] There is no significant alternative wedding movement, and temple weddings do not hold the same nostalgic place in the Japanese psyche as church marriages do for us in the European American West. In 1981 to 1982 the average cost of a Japanese wedding was the equivalent of 8,392 dollars, or if the costs of the honeymoon and furnishing the new household were included, 28,554 dollars.[186]

Whereas it is common in the Western world to descry the commercialization of weddings, Japanese weddings are unabashedly commercial. One of the most striking features of weddings in Japan is the dramatic flair with which traditional and commercial, Asian and Western, elements are integrated or juxtaposed. The Japanese readily appropriate selected Western items into their ceremonies, quickly coming to regard them as traditional.

Japanese weddings, to an even greater degree than American ones, are structured around a series of poses for cameras. Since the primary actors in Japanese weddings are coached on the spot (rather than put through a rehearsal the day before), wedding scenes are not action filled. Rather, they are relatively static tableaus designed to facilitate aesthetic contemplation and photographic access.

Cake cutting, a symbolic act borrowed from the West, uses an inedible cake made of wax or rubber. The cake is for seeing, not eating. The "sword" (actually, a knife), dramatically covered, uncovered, and re-covered by a cloth, is inserted through a precut slit. The entire scene, spiked with dramatic spotlighting, is bathed in dry ice vapor and taped music. The groom's hand leads, the bride's following on top of his. A taped female voice utters stylized bridal sentiments: "You have taught me love's true treasure. / Now, our hands together [are] poised above our wedding cake . . . / Take this hand gently, firmly. / Lead it always, and forever I will follow."[187] Applause and camera flashes greet the gesture. (No one says aloud what the action refers to; no one needs to.) Joint cake cutting is supposed to be "the first act of marital harmony." What takes ten seconds in North America is drawn out for a full minute in Japan.

The tenor of a Japanese parlor wedding is akin to Kabuki theater, in which actors strike and hold momentarily dramatic poses, freezing them in time and space for the audience to enjoy. In Kabuki, certain postures and gestures have as their primary motive showing off the costume—its color, folds, and movement. Similarly, costume is extremely important in Japanese weddings.

In Japanese Bunraku theater near-life-sized puppets are animated by two onstage masked puppeteers. Similarly, in Japanese wedding performances, couples are ushered about and coached by unobtrusive but omnipresent palace employees who ensure that participants do what they are supposed to do and say what they are supposed to say.

In a Japanese palace wedding, ceremonial space is photographic space. A professional video of the ceremony is shot and carefully edited so the family can relive the rite cinematically. The editing further idealizes the memories, since it can disguise, de-emphasize, or even eliminate glitches. Cameras are mounted above Shinto altars so as not to miss the most sacred moments when the couple are ceremonially purified and during which they exchange rings, recite vows, and share nine sips of sake in the presence of Izanagi and Izanami, the Shinto deities responsible for copulating the universe into being.

By North American standards Japanese reception speeches are not only protracted but noticeably stylized and idealized. Although there is occasional humor, the speeches do not aspire to the bawdy joking characteristic of North American weddings. Speeches, replete with ceremonial humility and self-deprecation, avoid references that might embarrass or be received as a slight. The speeches formally introduce, congratulate, and praise couples:

Although it is not my place to do so, I have been called upon to speak, so I would like to say a few words appropriate to this happy occasion. Neither am I accustomed to speaking in such formal circumstances, so I will simply speak in my usual manner. [To the bride and groom:] Mr. Hayashi, Noriko, congratulations on your marriage. I am certain that the parents who have raised you to this day are too happy for words. As the nakōdo [an exemplar, usually a stable, married man] has already explained, it is now over five years since the groom came to work in our company. In that time he has earned the confidence of both his fellow workers and our customers and has become a very responsible and capable worker. We have great hopes for him in the future, so I ask everyone for guidance and support on his behalf. . . . For a couple to truly love each other and build a good home it is best that they have common goals and ideals regarding work and life-styles, and work together to achieve their goals. I believe this is the basis of an ideal marriage. I hope the bride and groom work toward their common goals and build a happy home based on mutual understanding and faith.[188]

Regardless of marital success or failure *after* a wedding, *during* a wedding the bride and groom are exemplars. They embody a community's virtues, illustrating its ethics and incarnating its aspirations. Bride and groom become "the most splendid couple in all Japan" even though other couples are being similarly praised in adjacent banquet halls.

Among the guests at Japanese weddings are not only friends and family but business associates whose connections with the bride and groom must not be overlooked. In Japan one is not regarded as fully adult, therefore not entirely responsible or trustworthy, until married and ensconced in a household. A Japanese wedding not only transforms a man and woman into a husband and wife but also into full adults. The wedding celebrates a couple's participation in a large circle of relationships; it is not about the interior states of lovers but about social interconnectedness. Japanese adulthood consists of recognizing that one's life is not entirely one's own. To argue, as we in the West would be tempted to do, that marriage is the culmination of romantic love, and love a condition of marriage, would be to court moral outrage.[189]

Japanese weddings emphasize the debt that a bride and groom owe to society in general, to parents in particular. These debts are not limited to moral and economic matters but are infinite, beyond being discharged once and for all. The Japanese answer to the question often raised by American couples, "Whose wedding is this anyway?" is that it is the community's and the ancestors', for without them the bride and groom would not be where, or who, they are.

This sense of community is acted out in a candle-lighting ceremony in which a flame is carried from the couple's parents to the couple and then throughout the hall to candles on every table. After entertainment and the serving of food and alcohol, the groom and bride ceremoniously acknowledge their debts to their parents and present them with floral bouquets. This climactic moment often overflows with deep emotion.

The cake cutting, candle service, and flower presentation are elements introduced by commercial wedding parlors in the twentieth century. Parlor owners and staff not only work to increase their market share by multiplying the number of services and products offered, they are also sensitive to what the customers want and to their experience of the rite. As a result, twentieth-century Japanese weddings are more elaborate than Japanese marriage rites in previous centuries. Modernization does not necessarily imply a reduced place for ritual.

Rites of passage are often rife with rhetoric and idealized images aimed at animating the emotions and cultivating community values. Only the most naive of participants could fail to notice the discrepancy between the magic of wedding poses and the hard realities of marriage. It is difficult to overlook—but also to contravene—the blandness of congratulatory wishes and matrimonial advice. Speakers at Japanese weddings, like those at North American receptions, rarely say anything that audience members do not already know. Like the dissonance between lived and eulogized lives, the tension between the ideal and real is integral to most rites of passage.

Many cultures grant rites of passage a kind of performative license similar to that granted commercials. We all know that commercials exaggerate or even lie. They deliberately manipulate the public—albeit with its consent—by forging fraudulent associations: "Drink this brand of beer and live that kind of zest-filled, youthful life." The difference between commercials and nuptial idealization is that the latter, embedded in a rite of passage, is supposed to aim above rather than below the standards of everyday life. The question, of course, is whether the enacted ideals are skin or marrow deep.

The Sacred Fire Was Our Witness

The peculiarities of Western matrimonial aspirations and practices are highlighted by setting them alongside wedding rites based on quite different assumptions. A Hindu wedding is a *samskāra*, a sacrament. Among those of the Brahmin caste it is one of the expected rites undergone by males and the only sacred rite of passage undergone directly by females.[190] For Hindus of both sexes, marriage is a sacred social duty, a dharma.

In Hinduism, the proper, idealized model for a husband-wife relationship is that of deity and consort or deity and devotee. A marriage is supposed to be both hierarchical and mutual, in contrast to the supposedly egalitarian marriage of the West. In a Bengali wedding, for instance, both bride and groom become symbolic deities, Lord Rāmā and his consort, Sitā. An ideal husband is his wife's swami, guru, or deity and she, his devotee.

Although we in North America might think a lover "divine," the notion is metaphoric and a far cry from the Hindu ideal, which holds, "A woman's husband is her first god."[191] A Hindu wife is bound to her husband even after his death—if not in law, at least in religious theory and often in local practice.[192] He is not bound to her in the same way. Not only is a wife expected to act with deference toward her husband, but in the first years of marriage she should also display ceremonial shyness in the presence of his parents, her elder in-laws.

Reality is always more interesting and complex than the myths that are supposed to explain it or the ritual texts that dictate it. Nowhere is this fact more true than with weddings and marriages. No matter how traditional the culture, family structures, residence patterns, employment practices, and wedding rites themselves change. And ritual memories, which continue the work of weddings, themselves fade and change. K. Janardhana Iyengar and his wife, Vijaya, married on May 20, 1973 in Gorur, a small town in the province of Karnataka in south India. He was twenty-six; she was twenty-one. Shortly after their twenty-fifth wedding anniversary celebration in Montreal, Janardhana recalled the wedding:

My father and Vijaya's father knew each other for a long time. Every Indian parent with a daughter would be thinking, especially when a daughter is about ten to fifteen years old, "Who is the best boy to marry my daughter?" The parents begin early to look around for a nice, handsome boy from a good family. I was studious, getting good grades in school, chubby, smiling and hence was sought after by many parents in the community as a good boy for their daughter. One day Vijaya's father said to mine, "Your son, I understand, is a very bright boy. My daughter Vijaya is an equally intelligent girl. If we can get them married in the future, it could be wonderful. Can you please consider this?" When my father was about to leave, Vijaya was called to do prostrations before my father and to obtain his blessings.

Nearly two decades later, I had completed my master's degree in engineering at a reputable school, the Indian Institute of Science, and had started teaching in a college affiliated with Bangalore University. During the summer holidays, I was about to go to my village, which is about one hundred and fifty miles away. My brother-in-law casually remarked, "If your parents tell you to meet a girl, do not simply refuse. You should think of getting married within the next one or two years. Remember, Janardhana, getting a good girl is hard. Your parents are putting a lot of effort into finding a good girl for you."

Ours was a giant, joint family. We were about thirty people. I had been home for nearly a month when all of a sudden one day in the afternoon, my mother said, "A girl is coming to see you tonight. You have to be at home to see her." I was very mad and screamed, "I am not seeing any girl. I won't be home at all." My mother very consolingly replied, "You should not refuse. They have come a long way to see you."

That night, Vijaya, her mother, her brother and one of her uncles came to our house. After taking some soft drinks and snacks, Vijaya's mother started asking my mother, pointing to all my brothers and cousins, "Is that the boy? Is that the boy?" Finally, my mother pointed to me and said, "He, the shortest one in the family, is Janardhana; he is our eldest son." I had never seen Vijaya before. She was dressed in a very simple saree. We looked at each other but didn't smile or talk—not even one word! I just thought, "She's pretty and decent." Vijaya had just finished one term of her Master's in mathematics. She too had come home for the holidays, not expecting to have to see a boy. When her family told her their plan, she started crying and said, "I don't want to see anybody. I am not interested in getting married this early."

We took supper together, the adults talking on all sorts of topics. Vijaya spoke freely with my brothers, sisters, and cousins, but I did not participate in the conversations. I didn't say a word to Vijaya. After supper, my parents asked me, "Do you like the girl?" I felt very embarrassed and said there was nothing to dislike about her. The same question was asked to Vijaya. After a lot of resistance in responding to it, I heard her saying, "Oh, he's okay." And that was it! They declared, "They like each other; let us get them married." They were about to set the marriage date when I interrupted, "Let her complete her Master's degree. If she marries now, she will have to move where I am, and her studies would be disrupted."

Vijaya's uncle had a little problem with this proposal. Usually the marriage follows within two or three months after the agreement. Now the wedding would be two years in the future. The uncle said, "The boy has accepted her now, but what happens if he changes his mind?" But Vijaya's brother interrupted, "They are respected family people; they would never do this to us."

Vijaya's family left our village. I went with them in a bullock-pulled cart to drop them at the bus stop three miles from my village. When Vijaya left, my heart was heavy; I was feeling empty. A sort of affection had, in fact, risen in my heart. I was actually missing her and wanted to see her again as soon as possible.

In addition to teaching in the university, I was also working in a consulting company as a design engineer. We were designing and constructing a bridge near Mysore, where Vijaya was studying. I was really too shy to show that I was anxious to see her, and probably her family would not want me alone visiting her. But when her brother or any other family member was along, they did not mind if I visited Vijaya. I took every opportunity to go to Mysore on the pretext of supervising the bridge construction; I dared to meet Vijaya. She was very shy and too scared to meet me alone. In the first few visits, she even refused to go off campus. But slowly she developed confidence in me. Since both of us were religious people, we went together for prayers in temples. Her parents might not have liked it that we went out before marriage. Until today, we have not revealed these secrets to any of her family members, although everyone, including my twenty-two-year-old daughter, knows about our secret outings. Once, Vijaya came to Bangalore with her brother. He took us to a movie along with my sister and brother-in-law. They allowed us to sit together; it was fun. I liked to hold Vijaya's hand, but she was very shy and would not give her hand. Even after twenty-five years, she is the same shy lady who will not allow me to hold her hand in public. But she is very romantic in private.

After one year and six months—about five months before our marriage— the real preparations for the great day started. Vijaya's brother approached my father wanting to finalize the dowry agreement and other formalities. My father was very modern, although he looked very orthodox and traditional. He was very much against the dowry system. His conviction was that celebrating a marriage is the combined responsibility of both the families, not just the bride's family. Generally, a watch, a gold ring and a three-piece suit would be given to the boy. These were the minimum. But my father said, "Janardhana has a watch. What he would he do with two watches? He has a ring too. So you don't have to give him anything except your blessings and your daughter. If you are so keen, you can buy him a new suit." Thus, I got a two-piece wedding suit. Even today, I appreciate my father's vision and ideology.

I have a daughter soon to be finishing medical school. It is 99% sure that I am the one who will pay for all her wedding expenses. I am willing to do that, since, after all, I have only one daughter. Sometimes she asks me, "What if I meet a Canadian boy—do you have any objection?" I tell her, "If you meet someone, let us know who it is so we can check some things you may not see." I tell her that marriage is family-oriented. If you marry someone from a similar tradition, with interests in similar music and similar food habits, it is easy to have family get-togethers. If he's totally different, it is hard. You should realize that it is not just a boy and a girl who marry; but two families become connected. If you choose just for yourself, then our families won't get connected."

My mother tells me that her marriage was celebrated over seven days. Our marriage was celebrated over three days, Friday afternoon through Sunday evening. For inviting people to the wedding, you don't just send a printed invitation. My father or brother or one of my uncles went personally to every one of the relatives. They took the marriage invitation along with some yellow rice, which symbolizes an auspicious occasion. They gave these things to all the elderly family members, requesting them to bring the whole family to attend the marriage and bless the couple. To some close relatives, cash was also given to cover travel expenses. A similar process of inviting relatives and friends also occurred at Vijaya's house.

Vijaya's village and mine are about forty miles apart. We rented a bus to take all our relatives. From the village, at least one person per family attends a wedding. A number of friends and relatives who live close by in neighboring villages also come to ride in the bus. In a bus that has capacity of fifty people, about a hundred and twenty people traveled. We had to tip the driver and conductor generously.

We started out from our village late in the afternoon and reached Gorur by five in the evening. The bus stopped at the outskirts of Gorur, before the village temple. All the family members and relatives from the bride's side— but not the bride herself—came to receive us. They carried flower garlands, fruits, and coconuts and were accompanied by professional *nagaswarum* (a pipe-type musical instrument similar to a saxophone) players and drummers. They put garlands on all my relatives and friends. Then they put a huge garland on me and placed a coconut in my hands. After they washed the feet of all members of the bridegroom's side, they led us on a procession around the village, then brought us back to the temple. I broke the coconut at the temple, an act which represented the breaking of my ego and symbolized entering the marriage with humble feelings. We were then taken to Vijaya's home and served a hot, delicious snack.

After eating, a ceremony of worshiping the bridegroom started. Here the bridegroom is considered a divine person (Lord Narayana). The mother-in-law comes and performs a few rituals to remove obstacles and to purify me. Still, the girl is not there; I am not supposed to see her. There are three or four hours of rituals for the boy. I perform some rituals to thank my in-laws for choosing me as a husband for their daughter. Throughout the ceremony, the priest chants and tells me what to do.

Honestly, not everyone really understands everything that goes on. People sit and talk while the rituals are going on. Nobody pays much attention to them. Indian weddings performed here in the West have a more spiritual environment. Here people sit quietly, watching the celebration. Though there are not as many rituals as in India, the ones performed here are generally explained so that both the Indian and Western participants understand the ceremony.

At that time, I personally found the ceremony to be boring. I was wishing the ritual would end. The priest wants to do a perfect job, otherwise it is a sin for him. He tells you, "Put the water here. Sprinkle there. Do this; do that." The overall message is that he and others are blessing you and wishing you a happy married life. Even though the specific meanings of all the rituals are not understood by the boy or the girl or the parents, it is a general belief that, if the rituals are properly performed, the boy and girl will be happy and their marriage will be successful. As a young man of twenty-six, I was more interested in holding my wife's hand than in sitting in front of the priest and doing these rituals. But now, I understand their purpose and meaning, so I really enjoy performing them.

Then the worship of the bride starts. She is considered a goddess during this time. Vijaya was dressed very meticulously by her friends, but I was not allowed to sit there and see her.

These rituals finished at midnight, then there was an eight-course meal for about a thousand people. All the men sat first for food served by men who had volunteered. By two-thirty in the night the men had finished eating. Then the feast for the ladies began. It too was served by men. At four o'clock in the morning everybody but Vijaya's parents went to sleep. They had to start making arrangements for a hot breakfast.

On the day of the wedding, early in the morning, my mother-in-law gave me a castor oil bath. I was feeling shy, but they force you, because they want to remove the shyness in you, make you one of their family members, show you that your mother-in-law is just like your own mother. After this massage, I wore traditional dress (a silk-bordered dhoti). Vijaya was also given an oil bath and dressed formally (and still, I had not seen her).

The main part of the ceremony began like a fun drama. I was sent to Vijaya's house to request her parents to accept me as their son-in-law. The scene is very playful. Her father refuses my initial request. I act very disappointed, saying that I will go to Banares (also called Kashi) and take up sanyas [become a monk]. Vijaya's brother intervenes. He brings a pair of footwear and an umbrella as gifts for me and says, "No, no, please don't go away. I will convince my father. He will give my sister to you and she will be your wife." Immediately following this assurance, Vijaya's maternal uncle shows up, carrying Vijaya on his shoulder. She is holding a garland in her hand. My maternal uncle comes and carries me on his shoulder. Then we exchange huge, beautiful garlands. This is the first time during the wedding that the boy and girl are supposed to meet. In very traditional marriages the boy and girl would not have met until this ceremony. Of course, Vijaya and I had seen each other, but I had not seen her since my arrival in her village on Friday evening. She was dressed very nicely, like that [points to a wedding picture of her mounted on poster board for their twenty-fifth anniversary celebration]. She was very pretty. She looked fantastic, like a princess!

After the garlanding ceremony, all other rituals were performed by the two of us together. We sit together in front of the fire, because Agni, the fire god, is the witness of a Hindu marriage. I tie a *mangalya* around her neck. A *mangalya* is a very holy gold piece with religious symbols on it: a wheel, conch shell, and the footprints of Vishnu. Vishnu called the world into being by blowing on the conch, and now he holds the wheel of life in his hand. The moment I tie the *mangalya*, we are considered married. (When a husband dies, the wife is supposed to remove her mangalya, since she no longer has the right to wear it.) As I was tying the mangalya, Vijaya's family members became very emotional. Her parents, especially, got tears. Their daughter, whom they had brought up all these years, was going away from their home to another one, in which she would take on additional responsibilities.

Now there is a fire in the center, and we take the Seven Steps around it. During the first round we promise, "In good times and hard times we will stay together." In the second round we promise, "In everything I will support you, even in difficulty. I won't allow you to suffer. We will do everything to help each other." Agni, the sacred fire, is again the witness. Whenever Vijaya and I have arguments and fights, I always remind her, "We have promised your parents in front of the fire that we will take care of each other."

Before I was married, this [pulls his initiatory sacred threads from under his shirt] had only three threads; afterwards, six—three more to represent my wife. Now, when I do meditation, I hold all six of them in my hand like this. I pray with them, so it is a prayer not only for me but for her as well.

The ceremony finished around three o'clock. Then a big meal was served. Vijaya and I sat together for the meal. The priest chanted and then directed us to feed each other a little bit. Everybody watched, made jokes, and enjoyed this feeding ceremony. This is the only time a husband and wife sit together and eat. After the marriage, in day-to-day living in a traditional family, the wife never sits with her husband and eats. She serves food to her entire family and only then eats.

In the evening, there is a reception. The newly wed couple sit in a decorated swing. Other recently married couples come to sit on the swing. They take turns; every thirty minutes a new couple sits on the swing. We had a very nice music concert. Friends came and gave us gifts and congratulated us. The gifts were first handed to the priest, who chanted blessing hymns and then announced the name of the person who gave the gift. After the reception, there was a buffet, more food. But there was no dancing or alcohol.

Sunday was the day on which the bridegroom's family left Gorur. On this day no formal ceremonies were held, but the priests who had performed the wedding ceremony were honored. A special lunch was given for only the groom and his close family members. About a hundred fifty people attended, and many special dishes were prepared. Eight or ten types of sweets were served. After lunch, there was an exchange of gifts. They were given to all my brothers, sisters, uncles, and aunts. We reciprocated by presenting gifts to Vijaya's family. After this exchange, I unwillingly left Gorur with my parents and friends.

After a week or two, on an astrologically auspicious day, Vijaya and her parents came to my village. For this occasion my parents arranged a feast and performed some rituals. After the ceremony and lunch, Vijaya's parents left her with us and returned to Gorur. It was a memorable and emotional event.

For one complete year, on the last Friday of every month, Vijaya and I visited Gorur. Each time there was a small celebration. Vijaya would stay with her parents for a day or two and then come to join me. These visits smoothed the transition from her family into mine. At the end of the year, there was a reception to bless and celebrate our first anniversary. After that, we were regarded as a full-fledged husband and wife.

Marriage was the biggest ceremony of my life. I don't remember any other one as elaborate, with so many family people attending. Marriage meant a big change in my life. Before, I had never touched a woman's hand; I didn't know how a girl's hands or lips would feel, or how a girl's body would be. You are curious, shy, wondering how you will face it. I had the physical urges, but never had physical contact.

There is a clear difference between my experience and that of people here in Canada. One of my colleagues at work was going on his honeymoon, so I said to him, "You have already have kissed this girl, probably slept with her too. What will be exciting for you about this honeymoon?"

He said, "Oh, we are going out."

I replied, "Many times you two have gone out, right?"

"Oh," he said, "well, we are flying far away from home; I have never flown so far away on an airplane."

I laughed—not that I am criticizing the Western way of marrying; I am just noticing the cultural differences.

In the beginning, my wife and I were quite incompatible. I was very enthusiastic and excited about everything. She was very practical and got excited about nothing. I used to get mad because she didn't get excited. She got mad because I got excited about everything. I can tell you honestly that it took ten years for us understand and really love each other. In my opinion, real love won't develop by going to movies or having romantic times. Real love does not develop in good times. It is only after we face difficult times in life, share, and discover the divinity in each other that we really start loving each other. After our twenty-fifth anniversary, Vijaya is, for me, still a charming and romantic girl. I still feel that I am dating her now, looking forward to marrying her. Probably our fiftieth anniversary celebration will be our real wedding day![193]

The traditional Indian view is that romantic love is untrustworthy, too ephemeral to serve as a foundation for marriage. The primary defect of romantic love is that instead of deepening ties of community and kin, it restricts, even severs, them. Janardhana and his wife want their daughter's marriage to add to the size and quality of their family, not detract from it. Not passion and romantic love, but religious duty and family well-being are the ideal motives for marriage, so the contrast with American aspirations is sharp.

In the traditional Hindu view, improper marriages, for instance, those that cross caste lines, those conducted with Christians, Muslims, or Jews, or those that violate kinship rules, are called "love marriages." In fact, any wedding not performed in the traditional way is a love marriage. In India, when not arranged by families or performed by Brahmin priests, weddings can have devastating consequences. In rural India families may cut off relationships with the primary participants. Not only is the couple ostracized, so are the parents, siblings, and children of such marriages.

Love, instead of being a precondition for marrying, as it is in the West, is expected to develop after marriage. The differences between love marriages and arranged marriages are not absolute, and we of the West should resist the temptation to become self-congratulatory about the assumed superiority of marriages based on romance. Hindu marriages are no more devoid of love than Western marriages are devoid of kinship considerations. Just as it matters to a Western bride and groom how parents feel about a new spouse, so it matters to an Indian couple whether love takes root in a marriage.

However, love is not an ultimate requirement, the absence of which is grounds for divorce. If the eligibility rules are followed, the match astrologically harmonious, and the wedding auspiciously scheduled and correctly performed, love should develop—even between a woman and man who do not know, or even like, each other.

Married Already or Not Yet?

Originally, Buddhism was no more interested in marriage than Christianity was. In this respect both religions contrast sharply with their respective "parent" traditions, Hinduism and Judaism. However, Buddhist priests, like Christian pastors and Jewish rabbis, officiate at marriage ceremonies. In Thailand one is asked frequently, "Married already or not yet?"[194] There is no third option. As one ages, the "not yet" option becomes increasingly deviant. Despite the strong pressure to marry, Thai young people, even in traditional and royal families, are allowed considerable latitude in choosing a marriage partner. An American physicist tells this story about his marriage to an urbane Thai woman with a traditional background:

I was the groom in a royal wedding celebrated in Bangkok, Thailand. Several months earlier, the date and time of the ceremony had been chosen as auspicious by monks from a nearby temple. The ceremony itself was unusually traditional. In a traditional Thai wedding events do not necessarily happen sequentially or in a strict order as they often do in the West. People talk, coming and going while kids play and run around—all with no worrying about disruption, as would be typical in a Western ceremony.

My wife is a member of Thai royalty, her title approximately equivalent to that of a countess. While coming from a most traditional family and deeply respecting its traditions, she is decidedly modern. An art historian with a Ph.D., she does not pay much attention to Thai weddings or such events. I met her at Bangkok's National Museum where she was giving an English-language tour normally conducted by a foreign resident of Bangkok. It was nearly Christmas, and all the usual docents had left town.

On the eve of our wedding I still felt very much in the dark about what was going to be happening the next day. My careful request—echoed by her family—for a brief explanation of what I might expect for the next day seemed to upset her. So instead, her younger sister, who had been married in a similar ceremony some years before, took me to the main hall where the ceremony was to take place. It was already decorated with white flowers and was gently lit with incandescent bulbs hanging high from the ceiling in old hand blown globes. She walked me through the major steps of the ceremony, with advice on kneeling and bowing.

Even allowing for the stress of last-minute preparations, why had my wife reacted so strongly to the suggestion that I be informed about what to expect in the ceremony? The question remained. Later, after the wedding was over, it occurred to me that perhaps she herself had not remembered exactly what was going to be taking place. Maybe she was frustrated to be put on the spot for an explanation. Traditional ceremonies are rare, and her sister's wedding may have been the only one she had attended. Even Thai people are not always clear about what happens or what things mean at traditional weddings. Few weddings are performed traditionally anymore. Today, the norm is a ceremony featuring an elaborate white Western dress and a tall, mostly artificial cake served at a reception in a fancy hotel. In contrast, our wedding took place in the main hall of my wife's family compound along the innermost canal in the old part of the city. The compound dates back to the reign of King Rama II, and the central teak wood hall is the only such surviving royal structure in Bangkok outside the Royal Palace.

The ceremony began around 7:30 A.M. when an old station wagon full of monks arrived at the house of my wife's family. The monks filed into the 150-year-old main hall and began chanting. I was told the head monk, who was in his nineties, was from a nearby temple. The old monk directed the action, and because this was a royal occasion, he was assisted by a short, uniformed protocol officer from the Royal Palace.

My future wife and I first sat on chairs in front of the head monk, our hands pressed together in a *wai* (prayer) position, while the monks, seated in a line on a raised platform, chanted many blessings. A ball of string was unwound. Eventually, it was held by all the monks and by us. It was tied to the main Buddha image. Later, the protocol officer directed us to a backroom, where we filled the monks' alms bowls with offerings: scoops of rice, wrapped eggs, and so on. All of this my wife and I did simultaneously. I was careful to keep my hand on top of hers as we held the rice spoon, since her brother-in-law had told me the previous evening that by Thai custom this gesture determines who will be the dominant one in the marriage. We were followed by my mother, as well as my wife's parents and other family members who wanted to gain merit by giving alms to the monks.

Traditionally, there is a water-pouring ceremony in which each guest blesses the new couple by pouring water over their hands held out in a *wai*. Ours was abbreviated in the interest of saving time. Only the princess, who had been invited to preside over the wedding, along with our parents, poured water over our hands. The water, first blessed by the monks, was poured from a large, ornate conch shell decorated with gold.

My wife wore a simple, white saronglike dress. I had on a white Thai-style coat with brass buttons and trousers made from one long piece of silk expertly wrapped around me in the early morning hours by an ancient maid. I was advised that I had better not require any more bathroom services until after the ceremony! I imagined that if I were walking in the lobby of the Oriental Hotel dressed this way, people would expect me to open the door for them.

We sat motionless on the floor to receive more blessings. One sits with one's legs off to the side, since this is polite although not comfortable. Together, we then presented each monk with a stack of presents: incense, a new robe, eating bowls, some money in an envelope, each topped by a lotus flower. Each monk accepted the gifts placed on his cloth, which he then pulled toward himself. (Monks are not permitted to accept anything directly from a woman.) Following the presentation of each gift, we fully prostrated on the floor before each monk, touching our palms on the floor, until the protocol officer decided this gesture was taking too much time. So instead, he had us bow while kneeling with our hands pressed together. Since I teach yoga and had attended Buddhist services in the U.S. and Japan, I had no problem prostrating to monks and Buddha images. Several Thai guests remarked that I had performed quite naturally in the ceremony, "like a Thai," they said.

Together, my wife and I served each monk his breakfast in the same way. It consisted of eggs and sausage, a fact that surprised some of our Western guests. (My wife's father thought they probably got enough Thai food at the monastery.) At about the same time the guests ate breakfast outside. After eating, there was a ring ceremony presided over by the princess. My wife's father blessed each of us with three dots of wet, white clay on our foreheads representing the three jewels of Buddhism: the Buddha, the dharma (the Buddha's teaching), and the sangha (the monastic order). We were presented with leafy twigs from some sort of plant and were supposed to keep the twigs behind one ear, but mine continually fell off.

At the conclusion of the ceremony we made prostrations to the Buddha and then sat before the head monk as others gathered close around us. The monk blessed everyone by shaking a large quantity of holy water over the crowd with a whisk. Later, some of the aunts confessed to worrying that the water would spoil their hairdos.

Our entrance back into the house of my wife's family was ceremoniously blocked by pairs of people holding strings across our path. The groom is supposed to pay something to each person to be allowed to pass, and I had prepared envelopes of money in advance. For children and maids, to whom the money would mean something, I gave one hundred baht. On my wife's rich cousins and friends I played a little trick: I gave them envelopes containing a single American dollar bill. After paying for our passage into the house, I carried my bride up the stairs.

In the evening, following a tea reception and dinner along the Chao Phraya River, my wife's parents performed an abbreviated version of the Thai wedding-bed ceremony in our room at the Oriental Hotel. They left out the traditional bags of rice, sesame seeds, and rainwater, as well as the tomcat. But they covered the bed with rose petals and lay in it for a while, making the required ceremonial comments: "A happy marriage with lots of children will certainly result from sleeping in such a marriage bed." It worked: We have a set of three-year-old twins.[195]

Richard Breedon, who tells this story, is an American. The narrative is Western in its structure, and it frames the movement of a traditional Asian ritual process. In good Western literary fashion, the tensions of the plot thicken in the middle but are resolved at the end. The ending is happy; it is what we expect of wedding stories. The hero persists, learning what he needs to know to perform the great deed, marrying royalty. The rite works; the twins are proof of it.

Richard's tone is playful, so I do not mean to suggest that he thinks of himself as heroic, only that the structure of the story is as traditional as the structure of the rite. A Western-born and -trained physicist like Richard is not likely to believe that old couples acting out fertility farces on the wedding bed will cause the next generation to be conceived, but he plays along. An effective wedding, after all, requires performance, not belief.

I have overstated the case. The story does not quite resolve all the tensions it exposes. It only seems to if we let our joy at the twins' birth distract us from noticing the tension between bride and groom. Richard surmises that his wife becomes upset because she herself is unsure what Thai wedding tradition requires. The groom is not sure what constitutes ritually proper behavior in this situation. He tries to solve the problem the way an American physicist would, by asking questions, trying to discern the rules. His bride, her upbringing saturated in Thai sensibilities, deals with it in another way. In the form of symptoms she acts out the cross-cultural leap that the couple is making.

Richard does not confront his bride with direct questions about her behavior. He does not perform a stereotypical postwedding scene in which the sensitive young groom sits down with his new bride and says, "Now, dear, what was going on with you this afternoon?" Thus, there is no subsequent scene in which she comes clean, and in telling all, sets the stage for them to live happily ever after. In the actual story, circumspection, rather than pop psychology, reigns. There is a tender spot here. It may arise from cultural or gender differences or be the outcome of a tension between tradition and modernity. In any case, Richard treads lightly.

In Thailand so-called traditional weddings are becoming as rare as they are in Japan. Wedding traditions around the world are feeling the pressure of the Anglo-American white wedding, just as they feel the pressure of the American dollar. But what is a traditional rite? An unchanged sequence of actions? Or a set of procedures capable of adapting to changed social conditions and thus of staying alive?

Ritual traditions have a paradoxical way of evaporating more rapidly than we think they will and also of enduring longer than we imagine. Richard's wedding story illustrates the fragility of ritual traditions. They can be forgotten or their meanings become obscure or objectionable: Why, for instance, must money be paid to unblock the couple's way? Why the leafy twigs behind ears? Why can't a monk receive gifts from a woman? Does a male hand atop a female one really ensure his dominance? Should it?

The story also illustrates the resilience of a ritual tradition. This one tolerates the improvised and edited actions that suffuse the story. Richard offers American dollar bills, a jest played on well-to-do relatives. Animals are omitted from the bed-blessing rite. Buddhist monks eat meat. And the ultimate act of improvisation and editing: A Thai wedding is recast as a Western-style romantic comedy in which all turns out well at the end. The genre shift from ritual performance to wedding narrative is a major way of bridging religious and cultural chasms.

Every tradition is marked by a perennial tension between those who would keep things the same (and thus connected to sacred origins) and those who would update them (thus making them relevant to participants). Imagined as structures, rites can seem static and changeless. Some rites are, in fact, old. Others are merely portrayed as archaic by those who have a high investment in displaying continuity. In either case, rites endure both by changing and by resisting change. No one can deny that the ritual systems of the world's religions resist change, but those that survive find ways of embracing it too. Rites are always in the process of being forgotten and reinvented, exported and adapted, conserved and reimagined.

It is a serious distortion to suppose that ritual change is the prerogative of formally educated, technologically driven societies, or that ritual stagnation is characteristic of so-called traditional societies. Ritual change is sometimes more readily effected in oral, nonliterate societies not saddled with written, unchanging texts to prescribe the rites. Since ritual enactment depends on human memory, changes can occur, if in no other way than by selective remembering and forgetting.

Ritual change occurs not only by modifying actions and words but also by attitude and tone shifts and by selectively forgetting as well. Richard, for instance, greets certain actions with humor, irony, or fictive naïveté. His wife, I suspect, was able to participate not so much *despite* her lack of knowledge, but *because of* it. She is not only from a traditional Thai family but also educated and Westernized. Did she think about the meaning of having her husband's hand atop hers or of having to place gifts on a cloth rather than hand them directly to monks? If so, did she balk or have reservations? If she did, the meaning of the rite has changed even though we would not have perceived the change if we had been in attendance. Of course, we do not know the answers to all the questions this delicately balanced narrative raises. The backstage area is off-limits. After all, even in the movies, the newly married couple has a right to draw the curtains.

Old Enough to Be the Father of His Bride

Contemporary popular feelings about wedding ceremonies are polarized. On the one hand, weddings are, in the language of brides' magazines, "special moments," "sacraments of fidelity" to be "lovingly planned and slowly savored." On the other, they are annoying social conventions coupled with legal formalities and entangled in exploitative commercial pressures, all of which deserve to be cut through as cleanly as possible. Weddings can be simultaneously sacred occasions and empty formalities.

The tension between weddings experienced as sacred or civic, special or merely contractual, has a long history. A brief survey of key moments in Western wedding history can shed light on the paradoxical, even contradictory, impulses that couples feel about wedding ceremonies.

Couples sometimes insist that this event is "their wedding," yet many customs make it all too evident that the occasion belongs as much to families as to couples. Brides exercise free choice in selecting their mates, yet a bride seems like an object rather than a subject if she is "given away."

Paradoxes such as these have a bedeviling persistence about them, partly because of the comparative uniformity of Western assumptions about marriage. There may be more variation among the wedding customs of contemporary India than across all of Europe and North America, including the historical variations reaching back to ancient Greece and Rome. Scholars treat Jewish, Orthodox, Catholic, and Protestant wedding traditions as distinct, so it might seem inappropriate to speak of a "European American wedding rite," as if there were only one. But since the elements comprising these traditions are variations on a limited, fairly consistent set of themes, it makes at least as much sense to speak of a European American wedding tradition as it does to speak of a Hindu wedding tradition. There are important variations among Western traditions, but if one compares them with the diversity of practice in India, they appear minimal.

There are at least two basic ways of accounting for the persistence of Western wedding motifs. One is that historic traditions imitated and borrowed from one another—the Romans from the classical Greeks, the early Christians from Romans and Jews, the medieval Jews from Christians, and so on. Another way of accounting for uniformity is to note that Christianity, during certain periods of its history, successfully imposed both its rites and its ritual sensibilities upon the tribes and cities that eventually became Europe.

The contemporary European American wedding rite is not merely a degenerate or secular version of an earlier, purely Christian rite. The Christian rite itself has an impure genealogy; it is a motley mixture of Greek, Roman, Christian, Jewish, and European American folk customs. It is impossible to decide whether the most remarkable feature of European American wedding history is the longevity of some of the practices or the mixture of sources.

There is no full narrative account of an ancient Greek wedding, so scholars piece together the process from vase paintings, excerpts from plays, and other sources.[196] Marriage in Athens consisted of a betrothal ceremony, followed, usually several years later, by a wedding feast and procession. Athenian girls married young, having been promised long before entering puberty. The typical Athenian husband was literally old enough to be the father of his bride. By contrast, Spartan brides were closer in age to their husbands. Athenian men despised the Spartan practice, complaining that it encouraged Spartan women to become domineering.

Athenian betrothal was conducted between household heads, sometimes with the assistance of professional matchmakers. The betrothal was the occasion for negotiating the terms of the agreement and for settling the size and composition of the dowry. A substantial gift passed from the bride and bridal household to the groom and his household. A formal oath sealed the betrothal pledge before witnesses: "I pledge my child, _____, to _____, according to the laws of the Athenians." To which a formal reply was uttered: "I accept the pledge. . . . "

The subsequent wedding was preceded by a series of preparatory rites, including a sacrifice to the gods offered by both groom and bride. Brides sacrificed hair, as well as dolls, toys, and other symbols of the childhood they were leaving behind. Whether grooms sacrificed similar items is unclear. Anticipation of a coming wedding was not always joyful any more than it is now. Women sometimes felt their marriages, not just the rites preceding them, were sacrificial acts. Sophocles has one of his female characters complain, "*Parthenoi* [young women], in my own opinion, have the sweetest existence known to mortals in their fathers' homes, for their innocence always keeps *paides* [children, dependents] happy. But when we reach *hêbê* [maturity] and can understand, we are thrust out and sold away from our ancestral gods and from our parents. Some go to strange men's homes, others to foreigners', some to joyless houses, some to hostile. And all this once the first night has yoked us to our husband, we are forced to praise and to say that all is well."[197]

After the ritual preparations were complete, the wedding feast was held at the bride's house. Women sat apart from men, the bride wearing a veil throughout the feast. The groom and his family may not have been present for the meal. Worrying about whom to include and exclude from the guest list or how much food to prepare were ancient Greek preoccupations, just as they are preoccupations today.

Plutarch observed, "There is no occasion for a feast that is as conspicuous and much discussed as a wedding. For even when we sacrifice to the gods or send off a friend on a journey or entertain visitors, it is possible to escape the notice of many of our friends. But a wedding feast is given away by the loud cries of the Hymenaios and the torch and the pipes, things that Homer says are admired and watched even by women who stand at their doors. Therefore, since there is no one who is unaware that we are entertaining and have invited people, we are ashamed to leave out anyone, and we invite all of our relatives and friends and connections of any type."[198]

By the end of the fourth century feasting got so out of hand in ancient Greece that legislation was enacted to limit the guest list to thirty.[199]

Before her departure, the bride was blessed by those present. Then, after the feasting was finished, came the public, cross-town procession, which enacted the father's handing over of the bride to her husband. The procession was a physical and symbolic transfer from her natal home to her marital household. Accompanied by wedding hymns in honor of Hymen, the bride was accompanied by both her husband and a crowd headed for his home. The couple rode in a special nuptial cart (today's limo), the groom's best friend (today's best man) seated beside him. The noisy procession, replete with torchlight song and dance, was in part a mock abduction, perhaps a remnant of an earlier time in which actual abduction had been a way of securing brides.

Athenian weddings were public, not merely private or domestic, affairs, and the procession was its most public phase; anyone could join. The ancient practice of public noise making to call attention to a new couple continues today, as cars—honking, decorated, and towing a string of tin cans—drive across town.

Upon arrival at the groom's home, his mother greeted the bride as she entered beneath a shower of nuts and dried fruit. Today, we echo the practice with rice. The bride was presented with a basket of bread, a sign of welcome but also a reminder of her task and place.

The bride was then conducted to the family hearth and placed under protection of the household gods, to whom she was required to offer homage. His family's gods became hers as she venerated them before the flame on the family altar, the site of domestic observances. As a concluding public gesture, the bride removed her veil before accompanying the groom to the wedding chamber.

In the chamber, she was expected to do what brides everywhere are expected to do. The groom, like grooms everywhere, was expected to "perform." A song was sung, perhaps through the closed door, and a doorkeeper was posted, both to prevent entry by the curious and to block a reluctant bride's escape. This first night was known as the "camping out," probably because the bride had yet to bring all her belongings to this new location.

Though not a honeymoon, there was a postnuptial ceremony. On the day after the wedding, the two families met, sometimes for the first time. Gifts were given by the bride's father to the couple.

Ancient Greek weddings were thoroughly religious, infused with ritualistic actions and mythological allusions. The importance of marriage ceremonies to ancient Greeks is obvious from the many artistic depictions of weddings between gods. Like most of us, they too enjoyed festivity.

In sum, classical Greek weddings included elements still familiar to us: brides given away by fathers, veiling and unveiling, clamoring in the streets for public attention, the giving of gifts, showering a new couple (or the bride) with flowers or food items (dates, nuts, dried fruits, and figs). Other practices such as processing in a chariot as if one were a divine or heroic being and blessing the marriage bed are no longer typical of European American weddings.

Weddings in ancient Athens, like many celebrated elsewhere, were not only occasions for celebration but also for sadness. There was the obvious problem, then as now, of culinary excess. But there are the darker and more menacing possibilities suggested by several components of the Greek matrimonial scene: the bride veiled at her departure banquet, the young bride led here and there by a much older groom, mock abduction, having a guard at the wedding chamber door. Perhaps these elements were symbolic of death to an old way of life and rebirth into a new one. But even if they were "only" symbolic, the bride, not the groom, was put through a deathlike transformation. The requirement to die ritualistically was not shared equally between the sexes.

In the Greek *Hymn to Demeter*, told from a mother's point of view, a daughter, Persephone, is abducted to become the wife of Hades, the aged lord of the netherworld. Demeter, the mother, weeps and searches, mourning the loss. The story concludes with a compromise in which Persephone lives for part of the year in the household of her birth, and part-time in the dark household of her husband. Even this somber ending seems optimistic alongside the fact that Athenian women were not free to choose such living arrangements. There was likely real grief, as well as real joy.[200]

Lack of reciprocity between husbands and wives is a shadow that still hangs over the history of marriage. There are moments, of course, of equality and reciprocity, times when a young woman's choices are taken into account, when a girl is given jointly by her father and mother, or when a contract is negotiated that binds a groom as tightly and fully as it does a bride. But in general, the pattern of transferring a female between males, that is, from father to groom, permeates much global wedding history. From ancient Greece onward, there is a struggle with the so-called Greek "first law of conjugality, namely that the key to a happy marriage depends primarily upon a wife's readiness to submit unquestioningly to her husband's *kratos* [authority, power] whatever his qualities or defects."[201]

Passing the Torch, Blessing the Bride

Although there were different kinds of Roman weddings, the basic pattern imitated the Greek one: first a betrothal in which a dowry was agreed upon and consent obtained, then, sometime later, preparatory activity, followed by a feast and procession, culminating in a rite that incorporates the bride into the groom's home.[202]

As is the practice today, formal betrothal in ancient Rome was not a legal requirement, nor did it have legal force if violated, but since the promise was formal, there was great social pressure to act in accord with the words spoken. Since a betrothal ceremony assumed that the couple consisted of a young girl and an older man, the girl was promised to the man, not the man to the girl. Consent was the only legal requirement in Rome, as is usual in contemporary Europe and North America, but consent meant the consent of families, household heads, or guardians, not necessarily the bride acting on her own behalf.

The ancient Roman bride's family offered a dowry, and the groom and bride exchanged gifts. His betrothal gift, often a ring, was considered the seal of the agreement. Wedding rings came into use only much later. The ring was worn, as it is today, on the so-called wedding finger of the left hand, since Romans conventionally held that a sinew or nerve led from that finger directly to the heart.

As in Greek ceremonies, a Roman girl gave up childish things such as toys. She also made a sacrifice, for example, of a locket, to the gods of the household she was leaving. On her wedding day a Roman bride was dressed and assisted by her mother. The bride's hair was styled and decorated with a wreath of flowers or sacred plants that she herself had gathered; her groom wore a similar garland. Around the bride's waist was a piece of wool tied with the knot of Hercules (in common parlance, a square knot), which only her husband was meant to untie for obvious reasons. She wore a flame-colored veil.

Before the wedding, the omens were determined by reading a sacrificed sheep's entrails. Assuming the omens were favorable, the wedding proceeded. The use of divination dropped out of regular practice after the Christianization of Europe.

The house of the bride's father was the site of the primary ceremony, and it was decorated celebratively with flowers, boughs, and colored cloth. Guests arrived at sunrise, an auspicious time. The ceremony proper could take one of three forms. In the most elaborate one, called *confarreate,* a matron joined the right hands of the bride and groom in front of ten witnesses. The tradition of joining hands continues in many European and North American weddings. The Roman bride declared, "When—and where—you are Gaius, I then—and there—am Gaia."[203] The formula resembles Ruth's reassurance to Boaz, "Whither thou goest I shall go." An offering of spelt cake was then made by a priest to Jupiter, with prayers also addressed to Juno. As with many food offerings, the cake was consumed by the bride and groom and distributed later to wedding guests. We continue cake eating but without its offertory intentions.

Coemptio was a second kind of wedding rite, and it took the form of a mock, or fictitious, sale of the bride. A symbolic purchase price, a single coin, was placed on a scale. In this ceremony, the groom asked the bride if she would be his materfamilias, the mother of his family. The bride, in turn, asked him a similar question. The presence of a scale was considered definitive of this wedding style, just as spelt cake was regarded as definitive of the first one.

The details of the third wedding form, *usus,* are not well known but likely involved joining hands and speaking words of consent.

The wedding feast, which typically followed all three kinds of wedding rites, was given by the father; it concluded with the distribution of cake.

The procession that followed was as essential as the words of consent. Public display was a requirement, not an option. Led by torchbearers and flute players, the wedding procession conducted the bride and guests to the groom's house. With mock bravado the groom marshaled his bride, a movement that may have been associated with the story of the rape of the Sabine women. As with wedding processions from ancient times until now, the Roman one was replete with song, noise, and sexual jousting. The processing bride carried three coins. One she offered to the god of the crossroads (she was, after all, making a major transition in her life cycle). One she gave the groom, a token of the full dowry that would accompany her. And the last she offered to the gods of his household. The groom carried with him sesame cakes, nuts, and other sweets to distribute to the crowd.

At the entrance to his house, the groom carried the bride over the threshold, to preclude her tripping or falling, a bad omen with which to mark entry into this new phase of their lives. His house, like hers, was decorated. Colored wool was on display, and the threshold was anointed with oil, a symbolic easing of entry. We can only guess at the jests that may have been made about its "real" significance.

The bride repeated the words she had uttered at the wedding. Then, at the hearth, she transferred fire from the torch of her natal home to the wood waiting here in her new marital home. The torch was then tossed, much as a bouquet is thrown today, to guests, who scrambled for it. Persons and objects sanctified by the power of ritual could absorb and transfer that sacred power.

The wedding couch awaited the couple in the atrium. It was used once, on the wedding night, then afterward it was used as furniture.

The next night there followed another banquet. At this one the new bride made her first liturgical offering as a Roman matron.

In Roman weddings, we encounter practices that seem dated, strange, or unjust. If a bride is "given" to a groom, why isn't he the one who pays the dowry? Why is a bride's family expected to provide a double gift, that of a bride as well as a dowry?

Other actions and objects, though modified and reordered, continue in today's wedding repertoire: a tossed object, being carried across a threshold, feasting, the passing on of a flame, public display, the distribution of cake, wearing special garments, elaborately coiffed hair, a ring. Today's procession is down the aisle toward the altar, not away from the wedding site toward the groom's home. But much else is recognizable, including the most important feature, the one considered Rome's distinctive contribution, and the one that will become definitive of Western practice: the expression of consent in the presence of witnesses.

From Blessing Marriages to Making Them

Early Christians married according to Roman law but, for a while, they continued to think of themselves as Jewish. It is uncertain how much early Christian weddings borrowed from the practices of Jewish contemporaries. But it took time for Christianity to develop a distinctive rite of its own. At the very least, Christians seem to have inherited from Jews the custom of blessing marriages. Central to Jewish practice was a two-phased process in which a woman was first promised to a man and then later given to him in marriage. In this most basic way Greek, Roman, Hebrew, and Christian weddings share a fundamental similarity.

Jewish marriage was contractual, based on the model of an economic transaction. Marriage had two phases, *erusin* (betrothal) and *nissuin* (marriage). *Erusin* was a formal, promissory action. It typically preceded the second phase by a year or more. After negotiating with a family, paying the required amount, and obtaining consent, a man then formally declared a woman "sanctified unto" him. This formula enacted a binding contract to marry.

The contract was not mutual. A wife was symbolically purchased, and this ceremony set her aside for a specific man. Although she retained certain property rights, she belonged to her future husband. The asymmetry of the betrothal rite is consistent with the asymmetry of Jewish initiation. Whereas a male Jew entered the covenant directly by way of circumcision, a female Jew had covenant status indirectly, first by virtue of her father and then by virtue of her husband.

A groom paid a price either to the bride's father or directly to the bride in ceremonial exchange for her consent to marry. The bride price did not represent a literal attempt to determine a woman's cash value. The amount was token; it could be anything upon which both parties agreed: a sum of money, a cup of wine, a ring. The kiss, the joining of hands, and the giving of a ring were originally betrothal, not wedding, gestures. Like today's handshake, they were symbolic means of ratifying agreements. Even though a betrothal price or gift might be small, the agreement was sufficiently serious that it could be dissolved only by a formal divorce. A broken betrothal was an act much more serious than today's broken engagement.

The practice of betrothal, much reduced in seriousness, continues in contemporary Europe and North America in the form of engagement. It also continues in another way—as the opening phase of the wedding ceremony in both Judaism and Orthodox Christianity. The ceremonial seam, whereby two originally separate rites were stitched into one, is still visible in both religions.

When betrothal was separated from marriage by a significant lapse of time, being betrothed was the source of deep ambivalence. The practice created a limbo zone in which brides and grooms could violate promises, become unsure of commitments, or resist obligations. Al-

though the conventional view has been that sharing a common residence and engaging in sexual intercourse should follow rather than precede the wedding, the history of marriage in the West is replete with socially approved exceptions to this supposed rule. Common-law
marriages, for instance, were widely recognized.

By the first century B.C.E. a marriage contract, known as a *ketubah,*
was in use. It protected a Jewish wife, not her husband, who had no
need for such protection, by committing him to pay her a specified sum
should he divorce her without cause or become abusive to such a degree
that a Jewish court would grant her a divorce.[204] In effect, a *ketubah*
softened the absoluteness with which a man might possess and dispose
of a woman.

The second phase of the Jewish wedding rite, *nissuin,* means "the
carrying." It takes its name from the practice of transporting a bride,
sometimes on a palanquin, to her groom's residence. This second phase
concluded and fulfilled the betrothal agreement. This more solemn
liturgy was followed by a ritual feast, which, although festive, was religiously framed. In an earlier time the feast was not merely a delightful
appendage to the wedding rite, it *was* the wedding rite.[205]

By the Middle Ages Jewish weddings included most of the familiar
elements of contemporary ones: The *ketubah* was witnessed; the groom
put the bride's veil in place; *erusin* and *nissuin* were performed (now
back-to-back) under the *chuppah* (canopy) with each of the two phases
marked by wine blessing and sipping; the seven blessings were recited;
and the rite concluded with the smashing of a glass. Some of these practices were borrowed by or shared among medieval European Jews and
Christians.[206]

According to Christian teaching Jesus had no earthly father. And
when his mother appeared on the edge of a crowd, he is reported to
have asked, "Who is my mother?" The question is rhetorical. He
knows who his mother is. He is trying to expand the notion of motherhood. Spiritual, or metaphoric, mothers (along with spiritual fathers,
brothers, and sisters) were accorded clear ascendancy over biological
ones.

For much of Christianity's history, its leaders and writers com-
mended social arrangements *other than* the couple and the family, for
instance, priestly celibacy, monastic community, and voluntary virginity
within marriage.[207] Marrying and reproducing were tolerated but not
strongly encouraged or lavishly praised. As long as the apocalyptic end
was just over the horizon, marriage was a distraction or dangerous self-

indulgence. The metaphoric marriage of Christ to his church overshadowed the more ordinary kind of marriage between a woman and a man. Consequently, developing a marriage rite was not a high priority in early Christianity.

Early Christian marriages were influenced by Roman practices and, to a lesser extent, Jewish ones. Central to Roman weddings was the formal and public declaration of consent to marry. Originally, consent issued from family heads, later, from the bride and groom individually. Obtaining either one or both kinds of consent, along with ensuring that there are no "obstructions" (that is, legal or genealogical reasons why marriage should be forbidden), continues today in Western weddings, both ecclesiastical and civil: "If anyone present knows of reasons why _____ and _____ should not marry, please step forward, making your reasons known, or forever hold your peace." Although consent seems normal and obvious to us, it has not always seemed so to everyone else. As we have seen, the notion of individualized consent was imposed by American occupation forces on the Japanese after World War II.

By the second century Christians were being advised to consult their bishops before marrying, but there is no evidence that a bishop or other ordained clergy performed the ceremony. The bishop's function seems to have been pastoral rather than liturgical, perhaps to deter second marriages or marriages to non-Christians. The early Christian rite, like the Greek, Roman, and Jewish ones, consisted of two phases. But the Christian rite consisted of a betrothal followed by a matrimonial blessing.

The betrothal was a private domestic affair, minimally ritualized except in Spain and in Eastern Orthodox countries, where full betrothal liturgies existed. Christians debated which pagan and folk elements (decorating the bridal bed with flowers and blessing it, donning a bridal veil, presenting bride and groom with crowns, and so on) were acceptable and which were not. Whereas veils, for instance, persisted in the Christian West, crowns continued in the Christian East.

Through the seventh century, and especially in places distant from Rome, weddings among Christians varied according to local custom and were largely domestic or civil rather than ecclesiastical occasions. Even having concubines, though never advocated, was tolerated. Priests did not perform weddings but rather blessed them after the legal act of marrying had already been accomplished. Blessings were sometimes conferred only on the bride. They were also conferred with some frequency on same-sex couples. In fact, the earliest Greek liturgical manuscript contains four wedding-related ceremonies, one of them for unit-ing two men.[208]

As with Greek, Roman, and Jewish weddings, Christian ones were usually structured as the transfer of a woman from her natal family to her marital family, from her father to her husband. Treating brides as analogous to property, therefore as liabilities or assets, was an assump-tion not seriously challenged until the twentieth century.

Spatially, the basic structure of the heterosexual European Christian wedding rite was that of a two-phased procession: first from the bride's home to the church, where the marriage was blessed, and then from the church to the groom's place, where the marriage was celebrated with revelry and banqueting. As in Greek and Roman weddings, processions were accompanied by noise making so that the entire community could witness and participate in the making of a new union.

The church had been in existence for over six hundred years before weddings were regularly embedded in worship services. Even then, such a ceremony was not obligatory, and the liturgical act was not what con-stituted marriage. Even as late as the twelfth century priestly blessings of marriages were still being dispensed at the front doors of churches, a clear statement that, although the church had an interest in marriage, marriage making was not its purview. It was mutual, public consent rather than priestly pronouncement that effected a marriage.

Early Christian marriage, enacted by a couple at home in the pres-ence of witnesses, gradually evolved into an ecclesiastical rite enacted by clergy. From the ninth through the fifteenth centuries, the Christian wedding rite was gradually taken under the wing of the clergy. Wed-dings, originally kept away from the Sabbath so that it could be de-voted exclusively to worship, were now deliberately scheduled for the Sabbath, as if doing so could make marriages holier. The ritual center of weddings gradually shifted from homes to churches, and from out-side church doors to inside, then to places nearer the altar and farther away from the backdoor. Slowly, weddings were clericalized.

The ceremony now required a priest who "made" a couple in an al-most magical fashion. Clergy now effected the union both sacrally and legally. Sacred objects such as the Bible, bread, or wine were imported into the rite to sanctify marriage but also to assert the church's author-ity over it. Marriage and sexuality were interpreted as symbols of tran-scendent mysteries.

Expressions of marital consent were elaborated; no longer mere an-swers to questions, they became promises. In some regions of Europe, vows of wifely obedience came into vogue, but, like priestly supervision, vows of obedience, which echoed monastic vows, entered late into the history of the Christian wedding rite.

Throughout much of European history clandestine and common-law marriages were recognized under civil law. But in 1215 the fourth Lateran Council asserted ecclesiastical control over marriage. The church tried to prevent private marriages by requiring publication of the banns, an announcement of proposed marriages. The banns required a waiting period and issued a call for any who knew of obstacles to proposed marriage to make them known. The church also began to insist on weddings in daylight; it came to disapprove of clandestine or nocturnal marriages, fearing that such ceremonies were conducive to unseemly behavior.

The height of ecclesiastical intrusion into marriage rites came in 1563, when the Council of Trent declared that only marriages contracted in the presence of a priest and two witnesses would be recognized. The celibate priest, with his incantatory words, "*I* join you together in holy matrimony," became the master maker of marriage, effectively rendering secondary the agency of bride, groom, family, and state. Previously, the parties, with their agreements, exchanges, and transfers had effected marriage. Now the priest with his words and gestures wed.

Gradually, this clericalization of the wedding rite led not only to its relative uniformity throughout Europe but also to another important change, that of making the vows reciprocal. The idea that each is granted to the other began to the displace the notion that a woman is given to a man. But centuries would pass before the implications of this change permeated the marriage rite and gained public acceptance.

In summarizing this major shift in European wedding history, it is sometimes said that Western weddings were originally civil and that they became religious in the late Middle Ages. This way of putting the matter distorts it. If by "civil" we mean secular or nonreligious, then the claim is demonstrably false. Hebrew, Greek, and Roman weddings were permeated with religious symbols, ideas, and actions. Some wedding rites required sacrifices, others invoked multiple gods, and all were laced with prayers and blessings. In the history of Western Christian weddings it is almost impossible to separate religious elements from nonreligious ones.

A better way to describe what happened across the long stretch of history is to say that in the late Middle Ages weddings came under more centralized clerical and ecclesiastical control. The shift was not from law to religion but from domestic piety to ecclesiastical liturgy. The change was not in religiosity but in who controlled its expression.

Ecclesiastical wedding rites did not altogether replace domestic ones. Homes, along with churches and synagogues, continued to be important sites for weddings. Even today, when the act of marrying has in certain respects become secularized, weddings typically involve homes and banquet halls, not religious edifices alone.

At the height of the wedding's liturgical elaboration, a countervailing trend erupted. A profound deritualization of weddings and other rites of passage was set off by the Protestant Reformation in the sixteenth century. Weddings, though still important, were no longer accorded the status of sacraments, rites supposed to have been instituted directly by Jesus. Rather, they were reduced to "occasional offices," rites that facilitate life-cycle events. What Protestant weddings gained in economy of expression, they lost in "magic." Weddings became occasions for moral exhortation and edification. Bride and groom were not only getting married, they were also being taught about marriage, read to from scripture, and instructed on how to raise children. Protestant weddings were ritually simpler, but the lengthening of sermons often made them longer. Theologically considered, a wedding now became a covenant (mutual promises made in the presence of God) rather than a contract, blessing, or priestly creation. Simultaneously, betrothal lost much of its legal force; it became a weak social convention or was dropped altogether.

Major changes in Catholic wedding theology and practice emerged in the middle of the twentieth century. Vatican II once again ensconced Catholic weddings in corporate worship. Not only did weddings become more Eucharist centered, they also allowed for more active participation of laity and the community. The council granted more latitude for incorporating local customs. Although weddings continued to be sacraments, the priest no longer pronounced the magical formula, "I join you in holy matrimony."

Although contemporary Protestant weddings are not technically considered sacraments, Catholic and Protestant weddings since the 1960s have begun to resemble each other. In 1985 the Consultation on Common Texts, a group representing mainline churches in Canada and the United States, constructed an ecumenical wedding text, evidence of a growing sense of cooperation among Christian groups.[209] The rite assumes the equality of bride and groom and presupposes that they marry each other rather than being married by clergy or given away by fathers. It also assumes the separation of the church's ceremony from the larger social celebration of a new marriage.

Today, weddings held in churches are not necessarily religious. Churches remain preferred wedding sites partly because they are dramatic architectural spaces capable of holding large numbers of people. They provide atmosphere and lend seriousness to the rite. Couples may prefer a "religious" service not because they are religious but because they want to cultivate a traditional atmosphere or because they want a beautiful wedding.

Only after the middle of the twentieth century did alternative Christian wedding rites, consonant with the mood of the 1960s, begin to mention sexual delight and pleasure as reasons for marrying, thus challenging the Christian notion that marriage is a "remedy" for lust or that its sole purpose is procreation. A trend in contemporary revisions of Christian wedding rites is the elimination of asymmetrical promises, those in which one party promises to obey the other. Generally, churches have given up the practice of having someone give away a bride, although either bride or groom may be "accompanied" by someone such as a parent or friend. On some occasions the companionship of peers is replacing the authority of parents to give away their daughters. Also, there is a growing tendency to address ritual questions to family, friends, and church members about their willingness to support the couple. It is common, even in the more conservative Christian denominations, for couples to become actively involved in selecting hymns and scriptural passages.

Alternative Weddings

No one has carefully studied the ways in which North American popular culture classifies weddings, but the traditional/alternative distinction oversimplifies the contemporary wedding landscape. How-to manuals and wedding Web sites are adequate indicators, since their authors have to provide publicly intelligible categories that consumers can easily decode.

The term *white wedding* never appears on Web sites; the term is largely a scholarly one. Weddings labeled "traditional" are the nearest equivalent. A traditional wedding is assumed to be a first marriage performed as religious service in a religious edifice and followed by a banquet that includes a multitiered white cake. The bride wears a white dress and is accompanied by bridesmaids. A traditional wedding is not necessarily the one with the oldest elements in it. It is, rather, the conventional rite assumed by brides' magazines and etiquette books. "Traditional" is the imagined norm from which alternative and "other" weddings deviate.

Although the traditional wedding has denominational variants, the differences among them have steadily decreased. In popular accounts, the differences that matter are not theological or ritualistic but stylistic and mechanical, and they are usually reduced in magazines and Web sites to a few traits considered distinctive: Quaker weddings are simple and quiet; Catholic services require a dispensation if one of the partners is a non-Catholic; Jewish weddings use a *ketubah;* Hindu weddings are arranged, and so on.

"Alternative," the most common label for do-it-yourself weddings, includes everything but traditional, ethnic, interfaith, and civil ceremonies. Sometimes, "alternative" is further subdivided. For instance, there is a growing African American alternative wedding movement, and it includes "Nubian" weddings. Sometimes these are billed as "alternative," sometimes as "ethnic." But if the advertisers or magazines are proffered by African Americans, such weddings may be called "traditional."

"Civil" weddings, although every bit as traditional as "traditional" ones, imply the absence of clergy and a smaller scale of ceremonial elaboration. A civil ceremony is ordinarily a quickly performed, supposedly nonreligious act, even though many civil ceremonies are, in fact, laced with religious rhetoric. The proportion of civil ceremonies remains small, no more than a quarter of the total number of American weddings. Even though civil weddings are, in fact, alternatives to weddings in sanctuaries, they are seldom classified as "alternative."

"Ethnic" is a catchall category that occasionally overlaps with "traditional," because "ethnic" includes certain Christian groups, such as Italians and African Americans, whose ceremonies may have a special "flavor." Jewish, Hindu, Buddhist, and Muslim weddings are also sometimes slotted as "ethnic." One occasionally sees the undifferentiated "Asian" either as a freestanding category or as a subcategory of "ethnic."

"Pagan" is no longer used pejoratively. Pagans draw on American Wiccan and European occult practices, sometimes mixed with Spiritualist traditions. Pagan weddings are sometimes depicted as alternative, but if Pagans themselves are speaking, they too may refer to their rites as "traditional."

"Interfaith" weddings usually imply that the marriage partners are from different religious traditions. The most commonly addressed interfaith wedding situation is one in which a Jew marries a Christian. Weddings between such couples are not quite traditional, since they usually run counter to the heritages of both the bride and groom. But they are not quite alternative either, since the principal participants are often so busy trying to bridge their two backgrounds that they rarely have a free hand for experimenting and innovating.

There are other minor or implied categories in the popular classification of weddings, for example, same-sex commitment services (usually billed as lesbian or gay) and second-marriage ceremonies. The same-sex manuals are a distinct and growing genre, but second-marriage literature remains minimal, usually appearing as a few pages in standard wedding or etiquette books. Even though the remarriage of divorced and widowed people is widely accepted, the usual assumption is that these weddings are more modest affairs, low-key versions of "traditional" weddings.

Another minor kind of alternative wedding is based on geographical location—for example, high-altitude, golf-course, beach, and forest weddings. A similar type is the theme or period weddings: sports and horseback weddings on the one hand, Renaissance and Celtic weddings on the other. Finally, there are "event" weddings, those in which a couple performs some deliberately outrageous act such as diving, parachute-clad, off a bridge together.

Like most folk classifications, this one is anything but consistent or unbiased. In addition, it continues to change, but at least it provides a rough idea of how North American weddings are classified for the sake of being marketed.

At first the array of alternative wedding possibilities is dizzying. A recent alternative weddings book offers these one-line descriptions: "Nicola and Alasdair Saunders, who had a tenth-century Viking-style wedding; Maria Coello and Stephen Newton, who conducted their own pacifist ceremony in a forest; Janet and John Moorhouse, who held a Buddhist ceremony after a civil wedding; Christian Baker and Mark Willis, who had a Humanist celebration outside the Peace Pagoda in Milton Keynes; Margaret Gregory and Colin Wall, who had a civil service in the presence of their three-week-old son; Amanda Shribman and

Avril Hollings, who held a lesbian commitment ceremony with Pagan, Goddess, Jewish and Buddhist elements; Katy and Peter Clement, who married on a beach in Florida and had a non-denominational church blessing one year later; Nahid Moshtael and Peter Gregory, who had a Baha'i wedding."[210]

The eclecticism and bleeding of boundaries that characterize the alternative wedding scene testify to the permeability of what were once regarded as impenetrable social and religious barriers. Marrying across boundaries that were once defended as sacred has become increasingly mainstream and normal.

A repeated claim made by purveyors of alternative weddings is that each wedding is unique, "limited only by your imagination." In one sense, the claim is true and the variety bewildering. But in another, the alternative wedding scene illustrates how fully our imaginations are culturally constrained. The themes in alternative weddings are recognizable and the sentiments predictable. The variations are much fewer than the rhetoric makes it seem.

Makers of alternative rites draw on the same limited pool of sources. They quote one another and borrow shamelessly. The tone of how-to wedding books is surprisingly uniform. It is optimistic and upbeat, inevitably full of second-person rhetoric: "This is the most important moment of your life." The manuals are replete with couples—some invented, some real, but all abstract and typified: "Dick grew up Presbyterian, but Jane was Jewish." Each volume has several such pairs so that every reader will find a hook, a couple with which to identify. In addition, there are appendices: a schedule with suggested dates for having invitations printed, a budget distinguishing necessary from desirable items, and a list of resources (photographers and wedding consultants, for instance).

Ritual experimentation and eclecticism do not necessarily eventuate in creativity or evolve from insight. In fact, alternative ritualizing just as readily issues from confusion and self-deception. One popular wedding site on the Internet peddles its wisdom with this slogan: "Incorporating an age-old custom into your ceremony can add a whole new dimension to your wedding."[211] Without the slightest trace of irony, the old, cut short and radically decontextualized, becomes a commodity marketed as something new. The newly invented is sold as something ancient. In the alternative wedding market, the old and the ethnic become commodities, options that couples can choose. Alongside traditional weddings there are also Scottish and African and Medieval-Renaissance ones. It becomes impossible to know which categories ought to be placed in quotation marks. A couple picks a look, a scene, or an era and builds a wedding around it, thus avoiding a confrontation between heritages. Groom and bride purchase a matrimonial idiom off the rack, much as one would choose a pair of shoes. The North American alternative wedding scene can be fun, but it is difficult not to be skeptical about it too.

It has become fashionable not only in alternative weddings but also in standard ones to peek at other ways of marrying. Guidebooks advise couples to explore their roots, incorporate bits of their heritage. A recent issue of *Sposa: The Magazine for the Discerning Bride* included nine full-page photos, an editorial, and an article on "ethnic" ceremonies and costumes, presumably from around the world.[212] In arguing that there are more similarities than differences among weddings around the world, the editorial was not simply inaccurate but counting on the strength and hegemony of the Western model. In this new, supposedly cross-cultural wedding model, ethnic and "foreign" elements are adopted—but only as long as they can be dismembered and reassembled into the basic Western model without threatening it.

In a recent issue of *Modern Bride* "ethnic customs" were reduced to three or four traits per culture or religion:[213] During Arabic weddings, receptions are gender segregated. In African weddings the bride and groom jump over a broom. At Puerto Rican weddings money is pinned to the bride's dress by men who dance with her. The message seems to be, As long as the meat is American, a little foreign spice can only improve its flavor. Religion and ethnicity, as purveyed in mainstream wedding magazines and manuals, exist in small, consumable bits detached from people's histories and communities.

People have long borrowed practices from others; ritual imitation and ceremonial syncretism (patching together bits from various traditions) are nothing new. Humans learn to ritualize in whatever ways they can, and mutual influence is one of the most effective methods. There may be nothing unethical about rediscovering, or even reinventing, one's roots and subsequently adding, say, African or Celtic, or native symbols to one's ritual repertoire, but there are other kinds of problems. Borrowing, syncretism, and the invention of tradition can evoke self-consciousness, leaving participants with an uneasy feeling that the new rite is contrived.

Besides self-consciousness, there is the difficulty of *ritual introjection*, that is, ingesting tidbits that one cannot digest and absorb into one's spiritual or cultural bloodstream. Wedding services are often marketed as if they were a set of modules to be plugged in or pulled out at will. This kind of packaging enhances not only their portability but also their sales appeal. A buffetlike atmosphere is often the result. The lack of integral connections among the parts of a wedding can mirror the detachment of a wedding from a couple's history and community.

The frequency of interreligious, cross-cultural, and mixed marriages will probably continue to increase, making ritual borrowing and reinvention a necessity. But exploitation, contrivance, and self-deception are strong temptations, so we should exercise care. A serious ethical issue emerges when a more powerful group preys on the ceremonial resources of an oppressed group or when a dominant culture imposes its wedding fashions and marital aspirations on an oppressed group.

Reinventing Marriage Rites

When we considered birth, the challenge was that of imagining a biological and technological event as a ritualistic one. With initiation the problem was how to conduct adolescents into adulthood without violating important ethical principles and without the support of stable face-to-face communities. When it comes to wedding rites, people are already inventing and reinventing alternatives. The dilemma, as I see it, is that the ceremonies, both mainstream and alternative, have so little to do with the hard realities of marriage. The wedding process, which should be about divining mates, making kin, and bridging differences, focuses instead on the cultivation of feelings and the performance of images spawned by the advertising, greeting-card, and pop-music industries. At the heart of too many weddings is collusion in a fundamental self-deception. Shaun Poisson-Fast confesses that the bride is supposed to be a blemish- and sweat-free icon. Japanese weddings proclaim, "This is the most splendid couple in all of Japan." And Monty, by uttering Deborah Laake's new name, will be able to pull her through the great curtain of death.

These are images, the stuff of extravaganza, worthy of a Cecil B. De-Mille movie; they move us, but they do not convince. There is nothing wrong with ideals; we all need them, but not at the expense of the truth.

We need weddings that prepare couples and families to face what they will actually face. We do not need weddings that wash everyone in a limelight that blinds them to the great dissonance between premarital romance and postmarital trouble.

Herbert Anderson and Edward Foley call such weddings "mythic," as distinct from those that are "parabolic."[214] Mythic weddings cover up the tensions inherent in a situation for the sake of homogenizing, idealizing, and oversimplifying. Mythic weddings obliterate the questions and doubts that lurk at the heart of every relationship. By contrast, parabolic weddings articulate troubles and confront paradoxes, refusing to gloss over forces that would undermine a marriage. We need ceremonial recognition of the *social* dimensions of marriage that will temper the almost exclusive concentration of North American weddings on the *emotional* aspects of it.

Rather than become cynical or moralistic about alternative weddings, it is perhaps more fruitful to consider a specific couple and a specific alternative ceremony. Two women, Yael Lee Silverberg and Luana Lynette Willis, one Jewish, the other African American, celebrated a ceremony in which they took each other as partners. The rite included traditional Jewish practices such as the use of the *chuppah*, along with elements from the African American holiday Kwanza. For example, the couple used a *mazao*, an ear of corn symbolizing communal effort and kinship. Two cups of wine were blessed: the *kikombe* cup of Kwanza and the *kiddush* cup of traditional Judaism.

Before the wedding, the two women wrote letters to their families, and after the wedding, Yael's mother wrote a response. These are excerpts from their correspondence:

From Yael to her parents:
Luana and I will be having a ceremony that will speak of our love for each other. The ceremony will take place in our synagogue and is formally called a *kiddushin*, or sanctification.

The decision to create a ceremony came quite naturally. We are people who believe in the importance of ritual, and we each know that the other person is the one with whom we want to build a family.

I know that this is not easy information for you to hear, for you do not understand my life choices, yet I believe that you do understand a desire to celebrate, through ritual, the love between two people. . . .

This letter is a difficult one to write. It is a hard one to read. I am sharing my life's joys with you only because I love you all.

From Luana to her mother:

I didn't realize how much I wanted you to be part of my "wedding" until I started shopping and planning. You have been there for me for every rite of passage. You have been my friend and mentor. It would be great to have you here now. . . .

Not only do I miss you being here, but I miss having my history at the wedding. I know that these are all old fantasies, but I guess I still have them and regret that they are not being fulfilled. I want my childhood friends there. I want your friends there. I want you to be proud. I want my brothers there. I want all of the significant people in my present life there to celebrate with me. I know that one of my fantasies is coming true, but the others. . . .

Neither Luana's mother nor Yael's parents chose to participate in their ceremony. From Yael's mother, Evelyn, to Yael and Luana after the wedding:

There was nothing in my thoughts and dreams for you that included gayness. I had hoped you would be a dancer or a teacher or a housewife or a career woman or. . . . It wasn't that I saw anything wrong with gayness, it was just that I hadn't thought of *you* as gay. . . .

When you [Luana] and Yael ate your first meal out of the same plate, I thought I would die. I had never seen anyone do that in all my life. . . . It was hard, because I was constantly bombarded with the sound of "Honey," "Sweetheart," "Darling."

I had to ask to see you [Yael] alone. I didn't want anything in particular, I just wanted to know if you were still you, if we could still talk about the things that we had always talked about or if you would talk with me differently. Well, you were the same, and after you left, I began the adjustment. My daughter is gay. My daughter is gay. Get that through your head, old woman.

Then came the wedding. My daughter was getting married, and I couldn't tell a soul. Well, that isn't quite true, I could tell some people. But no one said, "That's wonderful," so I stopped telling people. I couldn't tell anyone at work. I mean when Rob got married I told everyone, including the bus driver (you know how I am). But when you got married, I had to keep it a secret, because people ask questions and want to see the pictures. . . .

I don't want anyone to think that there is anything wrong with my daughter, my loving, giving, beautiful, talented daughter. The interesting thing is that my gay friends are the most fearful for you. They have lived the way that they had to live, but they know it's a hard row to hoe. They say to me, "Evelyn, I am sorry. I would have wanted an easier life for your daughter."

There it is, not well written. Neither cruel nor gentle, just how it is for me.

. . . The paper is gone and I'm hungry—so I'll say good night, and Love, of course, Evelyn.

Yael, telling about a visit to her family after the death of her grandfather:
My mother didn't even let me get settled before she asked to see the wedding photos I had brought. She and I went through them together. With tears in her eyes, she said that after the ceremony she had called my Aunt Terry and talked for hours, asking about every detail. She needed me to know how much she cared and needed me to know that there were many reasons she could not be there, the biggest one being that my father couldn't handle it. She said that nothing was more important to her than my father and their relationship together. While it was hard for me to hear, some part of me understood, for I hold that same dedication to Luana.[215]

From these letters and accounts we learn less about the actual rite and more about the tensions between the temporary "world" of the ceremony and the "real" world outside it. We hardly know what to call it. Avoiding use of the term *wedding* for a same-sex commitment ceremony can be politically motivated. Some lesbians consider the usage to be an uncritical aping of conventional heterosexual assumptions. Others continue using the term as an act of resistance; they refuse to let heterosexual couples exercise exclusive rights over it. Luana and Yael's "wedding" (they themselves put it in quotation marks) crosses several divides long guarded as sacrosanct in North America: black/white and female/female and Christian/Jew. This rite negotiates more than the usual load of social tensions that characterize conventional weddings.

At marriage, more intensely than at any other Western passage, primary participants become ritually active in designing, deciding, and choosing elements for the rite. Not merely being put through their ceremonial paces, they conduct research, scour their traditions, consult friends and relatives, negotiate values, and invent ceremonies. Luana and Yael work overtime, because they not only have to plan their wedding, they also have to sell it, convince their friends and family that what they are doing is sane, right, fitting, and worthy of recognition. In the end, the two women admit that some of their friends and family did not come through; they were too firmly rooted in other traditions or their prejudices.

We are used to thinking of rites of passage as moments in which one can rest upon tradition, drinking deeply of its nourishment. Since major life passages are stressful both spiritually and socially, it is no fun questioning the very ground you walk on; you want it firm. But the notion that rites are built on tradition is half a truth. The other half is that rites of passage are constantly being reinvented in the very process of being enacted.

So far, few of the large historic Jewish and Christian denominations authorize clergy to solemnize same-sex marriages, so the work of inventing them goes on in the margins. In the story of Yael and Luana, the ceremonial leaps, combining African American and Jewish symbols, are breathtaking, but even in the midst of executing them, both women are counting on and appropriating their respective traditions. Traditions innovate, and innovations are traditional. The collection of lesbian weddings from which this account comes is itself now part of a nascent countercultural tradition.

Luana and Yael's wedding is both interethnic and interfaith. We usually imagine an interfaith couple as a heterosexual pair; she comes from one religious tradition and he another. But interfaith marriages are not limited to the heterosexually inclined. In one respect all weddings are interfaith. They mediate the ultimate concerns (faiths) and communities of the main participants, and these are *always* different from one another. A rich socialite hooks up with a threadbare academic; a French-speaking Jew from Quebec marries a Chilean Catholic; an American scientist weds a Thai art historian; a young gay activist exchanges vows with an elderly gay mystic. Weddings, whether straight or gay, are always about bridging chasms and establishing a common ground, but some chasms are more dangerous than others. The hope is that participants will discover or create a common ground with enough solidity that two ever-changing people can dance on it for a lifetime.

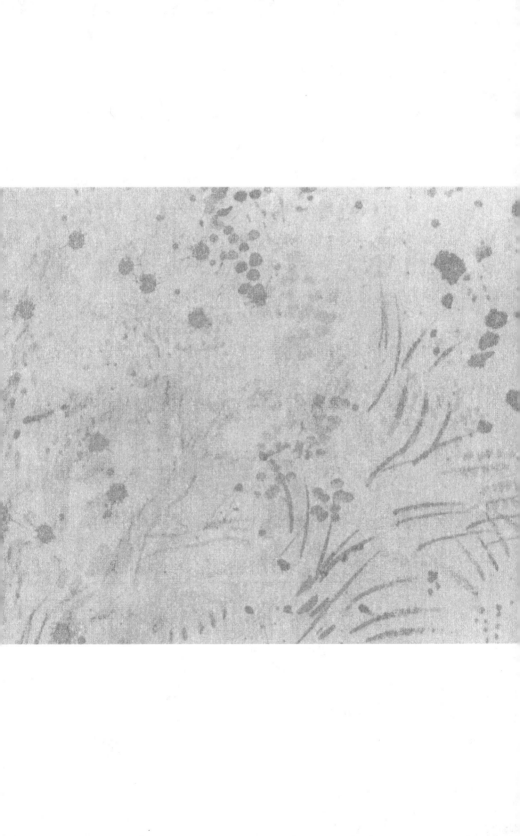

CHAPTER 4

Living with the Dead, Exiting Gracefully

Death is greeted with an outlay of ritual that far exceeds that of birth. More time, money, and resources are spent on funerals than on birth rites. Whereas few cultures have explicit birth ceremonies, many have elaborate death rites. Globally considered, having negligible or sparse death rites is exceptional. Even in urbanized North American countries where funerary sparseness is the reigning ideology, the decorum of death is sufficiently strong to command a temporary suspension of ordinary behavior. Whereas most of us have not experienced a birth rite, everyone knows what a funeral is. Funerals of important people are sometimes televised; births never are. Even if we in the technologically preoccupied West avoid talking about death, it is obligatory to respect the necessity of funerals. Failure to provide a decent funeral for a parent or mate is a ritual insult.

A few people such as the Mbuti of Zaire, the Hadza of Tanzania, the Baka of Cameroon, and the !Kung of Botswana and Namibia display little ritual activity at death. Christians in the Appalachian Mountains occasionally forego funerals, or they "funeralize," that is, put a dead body in the ground with no ceremony, waiting several months to have one when a preacher arrives.[216] The Navajos of the American Southwest expend few of their extraordinarily rich ritual resources on conducting death rites; strictures against touching or even speaking about the dead are exceptionally strong. Ritually resourceful in the face of illness, Navajos are nevertheless happy to turn deaths over to others, even white people.

Funerary sparsity in Europe and North America is often associated with memorial societies, most of which are consumer organizations. The Funeral and Memorial Society of America is a federation of non-profit societies.[217] The aim of memorial, or funeral, societies is to facilitate funerals that are affordable, meaningful, and dignified. They provide scanty resources on ritual but rich lodes of consumer information and practical advice.

Not only do death rites have a higher profile than birth rites, they also have left a more obvious historical residue than either birth or marriage. No other rite of passage inscribes such extensive markings on the landscape. Births, weddings, and initiations do not ordinarily leave enduring archaeological monuments. The Egyptian pyramids and the tomb of Chi'in Shih-huang-ti, China's first emperor, are visually impressive and rich sources of information about past practices, but birth, marriage, or coming-of-age rites leave few such remains.

I am often asked, "What sorts of things do people do around death, and why do they do them?" It is a simple, important, and difficult question to answer. There is infinite variation in the world's mortuary customs, but the motives for engaging in them are limited. As a result, the funerary gestures of others are largely recognizable to us, even though a few of them may seem bizarre if we do not grasp their meanings. Listed below are some of the most obvious motives for engaging in death rites, followed by examples of actions used to accomplish those aims. I refer to these actions as gestures rather than rites, because, even though they are stylized and convey meaning, some would not be considered formal rites.

anticipating death: listening to stories or sermons about death; contemplating or imagining one's death; learning to glorify, fear, or rationalize death; promulgating death wishes

segregating, observing taboos: wearing special clothing, for example, black "widows weeds"; using symbolic colors—black or white, for instance; not saying bad things about the deceased; refraining from public activities

mourning: weeping; wailing aloud; looking sad; avoiding laughter; walking slowly in processions; refusing to eat

marking an end to mourning: holding an end-of-mourning ceremony after a specified lapse of time; disinterring, cleaning, and redepositing bones; wearing regular clothes; remarrying

protecting survivors from the dead: verbally dismissing the soul; sending the spirit on its way; closing doors and windows; uttering protective spells to keep away ghosts; confining the dead to a specific, closed space

publicizing or announcing a death: publishing death notices; calling friends and kin; announcing a death; setting special times for observances

congregating, comforting: visiting or contacting the bereaved; coming together to enact a death rite; partying or orgiastic behavior; appealing to tradition, for example, by reading sacred texts or using religious leaders

showing gratitude, respect, or sympathy: attending a funeral; paying functionaries with gifts or money; sending messages of sympathy and condolence; offering to help; giving food; delivering or listening to a eulogy

demonstrating kinship or status, ensuring succession: being properly notified of a death; not remarrying too soon or at all; playing the role of widow or widower; writing wills; designating heirs; assuming roles— for instance, that of chief mourner, therefore, primary heir; being seen, being on display

dramatizing death's finality: making good-bye gestures such as touching or kissing the dead; putting the corpse on display; allowing signs of decay to be witnessed

maintaining and reconstructing social order after a death: placing limits on the expression of grief; displaying normalcy; demonstrating that "life goes on"; placing bereaved children in the care of relatives or guardians

denying death's finality: embalming; disguising the smell of putrefaction with perfume or incense; dressing up the corpse; using circumlocutions, for instance, "at rest" rather than "dead," the "deceased" rather than the "dead person"; believing in life after death; providing the dead with food, equipment, and clothing for their journey

releasing, integrating, embracing death's finality: laying a person on the earth to die; carrying ashes or bones to a final resting place; exposing a corpse so birds of prey may have their fill; pouring out water; breaking something, for instance, a pot or the skull of the dead person; burning, burying, exposing, or immersing the corpse; destroying clothing or possessions of the deceased; hugging or touching the bereaved; giving away possessions; speaking to the dead; saying good-bye

commemorating: making donations in the name of the deceased; conferring the name of a dead relative on a newborn child; retaining keepsakes—for example, locks of hair and photographs; erecting monuments, installing tablets, and setting up gravestones; lighting candles for the dead; honoring or praying to ancestors; visiting cemeteries; attending annual commemoration rites

In North America we place little emphasis on anticipating our own deaths. In fact, we avoid doing so with notable consistency. We observe few formal taboos at death and look askance at protracted mourning; therefore, it seldom occurs to us that we should formally mark its cessation. Since our public worldview does not include disgruntled ghosts, mainstream funeral rites assume little need to protect the bereaved from the recently deceased. When a death occurs, we announce it in newspapers, expect people to pay their respects, and congregate to garner comfort. At the funeral, the closest of kin receive special treatment, but there are no pronounced demonstrations of kinship status except perhaps at the reading of wills, an action normally separated from the funeral and burial. We have mixed feelings about the finality of death. On the one hand, we believe in its finality and urge each other to "get on with life"; on the other, we deny its finality by concentrating time, money, and energy on embalming, a way of denying death's finality. We believe in the private release of grief but not in the public or metaphysical release of souls. Even though funeral oratory often refers to "the other life," funeral rites de-emphasize gestures for sending souls elsewhere. On occasion we commemorate the dead, but we seldom regard them as ancestors whose advice and presence should be actively courted.

However many facts science has accumulated concerning death as a biological event, we in the West avoid occasions that would force us to contemplate death. We do not keep close company with the Grim Reaper. No matter how many murders lace the late-evening news or how many wars have been waged in the past fifty years, Old Death is not welcome at after-dinner conversations. With death held at bay, most of us expire unprepared, relying on professionals to do the work; they do it *to* us and *for* our families. In contemporary North America, death knowledge is professional knowledge, not personal knowledge.

Not only are we spiritually unprepared for whatever hereafter there may be, most of us know little about what happens at death in what our forbears used to call "this" world. Even the mundane actions surrounding death—embalming a body, building a casket, cremating a corpse, adapting a funeral rite—are foreign to us. Even though media and movies traffic in death, only a few of us preplan funerals. Not only do we ponder life insurance with circumspection and anxiety, we also postpone writing our wills.

Good Ways to Die

The dying process is implicit in being born. To be born is not only to be in the process of growing up but also to be on the road to death. But for most of us dying only slowly reveals itself as distinct from maturing. The curvature of life from ascent to descent is gradual. At least we would prefer it that way, so we organize much of our cultural and religious life to stave off the anticipation of death. But because we can anticipate our own deaths, even apart from a threatening attack, both the anticipation and the avoidance of death condition the ways we act. A culturewide refusal to imagine a good death tends to ensure that we will not experience one.

Death rites is a broader term than *funeral.* Death rites include memorials, exhumations, reburials, and even predeath ceremonies. The Bena Bena of Papua New Guinea have funerals for the very old before, not after, they die.[218] Narrowly defined, a funeral is only the most formal, liturgical portion of a postdeath rite. In funeral-home parlance, a funeral is the "service" that takes place after viewing and before burial. In popular speech the term *funeral* sometimes refers to all mortuary behavior from visitation through burial. Even the broad usage of the term *funeral* is still too narrow, since it excludes ritualized anticipations of death, preparation of the body, and commemorations of the dead.

In *Western Attitudes toward Death* Philip Ariès, a French cultural historian, bemoans the loss of the *ars moriendi,* the art of dying.[219] Trained in such an art, people presided over their own deathbed scenes. Ariès claims that doctors, not the dying, now preside over deathbeds. Some would argue that doctors more characteristically abandon deathbeds. In any case, dying people become largely passive and are no longer primary actors. Before the twentieth century, dying in Europe and North America was more consciously embraced and publicly performed. A dying person's deathbed scene was saturated with explicit death rites as well as ritualized social drama. Dying was a family, if not a public, occasion. Deathbed utterances were given special credence. To listen to someone straddling the great divide was considered an opportunity for spiritual growth.

In earlier times, says Ariès, not only did believers hear about death in sermons and daily discourse, they also actively contemplated the possibility of their demise. Not that our forebears looked forward to dying, only that they knew there were better and worse ways to face the inevitable, so they cultivated a good death, or perhaps more accurately, images of a good death. In prescribed ways they prepared themselves and their families.

Ariès's portrait is perhaps romanticized, a depiction of the exemplary rather than the average death. Not everyone achieved a good death. Some were lost at sea or dismembered. Others expired violently, accidentally, unexpectedly, or prematurely. Many died afraid and angry rather than speaking oracularly or departing at peace with their maker and neighbors. Nevertheless, people knew how exiting *ought to happen.* As with sex, so with death; they were ambivalent about talking too openly and frankly, but to avoid the powerful and inevitable was foolish. A good death, then, was one contemplated and prepared for. A bad death was the outcome of refusing to face your mortality until it was too late.

In the Middle Ages living a life permeated by awareness of death was most intense in monasteries, where certain religious orders encouraged their members to dwell on images of putrefying flesh and skeletal remains. The aim of monastic meditations on death was not to sadden or depress but to heighten your sense of urgency, your appreciation for the preciousness of life. You lived fully in the present because you had an eye trained on your ultimate destiny. Pondering death, far from being life denying, was meant to be life enhancing: "Stop and smell the roses today, for tomorrow, they—and you—die."

As late as the mid twentieth century, children were ceremoniously instructed in death awareness: "Now I lay me down to sleep, I pray the Lord my soul to keep. If I should die before I wake, I pray the Lord my soul to take." Perhaps the ritualizing of death's immediate possibility contributed to its routinization, but the intention was the opposite. Ritual preparation of the spirit was supposed to be a goad to readiness, a stimulant of spiritual alertness.

The notion that a death can be good may strike some as macabre. A death can be easy or hard perhaps, but good? The idea confuses us because we are prone to think of goodness in too moralistic a way. The idea of a good death is less about morality than it is about ritual practice. Dying a good death is a ceremonially stylized way of exiting gracefully. By ritualized means a grim necessity is transformed into a dignified and exemplary demise.

Because death is death, after all, the idea of a good or bad one may seem strange. But we still discriminate among kinds of death, even if we do so informally. We regret premature deaths and those of the promising young. We deplore mass deaths, suicides, and murders as well as deaths that take so long that they drain a family of its economic and emotional resources. We prefer deaths in ripe old age and deaths that appear peaceful rather than painful or regret filled.

Not just in early modern Europe and North America was preparing for death ritualized. Preparing to die is practiced in other traditions, even highly developed, in Buddhism, for instance. Buddhists not only tell enlightenment stories about awakening to the true nature of the self, they also recite tales about the deaths of masters. A master's death is exemplary. True mastery is not merely a matter of studying scriptures or teaching meditation. It is not even the supremely important art of living fully; it is the art of dying well.

Buddhist meditation is in one sense a death rite, although it is seldom called that. Meditation practice is about sitting attentively on the abyss between life and death without clinging to life as if it were good or fleeing death as if it were bad. Masterful dying, in meditative traditions such as Hinduism and Buddhism, is supposed to be harmonious with ritual meditation practice. As one practitioner puts it, "Die a little bit each day in meditation."[220]

Although the Soto Zen Buddhist dictum "Die sitting, die standing" is a metaphoric counsel of mindfulness, there are many stories about masters who died literally standing or sitting in meditation posture or who exited on cue at the strike of a meditation bell. The point of such narratives is not so much that Buddhists should imitate this way of dying as it is that people should live in ways that will eventuate in such a death. In Buddhism one's exiting is a summary, a grand metaphor, of one's life. Although meditation is primarily about living this life—here, now—life is inextricably wed to death. So it is that meditation becomes a ritualized way of preparing to die.[221]

Some Hindu and Buddhist dying stories are miracle tales, illustrating the spiritual prowess of the protagonist or legitimizing a teacher's successors. Others are parables meant to illustrate proper attitudes such as detachment or presence to the moment. Whether or not dying masters actually perform concluding ritual dramas, intending their deaths to be instructive, students nevertheless search their teachers' deaths for messages. Ritualizing, then, emerges from two sources: the ways in which masters perform their deaths and the ways in which disciples gather, invent, consume, stylize, and repeat stories about their teachers: "Sensing that death was near, Master Razan called everyone into the Buddha Hall and ascended the lecture seat. First he held his left hand open for several minutes. No one understood, so he told the monks from the eastern side of the monastery to leave. Then he held his right hand open. Still no one understood, so he told the monks from the western side of the monastery to leave. Only the laymen remained. He said to them: 'If any of you really want to show gratitude to Buddha for his compassion to you, spare no efforts in spreading the Dharma. Now, get out! Get out of here!' Then, laughing loudly, the master fell over dead."[222]

The good Buddhist death is sensed from afar. In traditional stories, death does not sneak up on the master unaware, since he is too well attuned for such an oversight. He neither shrinks back nor tips forward in anticipation. The master's death culminates in a posture, literal or figurative, that epitomizes the tradition. In this tale he falls over, consumed by laughter, but he could just as easily have died sitting in meditation posture or reclining Buddha-like on his side.

For the enlightened person, death happens; that is all. And one is in perfect accord with the event. Like breath, people come and go, but with practice, ritualized and regular, Buddhists determine *how* they go. Those who witness a master's death, usually disciples, are at once liberated (in this story, kicked out) and obligated (go teach; show your gratitude). The dying scene is simultaneously instructive and opaque. After it concludes, witnesses have something obvious to do, yet they will return again and again, peering into mysterious aspects of the demise in search of their meaning. A disciple's death ritual, then, does not begin when he or she dies but upon witnessing a teacher's death or hearing a graceful exit story that strikes home.

Do people actually die this way—laughing, instructing, quipping, sitting in full lotus position? Perhaps a few do. But these stories are myths of dying, stories told to inspire. The tales are not photographs of what masters do but portraits of what students imagine that masters, if they live consistently with their teachings, are capable of doing. The ritualizing of dying emerges not only from how "great beings" perform in their last hours but also from the telling and retelling of death narratives that bolster courage, evoke compassion, and instigate community. Dying myths are primarily about aspirations, secondarily about achievements. The question is less whether to believe such stories than it is whether their teachings permeate the lives of practitioners.

Even in the West we speak of one's "last breath," sensing the connection between living and breathing. In Asian meditation traditions, breathing is deliberately ritualized. Inhalations and exhalations are counted or imagined as having weight and color; the spaces between them are contemplated. Each breath is attended to as if it were one's last. Since one aim of practice is to extend meditative consciousness to everyday life, it is no exaggeration to say that breathing, simple inhalation and exhalation, is ritual preparation for death.

The possibility of an exemplary death worthy of emulation implies the possibility of a bad death. Zen Buddhists talk little about ways *not* to die, since doing so would imply "discriminating," clinging to distinctions that feed the illusion that life is good and death bad. Even so, an aspiring student would have to be dense to miss the point that a mindless, distracted, clinging way of dying should be avoided.

The Vajrayana Buddhism of Tibet is explicit about the terrors of dying badly. In this branch of Buddhism the art of dying is called *phowa*. *Phowa* is not a mere matter of bodily comportment and style—dying in lotus position rather than sprawled, mouth gaping open, on a hospital bed. Rather, it is a skill for negotiating the various levels of *bardo*, which one enters upon dying. The *Tibetan Book of the Dead* is not only a depiction of horrific scenes in the afterlife but a manual on how to survive the disorientation inevitable both during and after dying. This guide is not about funerary decorum but liberation. Whereas Zen Buddhist stories concentrate on the dying moment in the here and now, the *Tibetan Book of the Dead* focuses on the cycle of dying and being reborn. In both traditions death myths serve a preparatory function. Hearing and reading them ritualizes a practitioner's life so it can be lived with a heightened awareness of death.

In some traditions the enduring images are positive: Die like this if you can. In others, the more compelling images are negative: Whatever you do, don't go like Coyote. Coyote, or some other version of the native trickster, brings death into the world. Although death is an obvious necessity (otherwise, the world would be overrun with people), you do not want to imitate Coyote or Raven. You do not want to die as he does—self-preoccupied, oblivious of your connections to other people or the earth. He's a good example of what you should avoid.

It seems that North Americans of European ancestry have few compellingly good or disgustingly bad examples, that the medicalization and professionalization of death has neutered it. Not only does death lack a face or name, it is also neither good nor bad nor paradoxical like Coyote. We may have few compelling images or long-standing, powerful cultural myths about dying, but we do have values.

In *How We Die: Reflections on Life's Final Chapters,* Sherwin Nuland, a teacher of surgery and the history of medicine, describes death by cancer, heart failure, Alzheimer's Disease, and AIDS—ways of dying we would like to evade. He concludes with a chapter called "Lessons Learned." Eighty percent of Americans now die in hospitals, and he worries about the scene he sees repeated there, that of the solitary death. Nuland tells the story of his Aunt Rose's death and confesses his collusion in keeping from her the diagnosis of aggressive lymphoma. "We knew—she knew—we knew she knew—she knew we knew—and none of us would talk about it when we were all together," he admits.[223] Nuland questions what he calls the "rescue credo" of his own profession and weighs it against the patient's right to die. He wonders whether the physician's art of saving life should always assume the upper hand over the patient's art of dying.

In summarizing the lessons he has learned, Nuland proposes a credo of his own: "When my time comes, I will seek hope in the knowledge that insofar as possible I will not be allowed to suffer or be subjected to needless attempts to maintain life; I will seek it in the certainty that I will not be abandoned to die alone; I am seeking it now, in the way I try to live my life, so that those who value what I am will have profited by my time on earth and be left with comforting recollections of what we have meant to one another."[224]

As Nuland envisions it, a good death in contemporary America has several features. It is based on diagnostic truth but not dominated by medicine's need to be in control. It is devoid of needless suffering, and it is talked about openly, not weathered in loneliness. The aspiration, though compassionate, is bereft of ritual.

This picture is not, of course, how things actually transpire, but how Nuland would like them to happen. This contemporary credo is not quite a *vision* of the good death, since it lacks compelling imagery. It is not underwritten by a particular religion or even by the American Medical Association, and it is not the basis of a ritual system such as the medieval Christian or contemporary Buddhist one. So it is, rather, a *philosophy* of death that exercises prescriptive force.

There is no good reason why we should have either a single vision or a single philosophy of death. In fact, in societies as complex as ours, a multiplicity of images of the good death and the proper funeral are a necessity. Whether we think rites mask death or facilitate it, and whether we are inspired by visions or philosophies, we need occasions and places in which to contemplate death before it arrives.

Dying Scenarios

Most popular writing on death seems at first glance to be about how we *in fact* die and not about how we *ought* to die. In 1969 Elisabeth

Kübler-Ross's *On Death and Dying* popularized the notion that people negotiate the terms of their deaths in stages: First there is denial. Then one moves through anger, bargaining, and depression. Finally, one arrives at acceptance. Kübler-Ross's book was so popular that it became impossible to say simply "death"; one had to say "death and dying." But no one, Kübler-Ross included, has ever demonstrated that most people do in fact go through such stages, although no one denies that they *might* do so or that they *sometimes* do so. The notion of stages has been so influential that it sometimes functions like a talisman, drawing attention away from the actuality of dying and focusing instead on a scheme for analyzing a dying person's progress.

The fivefold scheme is occasionally useful for coping with death, because it conjures order in the midst of bewilderment, and it offers the possibility of a more or less happy ending, acceptance. Though radically different in intent and worldview, the Tibetan Buddhist idea of *bardo* and Kübler-Ross's scenario can take the edge off the fear and chaos that can make dying a terrible conclusion in the human life cycle. But like the threefold rites-of-passage scheme, this dying scenario can also distort the process.

Because they were named, schematized, and popularized, Kübler-Ross's stages have had considerable popular and therapeutic impact. The scheme has gone the way of most developmental scenarios, from description to prescription. It has became a tool for prodding dying people along the correct path. One *is permitted* to start with denial because one *ought* eventually to arrive at acceptance. Inspired by Kübler-Ross's phases, spiritual advice is tendered in the form of a supposedly nondirective question, "Don't you think you are in denial, dear?" But the interrogative mode hardly disguises the imperative lurking beneath the surface: "Hurry up and get through this phase; it is not good to die in a state of denial." Not only do others expect a dying person to follow the ceremoniously prescribed course, the dying themselves also expect their deaths to follow this course. If the trajectories of dying deviate, people may feel they have failed, died a bad death.

Is the application of credos and schemes ritual? Not exactly. But ritual action is prescribed (even though not all prescribed action is ritual). Ritual action is also sometimes based on mythic narratives or cultural values and the images that convey them. So in this respect, living a life calculated to eventuate in a proper death is ritualized. And when a particular kind of death is elevated to heroic proportions, held up for emulation, death is also mythologized. That such mythologizing and ritualizing may operate outside religious institutions does not dampen their effect.

Wouldn't it be better to approach dying naturally, without ritualizing, schematizing, and mythologizing it? Why is a ritualized way, riddled with oughts and traditions, any better than an unritualized way? Isn't there something artificial, even dehumanizing, about all the customs that crowd like vultures around a poor dying soul?

Protesting funeral rites is part of the American way of death. In the beginning of its nationhood the United States was infused with a Protestant ritual sensibility, one inclined to trim away liturgical excesses. First the frontier experience, then the experience of high mobility enhanced the American tendency toward funerary minimalism. But is it really "natural" to approach death without ambivalence—the attitude that drives much human ritualizing? Or to dispose of the dead without protracted mourning? What seems natural to us may seem anomalous to others.

In many societies death preparation is communal, distinctly religious, and laced with overt rites and explicit myths. In our culture, neither doctors nor funeral directors actively help us anticipate death, but their control during and after the moment of death is almost complete. Educators and psychologists now carry much of the burden once assumed by families and religious institutions. Since the 1970s the so-called death-awareness movement has attempted to educate the public.

Death education has become a legitimate topic, and there are journals devoted to the study of death such as *Omega* and *Death Studies*. The study of death now has a formal, academic-sounding name: thanatology. Like being suspicious of ceremony, preferring education to ritualization is part of the American way. Unlike, say, the Buddhist way, the American way places heavy emphasis on death research and therapy. Both are means not only of building cultural consensus and garnering support but also of mapping the terrain of death, insofar as it is knowable, and of advising travelers how best to walk it.

Every society has its avoidances—words you don't say, places you don't go, things you don't do. When sufficiently ritualized, we call these avoidances taboos. A taboo is not only something to steer clear of, it is also something charged and dangerous—potentially transformative, but also latently destructive. Most societies stigmatize certain ways of dying, so the death rites in which they culminate usually reflect these cultural judgments. Among the ways of dying we treat as taboo are death by murder, suicide, execution, torture, or lynching. Also, we do not want to go too soon or too painfully. More recently, Alzheimer's and AIDS have been placed on the list of stigmatized ways of dying, thus displacing older ways such as leprosy.

Certain ways of dying are borderline—sometimes tabooed, sometimes sanctified. A thin line separates martyrdom and suicide, for instance. In T. S. Eliot's play *Murder in the Cathedral,* Thomas Beckett struggles with the problem of doing "the right thing for the wrong reason." Deliberately getting himself killed could be an effective form of revenge against King Henry. But to die in this calculated way would not really constitute martyrdom, even if others were to interpret the event as if it were. Although we in the West find Japanese *sepuku* (better known as hara-kiri) baffling, we countenance heroic deaths on battlefields, even though running across a bullet-riddled zone in wartime can be suicidal rather than heroic.

To contemplate death in North America requires attention not just to the passive experience of dying but also to the active delivery of death, to killing. Because of the power of the media industries, we are most familiar with death in this form. Movies regularly proffer bad deaths as if they were good entertainment. Executions and lynchings, however devastating, are also theatrical; they are performed, witnessed, and consumed. In addition, they are riddled with the dynamics of scapegoating, a ritual process in which "others" are regarded as evil and therefore sacrificed to relieve "us" of our own burden of guilt. Although witnessing actual hangings is no longer fashionable, capital punishment and murder trials still draw media attention. We avoid thinking about our own mortality, on the one hand, but are drawn to the spectacular deaths of others on the other. The nightly witnessing of television deaths may not be a rite, but it is certainly ritualized.

It Took Two Funerals to Bury My Brother

If deaths can be good or bad, so can funerals. A good funeral is one that celebrates a life, comforts the bereaved, and facilitates working through grief. Some traditions accomplish this goal by making death seem the most natural thing in the world. Others do it by admitting death's absurdity and expressing the hope that it can be overcome. Whatever the strategy, some funerals are more effective than others. A funeral can stifle, amplify, formalize, or facilitate grief. The relation between the ebb and flow of human emotion and the forms and rules of ritual is complex, as Bill Myers's story shows:

When I woke up in this world, I was five years old and nobody else was there but my four-year-old brother, Terry. Nobody else mattered except Richard and Fox, our dogs. Terry and I were inseparable; he followed me everywhere. I was always going somewhere to fight somebody who had messed with him. Fighting was not in his nature. He loved life, loved things, loved everything, loved me. Nobody loved me unconditionally, without equivocation, like Terry. I loved him and protected him as if I were his father. I had to, because we had no mother or father to take care of us, just a mean old lady who hated us.

Then at thirty-four he was dead, shot in the head by a woman he was living with. And I wasn't there to protect him. Why wasn't I? I had always been there to protect him. During beatings in the middle of the night, I had covered him with my body. When others jumped him because he would not fight, I fought for him. When he was put in jail for something he didn't do, I bailed him out. I was always there to protect him.

I was eleven and Terry was ten when we abandoned that mean old lady in Mississippi. We moved to Cleveland to live with our mother, whom we had just met. We landed in a rat- and roach-infested tenement in the ghetto. But it was paradise compared to what we had left.

We met a man who would change our lives, the Rev. Cary McCreary. He wasn't looking for us; he was looking for a piano player for the storefront church he had just started. As providence would have it, he found us instead. He was a big man with a fast gait, a consecrated, old-style Baptist preacher who tried every day of his life to be like Jesus, a man who could predict future events in minute detail. He was not just our pastor and friend, he was the father we never had. He taught us hard work, love instead of hate, survival instead of self-destruction, respect instead of violence, education instead of hopelessness.

Rev. McCreary picked up Terry and me in his Cadillac and took us to Sunday school. He gave us work, loaned us money, baptized all three of us, ordained me, performed my first wedding, baptized and christened every one of my children, attended all my graduations. Then he preached Terry's funeral.

McCreary, God rest his soul, had always said that anyone missing more than ninety days of church without a "legal excuse" such as sickness or work and without putting some money in the collection plate could not have a church funeral. He declared that even if his mother belonged to this church and she broke that rule, he would not allow her funeral to be held in the church. Her body, he declared, would be sent to the funeral home.

On that cold February night in 1984, when Terry was shot, he died instantly. So the detective said. I went to my brother's apartment to gather up his things. There was blood on the wall, broken glass on the floor. I hadn't even given him his birthday gift.

When McCreary informed me the funeral would not take place in the church, I was shocked, then angry, embarrassed, and depressed. Terry and I had been like his very own sons. What would my students, some of them pastors, think? What would church members think? How would I act? How would a funeral-home burial affect the fate of my brother in the afterlife? Did McCreary, with his ability to predict the future, know more about running churches and conducting funerals than I did with all my training? When my children, students, colleagues, and friends asked me how I could be so calm during the funeral and trial, they didn't know how completely these questions consumed me. The pain was too deep, too theological, to be merely personal.

My oldest brother and a half sister I had never met came to the funeral. I was numb through it. I remembered that a colleague of mine had held the funeral of Count Basie and Moms Mabley in his church, and they didn't even belong to a church. I was trying desperately not to let anyone know what I was thinking or feeling. Despite my anger and embarrassment, I appreciated the eulogy. Rev. McCreary loved my brother and mourned his death greatly and openly. At the grave, McCreary allowed my friend Leroy to commit the body to the ground.

We returned to the church dining hall. Black Baptists have a long tradition of gathering to eat after a funeral. The meal is supposed to signal the end of mourning and the beginning of a celebration of a Christian life. Christians should not mourn like others, because their loved ones are better off being with Jesus than being here.

I wanted to go home. I preferred the other eating ceremony, the one in which people bring food to the house, the one that allows you to eat when and if you want, the one not disturbed by everyone coming up to you and saying the same thing over and over again, muttering how sorry they are and hurling some useless or misinterpreted scripture at you. I wanted to go to my mother's house. It was a stone's throw away from the church. But, no, to be respectful, I went to the dining hall.

Rev. McCreary was not a man to be delayed when it was time to eat. When he sat down, it was time for food to be on the table—right then. The family sat in a cramped space on hard seats as people streamed by our table to console us. I didn't want consoling or food; I wanted to be alone.

Finally, I couldn't stand the scene any more, so I did the unthinkable: I refused to eat, a clear sign that I was not celebrating in the way a Christian should. I stood, thanked Rev. McCreary, the church members, and all the others who had come. After I admitted I couldn't eat, McCreary displayed his anger by announcing in a loud and angry tone, "Let's eat."

I fled to mother's house, leaving the rest of the family behind. No one followed me. People were so stunned by such an audacious act that they didn't know what to do. Later, Leroy said that after I left, he couldn't eat either. So shortly thereafter, he left. So did a few others.

In the privacy of my mother's house I fell to mourning. My brother was gone—never to be seen again in this life. I would never hear his laughter, never hear him call me Bubba, never hear him ask me for a couple of dollars for gas. A part of me went to the grave with him, so I did in private what I couldn't do in public: I cried.

Thirteen years later, when my daughter Robin died, after years of struggling with lupus, she was the same age as Terry had been. Like my brother, she died within a week or so of her birthday. Robin had been my daughter Teresa's protector, just I had been Terry's. However, in Robin's last years, as her health failed, the roles reversed and Teresa became Robin's protector.

Robin's funeral was held in our church, where she had been baptized. Due to an illness, Rev. McCreary couldn't talk; therefore, he allowed me to run the funeral as I chose. I asked Leroy, who had known Robin since childhood, and he conducted the service in the way I wished. Colleagues, students, and friends commented on how beautiful the funeral was.

At the grave site, Teresa cried fervently, just as she had at her uncle's funeral. Then she asked, "Daddy, isn't this where Uncle Terry is buried?"

"Yes, it is," I replied.

"Well then," she said, "Robin is with Uncle Terry, and I know she's all right."

At that very moment I knew the final chapter of my brother's funeral had been written and concluded. After thirteen years, a funeral done right helped me find closure and peace, enabled me to gather my footing while standing on the slippery banks of the Jordan.[225]

The story of one funeral becomes the story of two. By telling the events in this way, Bill leaves us wondering, When does a funeral *really* end? If a funeral can be unfinished, requiring a second to complete it, why not a third or fourth? What if there is no end at all to the ripples created by a death? What if there is an insatiable need for sacred acts with which to resolve unfinished business left over from the past?

Terry's funeral is not hermetically sealed in the jar of ceremony. It is extended by means of Bill's memory and that of his daughter Teresa. Robin's funeral completes, even redeems, Terry's funeral. And Bill's telling extends the pair of rites even further. Even though death rites do their work by imposing definite limits in time and space, a ceremony's boundaries are permeable to the social forces surrounding it. A funeral rite is but a slender thread woven into a much larger social and spiritual fabric.

The second funeral, Robin's, brings closure. We are relieved when Bill lays claim to peace. But he is not naive, and we should not be either. His feeling of resolution notwithstanding, Bill knows he has not died and gone to heaven, where, we are told, problems are permanently resolved. Bill is standing, still, on the slippery banks of the Jordan, where things regularly slide back into indeterminancy.

There is, after all, the unfinished business of the Rev. McCreary's rule that determines who can and cannot have church funerals. The refusal of Bill's mentor to sanctify fully the death of one who didn't pay the expected Christian dues, along with McCreary's insistence that Bill demonstrate his faith by eating properly, sticks in the gullet. We have little choice but to believe this powerful preacher when he announces that he would refuse his own mother a church funeral if she failed to abide by the rules, his rules. So Bill's story of closure also opens up a new question, one about a third funeral, McCreary's. When he dies, what will his funeral resolve, and what will it leave dangling? Rites of passage do not always accomplish the tasks we assign them, and sometimes they accomplish others we do not anticipate.

What funerals actually do, or should do, is less obvious than we may think. Globally considered, there is a range of aims. Psychologically considered, there is a variety of consequences. Ritually considered, the official public ceremony may not be the most interesting or important one. So we do well to be cautious about overgeneralizing. Westerners sometimes reduce the work of funerals to facilitating personal grief. Our attitude is predictably psychological. Regardless of the otherworldly rhetoric of some funerals, we are certain that funerals are for the living, for comforting them and helping them work through grief. As a matter of fact, our funerals may suppress grief more often than they facilitate it. We leave serious crying for the home or the psychiatrist's office, not for funerals. Even though we conventionally say funerals do grief work, they are rarely cathartic.

Cross-culturally considered, the major aims of funerals are to support and protect the living; honor the dead; facilitate their exit from the society of the living; and initiate, if not complete, their incorporation into whatever level of existence or nonexistence the dead inhabit. Death rites may have other aims as well as other effects both intentional and unintentional. The effects do not necessarily coincide with the aims. Royal funerals typically become vehicles of state propaganda. Postfunerary meals afford families a chance to visit and hungry people something to eat. Sometimes the side effects and tributary events upstage the official performances:

About 1984, when I was a monk in the monastery of Entsuuji in the town of Imari in Kyuushuu, Japan, I became involved in the many memorial services and funerals that the monastery performed for the local families. One of the first funerals I conducted as the head monk of Entsuuji was for an elderly woman who had lived in a small farming village near the town of Imari. She must have been around eighty when she died. At a Japanese funeral there is a *chouji* instead of a eulogy. At *chouji,* a good friend of the deceased speaks, not directly to the assembled people, but to the deceased person. Of course, all the assembled people overhear, as they are meant to. Usually, the family arranges for someone to give an appropriately dignified and eloquent *chouji,* but anyone may come forward to say a final good-bye.

The funeral of this elderly lady was held at the farmhouse in which she and her family lived. The sliding partitions and exterior windows had been removed, so the interior of the house was completely open to the guests who gathered in the garden area outside. At *chouji,* an old man who had been sitting at the back of the assembled guests came forward. He wobbled on his cane as he approached. He sat down facing the coffin, and after a while, he started to sing in a low voice. I did not know the song and could not make out the words. After a few minutes, he finished and returned to his seat. I noticed then that a few of the women were crying. I did not know what to make of this scene.

A week later, I was back at the farmhouse to do the weekly chanting that follows a funeral for forty-nine days. After I finished and was drinking tea with the deceased woman's children and grandchildren, I asked about the old man and heard this story:

Both the old man and the deceased lady had been born in that little village. When young, they had fallen in love. But marriages then were strictly arranged by parents. And each was married off to someone else. Since the marriages had taken place in the village, they had lived within a short distance of each other for all of their lives. They saw each other constantly. Both had children and grandchildren. Then as they grew old, her husband died. A little later his wife died. In their old age they were single again, but since they were old, they no longer cared what anyone said about them. When she was not around, her children knew she was visiting him at his place. If he was not around, his children knew he was drinking tea at her place. The entire village knew the story.

The scene I had witnessed but not understood was that of the old man sitting before her coffin, singing a song to her. This was the first and only time he had been able to declare his love publicly.

Victor Hori, a Japanese Canadian and Buddhist monk, explains, "A *chouji* is not a eulogy. In a eulogy, the speaker addresses the audience. Everyone gathers to construct an ideal image of the departed person. People do not speak of the problems, the difficulties, the unfinished business they had with the deceased. Strangely, the deceased is lying there hearing this speech about him- or herself and is not really part of the conversation. In *chouji*, however, speakers come forward to finish unfinished business. Usually *chouji* express gratitude but quite often feelings that were never expressed while the person was alive. Some rites make the private into the public. A wedding stamps public recognition onto a love relationship which, before the ceremony, was private. The old man and the old lady in my story never got that chance while alive, so the old man made his love public at the *chouji*."[226]

To the Western ear this funeral has something of a matrimonial undertone, since it makes space for a love story. One passage can echo another. A wedding can feel like a funeral. Initiation can seem like a new birth. Birth can be a veritable initiation. Besides echoing one another, rites of passage sometimes piggyback. A parent's unfinished grieving over the death of a child can be finished at the funeral of someone else's child. Things left unsaid at one's own wedding can be uttered twenty years later at an anniversary celebration or while gossiping about someone else's wedding.

A Coffin Lined with Paper

Death rites serve several functions. For the dead, a funeral completes a life and facilitates a transition. A rite, however filled with personal remembrances, also depersonalizes the deceased, transforming a human into something else—a corpse, an ancestor, a god. For survivors, death rites offer consolation, garner support, facilitate grief, display loyalty, test the net of kinship, and declare hope in the face of meaninglessness. For the larger society, death rites are a patch stitched across a rip in the social fabric. Such ceremonies assert social control, reestablish equilibrium, and display social, economic, and political status. For professionals such as health-care workers, grave diggers, clergy, and undertakers, death rites provide work and remuneration. For religious traditions and institutions, death rites are an occasion on which to assert their relevance and confirm their privileged access to ultimate sources of meaning.

It is impossible to say with certainty whether funerals affect the destiny of the deceased. Despite myths of an afterlife, the promises of sacred texts, and the hopes of the faithful, none of us really knows *what* continues, and if it does, *where* it goes or *how* it gets there. People imagine life after death variously: as purgatory, as a final reckoning, as arrival in a longed-for paradise, as eternal suffering, as final liberation, as continual reincarnation into other forms, as reintegration with the elements, as entry into a world of shadows and shades, as becoming one with all that is. But in the end, what death is a transition *to* is unknown. Our knowledge about what's "over there" is a gaping void that we fill with imaginings or fears. Either that, or we resolutely determine to dwell in the middle of the void, refusing to imagine its contents.

Imagining is fundamental to the dying process, even if all we imagine is the final disintegration of a body. After an initiation, the community can watch to see if a girl behaves like a woman. After a wedding, people can observe whether the groom acts as husbands should. But after a funeral, one has to imagine the deceased as an ancestor or saint or devil or dust.

Death rites are squeezed between what we can imagine and what weighs upon us. A poverty-stricken Danish mother advised her son, "Poor people don't belong in heaven; they have to be thankful if they can get into the earth."[227] Not only is there a right way to prepare for death, there is also a proper way to be treated when you die. If death preparation is a sign of spiritual readiness, receiving a decent farewell is a symbol of a person's social standing. Even though we know that a proper funeral does not necessarily prove either love or respect, most of us act as if funeral rites accomplish or demonstrate things of considerable importance. A decorous send-off is as necessary for those who give little thought to heaven as it is for those who are certain about their postmortem destiny. However little a funeral may mean in the light of things eternal, most societies have not dispensed with them. However heaven tends its own gates, if those who tend cemetery gates won't admit you, you are less than human.

In Alto do Cruzeiro, a Brazilian shantytown in Bom Jesus da Mata, death is not the great equalizer; it is the great signifier of status: Poor in life, poor in death.[228] At one time the rallying cry of peasants there was, "Six feet under and a coffin of one's own."[229] Such modest requirements hardly seem to warrant rallying, but only from the point of view of the privileged who can take for granted the bare minimum.

People of the Alto cannot assume a burial of sufficient depth to prevent bones from working their way to the surface. Nor can the poor take for granted that their bodies will be left to rest in coffins. Coffins, unlined and hard, will be returned so they can be used again by another person too poor to purchase one.

The residents of Bom Jesus know well enough that as living people they have no land rights. Still, they would appreciate being granted tenure over the bit of soil in which they are buried. But the chances are slim; most will lack the resources to control even a postage stamp's worth of turf. Buried without coffins, they will be exhumed in a year if they are adults, six months if children. Their bones will be tossed unceremoniously into the municipal bone yard—ossuary we would call it, if our desire to be sensitive were allowed to override our knowledge of the indignity it is to land there. Even worse than having no plot is being unable to afford a decent coffin. Residents find it deeply shameful to have no proper coffin of their own. Some labor in abusive circumstances to ensure that enough money remains to buy a coffin. More often than not, their meager wages are insufficient to ensure they will be properly disposed of.

The people of Bom Jesus have a great fear of being dumped, without liturgical attention, into a dark hole. The rich are entombed, ensconced above ground rather than buried. They escape the rats, or so they imagine. The poor remember stories from the time of cholera, when people were buried so quickly that some were still alive. Driven by this historic memory, residents insist that a person not be buried on the day of his or her death. But to rules there are always exceptions. The rule is often overlooked in the case of infants. The children of the poor are at the bottom of the social order, less likely to have marked graves or sturdy coffins and to evoke elaborate ceremony or protracted mourning.

Dona Amor, almost ninety, tells Nancy Scheper-Hughes the story of her mother's death:

My mother, may Jesus and His angels embrace her, lost a bunch of children. Only a few of us survived. We suffered a lot in growing up, until everyone left and there was only me working to keep my mother housed and fed in her old age. . . .

Well, it turned out that it was only a week before my mother suffered this terrible fall that was to claim her life. . . . She called me to her side and said, "My love, I am not going to escape death this time, so don't forget about the little brass box where I have hidden away the money for my funeral." She wanted me to go and order her coffin and her *mortalha* [burial clothes and coffin decorations]. "My God," I thought, "what will I do now?" You see . . . , I had to spend a long time nursing Mama after the fall, and during that time I could not work. So from time to time I had to take out a few notes and coins from the brass box. I took out only what was needed, not a penny more. I could recognize the value of the bills from their colors. After all, was I going to let her and me die of hunger, *querida,* knowing all along that there was money set aside . . . ?

I felt very bad after this, and I walked the streets all that afternoon. When I came home my mother was very, very weak. I said to her, "Mama, I am not going to be seeing you very much any more." And we both cried. And all I could think of was that mother would die without anything put aside for her burial. But I lied to her: Don't worry, Mãe. I will go down into the street and order your funeral things."

"That's a good girl," she said. My mother was a simple person. It never would have entered her head that I could have spent the money from her special brass box.

I went to my old boss's house. "What is it?" he said. "Has your mother died?"

"Not yet," I said, "but she is at the portals of death, and I'm here to borrow the money I need so I can arrange her funeral."

"I don't have any money here," he said. Imagine that! And he was the manager of a big bank! But he said, "Just take this check, and with it you can buy what you need." Well, *minha santa,* ignorant race that I am, did I understand anything about bank checks? I thought my patron was tricking me, and so I took the check from him, but outside I tore it up and threw it away.

[When Dona Amor's mother finally dies, she does not know the money in the brass box is gone. Dona Amor has successfully hidden the truth from her mother and now has to bury her in "a piece of crap," a charity coffin decorated in paper rather than fabric and ribbons. By borrowing, improvising, and rationalizing, Dona Amor succeeds—more or less. She comforts herself by recalling that her mother had said she wanted to be buried in the same way as her husband. That much she gets. Dona Amor concludes the story of her mother's death by invoking a sacred story, one that relieves her of some of her guilt as well as the heavy burden of an expensive coffin.]

So I am content. If our sweet Savior could come into this world in a manger lined with hay, then my mother can surely leave this world in a coffin lined with paper.[230]

Few funerals escape compromise. One advantage in having strict traditions is that they relieve us of the burden of exercising choice. But for those who cannot live up to customary expectations, traditions are no relief. In fact, death rites may add to, rather than soften, the hard blow of death. Dona Amor, torn between the desire to feed and care for her ailing mother and the obligation to bury her properly, does what she has to do, even if some of her siblings are unhappy when they find out. The interests of the dead must be weighed against those of the living, the interests of one survivor against those of another, the interests of individuals against those of family and state. The necessities of the other, supposedly more real world have to be weighed against the requirements levied upon life in this one.

A Cloud of Earth for a Pillow

Subverting the wishes of a dying woman is dangerous, but death does not ensure that the danger is past. Even when dead, people clamor for attention, sometimes looming menacingly if the living do not pay it. In pre-Communist imperial China, the primary purpose of funerals was not mainly to comfort bereaved individuals but to enhance filial piety.[231] Death rites were not performed primarily for the sake of purging personal grief. Rather, mourning existed for the sake of cultivating enduring relationships between children and their parents. A child owed a dead parent at least three years of active mourning and, following that, less intensely focused ancestral veneration. It was popularly held that these years were repayment for the initial three years of the child's life, during which she or he was completely dependent on the parent.

Chinese death practices percolated up from a grassroots level to the imperial courts, but they also trickled from the top down, from rulers to peasants. Even when there is an imposed and accepted ritual pattern based on a widely read ritual text, as was the case in China, there can still be great local and regional variation in the way rites are performed. Ritual tradition and creativity are not mutually exclusive. The history of any mortuary practice, even in so-called traditional societies, is replete with debate and reform, cycles of ceremonial elaboration followed by movements toward simplification.

Before the twentieth century the pattern of Chinese funerals was widely standardized, having been propagated by the state and prescribed in ritual manuals such as the *Li Chi*, a copy of which was in many households.[232] Traditional death practices followed a pattern.[233] Death was announced by wailing and sometimes supplemented by pasting white banners on the house of the deceased. White was associated with death in China much as black is associated with it in Europe and North America. Although white clothing symbolized mourning, degrees of kinship were indicated by the kind of clothing put on.

In south China the corpse was bathed ritually with water purchased from the guardian deity of a well. The dead person was presented with play money, incense, and food, especially pork and rice. A soul tablet was inscribed with the deceased's name and installed on the altar of the family home or, in the case of the wealthy, in an ancestral hall. Specialists, funeral priests, were hired to manage the complex rites, since without monetary exchange the corpse could not be safely exported from the community. Piping and drumming typically accompanied the dead during crucial transitions. The deceased, packed so as not to move around, was sealed into a coffin with caulk and nails hammered in ceremonial order by the chief mourner. Finally, the coffin was carried in procession out of the city or village, concluding the formal part of the ceremony.

In Confucian China, *li* ("ritual") governed relationships between children and parents as well as between the people and the emperor and between the emperor and Heaven (one of the constitutive forces of the cosmos). Since ritual linked the cosmic and social orders, the proper way of behaving at death was, naturally, ritualistic. Chinese sages did not intend ritual forms to displace personal grief. Instead, they were supposed to facilitate it by providing form, without which only *luan*, chaos, would reign. *Luan*, the sages taught, was the natural consequence of a death, but it was potentially destructive. A ritual form without filial feeling could be empty, but bare feeling, unabashed grief

without ritual form, could eventuate in mental disorder and social an-
archy. In the Chinese view, ritual action, moral behavior, and one's
mental state were integrally related. Each reflected, and was reflected
by, the other.

Before the Sung dynasty (960 to 1279 C.E.), ancestor rites, including
those that marked death, were the purview of rulers and privileged
classes. Access to the gods was the exclusive right of such people. After
this period, however, peasants gained access to death rites. In fact, they
were sometimes punished if they did not observe them or if they practiced unorthodox, which is to say, Buddhist or Taoist, rites. Participation
in mortuary rites was a privilege in one era, an obligation in another.

Eventually, sponsoring elaborate and costly funerals became a means
of climbing the social ladder. The rules of decorum were elaborate, prescribing even the bodily details of feeling and demeanor that we think
of as private and psychological. Mo Tzu, a Chinese sage who lived
around 470 to 390 B.C.E., complains about, and caricatures, the expectations: "We are told that he [the mourner] must wail and cry in a sobbing voice at irregular intervals, wearing hemp mourning garments and
with tears running down his face. He must live in a mourning hut, sleep
on a straw mat, and use a clod of earth for a pillow. In addition he is
urged not to eat so as to appear starved, to wear thin clothes so as to
appear cold, to acquire a lean and sickly look and a dark complexion.
His ears and eyes are to appear dull, his hands and feet lacking in
strength, as though he had lost the use of them. And in the case of
higher officials we are told that during a period of mourning they
should be unable to rise without support or to walk without a cane.
And all this is to last three years."[234]

Mo Tzu complains that contemporary rulers believe they need outer
and inner coffins, jewels, weaponry, horses, musicians, and a long list of
other "necessities." He imagines that ancient sage kings were more modest, their grave goods simple and their funerals short. Today's officials,
he complains, "confuse what is habitual with what is proper, and what
is customary with what is right."[235] Mo Tzu's conclusion is that the family and state suffer unless funerals are conducted with more moderation.

Moderate or extravagant, funerals were of utmost importance to the
Chinese. Adhering to Chinese mourning customs became so essential
that it sometimes served as a key identifier of who was *really* Chinese.
Chinese death rites were more determinative symbols of Chinese identity than North American funerals are of our identity.

Living with the Dead

North American popular psychology places a great deal of emphasis on "working through" grief. The phrase does not quite imply forgetting, since forgetting would constitute repression, and repression is considered unhealthy. Still, "working through" connotes getting on with your life, not dwelling too long on those you loved: "Come on, Mom, why don't you try dating? Dad's been gone for a year."

When social scientists speak of "corpse disposal," we are reminded that we live in a society with a serious disposal problem, but should we speak of corpses, fetuses, or the senile in the same way we talk about atomic waste or urban refuse? All these topics are hedged by taboos, but they are of differing moral and spiritual orders. If the dead become merely part of our disposal problem, then our dilemma is not just practical but moral and imaginative as well. If we imagine the dead as "things," then hurried or truncated funerals designed to save time and cut through grief make sense. But if we imagine the deceased as people making a profound and mysterious transition, then we will construct funerals that take their time, becoming occasions for dwelling with the dead. If death is a quick commuter flight, we behave one way. If it is a picnic among relatives, some of whom have come on long journeys from afar, we act another.

Twenty-five miles southwest of Mount Olympus sons do not urge their mothers to get on with their lives by dating:

At the sound of the church bell calling the village women to vespers, I went out into the bright sunlight. A few minutes later a woman entered the graveyard dressed entirely in black, with a black kerchief covering her forehead, hair, and neck. She carried one large white candle and a handful of small yellow ones. After crossing herself three times she lit the white candle and one yellow one at the grave of the person she had come to mourn. Then she went up and down the rows of graves placing candles in the sand-filled containers at the foot of several other graves. Finally she returned to the first grave and began the elaborate procedure of preparing and lighting the oil lamp by the headstone.

Soon the graveyard was alive with activity, and a forest of candles burned at the foot of each grave. About ten women, all dressed in shades of black, brown, or blue, busied themselves lighting lamps and sweeping around the graves. Several women began hauling water in large buckets from the faucet in the church courtyard nearby. After watering the flowers on the graves they were caring for, the women began to wash the marble headstones with sponges and detergent kept in little plastic bags hidden carefully in the grass by the graveyard wall. So attentive was their care for the graves that some women would sift through the sand-filled containers throwing out clumps of melted wax or scrape old wax off the marble slabs with small knives kept just for that purpose.

After fifteen or twenty minutes, when most of this housecleaning had been completed, the atmosphere in the graveyard once again turned somber and quiet. Each woman sat on the grave of her husband, parent, or child, tending the candles and talking quietly with women at nearby graves. They discussed the crops, the weather, or the long-awaited summer visits of their children working far away in Athens, Germany, and the United States. Often their conversations dealt with matters closer at hand—funerals in neighboring villages, the expense of renting a cemetery plot in a large city, or the circumstances surrounding the deaths of their relatives who lay buried beneath them.

One woman stood near the head of a grave, staring at a photograph of a young woman. She rocked gently back and forth, sobbing and crying. Suddenly she began to sing a lament in a pained, almost angry tone of voice. Before she finished the long, melismatic line of the first verse she was joined by other women. The intensity of emotion in the women's voices quickly increased. The verses of the lament, sung in unison by the chorus of mourners, alternated with breaks during which each woman shouted a personal message addressed to her own dead relative.

"Ah! Ah! Ah! My unlucky Eleni."

"Nikos, what pain you have caused us. You poisoned our hearts."

"Kostas, my Kostas, the earth has eaten your beauty and your youth."

These cries were interrupted by the next verse, as the singing resumed. When the first lament ended, a woman sitting in the far corner of the graveyard immediately began a second. Finally, after singing three or four laments lasting perhaps fifteen minutes in all, the women stopped. The loud songs and cries were followed by quiet sobbing and hushed conversations.[236]

With minor variations this scene is performed once, often twice, a day in the Greek village of Potamia.[237] In 1974 Eleni was twenty years old when she died after a hit-and-run automobile accident. Because she had not yet married, she was buried in a white wedding gown, making her funeral—at least symbolically—her wedding. After the death, Irini, Eleni's mother, formally entered into mourning. She did not leave home to see people, attend church services and baptisms, or visit her own mother. She did not attend the wedding of another daughter. For five years, she left her house twice daily to visit the graveyard. Eleni's father not only mourned openly at his daughter's funeral, he also sang laments while herding sheep and goats in the hills.

Greek laments are not laced with sugar-sweet comfort. Some of them are extraordinarily graphic, depicting the earth and its creatures as consumers of buried bodies. Just as the living once ate off mother earth, so mother earth eats us. "Mother," complains a dead child, "here in the underworld where I have come / I found snakes twisted like braids and vipers curled like ribbons. / One snake, mischievous and smaller than the others, / came and built a nest above my head. / He ate my eyes, with which I saw the world. / He ate my tongue, with which I sang like a nightingale. / He ate my hands, with which I did my chores. / And he ate my feet, with which I used to come and go."[238]

The rural Greek cemetery is a primary space for carrying on relationships with both the living and the dead. Irini and Maria become neighbors by virtue of the fact that Maria's son Kostas is buried in the grave beside Eleni. At home Maria laments as she hugs her son's clothes. Neither woman is behaving abnormally. Both are acting in accord with tradition, so no one advises them to get on with their lives. At the cemetery the women share their grief and converse daily. The cemetery is a place for socializing, like coffee shops, malls, or city squares in other parts of the world.

North Americans fear emotional display at funerals almost as much as death itself. Distaste for funerals arises for two contradictory reasons: on the one hand, suspicion that ceremonial formalities stifle genuine feeling and, on the other, fear that funerals will not succeed in stifling emotional display.

The problem of managing the relation between ritual form and the onrush of feeling is persistent, but the relation among death, emotion, and ritual is not straightforward. We cannot be certain that ritualized mourning behavior is cathartic or even that such mourning is the direct expression of emotion. In some traditions there are professional mourners who are paid for their ability both to control and to let go of their emotions. The fact that their emotions are "theatrical" rather than "natural" reminds us that emotions of all kinds, not just grief, can be stylized, performed as expected. Likely most of us have been in ceremonial situations that required us to perform with solemnity or dignity or joy when we felt nothing of the kind. But in some cultures performed grief is standard ritual behavior, not hypocrisy.

Under the influence of Western romanticism, we sometimes imagine emotion as following a more or less causal sequence. Emotion is a well-spring rising up spontaneously from the heart. Emotion lodges in the throat, contorting facial contours and producing tears. The "heart strings" are tied directly to those we love, and when they die, their "downward" motion tugs at those strings, eliciting strong feelings. In this model the connection between the beloved's death and our emotional upsurge is direct.

Ritualized emotion, however, works differently. Weeping and wailing are not just personal expressions of affection but also social obligations: Greek women are *expected* to grieve. It may even be that the basic funerary emotion is not sorrow but togetherness or some other feeling such as relief. There is no reason to assume that emotion, on the one hand, and obligation or stylization, on the other, are mutually exclusive. It may be that a mourner, under social obligation, at first *performs* grief only to find that the performance itself elicits *felt* grief. My point is not that ritual mourners never feel grief but that we should not assume a one-to-one correspondence between what someone feels and what he or she expresses in mourning. We should be cautious about inferring either feelings or the lack of feelings from ritual performances.

After five years, as tradition requires, Eleni is exhumed, putting a formal end to mourning and releasing the mother from her tenure at the grave site:

Eleni's two brothers, who had started to dig down through the gravel and sandy soil, were soon overcome with emotion, as the intensity of the lamenting increased. When they began to cry, two young women took their shovels and continued digging. Eleni's brothers withdrew to the outside of the circle of women, where they stood quietly and awkwardly, men out of place in a women's world of death.

The loud chorus of laments could not mask the sharp ring of the shovels against the earth, nor could it blot out the increasingly violent cries and shouts of Irini and Maria. As the gaping hole in the middle of the grave grew deeper, Irini leaned farther over the place where her daughter lay, until she had to be pulled back by her sister. Eleni's father, much more restrained in the expression of his grief, though no less intense, would occasionally cry out: "You didn't live to accomplish anything, Eleni, anything at all."

When the earth in the grave turned a much darker color, and fragments of rotten wood appeared, the singing grew louder. The young women with shovels were replaced in the grave by an older widow with a small hoe. Some women shouted instructions to her, telling her to dig carefully: "More to the right. Find the skull first, then the ribs. Don't break anything." When she struck something solid with her hoe, she put it down and began to dig with her hands. The singing grew weaker; the melody was carried now by only a few voices. Irini, Maria, and the other close relatives continued their wild, angry shouting.

When the widow uncovered the skull, she crossed herself and bent down to pick it up. People threw flowers into the grave. All singing stopped, while the screaming, shouting, and wailing reached a new peak. The widow tried to wipe what looked like hair off the back of the skull before she wrapped it in a white kerchief. She crossed herself again and placed some paper money on the skull outside the kerchief. Then she kissed the skull and handed it to Irini.

Irini cradled her daughter's skull in her arms, crying and sobbing uncontrollably. The women behind her tried to take it from her but she would not let go. She held Eleni's skull to her cheek, embracing it much as she would have embraced Eleni were she still alive. Finally she placed more paper money on the skull and wrapped another kerchief around it, a kerchief which had been embroidered by Eleni as part of her dowry. Irini kissed the skull and touched it to her forehead three times before she handed it to Maria, who did the same. Irini and Maria embraced the skull together for several minutes, shrieking and wailing. Then they handed it across the open grave to Eleni's father, who greeted his daughter's skull as the others had before him. It was then passed down the side of the grave to be greeted by sisters, brothers, cousins, and others.

As more bones were uncovered, they were placed in the metal box by the headstone. Irini took the photograph of Eleni, which had stood for five years in the glass case at the head of the grave, and placed it in the frame on the front of the box. Women tossed small coins into the box as it slowly filled with bones. Eleni's skull was returned to Irini, who held it in her lap for the remainder of the exhumation. Some women commented on the blackness of the bones and on how well preserved Elenis's shoes, stockings, and dress were. Others offered advice as to where to find the small bones of the hands and feet. Irini reached into the metal box and picked up a severed bone from one of Eleni's legs, which had apparently been broken when she was fatally injured. She dropped it back into the box, crying: "You were a beautiful young partridge, and they killed you."

The widow was still sifting through the earth, in search of a ring, a cross, and a gold tooth. The lamenting gradually ceased, and women began to exchange fatalistic comments about human mortality and the inevitability of death: "That's all we are, a pile of bones. We are born, and we will die. Then we'll all come here." Two women counted the bones in the box and discussed the best way to arrange them. At last Irini was persuaded to let go of her daughter's skull and place it in the box on top of the other bones.

Suddenly all the women stood up and crossed themselves. The graveyard was filled with silence and the smell of incense. The village priest had arrived. . . . He poured a bottle of red wine over the bones, forming the shape of a cross three times. He continued to recite from the funeral service: "You shall sprinkle me with hyssop and I shall be clean. You shall wash me and I shall be whiter than snow. The earth is the Lord's and the fullness thereof, the world, and all that dwell therein. You are dust, and to dust you will return."[239]

These villagers are Greek Orthodox Christians, but their beliefs and practices are a mixture of Orthodoxy and traditional folk beliefs. A description of the official Orthodox rites that follow the events recounted above by Loring Danforth would present only a fraction of rural Greek death ways. The mortuary process in this part of rural Greece is complex, involving home, church, and cemetery, and there are several phases: preparation and laying out the body at home; procession to the church; the Orthodox funeral service; and memorial services on the third, ninth, and fortieth days after death and two more, six months and one year, respectively, after the death. Exhumation, the final rite, occurs five years after death.

In rural Greece, if rites are not properly performed, the deceased cannot be fully incorporated into paradise. The state of the bones at exhumation is indicative of the state of the soul.[240] If, on the one hand, the flesh has decomposed and the bones appear clean and white, the soul has completed its journey. The relatively permanent nature of bone symbolizes the eternal nature of the soul. If, on the other hand, hair and flesh continue to cling to the bones, the transition process is unfinished and the bones are reburied. Prayer, additional memorials, and more time are necessary. Flesh symbolizes the transient nature of the body. If the deceased died violently, unforgiven, or under the influence of a curse or excommunication, the decomposition will be tellingly incomplete. Although a few people, mostly men, insist that decomposition is the natural result of soil and climactic conditions, others hold that morality rather than nature determines the state of the bones.

Once bones are exhumed and deposited in an ossuary, the deceased gradually becomes part of the anonymous dead. This secondary burial more or less completes the funerary process. I say more or less because even after exhumation there are memorials and remembrances for the collective dead. They are held on Soul Saturdays. Each year several such ceremonies are held, and the names of the past few generations of dead are recited.

Except in the Orthodox funeral service, at which a male priest officiates, women are the primary actors around death. Between the first of the memorial services and the exhumation, bereaved women make one or two visits a day to the cemetery. Cemetery ritual is determined by customary practice rather than formally mandated by a ritual book. The more formal aspects of it consist of laments, many of which are conversations with the dead. The following example stitches together specific biographical details with general mythological themes and characters: "Eleni, you didn't cry out so that we could rescue you." / "How could I cry out? How could I answer your call? / My mouth was gagged. There was a kerchief around my neck. / And that vicious Haros [death personified, an angelic messenger] was raining blows down on me."[241]

Another lament takes up the widespread theme of death as a process of being eaten: "Tell me, tell me, my darling: How did Haros receive you?" / "I hold him on my knees. He rests against my chest. / If he is hungry, he eats from my body, / and if he is thirsty, he drinks from my two eyes."[242] By means of ritual laments death is made graphic and real, but at the same time the harsh split between life and death is momentarily overcome.

The Greek dead, like the living, desire human company, hence the importance of grave visiting. The dead have needs that resemble those of the living. Graves are homes, and candles provide light for the inhabitants. Food consumed by mourners feeds the dead. As one woman put it, an elaborate funeral sends a husband off "well fed and pleased."[243] A variety of symbolic foods and ceremonial meals are connected with the funerary process. Eating and being eaten are major themes linking women's activities in death to those in ordinary life.

Women bear the burden of washing, feeding, and caring for the dead, just as they do for the living. Because of Greek marriage and work patterns, wives regularly outlive their husbands, resulting in what one might call a widow culture. In a widow culture, death is a central fact. Death does not prevent women from carrying on relationships with one another or with the dead; if anything, death amplifies their relationships. Women typically bury their husbands, but widowers have no parallel responsibility for burying their wives or tending their graves. Instead, these responsibilities usually fall to a daughter-in-law, the wife of the youngest son.

The ritualizing of death in graveyards is carefully watched and overtly criticized by villagers. Proper grave tending is an obligation implied by the right to inherit. The primary activities are grave visitation and musical lamentation, but dreaming about the dead, naming children after the deceased, and hoping for the resurrection also keep the dead alive. Caring for the dying and dead is one way to repay an obligation; naming one's children after a grandparent is another. By preserving his or her name, the deceased will be remembered. Dead people feel joy at having their names passed as gifts to young people. In effect, the dead are resurrected by means of, or into, ritualized behavior.

Yet, these same rites also depersonalize the dead. The deceased are made more fully dead by the drama of a funeral liturgy and exhumation rite, so the ceremonial victory over death is only short-term. In the long run, even the Greek dead fade, becoming less and less individualized as time passes. Greek women learn to hold two paradoxically related attitudes. On the one hand, in their graphic laments they imagine the dark and dreary aspects of afterlife; they are blunt in expressing their pessimism about the future. On the other hand, they believe in, or at least hope for, eternal life by way of their participation in the resurrection-centered liturgies enacted by the Greek Orthodox Church.

In North America the dogged, long-term care of the dead by Greek women would be labeled denial, a refusal to come to terms with the finality of death. Some might wish the women spent their time caring for the sick, or even the dying, rather than chanting to and chatting up those already dead. There is an enormous difference, after all, between the five-year Greek mourning period and the typical three-day bereavement leave granted by American and Canadian employers.

But from the point of view of a Greek widow, the North American haste to get on with life is a blatant refusal to assume responsibility or act in a caring way. In one lament the speaker says of her grief, "I will go to a goldsmith and have it gold-plated. / I will have it made into a golden cross, into a silver amulet, / so that I can worship the cross and kiss the amulet."[244] Grief is not to be vetted but cherished; keeping grief alive is one way of knowing that you yourself are not dead. Cemetery visiting is a way of achieving catharsis, a method of purging grief, and a way of cultivating it. The culture of these rural Greek women is largely a culture of death, but their dead are alive. Although exhumation is supposed to incorporate the deceased into the world of the dead, grief, particularly that of a mother, is "a wound that never heals."

The Release of a Hungry Ghost

But what about those who die without healing? Like all rites, those surrounding death condense a people's cosmology, their most fundamental, taken-for-granted images and assumptions about the nature and destiny of human life. The European American West is comparatively dogmatic in believing that the line between life and death is clear and definite and that the dead do not require the ritual efforts of the living. Even though an occasional individual may be stranded, having been rendered a "vegetable" by mishap or medical error, we nevertheless cling to the clear distinction between the living and the dead with the tenacity of faith. An occasional smudge of the boundary line does not squelch confidence in its basic clarity.

Even reports of near-death experiences do not threaten the public's confidence that there are only two sorts of human beings, the quick and the dead, and that the latter are less than human. Ghosts, the restless and hungry dead, even though they are objects of contemporary popular fantasy, are considered figments of the imagination. They inhabit Gothic novels and horror films but not real life. Like figures of speech, these figures of the imagination fascinate but have not earned the right to be considered primary actors in Western funeral rites.

Faith in the distinction between the living and the dead is buttressed by the split between the self and others. A key Western dogma is that of the singular self. In our cosmology spirits neither "inhabit" nor "ride" the living by possession, reincarnation, or any other means. Except in fiction and in the gushy rhetoric of weddings, a person is definitely one—not two.

Or so it would seem. Even in the West we sometimes talk as if the self is divisible into a mortal part (the remains) and an eternal part (the soul or spirit). However we put it, or avoid putting it, death raises questions about the nature of reality and the constitution of the self, and death rites are predicated on the answers we give to such questions. It also works the other way around: Rites teach us the expected answers to such questions.

In any case, religions exist in which intermediate zones are interleaved between life and death, leaving human identity with fuzzy rather than clear boundaries. In such traditions, the work of death rites is not restricted to funerals or even ceremonies enacted close to time of death. Death rites may be retroactively performed:

Fifteen years ago, I was leading a meditation program at Rocky Mountain Dharma Center (RMDC), a retreat facility high up in the mountains near Red Feather Lakes, Colorado. We were conducting the program in a group of buildings owned by the Girl Scouts. One night, a participant heard someone cry out in a high, sharp-pitched, mournful voice. On subsequent nights, others heard it.

A woman who worked at RMDC said it wasn't unusual to hear this sound and that people had been hearing such cries for the past couple of years. She then told the story of a little girl, perhaps ten years old, who had been killed here a number of years before. She had been climbing on some rocks that tower up behind the camp. Her parents had been battling each other for years. The family, in tremendous disarray, was disintegrating. The girl's parents had finally decided to divorce, so they had sent her away for the summer to remove her from the situation. She was beside herself with anxiety, loneliness, and fear.

One day, the girl fell from the rocks and was gravely injured. Brought into a nearby cabin, she died there. After this tragedy, use of the camp by the Girl Scouts tapered off. There were even thoughts of selling the place.

The Tibetan teacher Trungpa Rinpoche, informed of this story, said the sound was probably a hungry ghost who was stranded, attached to this physical locale, unable to move on to a better rebirth. He suggested planning a Sukhavati ceremony for the little girl. The Sukhavati is a traditional Buddhist ceremony performed for people after they die to encourage them toward a favorable rebirth. It is also done to help a hungry ghost, stuck in a state of attachment and unfulfillment, on its way to better rebirth.

Those of us participating in the retreat, most of whom had been Buddhists for many years, decided that now was the time to perform the Sukhavati. One of my friends, well acquainted with the story, took me into the cabin and up to the room where the little girl had died. The air of sadness and grief in the room was palpable. It was upsetting to sit on her bunk and feel it.

I didn't lead the ceremony. In fact, I thought, "Well, maybe this is real and maybe it's a collective fantasy." I had my doubts. Whenever you are in this "flat world," you always have doubts. The only part you can prove is the flat part; the rest you cannot prove. The part that is not flat is accessible only through intuition.

I was sitting there with all my doubts, but I was paying attention because I was curious. At a certain point in the ceremony, the officiant snaps his or her fingers to release the trapped ghost. When the woman officiating snapped her fingers, I saw a being rush off to the east. A sudden sense of joy filled the room. I was taken completely by surprise and felt as if I had been hit by lightning. In that moment, I was sure that the notion of hungry ghosts had something objective to it, that it was not just a way of talking about a human state of mind. I understood why Tibetans feel so strongly about ceremonies that make connections with beings in other realms. For Tibetans, we humans are in a unique position to help beings in other realms who may be suffering terribly and are otherwise without recourse. I realized why Tibetans become so upset when Western Buddhists want to jettison any belief in realms of existence other than this flat, immediately visible, human one. When one is dealing with other realms, flat-world instruments don't apply.

Subsequent to our performance of the Sukhavati ritual, the air of sadness that hung over the room where the little girl had died dissipated completely. The mournful cries were no longer heard at night. People at RMDC stopped talking about the tragedy. The Girl Scouts began using the camp more frequently and a new board decided against selling the property.

The people who now manage the camp do not seem to be familiar with the incident of the little girl's death.[245]

Contemporary views of ritual would have us believe that rites exist for the sake of their psychological and social effects. Ritual is a flat-world device, but it can also be a way of interacting with the multidimensional world. Performers use it to connect with powers and entities on other planes, those that, although they exceed the human grasp, are tangible if approached attentively and with due ceremony.

In Reggie Ray's story above, *sukhavati* is not performed to make participants feel better about themselves, to consolidate group feeling, or even to inculcate the Buddhist moral value, compassion, even though the rite accomplishes all these. Its aim rather is to straighten out a warped state of affairs; to unhook a sentient being hanging from a shard at the edge of the universe. The *sukhavati*'s removal by several years from the time of the girl's death divests the rite of what we Westerners normally consider the usual funerary motive, that of comforting a family in its loss and of paying respects to the dead.

"Was a ghost actually trapped, and did the performance of a mere ceremony release her?" This is a flat-world question, to which the flat-world answer must be, "Who knows?" Reggie's doubts authorize us to articulate our own doubts if we are so inclined. But his conclusion also encourages us to consider the possibility that there may be more than two dimensions, or even three. Across the world it is a widespread view that the dying and deceased are susceptible to influence by ritual means, perhaps *only* by ritual means. How else could we humans even imagine assisting a dead, but still wailing, ten-year-old girl?

It would be ethnocentric to build into the definition of "rites of passage" the conviction that a funeral is the "last rite" or to require allegiance to a credo declaring that, after death, there are no further passages to be made. Our definition of death rites must be large enough to include not only ritualized preparation for death and rites performed near the time of a death but also ritual activities that follow long after the occasion of a person's death.

Dancing with the Dead

So far we have been considering rites of passage that mark the deaths of individuals. But not all death rites are rites of passage, ceremonies that mark a moment in a person's life cycle. Some are occasioned not by the event of a specific death but by a seasonal, or calendrical, recognition of the dead.

In the Christian world November 2 is known as All Souls' Day. Although part of the Christian liturgical calendar, this day is not widely celebrated in English- or French-speaking North America. The preceding day, All Saints' Day, is slightly better known. More widely observed than both is the evening of October 31, All Hallows' Eve, popularly called Halloween.

The Mexican counterpart of this festival is called *el Día de los Muertos*, the Day of the Dead. All over Mexico, even in rural areas, Day of the Dead symbols are bandied about for political, commercial, and artistic purposes, as well as religious ones. The day has become a national symbol of Mexico itself. Not merely a rite dutifully observed, the Mexican Day of the Dead is festive even though it celebrates death. Canadians and Americans have few occasions on which death and festivity, tears and laughter, publicly coincide, so to them the atmosphere of this Mexican fiesta is incongruous but intruiging.

The appearance of skeletons on Halloween as well as on *el Día de los Muertos* is an obvious iconographic link between the Mexican observance and that of Mexico's Anglicized neighbors to the north. But Halloween is child focused and rarely an occasion for contemplating the dead, death, or even horror, despite the masks that herald its arrival. In contrast, the Mexican Day of the Dead is about tending and nurturing the links of extended families with their ancestral dead.

On the Day of the Dead, Mexicans visit the graves of friends and relatives. The living picnic among the deceased, cleaning and decorating their earthy abodes, the graves. The living chat with neighbors and relatives, exchanging stories about the dead. The deceased—some sainted, most not—are, ritually speaking, an integral part of society.

Although names of the dead may be remembered for several generations, personalities of dead people begin fading after their funeral. But the anonymous collective, "all souls," continues its existence, requiring ritual attention from the living.

The Day of the Dead, although part of the Christian calendar, incorporates attitudes and images that are unique to Mexico, with its confluence of Spanish and indigenous symbols. The day triggers an avalanche of folk-art forms: toys, food, grave decorations, statues, paintings, songs, and poems. Families build domestic altars on which to display pictures of the dead, to whom are made offerings of drinks, incense, candles, flowers, water, and food (even if, in popular lore, disembodied souls can only smell, not actually eat, the food). Marigolds, chrysanthemums, and other brightly colored flowers are everywhere. Places are set at dinner tables for deceased family members, their empty chairs trumpeting their absence. Special foods are prepared: red or blue corn tamales, mole (meat cooked in a sauce made of cocoa, chili, and ground peanuts), pulque (a cactus liquor), and *pan de muerto,* "bread of the dead." One is especially favored if she or he bites into a piece of bread containing a tiny skeleton. Death toys are distributed to children, dead ones in their graves as well as living ones in their homes. Skulls and other reminders of death made of sugar are consumed with gusto. Eating death is at once a way of defying and submitting to it.

The Mexican relationship with death is not only respectful and somber but jocular, ironic, even defiant. *Calacas,* skeletons representing the Grim Reaper, are ubiquitous. *Calaveras,* "skull" verses, are satirical lines, often in the form of obituaries written by dead authors: "This gay skull invites mortals today / To go to visit the infernal regions. / There will be special trains as amusements during this trip, / And there won't be any need to wear a new outfit."[246] In cities as well as rural areas, *calaveras* lampoon the living—the town drunk or even the mayor— with ironic eulogies.

Day of the Dead iconography is less informed by heavenly bliss than it is by infernal irony. So statues of skeletons not only wear wedding dresses or ride bulls, they smoke and fall, bottle in hand, into drunken stupors. Hell bound, they forget their clothes and are less than modest.

Although there is probably some truth in the claim that the Day of the Dead arises from a unique convergence of native and medieval Spanish Christian elements, the contemporary forms became recognizable only during the Mexican revolution, between 1910 and 1930, a period when death was, in fact, at everyone's elbow. *Corridos,* ballads, were written to prepare people for the necessity of death in combat. So the first use of Day of the Dead death imagery was propagandistic and nationalistic, not mystical and religious. After the revolution, the media continued the iconographic tradition, putting the imagery to commercial use.

The Day of the Dead has had its literary and artistic popularizers. Octavio Paz, whose book *The Labyrinth of Solitude* was translated into English and widely read by English-speaking North Americans and Europeans, popularized the romantic view that many of us now hold of the Mexican love affair with death: "To the inhabitant of New York, Paris, or London," wrote Paz, "death is a word that is never uttered because it burns the lips. The Mexican, on the other hand, frequents it, mocks it, caresses it, sleeps with it, celebrates it; it is one of his favorite toys and the most permanent lover. It is true that in his attitude there is perhaps the same fear that others also have, but at least he does not hide this fear nor does he hide death; he contemplates her face to face with impatience, with contempt, with irony."[247]

But not all Mexicans are so happy with a portrait that casts them as death's lover. Aunt Guadalupe died in squalor on the Day of the Dead, 1962. Guadalupe's niece Consuelo Sánchez had prayed just two days before, on All Souls' Day, to San Martín de Porres for a miracle. If she was not to be granted a miracle then, please, at least a chance to see her aunt before she died. Consuelo got no such chance. Word of her aunt's death arrived before she could pay her a visit:

Then I looked directly at Saint Martín on his marble pedestal surrounded by lighted candles and I said to him, "Brother Martín of Porres, if it is true that you can perform miracles, I challenge you to heal my aunt—overnight. That is the only thing that will make me believe in you."

Saint Martín didn't take up my challenge and now I scolded him, "You are bad. I don't love you. You revenged yourself. Why? Why? I prayed so hard."

What can I say to express the pain that has drained away the last drop of joy from my heart? I have never been able to accept death the way it comes to people in my class. We are all going to die, yes, but why in such inhuman, miserable conditions? I've always thought there was no need for the poor to die like that. Their struggle is so tremendous . . . so titanic . . . no, no, it isn't fair. They can be saved. I refuse to resign myself to death in that tragic form.

There are authors who have written that the Mexican cares nothing about life and knows how to face death. There are jokes and sayings and songs about it but I would like to see those famous writers in our place, undergoing the terrible, hideous sufferings we do, and then see if they are able to accept the death of any one of us with a smile on their lips, knowing that the person didn't have to die. It's all a big lie. The way I see it, there's nothing charming about death nor is it something we have become accustomed to because we celebrate *fiestas* for the dead or because we eat candy skulls or play with toy skeletons. . . . No, the death of a loved one is not accepted, anyway you look at it.

. . . Why do we insist on carrying on that absurd masquerade, the gigantic lie that hides the real truth here in this "republic" of Mexico? "We, the Mexicans," amid "this prospering beauty with its politically strong, economically solid foundation . . . " Oh yes, we are making progress. We are advancing in technology and science; the steel structures are rising over the corpses.[248]

Here, Consuelo is still grieving for her aunt, but her grief does not authorize one to dismiss her anger. She knows there is a contradiction between *el Día de los Muertos* and the experience of dying in poverty. She reminds us that however willing death is to play the butt of verbal and pictorial jousting, and however well it receives jests and tolerates ironies, death is still not a loved one. Celebrations of death, even if they do remind us of our mortality, should not be allowed to cover up the fact that dying is neither cute nor acceptable, especially if you are poor. The story that Consuelo and her brothers tell Oscar Lewis, who recorded the narrative, reminds us of the distance between Day of the Dead coffee-table books, with their array of gloriously colored, taunting, playful images and the harsh realities of dying Mexican, female, and penniless.

Death rites never provide answers. In fact, celebrations often spring up around questions that are by their very nature unanswerable. Ritual is a way of performing, thereby becoming identified with, our most troubling questions.

The American Way of Death

In some respects scholarship on death is better informed about the rites of other cultures than it is about our own. Although there is an enormous amount of literature, much of it recent, on "the American way of death," it pays scant attention to death rites, focusing instead on general beliefs and attitudes toward death, grief counseling for the bereaved, or the economics of funerals. So not only is the general population distanced from the dead, but scholarly knowledge about death rites in the United States and Canada is scant.

One of the most widely used and respected textbooks on death is Robert Kastenbaum's *Death, Society, and Human Experience.* Originally published in 1977, the book is now in its sixth edition, and it is as near as one can get to a comprehensive survey of death trends and thanatological research in contemporary America. Kastenbaum introduces the idea of the death system, defining it as "the interpersonal, sociophysical and symbolic network through which an individual's relationship to mortality is mediated by his or her society."[249] He understands well the complex network in which death occurs. The people, places, times, objects, and symbols of a death system work together to achieve several aims: warning about and predicting death, preventing death, caring for the dying, disposing of the dead, consolidating groups after a death, making sense of death, and delivering death, which is to say, killing.

A death system, then, includes much more than death rites. But since our concern here is with death ritual, it is revealing to note the space Kastenbaum allots to it. Only one of his fifteen chapters is devoted to the funeral process. Within this chapter, half a page is spent on the funeral service, even though Kastenbaum calls it is the "centerpiece of the entire process."[250] If this authoritative textbook's representation reflects either the state of American thanatology (the study of death) or the state of American attitudes toward death, then death rites are of minor importance to both the American way of death and to American research on death. The American way of death is more focused on emotions, relationships, and ethical issues than on ritual processes.[251]

The popular avoidance of the topic of death, coupled with the intellectual focus on nonritualistic issues, makes it difficult to paint a full or accurate picture of American death rites. Our only alternative, then, is to understand the construction the "American way of death" and to pay close attention to how it works in the literature.

In 1963 Jessica Mitford's book *The American Way of Death* popularized the notion that there is a distinctively American way of dying. This idea is seldom challenged or even questioned. In her characterization, the most telling feature of the American way is its commercialization, the sale of expensive caskets and costly embalming services to the bereaved, who, in their moment of vulnerability, naively sign on the dotted line without reading the fine print. Writing in the tradition of journalistic muckraking, Mitford exposed manipulative schemes perpetrated by undertakers and railed against their overcharging. She counseled better planning and wiser spending. She said little about the structure and content of funerals. In the wake of her book's publication, burial societies were formed to resist the well-organized cadre of professional funeral directors, who are largely responsible for creating the "American way of death." Mitford's exposé did not substantially change American practice, which remains heavily determined by the funeral industry. And the alternative rites inspired by her criticism were not more elaborate or more effective, just shorter and cheaper.

Despite—or perhaps because of—the American tendency to avoid talking about or preparing for death, the "American way of death" and "death and dying" became popular topics, selling books and spawning university courses. Even so, there are few sustained descriptions of specific funeral rites in Canada, Mexico, or the United States. Not only are the ethnographic data scant, but sources that provide long historical views of death practices are in short supply too. Most of the writing on death consists of reportage and analysis of social trends, or it is psychologically oriented self-help literature. So describing a typical American funeral is not easy unless one is content to speak anecdotally.

From one point of view, it may not matter that no one has closely observed and fully documented death rites in America. Who, after all, needs a description of what everybody knows? Such a description would be a boring repetition of the obvious, wouldn't it? But suppose "what everybody knows" about the American way of death is wrong or a cliché? What if there is no such thing as *the* American way of death? After all, the bewildering variety of religious and ethnic groups in America should make it impossible to identify a single template as *the* American way of death. Surely, anthropologists with their penchant for cultural distinctiveness are capable of dispelling too homogenous a picture of American mortuary practices.

In *Celebrations of Death*, one of the most reputable cross-cultural treatments of death rites, Richard Huntington and Peter Metcalf complain about the lack of American data; there are richer, more plentiful descriptions of, say, Indonesian death rites than of American ones.[252] American death ways, they claim, are homogeneous. In view of the large population, as well as the ethnic and religious diversity of the United States, one would expect the range of funerary options to be great, but in fact, they argue, the range is small. From coast to coast, the funerary pattern is uniform. Predictably, it has three steps: embalming, display, and burial. A person dies in the hospital. The body is rapidly removed to the funeral parlor, where it is embalmed (even though embalming is not a legal requirement). After it is publicly viewed or visited, the body is buried.[253]

In the American way of death, the most important of the three phases is that of the wake, the ceremonial viewing of the craft of professional death workers.[254] Compared with other peoples, say Huntington and Metcalf, Americans have a pronounced tendency not to confront mortality. The primary expression of American avoidance is extensive embalming, which is nowhere else in the world practiced with the intensity that it is in the United States.

The apparent uniformity of American mortuary practice and the removal of death rites from the public eye make it hard to identify a coherent set of beliefs that undergird the rites. Americans show a pronounced vagueness of belief, an "indeterminate ideology."[255] Americans, despite their predominantly Christian upbringing, are unsure what they believe about death and life after death.

Huntington and Metcalf find in American mortuary culture several ironic reversals, if not contradictions. One is that in a country whose rhetoric emphasizes the family, little of the dying process actually occurs at home. Another is that a nation that so rigorously avoids contemplating death would let funerals hold a privileged place in its system of civil ceremonies.[256] A third irony is that a society stressing individual achievement prescribes so passive a role for the dying person. Funeral directors and doctors, both highly organized groups, are the primary actors in the dying process. Dying people are objects, not subjects, of action. Clergy, kin, and the dying play bit parts. "In the Middle Ages men and women made themselves masters of their own deaths. In America, the archetypal land of enterprise, self-made men are reduced to puppets."[257]

Huntington and Metcalf's summary of the American mortuary sequence is revealing for what it excludes: the funeral rite itself. Like Kastenbaum's portrait, their depiction excludes the obvious, the service at the local synagogue, temple, or church and the meal that often follows it. Even though the two scholars discuss the informal and unwritten codes of decorum that dictate who should be called first after a death, when to visit a bereaved family, and how to approach a corpse on display, they omit the most obviously and explicitly ritualized actions, those of the funeral itself. Such an oversight would be unimaginable if these social scientists had been reporting on a society other than their own. They do not explain their omission, perhaps do not even notice it.

The omission of the funeral liturgy is consonant with the assertion that American attitudes toward death are not shaped primarily by religious institutions, that is, by organized, denominational religion. The uniformity of American mortuary practices, say Huntington and Metcalf, is the result of the power and omnipresence of American civil religion.[258] By "civil religion" the two writers do not mean only Fourth of July celebrations or the religious rhetoric that laces inaugural ceremonies and state-of-the-nation addresses. Civil religion also includes American "faith" in medicine, the media, and the professions, especially funeral directing. American civil religion is death centered, even though it includes Christmas, Thanksgiving, and other holidays not focused on death. This civil religion has no proper name, so the "American way" will have to do. But this no-name religious complex has actual rites. Huntington and Metcalf present two specific examples of death rites in American civil religion: the funerals of Presidents Washington and Lincoln.

Even though I do not consider American death practices to be as uniform as Huntington and Metcalf claim, or as exclusively linked to the deaths of politicians as they imply, I agree that death rites in the United States are not contained or controlled solely by American religious institutions. In my view American funeral rites arise from the confluence of public civil ritual, religious death liturgies, and the embalming procedures of professional funeral directors. But a historical perspective is necessary if we are to understand this configuration.

Dead, He Presides Over Us

In *The Sacred Remains* Gary Laderman offers a historical perspective on the American way of death. He subtitles his book *American Attitudes Toward Death, 1799–1883*, but the book is really about northeastern, white Protestant attitudes. The dates of the subtitle are revealing: 1799 is the date of George Washington's funeral, 1883 of the second annual meeting of the Funeral Directors' National Association. Laderman tells what transpired between Washington's funeral and that of Abraham Lincoln, in 1865, as a way of explaining how embalming became an American "article of faith."[259]

Like Huntington and Metcalf, Laderman considers embalming and gazing ceremonially at the "restored" corpse the centerpiece of American death ways. As a historian of American religions, his question is, How did embalming and "viewing," or "visitation," come to be the dominant American practice? His answer is complex, as any good historical answer must be. It hinges on the convergence of several factors. The two central ones were the problem of disposing of the Civil War dead and the effect of Abraham Lincoln's death rites.

American Puritanism was heavily invested in contemplating death. In sermons the horrors of bodily decay—worms, rottenness, and putrefaction—were reminders of the reality of sin.[260] Actual corpses, in contrast to homiletically imagined ones, were buried quickly with little ceremony. The Puritan emphasis was not on the deceased or the memories of survivors but on the actions of God.

However, by the nineteenth century, Puritan theology, with its austere, sometimes harsh, attitude toward death, was giving way to a more romantic, sentimental one preoccupied with imagining "beautiful" deaths. Death was no longer a punishment for sin but a natural event. This newer theology emphasized the feelings of mourners, remembrance of the dead, and spiritual bliss in the next world.[261]

The deathbed scene, an emotional spectacle, assumed center stage, at least in the popular literary imagination. The proper homiletical aim was no longer that of frightening congregations into embracing salvation but that of consoling people. There arose a consolation literature, written largely by women with the support of liberal male ministers and replete with inspiring death stories. Such narratives constituted a new way of caring for the dead, one less overtly ritualistic and more imaginative or literary. However literary, this sensibility had its ritual moments, though, for instance, in the giving and taking of locks of hair from the deceased's head.

During the pre–Civil War period the northeastern Protestant way of death had three phases: the preparation of the body, transportation of it to the site, and burial. But like most tripartite summaries of rites of passage, this one is an oversimplification. Laderman's account actually implies other phases.[262] For instance, he describes a stopover at the church during the procession to the grave site, as well as a deathbed scene in which the dying person was surrounded by family, friends, and neighbors. The scene often involved an inquiry into the dying person's physical conditions and spiritual readiness.

Before the Civil War, death in the white Protestant northeastern United States typically occurred in the home, so the body was prepared there. It was laid out, washed, dressed in a winding sheet or sack, and put in a coffin, usually by women. Local cabinet makers or carpenters took measurements and built the pine coffin. Family and friends kept a vigil over the deceased for one or two nights—partly to ensure that the corpse was, in fact, dead and also to protect the body from being stolen, used for anatomical dissection, or otherwise treated with disrespect. Where ice was available, chunks were placed beneath the body to slow decomposition.

The funeral procession led from the home to the cemetery. It was marked by prayers at the beginning, then by a sermon at a church or meeting house on the way. Clergy were common but not essential. At the stopover, the larger community joined the primary mourners. Sometimes participants were afforded an opportunity to view the corpse. Afterward, the procession, now more ritually elaborate, continued. At the grave site, the body was either interred or entombed, the latter being mainly an upper-class option. For most families neither cremation nor embalming was conceivable. The final act of burial was accompanied by prayers and discourses briefer than those offered at the stopover.

Before the Civil War, urbanization was already precipitating changes in mortuary practice. Fewer people were being buried on their farms. An increasingly mobile population could not assume that their descendants would live on the premises and thus be able to tend their graves. The city was not a good place for burial either. With city space at a premium, and with growing fear that decaying corpses might spread disease, cities became less hospitable to the dead. The so-called rural cemetery movement emerged, advocating the establishment of space for the dead on the outskirts of urban areas rather than in churchyards. Suburbia originated as a way of distancing the dead from the living.

The dead were being distanced metaphorically as well as literally. The medical profession was young, attempting to establish itself as scientific. Anatomical dissection was crucial to its future. For research purposes it required cadavers. But first, says Laderman, the self had to be conceptually disaffiliated from the body, leaving it a mere corpse, an object. There was much Christian resistance to objectifying the body in this way. It was the temple and image of God, therefore difficult to divest of religious significance. There was also the matter of the doctrine of the resurrection of the body; God alone should reconstitute the dead body. Consequently, it took time to render the dead body theologically meaningless. It also required the Civil War to produce a surplus of corpses and thus disrupt the usual funerary routine.

Eventually, Christian theology and the new medical science succeeded in stripping the human body of its religious meaning. The body became "only" the body, mere remains, so its fate had no effect on the destiny of the soul. Then, and only then, did it seem natural for the body to be cut open or to reside in a grave that no family member tended.

The carnage of the Civil War was a national trauma in which one out of sixteen white northern males died.[263] The usual funeral—death at home surrounded by loved ones, a stately procession, burial in a marked grave—was no longer possible for many young men. Bodies were left unburied by the enemy, or they were heaped into poorly marked mass graves. A few corpses were mutilated; trophies were taken. Baby rattles made from enemy bones were sent home; skulls became drinking cups.

The horror of a civil war was great enough, but it was compounded by the absence of the dead from funerals. Some families went to look for the bodies of kin, or they paid others to retrieve them. When bodies were found, how might they be transported home for a decent burial?

Previously, embalming had been a repulsive notion to Christians; its purview had been strictly medical, a means of preserving corpses for dissection. But now, embalming came to be regarded as a practical necessity for transporting the war dead across great stretches of time and space.

This necessity was supported by a powerful example. When President Abraham Lincoln was killed, a decision of major ritual importance was made: to embalm him, put him on a train, and let citizens greet their dead president on the long journey from Washington, D.C., to Springfield, Illinois, his home. The Civil War, over which he had presided, and his assassination, which traumatized the national psyche, required desperate measures. There was no gentle death at home, no washing by his wife Mary Todd, rather, embalmers, professionals, prepared him in quite another way. They sawed off the top of his head, performed an autopsy, and removed not only the bullet but the brain itself. They flushed the blood from the man's veins, replacing it with embalming fluid.

Reduced from a man to a puppet, Lincoln was nevertheless dramatically elevated into something more than a man. He was "sacredly preserved" and in this state became the "father of his country." As Laderman wryly puts it, Lincoln hollowed became Lincoln hallowed.[264] The president's paraded body was deified, a source of healing for a wounded nation (even though it began decomposing and had to be repaired on the journey). The train trip, much longer than the usual procession to the cemetery, was so successful that within a few years embalming had become desirable, *the* preferred, the *American,* way of death.

Laderman argues that the crux of the transition to embalming was short, concentrated into the five years of the war that culminated in Lincoln's death.[265] In a brief time, public attitudes shifted from revulsion and disgust to sentimental acceptance of embalming. Lincoln's death journey was a watershed, after which dissection and embalming lost the power to provoke public moral indignation.

Lincoln's death contrasted considerably with George Washington's in 1799. Washington had been buried on the grounds of his home. His body belonged not to the nation but to his family. His corpse was absent from the many ceremonies that marked his demise, and his survival of death was largely portrayed in heroic narrative and mythic art. Ritually, his presence and absence were simultaneously symbolized by a riderless horse, but he was never a preserved corpse presiding over the nation from a chair.

By 1882 entrepreneurial death workers had organized themselves into the National Funeral Directors' Association. They began lobbying and publicizing to convince consumers that embalming was essential, not just for lab use in anatomical studies but for "home" use. Eventually, their place of work would become a funeral "home" and embalming a ceremonial way of creating a "loving memory." Embalming would not have been saleable for long if its only value had been that of preserving medical cadavers or transporting war-torn corpses from the South.

Embalming would not have become widespread if bodies had retained their value to organized religion. Churches had to be willing to abandon the body as a site of religious meaning if funeral homes were to exercise squatters' rights over them. The doctrine of the resurrection of the body had to be displaced by an exclusive interest in the fate of the soul. But if bodies lost *all* their sentimental value, people would not pay to make their loved ones viewable.

At its outset funeral directing required a delicate balancing act. Quasi-religious ritual concerns had to be played off quasi-scientific and esthetic ones. "Undertakers," priests of a peculiar sort, became "funeral directors." They had to become, and to sell themselves as, experts. Whereas American communities had previously entertained a mild curiosity about viewing dead bodies, now the public would learn to desire a final, almost pornographic gaze at a body in repose, a body not decaying or in pain but "at rest," "natural."

In addition, embalming promised to curb the much publicized, often exaggerated danger to public health posed by decaying corpses. Public desire and salesmanship, rather than theological correctness or ritual sensitivity, colluded to shape the American way of death. Intimacy with the bare bones and naked reality of death was no longer the American way.

Mortuary photography, like embalming or wedding photography, might have become a ritual necessity. Photographs of Civil War battlefield scenes, before the dead were removed, became popular items. Some of these scenes, replete with close-ups, were even staged. The worth of these photos was not mainly utilitarian, that of helping families identify their unlocated dead, but of satisfying the curiosity of a people increasingly removed from their dead. The real money was in casket making and embalming. As a way of preserving memories, embalmed corpses were more successful than photographs of them. Photographing the violently killed continues in photojournalism, but photographing those embalmed and "at rest" in funeral "homes" has largely disappeared.

The picture Laderman paints is a powerful one but, I believe, too enamored of wars and heroically mythologized presidents. It is striking that he does not examine specific funerals rites other than those of presidents. The ordinary ones transpiring in either religious sanctuaries or funeral homes hardly appear in his account. Of course, Laderman is studying American *attitudes* toward death, not American death *practices*. But rites reveal attitudes, and rites often leave substantial traces, for instance, in ritual texts that instruct people on what to do and say. Historical data on American funeral rites do exist, and Laderman largely ignores them as a source of understanding American attitudes toward death. Like Kastenbaum's important textbook on death or

Huntington and Metcalf's reputable cross-cultural study of death, Laderman's history marginalizes death rites and overemphasizes death attitudes.

The best we can do, therefore, is to conclude that we know much about the American way of death, but little about American funerals. We know that Americans have explicit death rites in a way that they do not have explicit birth rites. We know that during some periods in American history, death rites have been more elaborate than in others. We know it is not true that Americans have gone from much death ritual to little. The shift from the Puritan era to the present is in the direction of increasing, not decreasing, ritual. It is also clear that the American dead, once in the hands of women, are now largely in the hands of professionals, mostly men. Also, it is obvious that neither families nor religions play the role they once played in caring for the dying and the dead, their place having been taken by medical professionals and mortuary institutions. It seems fairly certain that Americans, who once stared death more or less hard in the face, began in the nineteenth century to sentimentalize it, cover it up, distance themselves from it, and then in the twentieth century to become intensely interested in reading about it.

There is a pronounced tendency in the research to claim or imply that the American way of death has little to do with religion, ethnicity, or region. African American ways, Jewish ways, Sikh ways, the New Orleans way, the Hispanic Catholic way—all such configurations fade into mere background for scholars who write on the topic. I have little doubt that the professionalization and medicalization of death have influenced, and in some cases, displaced other practices. But I also have no doubt that death rites in North America are poorly understood because they are so seldom explicitly and carefully studied. If we attempt either a global or an American perspective, we should regularly ground ourselves in the local, stubbornly particular stuff of actual deaths and their attendant ceremonies. The problem with concentrating on *attitudes* toward death or the funerals of *presidents* is that we seldom descend from such altitudes to ground level, where most people die. At ground level, there is, I believe, both more tradition and more experimentation than standard portraits of the American way of death would lead us to believe.

The dearth of detailed ethnographic studies on death rites in North America prevents us from drawing reliable conclusions about funerals. However, the research does support a broad-stroke portrait of contrast-

Simple or minimal rites	Elaborate or protracted rites
Single disposal of the corpse	Double or multiple disposal patterns, e.g., burial/exhumation/reburial
Emphasis on the expression of personal feeling	Emphasis on the adherence to social or ritual form
Optional or minimal mourning	Required or protracted mourning
Minimum philosophical or mythological attention paid to the afterlife	Elaborate conceptions of life after death
Minimal interaction with the dead	Active veneration of ancestors
Little fear of the dead displayed; death not regarded as polluting	Considerable fear of the dead displayed; death regarded as polluting
Death avoided; hands-off approach	Death embraced; hands-on approach
Emphasis on the preservation of the remains	Emphasis on the destruction of the remains
Ways of dying not fully or clearly distinguished	Clearly identified "good" and "bad" deaths
Death rites that "level," de-emphasizing hierarchy and status	Death rites that emphasize hierarchy and status

Figure 3. Polarities in Responding to Death and the Dead

ing attitudes. Figure 3 summarizes the major contrasts in mortuary practice found in the world's religions and cultures. These are not all the alternatives, only major ones that distinguish one tradition or group from another.[266] In general, the left column more nearly summarizes mainstream North American practices. The usual rites are relatively simple; they do not take days or years to complete. We bury once and would consider exhumation a horror unless it were for forensic purposes. As a society, we emphasize the expression of personal feelings but not the public expression or sadness or grief. So, although we are suspicious of formalities, our rites, in fact, emphasize form as well as feeling. We do not require mourning, although the absence of tears can be taken to signal denial in someone especially close to the dead person. We pay only a little attention to myths and ideas of the afterlife. We interact minimally with the dead, having buried them in places removed from centers of commerce and residence. Too much speaking of or with the dead is considered deviant. Although we fear death and it is considered impolite or morbid to talk much about it, we have little fear of the dead. Although we do not think of death or the dead as polluting, we nevertheless have a hands-off approach to death and hire professionals to handle the dead for us. Although we are uncertain about the fate of the dead, we place strong emphasis on the preservation of their remains. Informally, we distinguish kinds of death, for example, the timely from the untimely, the suicide from the nonsuicide. A certain amount of display separates rich from poor or lower-class from upper-class funerals, but too much display or emphasis on status evokes gossip or criticism.

It is dangerous to summarize what we do, not only because there is great variation in who "we" are but also because what we "do" is not necessarily what we did or will do. Death rites can change. Ritual is reputed to be the most conservative cultural activity in which humans engage. Death rites are said to be the most conservative kind of ritual, the most stubbornly resistant to innovation. In contrast with funerals, European American weddings are sites of experimentation. Somehow, ritual creativity seems more consonant with the promise of marital bliss than with the somber duty of laying our dead to rest.

It not easy for people to marshal the energy to reinvent rites when they are racked with grief. But we have seen how American funerary practice did, in fact, turn on a dime (or maybe a silver dollar—the death, after all, was Lincoln's), so mortuary change is not impossible. Despite their reputation, funeral rites, in North America and elsewhere, have histories, and they are marked by the kind of substantive changes that require significant reimagining.

Before 1949 China had a rich history of death rites and ancestor veneration, but after that date, in the hands of the Communist Party, Chinese death rites underwent a major revolution. The cautious reinstatement of a few traditional practices in more recent times has not negated or reversed that ritual revolution.

North American mortuary history, too, continues. It did not end with, or even culminate in, the introduction of embalming and professional death workers. Two of the most visible mortuary innovations in recent decades, the growing acceptance of cremation and the establishment of hospices (places dedicated to caring for the dying), are evidence that death rites, like other rites of passage, evolve.

The Western debate over cremation lasted for almost two millennia. During that time Christian burial gradually displaced cremation, the usual pagan practice. By the late eighth century, Charlemagne made cremation a capital offense. Burial became *the* Christian, thus *the* European, way of disposing of the dead. By the seventeenth century, however, the wheel of history was turning again. French republicans and other Europeans began promoting cremation as the more enlightened way to dispose of bodies. Within the last half century we have witnessed the doubling of the life expectancy of middle-class North Americans. This fact and the crisis of overpopulation have helped cremation gain ground despite the long history of religious strictures against it.

In 1963, the year of Jessica Mitford's attack on the American way of death, the Roman Catholic Church, in its *Instruction with Regard to the Cremation of Bodies,* relaxed its absolute ban on cremation (although it still prefers burial). For centuries the change was slow, but in the mid twentieth century the pace became rapid. By 1997 the cremation rate in England was over 70 percent. In the United States, in 1995, it was 21 percent and still rising.[267] In China, in 1983, 90 percent of city dwellers and 15 percent of rural people were being cremated, resulting in a national average of 30 percent.[268] The near-global shift from burial to cremation, as simple as it may seem, is having an enormous impact. Cremating rather than burying transforms land use, changes the employment demands for funerary specialists, and precipitates fundamental shifts in one's image of the self, family, and afterlife. So it is possible, whether by legislation, imagination, or some combination of both, for death rites to be reimagined, reconfigured, or reinvented.

Mortal Acts

Social, economic, and political forces only partly account for shifts in death ways. Rites also emerge or decline when a people's way of imagining a passage changes. How death is imagined in America depends on who is doing the imagining. For instance, funeral directors paint death as a kind of restful sleep. Filmmakers portray it as a dramatic event replete with guns; death is delivered to "others" who deserve it. Clergy mythologize death as a preliminary step in a long journey, rendering death not so much a cessation as a transformation.

More recently, therapists have tendered other ways of reimagining death. Just as initiatory fantasy is driven by images from movies, novels, and stories, just as weddings are pressured by fashion-magazine imagery, so funerals are conditioned by doctrines, myths, and images of life after death. Death rites are occasions for performing fundamental cosmological tenets—for asserting what a self is, counting out what a life is worth, speculating about our origins as a people, guessing where we are going, declaring who we are. We do not have the whole view of things until a life is finished, so when we bury or burn our dead, we often do so in a setting adorned with ultimate postulates.

An ultimate conviction of many Americans is that individuals are sacred. Accordingly, Americans continue to individualize and privatize death and its ritualization. *Mortal Acts: Eighteen Empowering Rituals for Confronting Death*, a book by David Feinstein and Peg Elliott Mayo, is based on a guided-imagery technique in which a reader guides a relaxed listener's imagining. This approach does not depend on templates for designing your own funeral rites but rather on exercises for coming to terms with your mortality. The intent is preparatory rather than funerary. Feinstein and Mayo refer to their exercises as "therapeutically informed rituals" and "internal rites of passage." When the authors talk about "postmortem life," they are not referring to life after death but to living after imaginative and emotional acknowledgment of one's own mortality.

Feinstein and Mayo are convinced that Americans are no longer well prepared to meet death. What these two guides offer are not cultural or religious alternatives but personal growth–oriented ones. American culture, they assert, no longer provides a way of dying, so individuals must now find it for themselves. They claim that their "personal rituals" are also universal.[269] Their treatment implies that cultural differences regarding the great themes—birth, maturation, bonding, decline, and death—are insignificant in comparison to the commonalities. This tactic, which equates the personal with the universal, thus bypassing the local, ethnic, and national, is a familiar American New Age conceptual move.

The aim of the book's eighteen "mortal acts" is therapeutic. It is to facilitate self-examination of one's "death-denial system" and to transcend it. In an early guided-imagery exercise, Feinstein and May direct us:

When you were a child, you had many fears about death. You may remember the terror of a nightmare or of a monster that you imagined had crawled under your bed or into your closet. . . . Pull yourself back to being very young and feeling your fear. (Pause.) Feel yourself moving back in time now to this early experience of your fear of death. (Pause.) Where are you? What is occurring? Who is there? (30-second pause.) You are about to find a symbol of these fears. Focus on a sensation in your body that relates to this early experience. . . . This symbol represents your fear of death, and you will be able to remember it so you can, in a little while, draw it on your shield.[270]

[In a later exercise, having concretized our fears, we have now faced, incorporated, and overcome them. We are at peace. Our guides encourage us with the power of positive thinking:] From this heightened awareness, your appreciation of life is amplified, along with a sense of peace about death. You can feel yourself, now, moving forward in time. You are moving forward to the occasion of your own death. In this death scenario, precisely the atmosphere you would desire for your last moments on earth already exists. (Pause.) As you survey the situation, you can vividly see or sense yourself in the scene, along with any others who are there. People are relating to you and to one another just as you might wish. (Pause.) You are about to imagine a ceremony or ritual to maintain or heighten the mood. It may be performed by you alone or with others. (Pause.) In the following silence, you will experience the entire ceremony. (45-second pause.) As the moment of death approaches, you begin to recite your death chant. Start to use it now and continue it as you imagine your consciousness moving out of your body. In your imagination, allow your death chant to be the bridge as you leave your body and come into a space from which you will be able to view your funeral or memorial service. . . . Again, the atmosphere is exactly as you would like it to be.[271]

Just as we would like it to be. . . . This vision is a far cry from the Puritan hell, a place where one would *not* have wanted to be. No longer sinners in the hands of an angry God dangling our feet over the fires of hell, Americans can now soar on the power of positive thinking, taking comfort from their spirit guides and death chants.

Funeral rites can take days, months, or even years to prepare, execute, and finish, yet here we are given a forty-five-second pause. Perhaps other people's imaginations are more concise than mine. Or maybe the authors have no experience with, or faith in, rites that require heavy outlays of time. I am not an advocate of the Puritan vision, but if I had to choose, I would opt for it. For the Puritan vision had courage and integrity. This one is not only a far cry from the realities of hell but also from those of dying. Placed beside the Mexican and Brazilian death scenes described earlier, this kind of fantasy is self-indulgent, luring us into the future with positive, personal, mood-enhancing armchair fantasy.

Do the exercises work? Perhaps some people are comforted by them, but the emphasis is on "comfort." I am disturbed not by the idea of imagining death or personifying someone's fears of it but by the lack of irony and humor as well as by the utter failure to recognize how ethnocentric these supposedly universal ritual exercises are. The images are stereotypical and the plots predictable. If in reimagining death, we domesticate it, we have failed.

Cyber Ritual and Death on the Web

All the major rites of passage are making their appearance on the World Wide Web, but none with such persistence and verve as death. There is much talk these days about "cyber ritual" and the revolution it promises to precipitate in our conception and practice of ritual. Aficionados insist that cyber ritual is real, not merely imaginary, ritual. Virtual reality is its own kind of reality.

The question is not *whether* cyber ritual is real, but *how* it is real. How does it work, and what does it do that is different from "normal," embodied ritual? Just as there are similarities and differences between the real and imagined, there are continuities and discontinuities between virtual and embodied rites. Virtual ritualizing is not completely disembodied: Someone sits at a keyboard; someone else stares at a monitor.

Actually embodied rites are not without their virtual dimensions. Some rites, when they are not being enacted, have what we might call a virtual, or latent, reality; a ritual text is, we might say, a virtual rite. Virtual reality is not the invention of computers but of ritual, literature, art, and theater. These are the original multimedia that enabled the appearance of gods, demons, and other hyperrealities. As-if, or subjunctive, realities are nothing new to ritual. What is new is the solitude and anonymity with which cyber ritualizing can be enacted. A couple can now be married without even being in each other's presence.

A prominent feature of death ritualizing on the Web is imagery. What meets the Web surfer are first of all the images—not the words or enactments. Even the words are images.

Behind the images are the persons, places, companies, and groups that create and maintain them. However much we may celebrate virtuality, reveling in images for their own sake, one is inevitably forced to ask what is behind them. Are their signatures and facts to be trusted? Will their downloads infect my files? How might I contact the designers and writers? It is the net-linked computer's promise of a person coupled with the absence of a face and tone of voice that gives cyber ritualizing its peculiar quality.

The cyber world is as important for the "places" you can "visit" as it is for the things it enables you to "do." In this sense, it is a better substitute for a cemetery than for a funeral. The World Wide Cemetery, established in 1995, contains "monuments," entries concerning persons who have died.[272] They are listed alphabetically as well as by region and year of death. Many include not only the usual facts of death (birth and death dates, name, and so on) but also photos, eulogies, and stories. Each "monument" costs between ten and twenty dollars, depending on what you want it to contain.

"Flowers" are notes of consolation left by "visitors." Flowers can be left in response to the dead in general, to specific dead people, or, more often, to their survivors. The site also has "memorials," deaths grouped into categories: World War II, Vietnam, AIDS, cancer, organ donation, and suicide.

The World Wide Cemetery site bills itself as a permanent marker and boasts that unlike real cemeteries it is accessible from anywhere in the world. Not only is it eternal and virtually omnipresent but it does not weather with time. At least that is what the site writers tell us. Writers of the World Wide Cemetery's statements are enthusiastic about the possibility of creating hypertext links among family members. They imply that using these links constitutes a new, virtual form of kinship. Furthermore, the cemetery is open to all faiths; there are no spatial markers of religious discrimination here.

On the same page as the claim to permanence, the site's managers solicit sponsors to help keep the site alive. This site, then, like most others on the Web, has about it both the illusion of permanence and a distinct feeling of ephemerality.

Do the World Wide Cemetery and sites like it help people ritualize death? What are the ritualistic implications of virtual-passage sites? There are testimonials illustrating that the World Wide Cemetery can have real effects. On March 7, 1998, one person wrote, "I surfed into this site just for a curiosity, but now I feel a great commotion. I remember all my deads, and I ask my grandpas and granma to watch over me. . . . "

Another person posted this in December 1996: "This site is strangely moving . . . that one of the unanticipated uses for electronic communications has turned out to be a digital columbarium is, to me, quintessentially human."

Another, identified only by a numerical code, left on Sunday, June 18, 1995, a simple note: "A bouquet of yellow roses, always fresh."

It is, I suppose, no more bizarre that we should remember our "deads" while searching the Web than remembering them while wearing masks or reading tombstones. Electronic roses, despite their lack of fragrance, are perhaps no stranger than the plastic or stone ones left in Mexican cemeteries or etched into medieval edifices.

Even so, the further disembodying of death that is possible on the Internet is, especially in a society already distanced from death, potentially dangerous. Virtual, like fictional, realities always work both ways, as substitutes, on the one hand, and as feeders back into lived life on the other. In my view we already have too many ritual substitutes. So the question is, What ways of reimagining death lead us closer to, rather than farther away from, a death that not only entertains but stings?

Reinventing Death Rites

It would be easy to make the World Wide Cemetery look silly and superficial by setting it alongside the death of Dona Amor's mother or Bill Myers's brother. So I will resist the temptation and turn instead to a funeral with a significant virtual dimension. Media, with their as-if qualities, are here to stay, and the ritually minded will not be able to avoid them.

When Princess Diana died in 1997, a news commentator referred to it as the funeral of the century, and a colleague labeled it the best example she knew of a truly postmodern ritual. It not only overshadowed Mother Teresa's last rites, it also successfully undermined traditional rules of decorum that governed English royal ceremony.

The day of the funeral my daughter asked, "Dad, did you know her?"

"No, not really," I replied.

"I don't mean did you *know* her. I mean did you know much about Princess Diana before she died?"

"Only a little. I saw her on TV occasionally."

"Well, I didn't know who she was or anything about her until last night and today, but, still, it makes me sad, really, really sad," she confided earnestly.

"She was a princess. I guess that would be enough to make a nine-year-old girl sad," I said.

Not about to let me explain away her feelings, much less with a stereotype she's already learned to criticize, Cailleah set me straight:

"No, I don't mean that kind of stuff. I mean all these things they are saying and doing make me sad." Then she added, almost as an afterthought, "And that she died, of course."

Sunday morning, the day after the funeral, Michael Enright of CBC Radio pronounced in his sagely manner, "We kept distracting ourselves with ceremony."

Enright was half right. Funerals do distract. In the midst of chaos and loss, they construct a countervailing order—in the British case, one marked by a slow and stately rhythm. After a high-speed chase through the streets of Paris, what could be more comforting than a slow-speed walk through the streets of London behind a gun carriage accompanied by Welch guards? Funerary decorum is hard to break in public and difficult to criticize openly. The distraction it provided was tranquilizing. Like any rite of passage, a funeral erects a safety net, allowing participants to fall—but only so far. After that, the net of ceremony yanks us up, just short of hitting hard ground at too high a velocity. Perhaps it is true that Diana's funeral rite, cobbled together—it was part tradition, part invention, part adaptation—helped to anesthetize grief and pain.

But Enright was also wrong. What the princess's funeral did for my daughter and for millions of others who knew little of the person Diana was not only to distract them from pain but also to take them to a place where it hurt, even if it did not need to, even if they never knew the woman.

Among television and radio commentators, it sometimes seemed as if there were only two possibilities: Either you cried for Diana or you distracted yourself. If you distracted yourself, you had two options. You could wrap yourself in the soft blanket of the funeral, or you could put your face to the hard wall of reality by pondering Diana as a collectively imagined media creation. We all know—at least we were told repeatedly—that Diana was a creation of the media, that she used the media and the media used her. So it was obvious that not only did Diana make us weep, but that the media made us weep as well. Without TV sets, fewer would have cried.

On the day of, and day after, the funeral you could not buy blank videotapes in Westmount, Quebec, where we were living for the year. People in this English-speaking enclave on the French-speaking island of Montreal were at home. Not just watching, they were taping so they could relive the funeral until their grief was fully spent. I know of people who've watched the funeral half a dozen times now. By making videotapes, not only could they take a souvenir of a historic event, witness a spectacle, peek at royalty and aristocracy stumbling in public, they could also wail—privately, with the public. Diana was not necessarily the only object of our keening, but she—rather, her funeral—was its occasion.

The afternoon of Diana's funeral my son, Bryn, and I walked through a large department store in downtown Montreal. An elderly bag lady had come in from the street. She sat on the floor eclipsed by three large-screen television sets and her array of plastic grocery bags. From Montreal, she was leaning into Westminster Cathedral, her face flushed, her eyes swollen, her cheeks wet with weeping.

For a while there were two camps. In the camp of the softhearted, we cried shamelessly in our innocence, British or not. The tears, I believe, were genuine, heartfelt. They needed no justification. They made perfect sense of Diana's physical beauty, regal bearing, candid observations, premature death, and obvious humanity toward those less fortunate than herself. She was saintly, or if not that, then a warm human being and a good mother. So why shouldn't we weep at such a loss?

In the camp of the hard-hearted, where critics huddled around their television sets, Diana was an empty cipher, the algebraic X, a mirror devoid of content. Never really knowable, because she had no real self, this Diana was a creation of the media. Bereft of cameras, she was nothing—less than a squashed pumpkin at midnight lying on a cobblestone road leading away from the ballroom. Why weep any more at this loss than at the loss of any other human being? What kind of mourning is virtual mourning anyway?—just another form of sentimentality, not at all like real grief. "Sad she died," the cynical said, "but that's life; no TV, no tears."

The way of innocence would have us pretend there was no camera between Diana and us. The calculatedly innocent would require that we ignore the obvious: Most of us hardly knew the woman or cared about her life before the funeral. The way of naïveté would make Diana a saint and her death a revelation, the appearance of absolute being.

The way of cynicism would make of Diana's life, death, and funeral a show, or worse, a sham. This way tempts one to forget there was a real human life on the other side of the cameras and to believe that the emotions of those on this side of the cameras do not matter.

The skeptical eye, I remind myself, would do the same to my daughter's life if the cameras were turned on her. So do we really have to choose between theatrical sham and revelatory purity? Only if we forget the ceremony; it mediated between the extremes. That Diana's funeral was a media event no one doubts. But it was also a ritual event, and this utterly basic fact went almost unrecognized and certainly unanalyzed.

During the televised funeral proceedings, the network anchors were accompanied by specialists in British politics, royalty, and society but no one who knew much about ceremony. The commentary on the ceremony was banal and uninformed, whereas the analysis of media performance was reflective and debate filled. In contrast to media analysis, the analysis of ritual was nonexistent. Commentary took the form: "And now here is so-and-so, the duke of . . . " "There go the guards." "This is Westminster Cathedral where such-and-such is buried." What little discussion there was of the ceremony took the form of an inquiry about which actions and objects and places were typical of a royal funeral and which were innovative. But even this kind of analysis was sporadic and piecemeal. Recognition of the elements of the ceremony, explanation of the ways rites work (or fail to)—this kind of analysis was utterly missing. After the ceremony, commentators dwelled on the content of Diana's brother's eulogy and the emotional impact of Elton John's "Candle in the Wind." The commentary was, functionally speaking, "protestant." Word and song were treated as the real stuff; the rest, the gestures, the movements, was window dressing—great to shoot but not worth analyzing.

In one sense it was a relief to have so much dead air time; silence is rare on television. The silence arose mostly from ignorance, not from reverence. Although it may not be appropriate to hear analysis *during* a funeral, afterward surely someone needs to think about the cadence of the walk, the tones of voice, the mediation of public and sacred space, the effect of dressing up and dressing down, the relationship between ceremonial traditions and spontaneous actions. For instance, what should we make of the fact that applause arose outside and rippled from the periphery through the doors of Westminster Cathedral, where, instead of being ignored, it was taken up by those most privy to the mortuary proceedings? No mere breach of decorum, applause, a performative gesture, overtook a liturgical one. Another kind of question that we should raise is, Where does the rite end? After the ceremony in Westminster Cathedral? After the private burial on an island? When the condolence registers are finally closed? When the last flower is laid at the tunnel in Paris? Or when the last person weeps while watching a video rerun of the funeral?

Deaths do not make most of us cry unless we are closely related to the deceased. But perhaps it is good to mourn those we don't know. One of the reasons we human beings enact funeral rites is to train ourselves in the art of grieving. It is better to grieve than not, and some grieve with more facility than others. Grief is learned, thus taught, and funerals are one means of instruction. To say that grief is learned is to say that it is cultural. But saying that something is cultural doesn't mean that it isn't also biological, psychological, or spiritual. Some of us learn not to grieve or at least to minimize grieving. Some are taught not to display grief (even to themselves). It is a widespread ritual, therefore cultural, convention for men to control or suppress grief and for women to have the cultural obligation or freedom to display it. None of this is to deny the reality of the human experience of grief. It is just to say that almost every physical activity from breathing to eating to defecating to weeping is choreographed. However natural (or supernatural) all these actions are, they are also canvases on which traditions put their stamp.

Did Diana's funeral work? If so, for whom? And how? What does it mean to say a funeral "works"? What are funerals supposed to do? The current, popular answer is that a funeral's job is to expedite grief. With what sounds like very Protestant rhetoric, we like to talk about "grief work." With the British weeping openly in the streets (a scene never witnessed by most of us before), Canadians, and even some nonroyalist Americans, crying in front of their TVs, you could say that Diana's funeral "worked." In fact, it worked better than expected. What we expected was the stiff upper lip, cold formality; what we got was weeping in the streets, anger at the queen and the media expressed inside Westminster Cathedral, and applause outside the cathedral. What we got was ritually framed social drama. With the help of television, the funeral was global, overshadowing even that of Mother Teresa, who was perhaps more deserving but less in need of a global funeral that somehow redeemed a troubled life.

However much poor ceremonies stifle grief, effective ones liberate us to the gift of tears—if not in public, then in private. Funerals help us find our grief, even if that grief is left over from some other death and our mourning for someone other than the deceased. Even if you didn't know the woman, even if you couldn't have cared less, it felt good to feel so bad watching Diana's funeral. It was good to grieve with the world, the one that includes our daughters and sons who pry us with questions when Old Death arrives. Princess Diana's funeral rite did not just distract people from pain, it conjured pain.

Because Diana was divorced and not quite a princess, elements of her death rite had to be invented. The ceremony was partly royal, partly not. The recasting and performance of a popular song by Elton John, the critical speech by Diana's brother, and the outbreak of applause all signaled some remarkable ceremonial revisions and inventions. In addition, the worldwide broadcast of the ceremony led not only to its global extension but also to its reconstruction. Literally, before our very eyes, a funerary tradition was being reinvented.

A major question that bedevils death rites more than the other passages is that of belief. *Chouji*, the Japanese practice of addressing the dead (illustrated in the story told by Victor Hori), may or may not imply a belief in the continuing presence of the dead. But the death rites of rural Greeks and Chinese, as well as of Brazilian Catholics like Dona Amor, assume a belief in life after death or at least a conventional compliance with the notion that the dead persist, either as venerated ancestors or as vaguely troubling shades. Even Reggie Ray, in telling about the performance of *sukhavati* to put to rest the restless spirit of a deceased girl, resists foreclosure on the belief question, since doing so would amount to a premature, "flat-land" pretension.

As the veneration of both Abraham Lincoln and Princess Diana illustrate, it is possible to participate in death rites and to commemorate the dead without necessarily implying belief in their metaphysical persistence. For ritual purposes it is enough that the dead persist in memory, imagination, or in the form of visual icons and that we approach them with empathy or respect. Belief, it seems, is not an absolute requirement.

In all likelihood Bill Myers, who shared his account of his brother's funeral, is a believer. But his story does not invoke articles of Baptist faith or depend on the acceptance of Protestant dogma. Whether or not there is "another side," and whether or not funerals are necessary for the dead to make it to that other side, the rites in Bill's story matter. Either they facilitate grief or they obstruct it. Whereas Reggie Ray's narrative suspended the question of belief, Bill Myers's story circumvented it. Ritual effectiveness does not depend on literal belief.

Several other attitudinal possibilities emerge from the descriptions and narratives we have considered. For example, Feinstein and Mayo, in the exercises from *Mortal Acts*, render death and the human confrontation with it in purely imaginative terms; the rites they offer are only "in the head." Another variation appears among Mexicans, some of whom greet death not only "beliefully" but playfully and ironically. A final example of alternative funerary attitudes: From Jessica Mitford's scathing attack in 1963 until the present no other rite of passage has been approached with a more critical attitude than the European American funeral. Ceremonial effectiveness is not undermined by sustained critique.

So the moment of passage that would seem to demand the most metaphysical credulity turns out to have generated the most interesting array of alternative ritual attitudes. People may participate in death rites not only feeling grief or expressing belief but also critically, ironically, playfully, imaginatively, pragmatically, or in a state of suspended disbelief.

Reinventing death rites, like reclaiming birth, requires not only experimenting with less conventional ritual attitudes but also a wrestling match with the institutions that control them. We are more fundamentally out of touch with the dead than with the newborn. At least the newborn, when carried home, swamp us with their utter tactility and ever-demanding presence. The dead, on the contrary, continue to recede, so there is urgency for us to lay hands upon them. The dead do not come home with us but are driven to the edge of town and laid to rest at a considerable remove from where we reside. Certainly, the dead should be laid to rest, and the bereaved deserve to be comforted, but the great haste with which we turn our backs on the deceased is one of our major ritual difficulties.

We are in dire need of doing hands-on work—at the very least, washing, dressing, and burying, perhaps also coffin building and grave tending. Otherwise, death itself becomes ethereal and abstract, prolonging grief and severing our felt connections with the earth in which they rest or with the sky in which they float as particles. As long as we pay funeral directors to shield us from the smells, touch, and sight of death, there is little hope that the so-called final passage will be any more than an exercise in decorum. If death rites are to become celebrations, there must be not only space and time for dwelling with the dying and the dead but also myths and images that support communication with the dead. I am not talking about seances, which are far too literal for most of us but about what we might call "subjunctive" communication: talking and eating with the dead *as if* they had presence and counsel to offer.

A truly reinvented funerary sensibility would require us to imagine the dead in a much more serious way than we do, and it would lead us to enact rites based on such imagining. In effect, we need a renewed mythologizing of death and the dead, one that does not require naive belief but depends on dramatic storytelling and bold, performed images of Old Death. I am no advocate of a women's cemetery culture like that of rural Greece, but we must overcome excessively pristine and falsely hopeful images of death. We need funerary, not cinematic, images as stark and compelling as that of Eleni's mother holding her daughter's exhumed skull or that of the lament in which the dead daughter is made to say of Haros (the death figure), "I hold him on my knees. / He rests against my chest. / If he is hungry, he eats from by body, / and if he is thirsty, he drinks from my two eyes."[273] We need graphic myths rooted in tactile rites and passionate engagement without the requirement of literal belief.

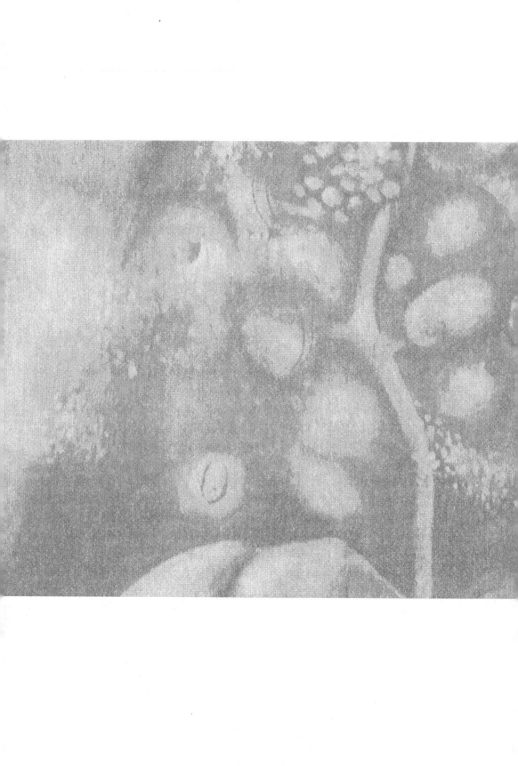

CHAPTER 5

Passages,
Troubled and Uncharted

In the last twenty-five years, the middle-class life cycle in North America has made stunning shifts. Both the number and length of life stages have altered drastically, rendering ages twenty-one and sixty-five almost meaningless as markers of adulthood. The age at which most girls experience the onset of menstruation has steadily declined in the West. Not only is biological puberty arriving earlier, it also lasts longer. Marriage now occurs closer to age thirty than to twenty, and childbirth can be deferred from ten to twenty years longer than it could in the middle of the twentieth century. In addition, we live longer, thus widening the gap between retirement and death.

As a consequence of striking demographic changes, Gail Sheehy, author of *New Passages,* has revised the life course, subdividing adulthood into "provisional adulthood" (eighteen to thirty), "first adulthood" (thirty to forty-five), and "second adulthood" (forty-five to eighty-five plus). Accordingly, she sets midlife passage at fifty rather than at forty.[274] Such drastic changes of definition within a single generation make the notion of "the" life cycle seem utterly arbitrary. The idea of either a standard Western or a general human life cycle has all but collapsed within a single generation. The idea of the life cycle is the foundation upon which Western rites of passage theory is built. When it trembles, the rites themselves may become troublesome and questionable.

It is remarkable that Sheehy can write a five-hundred page book on life passages without paying attention to ritual. Not only are "rites of passage," "ceremonies," and other such entries missing from the very full index of a heavily documented book, but so are several others such as "funerals," "weddings," and "initiations." To treat major life transitions without significant reference to ritual ways of handling them illustrates how much passage has been psychologized and privatized in the contemporary United States. Even when Sheehy writes about celebration, she treats it as an individual feeling rather than a community activity.[275] The portrait she paints is of an America besotted with life-cycle transitions but bereft of rites with which to negotiate them.

The belief that human life follows a developmental course or map is a long-standing feature of Western conceptions of self. We widely assume that individuals develop in stages more or less predictable and uniform. Under the influence of psychologist Jean Piaget and other developmental theorists, educators organize teaching and learning on the premise that cognitive ability gradually emerges in a human being and that success in mastering higher, later stages depends on mastery of lower, earlier ones. Religious studies scholar James Fowler and his associates claim that faith too—regardless of religious affiliation or geographical location—develops in stages that parallel the stages of rationality. Psychologist Erik Erikson argues that the capacity to engage effectively in ritual action likewise emerges in stages of ever-increasing maturity.

Articulating a set of stages is supposed to orient us, enable us to predict what comes next and to measure how far we have come on life's journey. But there is no consensus on what the stages are, and it is difficult to know which versions of the life cycle are grounded in reliable theory and which are merely the outcome of popular speculation and convention.

When a well-known institute of science first proposed to mount an exhibition called "Celebrations: Cycles of Human Life,"[276] one draft of its prospectus stated, "Human lives are composed of cycles of birth, childhood, adolescence, maturity, old age and death. We find it remarkable that the celebrations marking these milestone events transcend divisions of nationality, culture and ethnicity, uniting us in our shared humanity even as they help us form our own, unique identities." This statement defines two *events,* birth and death, as bookends holding four *periods* between them; it also assumes the universality of such a scheme. But can we be so sure that there are only four stages? For every religion and culture? For both sexes? For every individual?

There is no agreement on the nature or number of developmental stages. Even within European American cultures, childhood and adolescence have not always been recognized as distinct phases, and it is doubtful that females go through the same stages as males. Asian and African peoples have their own ways of reckoning phases. So the obviousness of a panhuman life cycle disappears. The stages of the life cycle seem as arbitrary and culturally relative as astrological images in the sky.

Even the truism "People are born, then they age and die" evaporates if we take into account the variety of ways in which the self is understood. In some worldviews, a person is not only born but reborn. A person is not just who he or she appears to be physically. A person is also a version, a reincarnation, of someone else. In some religions, only certain aspects of a person age; others do not. In most Western cosmologies bodies age, while souls do not. In some traditions, death is an illusion or just another kind of birth, so the real self does not *develop;* it just *is.*

Only by refusing to think comparatively can we get away with regarding the human life course as if its structure were obvious and universal. However natural a life-cycle scheme may appear, it is not a given, not "the" life cycle. The sequence of life stages is not genetically determined, regardless of how biological the underlying processes are.

The most widely practiced and thoroughly studied rites of passage are those marking birth, coming of age, marriage, and death, but these are not the only possibilities. Just as actual rites may have more or fewer than three phases, so actual lives may have two or ten or any other number of actual stages. Further, ritualizing all of them is anything but universal. A society ritualizes only a few of the possibilities, not always the ones we in the West consider obvious.

Hinduism probably has more rites of passage than any other large-scale religion. It espouses a life cycle of four stages—student, householder, forest dweller, and renunciate—punctuated by a set of rites called *samskāras*. The number varies, but sixteen life-cycle rites is fairly common. Most traditions have fewer—three or four, perhaps.

Life passages are marked by varying degrees of ritual attention. In the West there are many passages in addition to the "standard" four. Most attract little ritual attention; a few attract more. Among the minimally ritualized ones are defloration (losing one's virginity), conception (as distinct from birth), abortion, naming, adoption, incorporation of new family members into a divorced family, leaving home, moving, buying a new house, induction into office, immigration, incarceration, midlife (turning thirty, forty, or fifty), divorce, name changing, falling ill, being healed, leaves of absence, vocation changes, menopause, job loss, becoming a widow or widower, retirement. Graduation, vision quests, joining a secret society, execution, declaring or going to war, ordination, and same-sex commitment ceremonies seem to attract a bit more ritual attention.

In most societies there is a ritually barren wasteland between marriage and death. Between these two points, roughly from a person's late twenties to his or her midseventies, there are few if any rites of passage to facilitate transition. Adults in this age range may engage in ritual activity, of course, but seldom in rites of passage. During adulthood, we are less likely to be subjected to a rite of passage than to be obligated to organize, attend, or pay for one. As a child or young person, one undergoes rites of passage, but as an adult one does them for others or not at all.

Since coverage of the life cycle is sporadic, not systematic, the typical passage system overlooks many of a person's most taxing transitions. In the European American West, rites of passage are usually predicated on the generic idea of a life "course," which is imagined as either a life "line" or life "cycle." Both images appear in theoretical as well as in popular forms. A crude version of the lifeline metaphor is this: You are born; then you age; finally you die. A line moves from point A to point B to point C. We can turn this linear sequence into a cycle by adding: Then you are reborn at A-prime—either in some other place, on some other plane, or as some other person. A cycle returns, more to less, to the place from which it started.

Imagine a life course laid out like a detailed map. Then imagine a set of corresponding rites, sketched onto a transparent sheet and dropped down neatly upon the life-course map. Everything fits. Every major transition on life's way is overlaid by a template, a rite appropriate to every demanding moment. Unfortunately, no existing passage system accomplishes such a feat. Even if it did, neither the life course nor the rites would likely fit individual lives perfectly. Whether traditional and collective or recently invented and personal, rites are imperfect means.

In contemporary North America there is a trend toward ritual individualism, the conviction that rites can be invented by individuals for the sake of individuals. We have already encountered two authors, who in instructing readers how to confront death, claim that major life issues are "hammered out on the anvil of individual lives. Even what it means to die, once insistently established by religious canon, is left for each individual to puzzle through."[277] Although it may be true that individuals now have freedoms and obligations their forebears did not, it is untrue that most of us puzzle through death and other life passages entirely by ourselves. The vast majority of individuals rely on convention. Even alternative rites become conventionalized among those who enact them.

The Spilling of Boys' Blood

Because it is so evident that there are considerable differences in the ways cultures map the life course, and because of recent, drastic changes within the Western life-cycle pattern, we can no longer regard either life-cycle schemes or rites of passage as cultural or divine givens. Rather, they are constructions that are not only invented but also questioned and revised. As difficult as it is to evaluate a rite, evaluation happens. It transpires across cultures as well as within them, and it happens implicitly as well as explicitly.

Suppose we become interested in constructing an initiation for boys. We begin reading ethnographies that describe these rites elsewhere and run across some of Gilbert Herdt's writings. He provides a disturbing portrait of a boys' initiation among the Sambia of Papua New Guinea. Called *iku mokeiyu,* this sequence of rites aims to make boys into strong and aggressive warriors, to purge them of everything feminine, and to fill them with *jerungdu,* phallic power. The rite's two most controversial actions are ritualized fellatio, in which boys ingest semen to make them more manly, and nose-bleedings, which have the same aim. The boys become so terrified by the bleedings that they cry repeatedly; some involuntarily defecate, while their mothers vacillate. Since they want their boys made into men, they comply and empathize, but since these are their sons, there are outbursts of rage, fear, and resistance.

Now the initiates are grouped round the pool of a small brook flowing down from a thicket. A huge crowd of men assemble, fencing in the boys. The nosebleeders themselves take center stage. Several are wearing upturned pig's-tusk noseplugs (worn with the tusk points turned up only during war and these rites). The men are serious; even as their tense bodies strain forward in anticipation of bleeding the boys, some of them actually grimace. A "strong" man—an aggressive war leader—steps forward and silently plunges cane grasses up his own nose: in full view of the shocked initiates, blood streams down his face. He betrays not the slightest emotion. He bends over into the water to let blood. Somewhere still out of sight, the flutes hauntingly serenade his feat. The crowd of men respond with a loud war cry, a signal that they want more. Only now do the boys grow truly alarmed, realizing what is to happen.

The first boy is quickly grabbed. He struggles and shouts but is held down by three men. Before we can catch our breath the initiator, Karavundun, rolls cane grasses, pushes the initiate's head back, and shoves the grasses repeatedly into the boy's nose. Tears and blood flow as the boy is held and then relaxed forward over the water. Next one and then another boy is grabbed and bled. One lad tries futilely to run away. Seemingly as a punishment, he is bled harder and longer than the others. The next initiate resists fiercely, so four men lift him off the ground and, there suspended, he is forcibly nose-bled. Af-

ter each boy is penetrated until blood flows profusely, the men raise the rit-
ual/war chant time and again. The smell of blood and fear sours the air. The
act is almost mechanical for the initiators, who are the boys' clansmen, cross-
cousins, and matrilateral kin. The guardians passively assist by holding the
boys. The initiates' fathers stay removed. . . .

Last, Merumie [one of the leaders] lectures the boys on their mothers'
harmful effects and the value of letting blood: "You [initiates] have been with
your mothers . . . they have said 'bad words' to you; their talk has entered
your noses and prevented you from growing big. Your skins are no good.
Now you can grow and look nice."[278]

Whereas ritual fantasies let us conjure beautiful images of what we
wish were the case, this is a quite real, quite specific initiation. The account transports us into the stench of blood-soured air and the sound
of boys weeping. The participants are not characters in a movie but
people in an actual place. The deeds have about them a shocking phys-
icality that resists any impulse to haul them across the Pacific in the
hope of importing them for domestic use. They belong there, in Papua
New Guinea, not here, in our own backyards. Thus, we exercise,
rightly or wrongly, our critical judgment about the appropriateness of
certain actions.

The danger is that in making such judgments we distance ourselves
from the Sambians, think of them as primitive and ourselves as civi-
lized. We may even be tempted to dismiss this, perhaps all, initiations as
crude and violent. Either that or we venerate tribal manhood making
with romantic zeal, using images of it to criticize the banality of manhood in contemporary culture. But the fuller picture, which can be
glimpsed only by reading the rest of Herdt's ethnography, helps one understand how like the Sambians we are while teaching us how different
we are as well.

Like us, Sambian parents are affectionate with their children. They
joke, suffer, and worry the same as we do. Like Sambians, we want our
children to have the right attitudes and skills to ensure survival. The
Sambian initiation contains much that is utterly ordinary and unthreat-
ening, much that we might, in fact, emulate, but this scene warns us
against trying to domesticate and market the rite. So, in effect, we make
two judgments about the rite: that we should not be in a rush to appropriate it and that we should not be hasty to condemn those who perform it.

To avoid thoughtless self-congratulation, posing some challenging comparative questions for ourselves can be instructive. The forced and repeated nose-bleedings are harsh, but are they harsher than ritualized induction into military service? And how do Sambian "surgical" procedures compare with episiotomies and circumcisions conducted at North American hospital births? Keeping Sambian boys sequestered against their wills could be considered child abduction in North America. And keeping their mothers away would be seen as sexist. Teaching boys to mouth flutes as a prelude to mouthing their elders' penises translates as child molestation. But are Sambian practices more damaging to the child psyche than the noninitiation or peer initiations of industrialized Western societies?

There is little that would tempt most of us to imitate this initiation scene, but it raises some probing questions: How much compulsion is necessary to underwrite effective initiation? When does initiatory hazing become violence, abuse, or brainwashing? How important is it to maintain and cultivate strong gender differences? If we were to take up the task of initiating the young, what forms of violence might arise in Western societies? What protections should be in place?

As both a father and a scholar, I would not tolerate physical initiatory violence in any form, nor would I consent to tests that would risk my children's physical health. I cannot imagine that most other North American parents would be any more willing than I. So the real questions concern not acute physical violence but chronic psychological violence. What will happen, or not happen, if we do not initiate our children?

Before my son, Bryn, was born, I remember contemplating circumcision. The act of cutting off the foreskin made no sense whatever to me. Of course, I had no memory of the actual procedure, since it had been performed when I was a baby. I had been subjected to it because it was the convention of the day, rationalized to my parents by doctors who declared it hygienic.

Shortly after Bryn was born and I was checking to be certain that all his parts were intact, I winced, again imagining his being cut, a procedure few doctors thinks of as ritualistic. Although I did not regard my parents' decision as irresponsible, since they believed they were acting in my best interests, I would have experienced the act of circumcising my son as a form of child abuse. I could marshal no credible religious or medical reason for allowing it. Why not celebrate those parts rather than slice them? Why not paint them red with cherry juice or tie a yellow ribbon around the old oak tree? Anything but cutting. The ritually imaginative moment and the ritually critical moment were simultaneous. Imagining enabled me to say no.

Ritual criticism is the interpretation of a rite or ritual system with a view to implicating its practice.[279] Such criticism is possible only if we consider rites to be human artifacts subject to the usual human flaws and manipulations. Ritual criticism is not always negative, but it is based on the premise that rites—however noble in intention or sacred in origin—are imperfect.

Rites may become not only irrelevant but oppressive. In the wrong hands, they can be tools for oppression as surely as they can be instruments of healing. During moments of passage, people are peculiarly vulnerable—not only open to the transformative power of ritual but also subject to ceremonial manipulation. Since rites of passage have been employed to mystify the sources of power and therefore to control others, we cannot assume they are above critique, even when they appear sacrosanct.

Even if ritual is not usually considered a proper object of criticism, ritualists do evaluate rites, both formally and informally. They may not make their evaluations public. But ritual criticism occurs, and it happens among practitioners and believers, not merely among scholars schooled in critique and debate.

Ritual has probably been evaluated for as long as it has been enacted, since, in prescribing ("Do it this way"), one is implicitly criticizing ("Don't do it that way"). In the eighth century B.C.E., God is said to have declared through the Hebrew prophet Amos, "I hate, I despise your feasts, and I take no delight in your solemn assemblies" (Amos 6: 21). Amos's criticism is offered as if it were God's, and it is aimed at the ritual practices of his contemporaries. The critique evokes two explicit criteria, justice and ritual purity. "Solemn [ritual] assemblies" were displacing basic concerns for social justice, Amos declared, and they were becoming tainted by non-Hebraic elements. Different ritual traditions invoke differing criteria by which rites may be called into question. Some traditions shield their practices from public criticism, but it would surprise me to discover a ritual system in which critique did not occur at all.

Most insider criticism of ritual, even when it takes the form of polemical attacks, is usually selective—a critique of this rite or that practice, not of ritual in general. During the iconoclastic controversies of the eighth and ninth centuries, as well as during the Protestant Reformation of sixteenth-century Europe, reformers criticized elements of the church's ritual system. But even Protestant traditions that denied they had ritual typically engaged in it under some other name: "worship," "services," "meetings," and the like.

Criticism can come from either inside a tradition or outside it. An insider is more likely to have access to backstage elements of ritual performance, to be positioned so as to observe the political jockeying that permeates a rite, but it is difficult, psychologically and politically, to question the ground you walk on. For this reason, it is tempting to deflect criticism of your own rites by criticizing someone else's. Outsider criticism can be experienced as a cheap shot, the exercise of unearned authority, but an outsider may also have less vested interest.

Female Genital Mutilation

Globally, there is more outrage over ritual surgery on girls than over the circumcision of boys. One reason is that the procedures and consequences for girls are much more drastic. Ceremonially conducted genital "mutilation" is a current practice in Africa and a widely debated issue. I use quotation marks not because I disbelieve genitals are really being cut but because using such a term bespeaks a specific point of view. Although one may on moral grounds hold that ritual surgery of the genitals constitutes mutilation, others regard it as beautifying and purifying.

The whistles pierced the early morning as the procession slowly circled the *mabwaita* [a structure of poles and leaves upon which rites occur] twice to the right. Suddenly, the girls sat on the ready leaves with their legs spread wide, each grasped firmly from behind, and the three surgeons began their work excising each girl's clitoris and labia majora. The result, as Okiek see it, made their genitals "smooth" and "clean," as adult women's should be.

People edged forward until young women with switches forced them back from the women quickly cutting the girls' genitals. After what seemed to me a long time, the whistles began again. The operations were over, without a blink or a sound from the six girls. Men and women both rejoiced in song.

The girls were stripped of dance costumes by their mothers and the women they were leaning against. They lay collapsed, at least one looking as if she was in shock, but all the time blowing their whistles. Wrapped now in blankets, they got up with some assistance and stood, legs apart and blood dripping. Their leg bells were jingled until the costume owners claimed them; they were tied with *sinenteet* vines as a sign of the girls' success. Finally, the girls walked, awkwardly stooped and with their legs apart, to the small house in the compound where three of them would later be secluded. Some had to be carried. Women sang "We want to rejoice," their song of celebration, with punctuating ululation and shouts of thanks for the girls' bravery and success. Men danced in a line, singing their own celebration song, *riret*. Nini's father looked like he had been crying a bit. The jubilant turmoil of this immediate celebration continued for some twenty minutes before people started to quiet down.

. . .

While others rejoiced, the girls lay on their backs in the seclusion house, knees bent and legs wide apart. Their pain showed. A blazing fire kept them warm. When they came in they had been fed milk; porridge was cooked later as well. Close female relatives and other older women visited the girls soon after the operation. When they entered, they spat toward them lightly, as to a newborn child. The girls were *taarusyeek* (initiates), no longer children but not yet adult women.

. . .

Late in the night, the initiates were lectured a final time about how adult women should behave, respecting people and staying at home, not roaming to look for men. The speech can be quite loud and abusive. They were also told not to tell women's secrets; a curse was said which would kill them if they did. The remaining secrets . . . were revealed to the initiates before they went to the river.

. . .

After four months together hiding from adult men and learning the secrets of adult women, the girls had become young women. Prospective suitors continued to visit their parents, though marriage arrangements were in the last stages and were expected to end as soon as possible with a wedding. Ideally, the young women would become new wives within the week.[280]

This kind of procedure occurs at an intercultural frontier where indigenous practitioners and outside observers engage in considerable debate. Western anthropologists, especially feminists, accuse practitioners of genital mutilation. The accusation is harsh, so some argue that observers who level it are ethnocentric. A more neutral word is *circumcision,* but applying the single term to all forms of genital surgery leads to confusion. Overly simplified usage glosses over differences in gender and in the seriousness of the surgery. Since the word *circumcision* means "to cut around," the action presupposes a penis, therefore a man. So if we speak of "female circumcision," we are inflating the male version to generic status.

Whatever one thinks of ritual surgery of the genitals, the consequences of, say, Jewish circumcision at a boy's birth are minor in comparison with the effects of removing a teenage girl's clitoris and labia majora in a puberty rite. Since some versions of female "circumcision" have major sexual and health consequences, it is imperative to distinguish different kinds of operations and identify examples of groups that practice them:

circumcision: exposure of the glans (head of the penis) by lateral or circular incision. Practiced among Jews and Muslims for religious reasons and North Americans for health reasons. Among some groups such as the Masai a vestige of the prepuce is left to hang below the glans.

superincision: longitudinal incision on the dorsal (top) side of the penis. Practiced by the Tikopia (in the Pacific).

subincision: longitudinal incision on the ventral (lower) side of the penis. Practiced by the Aranda of Australia.

clitoridectomy: surgical removal of the clitoris. Practiced by the Okiek of Kenya (cited in the example above).

labial excision: surgical removal of the labia (also narrated in the above account).

vaginal infibulation: surgical scarification of the sides of the vulva causing them to grow together during the healing process, leaving a small hole for urination. This version is sometimes called pharaonic circumcision, presumably because it was practiced by ancient Egyptians. This practice is found in Somali and Sudan.

Whereas ancient Romans regarded the circumcised male body as ugly, contemporaneous Jewish rabbis considered the foreskin ugly. So even though the Jewish rationale for circumcision was not mainly esthetic, circumcision was considered a beautifying procedure. In many places where ritual surgery is practiced, the surgically altered genital, whether male or female, is considered more pure, more beautiful, more mature. The bearer of such organs are adults with the means for having proper adult sexual relations. Since they have endured ritual surgery, they are considered brave and in control of themselves.

Europeans and North Americans struggle to comprehend why these practices are not only permitted but encouraged, perpetuated by women as well as by men. Because so much more is at stake for African women, they consent to such operations for some of the same reasons American and Canadian women consent to routine episiotomies in hospitals: It is the way things are done; you have to do it, there is no option; the authorities say so. If you don't no one will marry you. The Western medical establishment claims that episiotomies make births easier. Surgery, doctors assure mothers, ensures that the vaginal tear will be smooth rather than ragged. Straight cuts may be aesthetically neater, but they take longer to heal than jagged tears and often result in third- or fourth-degree tears into the rectum. Women routinely consent to these surgical procedures even though midwives and mothers from other cultures consider them unnecessary.

What seems common sense in one society appears bizarre or unethical from the point of view of another. Many contemporary Western activists have worked to abolish female genital mutilation. In this respect, they stand where nineteenth-century Christian missionaries stood, having to balance moral commitments with their desire not to interfere with cultural values they do not fully share or entirely understand.

Corinne Kratz, who wrote the above account of initiation among the Okiek of Kenya, discusses the procedure. Although she does not advocate it, neither does she criticize it. Instead, she counsels the development of a more fully contextualized understanding of the ritual practice, warning, "Were Okiek girls' initiation to be abolished because it includes excision, the primary context in which women come together as a group, constituting a ritual community and a forum for social critique, would also disappear."[281]

Genital surgery in Africa sometimes becomes a prominent symbol of resistance to colonialism. The procedure has been cited as justification for Western powers to engage in further colonizing; Westerners have felt compelled to instruct natives about the immorality of their actions. But when undergoing ritual surgery begins to serve as a symbol of resistance of Western domination or intrusion, it is difficult for Western observers to balance respect for female bodies with respect for a community's cultural and religious autonomy.

Kratz is right to caution against decontextualizing. In fact, the context should be even broader. It should be global, taking into account both African and European American ways of rationalizing ritual procedures. Episiotomies in the West are rationalized in ways that are decidedly aesthetic and symbolic, making "our" practices just as strange as "theirs."

But the ethnographic question of understanding female "circumcision" in its local and global context must not become a way of evading troublesome moral questions: Do observers have the right to criticize indigenous ritual practices? Do they have a right *not* to criticize them? Should parents lend support to those conducting such rites on their children? The questions remain, just as they did when the issue was slavery rather than genital surgery.

Questioning ritual surgery on the African continent can be specious if it does not lead to questioning other forms of ritualized surgery closer to home. The growing global opposition to ritualized surgery on female genitals has sparked a debate over Jewish male circumcision as well as its secular, medical counterpart. Some doctors and insurance companies have declared circumcision medically unnecessary, making it difficult for observant Jews to underwrite their practice by claiming a consensus among medical practitioners. There is a vigorous Jewish defense of the practice, but it is increasingly argued on ritual, rather than medical, grounds. In addition to criticism there is an increased willingness to improvise naming ceremonies for boys that eliminate the act of circumcision. The question debated among Jews of various persuasions is whether the rite can be bent without being broken.

Jewish circumcision is sometimes called a rite of passage or birth rite. But the ceremony is not quite a celebration of birth, and even if it were, it does not do everything that needs doing to recognize and honor a birth. The rite is mainly about the incorporation of a male into the covenant between God and Israel. Only because it follows quickly upon the heels of birth is it conventionally treated as a birth rite. As it stands, the rite has little to do with female fecundity or parental nurture; it is about patriarchal succession.[282] For much of its history the circumcision ceremony has either excluded or marginalized women. Historically, not only have women been refused a corresponding mark of the covenant, but mothers were sometimes kept from holding their infant sons as they were being circumcised or even kept out of the actual circumcision room.

Not long ago a Montreal newspaper published comments by a female medical doctor calling for an end to the circumcision of boys. The procedure, she said, was worse than superfluous; it was abusive. A few days later a nearby Reform synagogue held a lunchtime discussion of the issue and of *brit milah,* the Jewish rite of circumcision. What surprised me was not the defense of circumcision but that women, rather than men, were among its most strident proponents. Two young parents-to-be said they feared *not* having their boy circumcised would create more psychological damage than the physical damage that *might* result from surgery. What would they be doing to their son if, ritually speaking, they made him *not Jewish?*

Asked if there were alternative ways that the community could imagine for marking entry into the covenant, many said that even imagining alternatives to the circumcision rite was threatening, more painful than continuing the practice. Of course, such a view of the relative painfulness was that of parents and grandparents, not that of infants undergoing the rite.

In the noontime discussion it was obvious that reimagining and criticizing the circumcision rite were equally threatening. To reimagine is implicitly to criticize, and to criticize, implicitly to reimagine. Resistance to ceremonial change is not just political and social, it is also imaginative. The project of reinventing ritual requires both imagination and criticism, but neither creating nor criticizing is comfortably or conventionally associated with ritual.

Ritual Criticism and Widow Burning

A telling example in which a rite of passage comes under critical scrutiny from both inside and outside a tradition is sati. It is not widely practiced now, so I will speak of it in the past tense. Centered mainly in Bengal, sati was the rite of a widow's burning herself to death on her husband's funeral pyre, thus committing an act euphemistically called co-cremation.[283] The term *sati* refers both to this self-sacrificial rite and to the woman who performed it.

A sati was mythologized as the ideal Hindu wife. Neither shunned nor impure like the widow who opted to survive her husband, a sati was popularly venerated as heroic. By her devoted action, she became a goddess. Her self-sacrifice constituted a meritorious deed capable of ensuring her salvation as well as that of her husband. Although the act was supposed to have been voluntary, there is evidence that some instances of it may have been pressured or coerced.

In eighteenth- and nineteenth-century Hinduism, a husband was deified, so a wife was supposed to act out of absolute devotion to him. Ideally, she should precede him in death. The premature death of a husband implied the failure of his wife, whose bad karma contributed to his early demise. By committing sati, she was able to transform not only her destiny but his.

When a Hindu husband died, his funeral made him an ancestor, but unless the wife committed sati, it ritually transformed her into a widow condemned to a life of social avoidance. Her head was tonsured, making her ugly and visible to all. She wore no jewelry, donned only prescribed colors, went barefoot, and avoided social gatherings, rich food, and entertainment. She denied herself not only remarriage but all the joys and symbols of the married state. Not only was she to engage in perpetual mourning, she also became to others a living embodiment of inauspiciousness and bad luck. To enter widowhood was to become symbolically dead.

Whereas a bereft woman's choice was between the living social death of widowhood and the martyr's death of sati, a widower was not held to be karmically responsible for his wife's death. He was expected to remarry, not burn himself on his wife's funeral pyre.

Although the term *suttee* came into use only in 1787, and the peak of its practice seems to have been in the eighteenth and nineteenth centuries, the earliest account of it, dating to 316 B.C.E., is Greek, thus that of an outsider. A man has died. The senior wife, it seems, has opted for widowhood, while a more junior wife has chosen sati:

The elder wife went away lamenting, with the band about her head rent, and tearing her hair, as if tidings of some great disaster had been brought her; and the other departed, exultant at her victory, to the pyre, crowned with fillets by the women who belonged to her and decked out splendidly as for a wedding. She was escorted by her kinsfolk who chanted a song in praise of her virtue. When she came near to the pyre, she took off her adornments and distributed them to her familiars and friends, leaving a memorial for herself, as it were, to those who had loved her. Her adornments consisted of a multitude of rings on her hands, set with precious gems of diverse colours, about her head golden stars not a few, variegated with different sorts of stones, and about her neck a multitude of necklaces, each a little larger than the one above it. In conclusion, she said farewell to her familiars and was helped by her brother onto the pyre, and there, to the admiration of the crowd which had gathered together for the spectacle, she ended her life in heroic fashion. Before the pyre was kindled, the whole army in battle array marched round it thrice. She meanwhile lay down beside her husband, and as the fire seized her no sound of weakness escaped her lips. The spectators were moved, some to pity and some to exuberant praise. But some of the Greeks found fault with such customs as savage and inhumane.[284]

This description was written by an outsider who was both admiring of the sati's courage and repulsed at the ceremony itself. We should remember, though, that Alexander the Great was at the time invading India, thus the Greeks were not without their own form of savagery, that of ritualized conquest. The ambivalence in this report is typical of subsequent European reactions, even among those who sought to suppress sati in the eighteenth and nineteenth centuries. Under the influence of British government officials, missionaries, and indigenous Indian opponents such as Raja Rammohun Roy (1772–1833), widow burning was outlawed in 1829, although sporadic illegal performances of it continued well into the twentieth century.

Sati was never widespread. Statistics compiled by Baptist missionaries declared that in 1803 there were about 275 satis in and around Calcutta. Even though the numbers were not great, the ceremony was public and had a profound impact on the crowds who witnessed it.

There is no satisfactory answer to the question, How and why did sati originate? The rite has little or no warrant in the Vedas, the most ancient sacred Hindu writings. The tenth chapter of the Rig-Veda describes a cemetery practice in which a wife lies down beside her deceased husband. Then she is called forth: "Rise, come unto the world of life, O woman; come, he is lifeless by whose side thou liest." She is beckoned *away from* her dead husband.

The eighteenth chapter of the Atharva Veda, apparently depicting the same practice, says, "This woman, choosing her husband's world, lies down by thee that art departed, O mortal, continuing to keep her ancient duty; to her assign thou here progeny and property."

Although a wife expresses loyalty to her husband by performing the expected ceremonial gesture, in this account she does not enter the cremation fire. The life to which she is called does not seem to be that of another world, but rather of this world, where possessions and succession matter. These verses appear to depict a ritual drama that legitimizes a widow's access to property and her jurisdiction over her children, a fate considerably more attractive than a forced choice between sati and despised widowhood. Here, the wife joins her dead husband symbolically and temporarily rather than literally and permanently. Having done so, she carries away what she and her husband produced together.

For Westerners the political and ethical issues surrounding sati were entangled. The ethical issue was whether it was moral for Christians to witness the rite without attempting to prevent it. But Christian opposition to sati was seldom mounted on the basis of purely moral motives. Missionary intervention was part of a grand plan to convert all of India, displacing Hinduism with Christianity. Missionaries believed that only an evil religion could produce such an obviously evil practice. Of course, they did not draw the same conclusion about Christianity on the basis of the European Crusades or witch burnings, both of which were supervised and sanctioned by the church.

The basic political question for the British was whether it was wise or just for government officials to intervene in local religious affairs, forcibly legislating an end to sati. Indians, too, struggled with the moral and political tangle. Some felt sati was authorized by tradition; others argued that the most authoritative and ancient texts did not sanction or require it. Indians sometimes found that the right moral choice (against sati) implied the wrong political choice (appearing to support the British). For a few Indian nationalists sati provided a self-sacrificial image that could be used to bolster resistance to British meddling in Indian religious affairs. For British imperialists, the practice of sati was justification for intensifying Christianization and continuing British domination in India. The meaning of sati as a rite of passage, then, was as inseparable from politics as it was from religion.

Satanic Ritual Abuse

In North America we have our own forms of "ritual abuse." Here, the phrase usually connotes satanic or sexual abuse. Fantasies about secret rites involving orgies, forced sexual acts, blood drinking, child sacrifice, and the cannibalizing of human flesh have a long history. Early Christians were accused by Romans of committing such acts. It mattered little that Christians practiced secrecy in order to evade Roman persecution or that the flesh and blood eaten by Christians were symbolic. Later, when Christians were in power, they accused Jews and nonconforming Christians of similar ritual crimes. Stories about bizarre uses of ritual have never died out entirely.

On June 25, 1995, Geraldo Rivera invited several victims of satanic ritual abuse to his show:

The third guest was Carol, an obviously distressed woman in her early twenties. She remembers being lured into what was apparently a Christian prayer meeting at the age of ten and abused by the cult for three and a half years. She believes that she repressed the memories and recovered them during therapy. She said that the cult told her that they were her family now. They allegedly put her in a casket, lowered her into a grave and threw earth on the casket. After a while, they freed her, saying that her family of origin didn't rescue her, Jesus didn't rescue her; they (her new family) did. These are typical false memories that often arise during recovered memory therapy (RMT). Carol was close to breaking down completely on the show. She appeared to be an all too typical example of a woman who had been functioning well in life, who entered RMT and became disabled by the results of the counseling.[285]

On December 12 of the same year Geraldo publicly apologized for having believed and encouraged others to believe those who told stories of satanic ritual abuse. Repressed memory therapy, he declared, is crap. The Ontario Consultants on Religious Tolerance, who summarized Carol's story above, are obviously on the side of the repentant Geraldo.

A wave of satanic ritual abuse stories began in 1980 with the publication of *Michelle Remembers* by Michelle Smith and Lawrence Pazder. Their exposé supposedly revealed extensive satanic ritual abuse in North America, but subsequent studies show that the book was a fraud, its rites pilfered from various African sources and modified to horrify and attract Western readers. The wave of accounts was amplified by talk shows and news reports across North America.

The question that obsesses satanic ritual abuse researchers is whether or not it even exists. The "it" is sometimes Satan, sometimes satanic groups or satanic rites, child sacrifice, or large-scale ritualized sexual abuse. Much confusion arises from the lack of clarity about the object of investigation.

If the scale and severity of ritualized sexual abuse is as great as some claim, the misuse of ritual is a more pervasive problem in North America than in India or Kenya, from which our previous examples come. If there are tens of thousands of members of satanic ritual cults in twentieth-century North America, we have a very serious problem.[286] Even if the phenomenon is only an expression of mass hysteria and collective projection, we still have a serious problem, though of a different kind. However one explains satanic ritual abuse—as fantasized, real, or some combination of both—it is remarkable, because it shows that we are both less rational and more ritualistic than we like to believe.

Our fear of ritual leaves us fantasizing about it. Even if the ritual-abuse scare proceeds primarily on the basis of stories told rather than ceremonies performed, its social consequences exceed those of the Salem witch trials in Puritan New England. In comparison, we have witnessed more trials, more widespread paranoia, and more lives ruined by speculation and accusation. So it is imperative to recognize the power of fictive ritual whether or not it is the root of satanic ritual abuse.

The witch trials of medieval Europe were conducted on a much larger scale than those at Salem. The trials themselves were ecclesiastical scapegoating rites aimed at rooting out, among other things, those participating in alleged satanic and demonic cults. Contemporary religion scholars and historians do not generally think there were widespread, devil-worshiping covens of witches in which participants sacrificed children, dispersed curses, and blasphemed the church. These acts existed largely in the fantasies of prosecuting clergy and the gullible populace. Devil-worship rites were fantasized, then projected, not uncovered or discovered.

Fantasized or not, the accusations resulted in trials, and the trials eventuated in ritual murder, very real destruction of human, predominately female, life, and this destruction was authorized by functionaries of the church. The trials, like Hitler's highly ritualized Nuremberg rallies, illustrate the ways in which ritual fantasy can eventuate in both deadly social ritualization and in explicit ceremonies, the outcome of which is genocide. Rites do not merely illustrate or augment military, political, or economic power, they also sometimes constitute and focus it.

Current North American ritual-abuse stories have resulted in social and psychological damage among both the accusers and the accused, but in few trials and in even fewer convictions. Evidence that will stand up in court is exceedingly rare. Between 1992 and 1997 several large-scale studies commissioned by various government bodies concluded that actual satanic rites do not exist on a scale large enough to constitute a significant social problem. There is little or no proof that multigenerational satanic ritual groups exist.[287] But these studies leave open the possibility that an occasional story or accusation might, in fact, be true or contain elements of literal truth.

A widespread tendency is either to believe or disbelieve stories of ritual abuse *on principle,* which is to say, without benefit of either reliable research or personal experience. Principled belief and disbelief are closed, therefore dangerous, postures to assume. Colin Ross, director of the Dissociative Disorders Unit of the Charter Behavioral Health System in Dallas, is the author of *Satanic Ritual Abuse: Principles of Treat-*

ment, one of the most cogently written books on the topic. Ross advises, "Ritual abuse is a complex and perplexing phenomenon, and we simply do not know what percentage of survivor memories are real. Given the history of man's barbarity, and the large-scale atrocities committed by all races in the twentieth century, it is important that we not adopt the role of good Germans who looked the other way while the Nazis carried out their human sacrifices. It is equally important not to foster a hysterical witch hunt. Satanic ritual abuse should be a subject of dispassionate intellectual and scientific inquiry and serious law-enforcement investigation. We should expect to discover a complex, heterogeneous, and fluctuating combination of fact, fantasy, and fiction as we learn more, and we should not endorse any one hypothesis prematurely, to the exclusion of others."[288]

Some cases of satanic ritual abuse can be accounted for in ways other than assuming the existence of actual groups of satanically oriented ritual practitioners. False-memory syndrome, urban legend–making, and psychic contamination by therapists and the media are among the alternative explanations. No one of these can explain every case, but then neither can assuming the literal reality of the cults. So explanations are necessarily complex, varying from case to case.

Because of the containment of their work in a special place and time, therapists, like scholars and readers of fiction, can afford to suspend disbelief. They function more effectively when they can assume that it doesn't matter if a ritual-abuse story is true or false. What matters is that the person telling it *believes* it to be true. The question for a therapist is not whether ritual abuse happened but how people feel and act if they *believe* it did or *believe they remember* that it did. By assuming a neutral but supportive posture, therapists can resist being drawn into the elaborate chains of double binding typical of satanic ritual-abuse stories, thereby being rendered ineffective. Drawn into the narratives, then lured into taking sides with one of the "characters" (usually the hurt child in the story) and becoming antagonistic toward another (usually the satanic figure), a therapist loses sight of *the whole person,* in whom these figures reside as memories or figments of imagination. Only if one takes seriously the power of the unconscious and embraces *all* the images produced by it is it possible to create the conditions for healing.

Outside counseling offices and psychiatric hospitals, it is not easy to suspend belief or disbelief. What occurs when whole families or communities come to believe that satanic ritual abuse is rampant in their neighborhoods? What happens when they refuse to believe? Family members and friends do not have the rules, closed doors, unlisted phone numbers, fees, and procedures that therapists employ to create clear, protective boundaries. If it is common for therapists working on satanic ritual abuse to show signs of posttraumatic stress, families and friends of people who tell ritual abuse stories are bound to suffer even more acutely.[289]

One difficulty for sensitive but skeptical inquirers is the fact that only a few decades ago the sexual abuse of native children in boarding schools was invisible. It "did not exist." Now, there is incontrovertible evidence that widespread sexual abuse did occur on a large scale.[290] So it is important to remain open to the possibility of satanic ritual abuse, while at the same time resisting the compulsion to believe and take sides.

However, when one tries to suspend judgment, others caught up in stories and experiences of sexual abuse may conclude that one's inaction amounts to complicity with abusers. So there is no perfectly safe position. Belief on principle, disbelief on principle, and suspension of judgment all have their dangers.

It would make no sense to expect sexually abused people to disbelieve their experience. It also makes little sense to expect those without such experience to believe readily. So what does one do? How does one respond to stories of ritual sexual abuse? In another era the church might have resorted to exorcism, a ritualistic counterattack. Exorcism rites are occasionally performed, but often without official church sanction. The Roman Catholic Church recently revised its exorcism rite, but in Europe and North America it remains cautious in allowing resort to the rite.

The results of exorcism can be as devastating as the abuse the rite is supposed to rectify. Assault on the assaulted does not work. The ritual cure may only heighten the disease, because exorcism in the West usually takes the form of a ceremonial assault on some "bad part" of a person, the devil within. The rite is less about integration than expulsion.

Colin Ross is a specialist in multiple personality disorder who works on ritual abuse cases. He is critical of "high drama" between therapist and client. Avoiding ritualization and dramatization, he prefers "behaviorally unremarkable conversation between two adults," even when the client is switching among different personalities.[291] He prefers conversation and cognitive therapy to counterritualizing, a strategy some therapists take. It may be that North American culture in general is so little attuned to ritual means that the use of rites in satanic abuse cases would only complicate matters. But there is little reliable research on ritualized forms of therapy for the ritually abused.

The popular literature on satanic ritual abuse has been accompanied by an escalation of scholarly study, but research, like popular interest, is spasmodic. Even though cultic uses of ritual have long been with us, academic interest in them is occasional, usually sparked by highly publicized stories about ritually framed deaths or suicides. The research peaked in 1992 and began tapering off, so likely public fear and fascination have crested as well.

Never "Instead of," Always "in Addition to"

The difference between using ritual to abuse and using it to serve or heal is not always clear, especially when money is involved. And money is involved as soon as we shift from enacting rites for ourselves and families to providing them to others for a fee. When talking about ritual creativity and criticism, it is easy to conceive of rites as transpiring in a protected zone much in the same way that art and research are imagined as insulated from the struggle for economic survival. But economics plays a significant role in rites of passage, even newly reinvented ones.

Since they are not entirely controlled by religious institutions, rites of passage attract entrepreneurs such as funeral directors. More recently joining the growing number of professionals are wedding planners, caterers, and photographers, who have become a standard part of many ceremonies.

Currently, another kind of professional is emerging. Whether these entrepreneurs are exploitative or creative or both is difficult to determine, but the current religious, legal, and economic climate supports their emergence. If alternative healing can become a business alongside mainstream medicine, why not alternative ritual entrepreneurs? If mainstream rabbis and priests can be paid, why not earn a living by marketing ritual goods and skills to the religiously disaffiliated and the affiliated but dissatisfied?

Joyce Gioia sells ceremonial services in the New York City area and is authorized to perform weddings in the states of New York and Massachusetts. She calls herself as a multifaith minister.[292] Educated at The New Seminary and now working on a degree in rabbinical studies, she has a Master of Spiritual Counseling (M.S.C.) as well as a Master of

Spiritual Theology (M.S.Th.) degree. The New Seminary's curriculum focuses on religious similarities, not differences. All religions, Joyce declares, "even Yoruba, the African religion that involves animal sacrifice," is accepted there. The board of directors, she tells prospective customers, includes a Reform rabbi, a Catholic priest, a Methodist minister, an initiated shaman, a disciple of Swami Satchidinanda, a representative of Islam, and a Sufi master. The motto for the seminary is "Never instead of, always in addition to."

Joyce does not specialize in a particular faith but in "customized" weddings. Having performed over two hundred of them, she "bonds" over fifty couples a year. She has performed not only a baseball wedding in the Bronx (during which the "audience" sang *Take Me Out to the Ball Game*), she has also conducted Muslim, Catholic, Protestant, Jewish, Hindu-Jewish, Muslim-Jewish, Muslim-Catholic, Rastafarian, interfaith, co-officiated, humanist, Native American, civil, and Buddhist weddings. Her multicultural and interfaith wedding ceremonies are often laced with words from sacred languages: Arabic, Latin, and Hebrew. According to her advertisement, "She finds unique ways to incorporate the languaging of the words within each religion, so that *everyone* feels comfortable and 'taken care of' and no one is ever offended."

Regarding fees, her ad says, "Because Joyce invests so much time to give couples exactly what they want, her fee is higher than some of her colleagues. Her basic fee is $500. This fee includes the initial meeting (in person or by phone), a customized ceremony and FAXing or e-mailing back and forth until the couple is delighted with the ceremony. It does not include a travel fee for travel more than 30 minutes away from her location in New Rochelle. The travel fee is $50 for each 45 minutes (or portion thereof) of travel to and from the location of the wedding. For weddings in New York City, couples also pay parking costs. Joyce also provides a unique, personalized gift to each couple after the ceremony."

Alternative ritual entrepreneurship is appearing in other Western countries as well. In Australia it is government supervised, and the image of a religious free market from which nothing is excluded is less pronounced. Since 1973 the Civil Marriage Celebrant (CMC) program has authorized certain individuals to perform weddings outside religious institutions. Some 1,550 celebrants now perform over forty thousand weddings a year—47 percent of the total of Australian marriages in 1995.

Jim and Meg Boswell run a business called Celebration Ceremonies.

Meg is certified by the CMC program and is authorized to perform weddings all over Australia. She bills herself as a marriage and naming celebrant, while Jim is described as a master of ceremonies and management consultant as well as a naming and funeral celebrant. She specializes in family life events such as weddings and vow renewals, while he is more deeply involved in business and community celebrations such as retirements, achievement and service recognitions, and the induction of new officers.

Jim articulates their view of myth and ritual. Ethics, he insists, are as "dry as dust," but myths and rites give them emotional and imaginative clout. "One of our great problems at the end of the twentieth century," he says, "is that we have become such a pluralistic society. We have replaced the value systems of traditional cultures with a pluralism of competing value systems. Myths and rituals once central to the entire society have lost their wide appeal. But pluralism does not lessen the need for ritual and myth. It underscores their importance. Modern Western society has become a battleground of competing rituals and myths struggling for power. In our society rituals and myths are battling to possess the souls of people but their messages are so much a part of life that they are taken for granted. This is the source of their power. We are so emotionally engaged in what is happening that we suspend disbelief and buy the message. Ritual and myth are so much a part of our lives we take them for granted. We are shaped by values and we rarely recognise it."[293]

On the one hand, we have an apparently unregulated American alternative ritual market and on the other, an Australian government-sponsored community service. I confess that Joyce's version, although provocative, also makes me nervous. I worry about the ease with which she claims ritual competence in so many traditions. I question the wisdom of unprincipled inclusion, of her principled refusal to exclude. There is a growing need for people who work in the interstices between religions, and Joyce displays a flexibility not typical of clergy, but this adaptability also means she has fewer loyalties. Who can call her into question? Perhaps only her customers. The attorney general of Australia looks over the Boswells' shoulders, but to whom is Joyce accountable? To a purely market-driven ritual economy? Would an association of ritual consumers be any wiser and more humane than an ecclesiastical or government bureaucracy? However much one might applaud interreligious sensitivity, we should also ponder capitalism of the spirit.

Evaluating rites and ritual entrepreneurs is not easy, since the capitalism implicit in globalization is everywhere. There are pressures on the Australian system to change. In 1997 the attorney general's office issued a discussion paper calling for greater self-regulation within the civil celebration industry and for the development of a code of ethics. The paper urged the writing of a statement of service standards for civil celebrants and proposed that they be appointed for a five-year renewable term rather than for life. The writers of the discussion paper seem ready to allow the entrepreneurial model to displace the community-service model. For instance, the authors suggest that fees would no longer be regulated and that advertising beyond the yellow pages would be permitted.

When the Australian celebrant program first started, it presumed a clear line between religious ceremonies and civil rites; civil celebrants were not allowed to use religious references. But their clients began to complain. They wanted to have celebrations that were neither secular nor institutionally religious, but rather, spiritual. The attorney general's office now seems willing to compromise, allowing for spirituality as well as religion, business-driven as well as community-service ritual.

Abortion Rites in Japan

We are used to thinking of funerals and weddings as services that can be sold, but what about abortion rites? Abortion has a history that encompasses the globe. Approximately 350 premodern societies have practiced it.[294] In Canada and the United States abortion is a lightning rod for ethical debate and legal wrangling, but in Japan the occasion is also handled ritually. The first precept, to which all Buddhists subscribe, is a vow not to take the life of a sentient being, so there are moral controversies in Japan, but they have not displaced ritual means of handling abortion.

Kuyō means rite and *mizuko*, water children. *Mizuko kuyō*, a rite for aborted fetuses, emerged in the 1970s, attracting 15 to 20 percent of women seeking abortions.[295] The ceremony is not Buddhist; Buddhism eschews killing. Nor is it Shinto; Shinto's preoccupation with purity usually implies a ritual avoidance of blood and death. The largest Buddhist denomination, Jōdo Shinshū, rejects the rite altogether.

Mizuko kuyō assumes many forms and contains both Buddhist and Shinto elements. From one viewpoint the rite is exploitative and thus an object of criticism; from another perspective it is an extraordinary example of contemporary ritual creativity. Because of popular demand, it is performed at Shinto shrines and Buddhist temples as well as at centers with shamanic or spiritualist leanings. It is remarkable that a rite so controversial, so largely patronized by women, and so lacking for a basis in sacred texts has been able to traverse so many denominational lines.[296]

Although both men and couples participate in *mizuko kuyō*, women are the primary participants. Some perform the rite in regions distant from their homes so they can keep their abortions secret. Others publicly post their names and those of their unborn "children." As with genital "mutilation," the quotation marks flag a controversy: Are they fetuses or children?

An anonymous Japanese woman tells of her visit to a spiritualist:

When I asked Shōzaki Sensei to perform the kuyō for the miscarried children, mizuko appeared to her in a spirit message, complaining that they were in a cold well and were very cold. Her voice was exactly the voice of a mizuko. I was filled with the feeling, "I'm so sorry I didn't perform kuyō for you." Shōzaki Sensei told me that I should bring candy and milk to offer to the mizuko the next time I came, so I went to visit her again, bringing these things. The sutras [scriptures] used in mizuko kuyō and Jizō *wasan* sank into my heart, and I could not stop crying. When Shōzaki Sensei said in a spirit message (in the voice of a mizuko), "Thank you for the kuyō. Thank you for drawing us up [to a higher level of existence]," my feelings were finally settled.

However, I could not help feeling that this wasn't the end, and I realized that I could have Shōzaki Sensei perform kuyō if I went to her again. In later spirit messages the mizuko made me understand the vital importance of *senzo kuyō* [memorial services for ancestral spirits].

On one occasion, Shōzaki Sensei said to me, "I think you have something like a hanging scroll. Please search for it." I recalled a scroll that I had put away and forgotten about. It was a scroll of the Bodhisattva Manjursi. At work I had been instructed to throw it out along with other things, but I held it back. When Shōzaki Sensei prayed over it, the following revelation came to her: "I wanted to appear in this world. Pray for me, and I will protect your family for future generations." I had the scroll repaired and hung in my house as a family treasure. Since then I have been protected by this scroll.[297]

The teller of this story says she miscarried. Perhaps she did, but since it is not easy for Japanese women in their fifties to confess to abortion directly, they sometimes resort to euphemisms. That they tell of the deed at all is partly because they have been taught that *mizuko,* disembodied spirits of aborted children, become angry at their fate and wreak havoc on mothers and living siblings or even unrelated people. This woman's anxiety about her unborn children is ceremonially placated. Then it is transposed into more socially acceptable directions, first toward the ancestors, then to a bodhisattva, a compassionate being.

As in many other *mizuko kuyō* stories, this narrative completely omits male agency and responsibility. The *mizuko kuyō* rite is predicated on the folk idea of women's karma, a conviction that the problem of unwanted births belongs to women and does not seriously implicate men. However therapeutic the rite may be, many versions of it reinforce the pattern whereby women, or women and their families, bear sole responsibility for pregnancy.

Officially, Buddhism rejects belief in a soul, but the no-soul doctrine is sometimes overridden in practice by the need to ritualize traumatic events in a way that provides a concrete focus as well as a myth to underwrite the ceremony.

Mizuko are most effectively placated if rendered in material form. For Japanese women one visible way of concretizing their feelings about abortion is to purchase, install, and care for a small, gray stone statue. Jizō is a figure known for his compassion and ability to navigate the six levels of the cosmos. To save those who are suffering, he even descends into hell.

Traditionally set up at roadsides and intersections, Jizōs are also installed in homes, temples, and cemeteries. The statues mark boundaries and offer help to weary travelers and children. Jizōs are bald like monks, but since they also wear red bibs and are given colorful pinwheels and other toys, they are symbolic children too.[298] Despite his adult demeanor, a Jizō assumes certain childlike characteristics. He is small in size, people say, so he can go anywhere to deliver helpful messages and also because he identifies with the suffering of little people. The pious clothe Jizō statues in knitted garments, decorating them with inexpensive jewelry.

The statue of Jizō is, then, both caretaker and cared for, deity prayed to as well as fetus prayed for. Both adults and children visit Jizōs, pray before them, and decorate them. Though both spirit and stone, they have human needs, so they are provided with umbrellas to protect them from rain or sun. Ceremonies directed through these statues to the never born simultaneously put *mizuko* to rest and keep them ritually alive.

Mizuko are talked about as if they were toddlers rather than fetuses. In a widely known story, they congregate in a mysterious stony riverbed where they build stone pagodas, expressions of devotion to their parents. Their labor is endless, since demons knock the towers down, forcing the children to start over again and again. But innocence and perseverance are not the whole story. Eventually, pain drives *mizuko* stranded in limbo to seek *tatari,* spirit revenge. These stranded souls, like ancestors not ritually honored, become restless and destructive. To placate them, one must approach intermediaries or visit places where spirits are accessible and cosmic realms intersect: cemeteries, temples, crossroads, riverbanks, or the seashore.

Although *mizuko kuyō* is not practiced by most Japanese, and is thus not "the" Japanese way of handling abortion, it has nevertheless been widely publicized and discussed. Generally, the Japanese discussion has avoided the split that drives the North American debate, that is, the claim that a fetus is mere matter, on the one hand, or a real person, on the other. "Water children" are spirits, thus not quite people but not mere matter or mere figments of the imagination either.

Mizuko kuyō characteristically takes the form of a ritual apology. William LaFleur explains the logic of the rite: "Many Japanese who make ritual apology to an aborted fetus do so to retain their sense of their own humanity. . . . The terrible fact of abortion makes it all the more important for the 'parent' of the fetus to find concrete evidence that she—and sometimes he as well—still remains a person who cares and who has human feelings. The hardness of the fetus-destroying act makes the excavation of a fundamental softness in the actor a matter of crucial importance. The guilt, then, can be a welcome sign, a gratifying testimony to the perdurance of a humanizing sensitivity still at the center of the self. The Japanese have a very basic word for this softness; they call it *kokoro.* Very often tears will be the outward signal of its presence. Rituals, especially rituals of guilt and apology, are often the forms that confirm the sense that, in spite of everything, the person that one wants oneself to be is *still intact.*"[299]

This way of describing the function of *mizuko kuyō* makes it sound humane, ritually enlightened alongside the polarized, morally obsessed debate in the West, where snipers shoot abortionists and terrorists bomb abortion clinics. But there is a dark side in Japan just as there is here. *Mizuko kuyō* was initially popularized by religious entrepreneurs in tabloids using fetal photography. So even though a description of the rite may sound to the Western ear like a therapeutic strategy devised by pro-choice advocates, the call to engage in *mizuko kuyō* can also echo anti-abortion calls for repentance. *Mizuko kuyō* was first introduced in advertisements that portrayed aborting women as selfish, deserving of spirit attacks, and thus in need of confession and ritual protection. *Mizuko kuyō*, then, is not only a therapeutic ritual enactment but also a commercial enterprise propelled by advertising campaigns designed to stoke guilt and generate income for ritual entrepreneurs. Seen from this perspective, fetal resentment is a myth recently invented in order to capitalize on women's guilt feelings. Helen Hardacre describes the advertising: "Outsized, lurid images of the full-term fetus, detached from the female body, turned head-up and snarling, were created through the interpretive lens of fetocentric rhetoric that construed any termination of pregnancy as an act of homicide by a woman, for which she would be punished by fetal 'spirit attacks.' Mizuko kuyō was advanced as the 'answer' to a problem created mostly by those purveying the rites in question."[300]

The history of reproduction in Japan illustrates how the same act, abortion, can be deritualized in one period and reritualized in another.[301] Before 1868 birth was almost entirely in the hands of midwives, whose birth practices were thoroughly ritualistic. Giving birth was a rite of passage into adult womanhood. Midwives were representatives of the gods and conductors of souls into the material world.

Women, in consultation with their families and midwives, decided whether to abort. Midwives were custodians of knowledge usually restricted to women—knowledge about conception, pregnancy, and birth as well as contraception, abortion, and infanticide. Neither religious institutions nor men were significantly involved, and "returning" a baby was not considered "killing."[302] Midwives were given feasts, and they attended the life passages of children whom they delivered. Children presented their midwives with gifts during appropriate seasons. The midwife, not the mother, sewed a newborn's first clothing. After birth, mother and child were regarded as living in a dangerous, even polluted, state, but after this period had passed, the newborn was presented by the husband's mother to the *kami*, deities of a Shinto shrine.

State regulation of Japanese birth began in 1868. In 1873 infanticide was criminalized, treated as a species of homicide. By 1945 birth was becoming medicalized and deritualized. Postwar economic stress brought with it widespread abortion as a means of birth control. The Eugenics Protection Law of 1948 legalized abortions performed by licensed doctors under specified circumstances, including economic hardship. Thus, abortion became a primary means of birth control, and the climate for *mizuko kuyō* was ripe.

The emergence of *mizuko kuyō* in the 1970s was both a reritualization and a commercialization of abortion. The rite brought with it an intrusion of religious organizations and male priests into what had once been the domain of women and their families. Currently, *mizuko kuyō* includes a broad range of ritual practices and practitioners motivated by compassion, moneymaking, or both. Some ritualists perform the rite only on the condition of deep repentance; others do the rite for anyone who pays the fee. Just as the motives of those who enact *mizuko kuyō* vary, so do the motives of those who seek its benefits. Most women resort to abortion with great moral ambivalence and only under duress. Some have *mizuko kuyō* performed only once; others use the rite with more regularity.

Helen Hardacre, who conducted the most thorough field study of these abortion rites, believes that *mizuko kuyō,* after flourishing for two decades, is in decline.[303] Even if it is, the presence of such a rite gives one pause to consider that preoccupation with abortion's moral dimensions blinds us to its ritual ones.

Until Grief Leaves the Forefront of My Being

Abortion rites are beginning to emerge in the West, but seldom under the aegis of religious institutions and not yet, as far as I know, in the hands of ritual entrepreneurs. Instead, individuals and abortion recovery groups are producing self-help materials. Kim Kluger-Bell's *Unspeakable Losses* even takes the Japanese *mizuko kuyō* as its model, but Jizō is probably too removed from the experiences of North American women for statues of him to be effective.[304]

An abortion rite need not morally condone or condemn the act of abortion. A rite, unlike an ethical principle, can thrive on ambiguity. A rite can acknowledge the seriousness of the act and grapple with the guilt precipitated by it without having to resolve the moral issues.

All the abortion rites I know about have been improvised by women, some of them determined to avoid the oversimplified moral polarization that plagues the Western abortion debate. When in her early twenties, Marie Snyder wrote this account in her journal:

It is June 6th, 1991, my due date, but I'm no longer due. Walking into the maple forest behind the house I lived in as a child, my backpack is weighing heavily on my shoulders. Finding a small clearing in this sacred space of mine, I tidy up somebody's empty beer cans before unpacking. First, come the perennial and the candles gingerly balanced together at the top of the pack in a slightly squashed peach basket, handle removed. Next, comes the Cool Whip tub which has made a nest for itself in the bed sheets that I struggle to pull out of the pack. Finally, my folding shovel escapes as I shake out the last of the sheets.

I arrange the three candles and light them, though the morning sun is already dappling through young leaves. I untape the Cool Whip tub and dip a finger into the water contained there, then cross myself. It just seems the thing to do. A warm breeze steals the drop of moisture from my forehead. Opening the shovel to its full length, I begin to dig. The ground is moist but packed under my bare feet. I hope to dig down only three feet or so. I hit tree roots long before I expect to, and the digging becomes an arduous struggle. Now, I'm on my knees digging with my hands, determined to make a place for myself without harming any roots. The candles are arranged and rearranged each time they get in the way of my work. Negotiating with the earth and trees, I resign myself to taking some of the sheets back with me, to be thrown out instead of buried.

I pick up an edge of the worn linens we conceived on and start to rip them. With each tear I attack him for his unrealistic promises, for agreeing with me before and then denying ever agreeing after, and for leaving me with the burden of this decision. I curse myself for insisting that everything was fine when he knew something was amiss. I berate myself for putting school and my own life ahead of the life of one unborn. I leave some of the shreds in the pit I've made. More supplies come from my back pocket. I use my pocket knife to stab and shred the useless diaphragm, and I am sorry I didn't surreptitiously save the condom that shred of its own volition. The wire edge of the gadget won't break despite my efforts at bending it back and forth. I relent and allow it to remain intact, a perfect circle nestled amid the strips of cloth in the hole. Leftover jelly squeezed on top completes a satisfying mess.

The rest of the sheet remnants are rolled up and wrapped into a bundle that I cradle in the crook of my arm. Instinctively rocking, I tell the bundle how very sorry I am for cutting its life so short. I confess that no matter who may have encouraged me in this direction, the final choice was mine alone. I chose to do this. I wanted its life to end. I sincerely promise the unborn child that I will love and care for it if it can return to me in a different state or at a different time. I hold it dearly and tell it how I've longed to hold it, smell it, call it by name—Emily maybe or Joshua. I tell it that I regret not having seen it, knowing what he and I would look like combined into a single person. I nuzzle the bundle to my cheek and kiss its soft, warm forehead. The dense forest envelops me, the only audience to my tears, some dripping off my jaw and others bringing moisture to the word "good-bye" uttered softly to my almost-first little love.

I gently lay the tiny bundle into the peach basket. Releasing the basket to the hole in the earth, I hear the words, "Ashes to ashes, dust to dust" escape my mouth.

I give myself some time before using my hands to cover the tiny casket with dirt. As I bury it, I bury my anger, telling the trees that I forgive him. He was just coping with this hideous situation. I forgive myself as well; I did what I needed to do, and I don't regret my decision. From my front pocket I dig out a black hair ribbon which I will wear until the grief leaves the forefront of my being.

The shovel fills in the rest of the hole, except for a dent left for the perennial. As I plant the flower, I talk of finishing school, of being able to finance myself instead of depending on him for allowance money, of the children I will have in the future when the time is right and I am better able to support and nourish their growth. I use the tub of water to wash the dirt from my hands and the tear stains from my face. Then I pour it on the trillium. This forest is full of trilliums. Next year I probably won't be able to recognize this one among the others. All of them will take on a special nuance now. They bloom every seven years, but even if this one isn't in bloom, others will be. The trillium is a perfect lily-white triad, and it grows wild, without intent, against all odds, as long as no one rips it prematurely from its home in the ground.[305]

Later, when Marie became a teacher in a local high school, she encountered young women facing the same hard, lonely decision. Some were willing to see counselors and involve their parents, but others were not. A few realized there were spiritual and ritualistic dimensions to their dilemma, but many could not articulate them. Certain that both silence and lack of spiritual direction would make tragic situations worse, Marie crafted a brochure identifying the emotions a woman might feel after an abortion (see fig. 4). The brochure also poses questions a young woman might need to ask as a way of allowing healing to begin. Marie's pamphlet links both the emotions and the questions to corresponding ritual actions that one might consider enacting. The language is simple and direct, as any brochure must be, but the reasoning behind

1. Emotions	2. Questions	3. Ritual Actions
1A. Emotional numbing and partial memory loss protect you from having to cope with the overwhelming nature of this event. These feelings can last for days, weeks, or even years.	2A. What do you remember about the abortion? What made you finally decide to have one? How will you mark it? Who will be willing to help or attend?	3A. Write or talk about the experience. Begin to document the details so it can become real to you again. Collect articles and locate a space in which to enact the rite.
1B. It is common to experience intense rage and anger at your partner, friends, and family as well as yourself and your body; perhaps even at faulty birth-control methods, at having to make this decision, or at life in general.	2B. How has your partner made you angry? Your family and friends? What have you done to enrage yourself? What did the circumstances do to you?	3B. To tap into your anger, you might shred bed sheets or receiving blankets, break eggs, write out your secret fantasies around having a baby and burn them.
1C. Guilt, shame, and remorse follow decisions to abort. Unresolved, they can result in self-destructive behavior and prevent grieving from taking place.	2C. What is it about abortion that evokes guilt? How can you be relieved of this feeling? Can you apologize to the unborn? Can you confess the decision and the act?	3C. To make the event tangible and real, create a symbol of a baby to apologize to, perhaps out of clay, rolled up blankets, or a teddy bear dressed up in child's clothing.
1D. Expect grief, sadness, loss, and despair at what could have been but will never be.	2D. What ideas and images did you have of the baby? As a result of the abortion, what will you miss?	3D. To comfort yourself, hold and clutch the symbol of the baby; sing to it and play with it.
1E. Forgiveness of yourself and others, as well as acceptance of the abortion are key to mental and spiritual health.	2E. How will you forgive yourself and others? What will it take for you to accept this situation? Can you say good-bye to this near-baby?	3E. Release the baby symbol in a meaningful way, maybe into a casket to be buried or onto a raft to be floated away.
1F. Renewal and increased participation in life will come in time, though some grief may always exist quietly in the background.	2F. How have you grown from this action? What can you do now that you would not be able to do if you had continued this pregnancy?	3F. Celebrate life, plant a tree, blow bubbles, fly a kite, choose something from the rite to keep as an aid to remembering that grief is a process.

Figure 4. Cultivating Health after Abortion: Using Ritual to Heal Ourselves (Written by Marie Snyder. The original version is not in chart form and does not contain these numbers. I have added them here to facilitate discussion and easy reference.)

it is sophisticated. The scheme is a remarkable condensation of a complex psychological, social, and ritualistic process.

Since Marie decided to make public the stories of both her abortion and abortion rite, readers can see the autobiographical roots of the actions she suggests in the brochure. Even so, the suggestions—and they are no more than that—have broad appeal. They are sufficiently generic that they can fit a variety of situations, and they are sufficiently evocative that they can stir the imaginations of those whose situations they do not fit so well.

When Marie first asked if she might perform an abortion rite as part of the seminar requirement in my course "Ritual, Illness, and the Body," I talked with her about the difficulties of in-class ritualizing on such a topic. "A rite in a class inevitably becomes a ritual demonstration," I said, "and, remember, the class will be evaluating your presentation. Are you prepared for that?" She said she was and planned to proceed even though I worried that her presentation might provoke more than she anticipated.

On the night she presented the rite and the rationale behind it, she explained that the original ritual enactment (the story of which she did not tell) had not been thought out, merely done, and that the rationale had come later. Marie's performance left the class speechless; some were in tears. Eventually a student recovered enough to ask her, "How did you feel doing that? I was blown away. I can hardly talk now. I was right there with you."

Marie replied, "The first few times I practiced the rite for this seminar I couldn't make it through the ceremony without crying, but after several run-throughs the presentation became a performance."

Marie's performance both was and was not a reevocation of the original enactment in the woods. Insofar as it *was,* the event was charged, and we, the class members, were drawn into its orbit. Insofar as the demonstration *was not* the rite itself, the presentation was controlled. Effective ritualizing, like effective drama, requires both the charge of a live connection and the insulation of a well-wrought structure.

There was no need to discuss the effectiveness of what Marie had done, so instead the ensuing class discussion centered on the question of isolation: What are the virtues and liabilities of private ritualizing around events like abortion? On the one hand, it ensures privacy, avoids public stigma, and, for some, facilities a fuller release of rage and grief. On the other hand, it may be that no rite is complete unless it is witnessed.

Some students of ritual have claimed that an internalized or divine audience is sufficient. I do not think so. I believe the capacity for self-forgiveness is inextricably bound up with being forgiven by others. In my view, Marie's ritualizing in the woods was brought to fuller completion by her decision to go public both in writing and in performing.

The Roller-Coaster of Joy and Woe

Like abortion, divorce is not a happy occasion, and we do not often think of it as an occasion for ritual. But like individuals and institutions, relationships have life cycles. The life cycle of a marriage, although influenced by the cycles of the husband and wife, constitutes, one might say, a third rhythm. The life of a marriage is not identical to the life of the man and woman who enter into it. Since half of North American marriages now end before "death do us part," it may be as incumbent upon us to ritualize divorce as to solemnize marriage.

Because ritual systems are incomplete and flawed, they require adaptation not only to cultures but also to individuals. Sometimes there is nothing to adapt, and invention is the only possible recourse. A growing number of invented divorce rites have appeared in North America, even though we are a culture with little experience of rites that nullify. Divorce is a rite that, in effect, undoes a previous rite, a wedding. There are other reverse passages: An excommunication cancels an initiation or conversion; defrocking voids ordination. Such ceremonies are usually hidden from public view and not included in standard ritual texts for use by ordinary practitioners. But the escalating divorce rate and growing social tolerance for divorce has brought divorce rites into the public domain.

Few traditions have well-developed divorce rites. Judaism and Islam have long-standing but brief ceremonies. Christians do not, although a few denominations have begun to construct them. Most contemporary divorce rites are made up:

My first marriage ended in divorce. After a year of weekly meetings to cry, rage, comfort, and negotiate, my former wife and I planned a ceremony of divorce and invited our friends and colleagues. We asked them to bring food or beverages to share, also something they needed to leave behind.

The music set the tone, recalling some of the good times in our life together. Some of the music was hers, some was mine, some was ours. One song was a duet by Roberta Flack and Donnie Hathaway. We had listened to it as we drove across the country in her red VW beetle.

We welcomed our guests and said why we were gathered: to celebrate and mourn, to say goodbye, and to move on. We talked about the difficult work that had led up to this moment. We acknowledged our need for courage, compassion, grace, and hope. We said we could not get through this event without our friends.

Our differences had led to a divergence. She became a Sufi, I remained a Unitarian Universalist. She wanted to live in community; I liked living alone. She was a former Catholic; I was a former Protestant. So Sufi and Unitarian jokes were told to spice the soup and release tension. How many Unitarians does it take to screw in a lightbulb? At least six, in order to hold a discussion group first and put the matter to a vote. How many Sufis does it take to screw in a lightbulb? It doesn't matter; they're all one anyway. What happens when you cross a Jehovah's witness with a Unitarian? You have someone who comes to your door but can't remember why.

We said a few words about why and how we had come to part. I told of performing a skit in which I brought a typewriter to bed. It turned out to be prophetic. On many days I spent more hours at the keyboard or library than with my wife. We acknowledged that there were many things we did not yet understand about our parting; some we might never understand.

After we ran out of explanations we stood together and reversed the language of our wedding vows: "I divorce you. You are no longer my wife / husband. I divorce you. You are no longer my best friend. I divorce you. You are no longer my lover."

After the words, each of us took back the gift that had sealed our vows. She reclaimed her ruby pendant. I reclaimed my turquoise ring. In retrospect, I'm amazed that we got through this exchange without falling apart. Were we lucky? Was the wind with us? Was our composure the reward for all that Wednesday night sobbing we had done?

A big fire had been built in the communal hearth behind us. We lit the fire together, feeding it old papers, love letters, photos—remnants of our life together. We named aloud what we were able to let go of. Then we invited our friends, silently or with words, to cast into the fire something they needed to leave behind. There was no shortage of words. Some testimonies were sad; others were funny. Among the items tossed into the fire were: chicken fat, an old draft card, mementos of various addictions (most of which burned well), photos of former selves, relationships that had been outgrown, and rejection letters from churches, colleges, publishers, and old lovers.

Clock time disappeared as the burning continued. By connecting the private sphere (one failed marriage) to the public sphere (shared failures and griefs), our community was deepened.

Cris Williamson was not a Unitarian Universalist, but her "Song of the Soul" was at that time an unofficial anthem for many of us. We sang it with gusto and few dry eyes: "Follow your heart. Love will find you. Truth will unbind you. Sing out a song of the soul. . . . "

My former wife invited us to form two concentric circles for a Sufi dance. We then blessed each person with our eyes, with gestures and a song: "May the blessings of life be upon you (our hands passed over the crown of each other's heads). And may peace abide with you (we clasped hands around each other's waists). May God's presence (our hands touched each other's hearts) illuminate your heart now and forever more . . . " (we bowed with hands clasped).

After riding the roller-coaster of joy and woe, we ate with more joy and tenderness than words can convey. It was a love feast in every sense of the word. As music and singing played in the background, we were fed in body, mind, soul, and spirit. It was a wedding feast and an Irish wake all at the same time. William Blake put it well: "Joy and woe are woven fine, / A clothing for the Soul Divine."

The trust built up by a year of hard work between my former wife and me, along with the gracious resources of our beloved communities, made this event possible. It hastened the healing process. I would not perform a divorce rite without similar groundwork. Our marriage, built on personal, social, and spiritual foundations, was publicly broken in all three ways. We felt empowered, even blessed, to begin again. I will always be grateful for the powers, visible and invisible, that made the divorce possible.[306]

Some who divorce do not want ritual attention drawn to themselves. In a bygone era the shame of being divorced would have prevented even imagining a public ceremony. The few who underwent divorce rites did so because they were required to. Few went looking for such ceremonies, much less considered them therapeutic or cooperated with their spouses in designing and performing them.

One version of the Jewish divorce ceremony (*get*) speaks of disentangling a wife's soul, as if it were wrapped around and threaded through that of her husband.[307] Psychologists speak of *fusion,* the loss of psychosocial boundaries between personalities in a marriage. Fusion is sometimes followed by an explosion, a dangerous way of trying to reestablish boundaries. After fusion and explosion, healing is required if people are to recover from the dismemberment. Healing is not necessarily ritualistic, but historically and cross-culturally, it often has been so.

The rite that Ted Tollefson and his wife enacted was the culmination of a long process. He would not have had it otherwise. He and his spouse parted, having danced with and blessed each other. Drawn into the story, I imagined the rite as leading them to fall in love again. Can't you just hear the one whispering in the ear of the other, "Such a beautiful thing we have created here, together, this love feast, this. . . . " In Ted's place, I would have required anger or resentment for fuel, something that would burn, propelling me in an outward direction. Ted chose the we-can-still-be-friends model, but there are other kinds of divorce rites, those enacted separately because hostility, pain, or alienation preclude cooperation.

Many divorces, because of the laws that bear upon them and the torque that drives separating individuals, are ritualized without ever crossing the threshold into explicit ritual. Dividing up the furniture, selling the house, and arguing over custody and support become forms of ritual combat. The danger with an unconsciously ritualized parting is that it never quite finishes socially and psychologically. In contrast, "I divorce you" uttered face-to-face before witnesses, puts a period, not a comma or even a semicolon, at the terminus of a relationship. Saying it makes it so.

The magic of ritual takes effect only if there is work *behind* a rite. If the only work is that which appears *in* the rite, the result will likely be self-deception, a saying that only makes it *seem* so. Saying can make it really so, but only if the saying *is* a doing or if the saying is *underwritten by* a doing.

Cutting the Cord of Employment

Besides abortion and divorce, retirement is the other moment of severance that cries out for ritual recognition. A few years ago I was asked to design the retirement celebration of a colleague. I am no fan of public university occasions, either the relatively informal wine-and-cheese parties or the high-flown commencement ceremonies studded with honorary degrees and "now you have arrived" rhetoric. I participate reluctantly like many other academics. We are a critical lot, not only schooled in debate and argument but also skeptical of platitudes, so we do not suffer ceremony lightly. We understand its necessity, especially for students and their families, so we let ourselves be pulled along by the flow of processions, having donned our tasseled hats and flapping hoods. We strut and kibitz and shake hands and, if the truth be told, we are even a little moved that some of our "kids" have, in fact, become adults in the process. Occasionally, we admit to being proud, but still, it is hard to swallow the oversimplifications to which such ceremonies are prone.

Faculty retirements are a cut above wine-and-cheese parties but several cuts below commencement. If retirees are lucky, they are treated to some good humor (usually at their own expense), and they hear perhaps a few honest testimonials about the care they exercised with students. If they are not so lucky, they hear eulogies, speeches so distorted by idealization that even the retirees are embarrassed by this overblown misrecognition of themselves. The verbosity of such occasions is matched only by their characteristic awkwardness and the incessant trips to the punch bowl and cheese trays.

Some retirees do not want their exit made so public, and thus, so conscious. A retirement gathering really is an end, not just a new beginning, and sometimes a paltry end at that—not even a gold watch by which to count the hours that will now pass all too slowly or all too rapidly. Upon retirement, one colleague declared that we were not to do anything whatsoever to mark it. He was firm in his insistence that we not make an occasion of it. But when Bob Fisher retired, it was quite another matter.

Bob had served thirty or so years, many of them as department chair. He began daydreaming about his retirement party for well over a year before the occasion. We would see him wandering the hall, suddenly darkening our doors to gab about what kind of music or food would be appropriate. At first the suggestions were oblique, but by the middle of his last year, they had become overt. No longer "what ifs," his comments became directives—he was, after all, still chair—although he was obviously feeling the disorientation of being in a lame-duck position. Bob began making more and more noise about the courses he would teach after retirement and what kind of person ought to replace him, even though it was department practice not to include retirees in decisions about their replacements. Occasionally, Bob said he would not cling or intrude, but more often than not he found the temptation too much to resist.

All his colleagues felt under considerable pressure to mount a big party and to promise Bob postretirement teaching opportunities to make the event seem less terminal to him. Once I heard him mutter that he would be relieved to get out from under all the administrative crap, but he admitted that he was having a hard time with his impending retirement. The department, he declared, was his life.

Another colleague was busy arranging food and music. He and other department members drafted me, insisting that I could not stay out of the fray or hide behind the books I wrote on ritual; I had to *do* something ceremonial. By consensus, the job of designing a retirement celebration was assigned to me. I consented, warning that they, and Bob— God pity him—had to live with the results. The threat did not deter them.

When Bob heard who was to be emcee, he was elated at first but later worried. I teased him, saying that in rites of passage, you have to *be passed over* the threshold; you don't get to *pass yourself through*. So, I told him, you have no choice but to trust your colleagues; the ceremony would have to be a surprise. He assured me that he trusted me; I was his friend. But he lost sleep over the upcoming event.

Around universities irony plays better than solemnity, but this was a serious event, and there was now an obvious and serious need for the right kind of celebration, so the ritual irony could not be merely empty. It had to have teeth as well as humor, respect, and affection. Students and faculty were invited to offer testimonials. I met with some of them, urging them to write candidly, not indulging in empty rhetoric or mere sentimentality. Some took my advice; others did not.

During closeted discussions about the occasion, someone remarked—I don't remember whether it was one of Bob's family or one of his students—"Bob is having a really hard time cutting the cord." As soon as I heard the metaphor, I knew it was the key. My job was simply to wrap it in the tactility and concreteness of ritual.

Although I complain about paper-induced ceremonies, those performed with an "order of worship" in hand, I produced a booklet. Academics love paper and words, and Bob, after all, was a scholar of ancient Near Eastern texts. Figures 5 and 6, edited for publication, are from the script that guided Bob Fisher's retirement ceremony in 1997.

During the "Words of Appreciation, Recollection, and Bedevilment," students and colleagues offered their reflections. Some were deeply appreciative: "For his first textual assignment he asked us to read a portion of Genesis and critique it as if we were high-school

> The Long-Lasting, Loosely Lyrical Legacy
> of
> Dr. Robert W. Fisher
> B.A., M.Div, Ph.D.
> Several times Chair, willingly
> At WLU since 1967 (the sixties, remember?)
> Currently, Associate Professor of Religion & Culture, and
> Retiring from servitude . . .
> Willingly (more or less),
> &
> Gracefully (on rare & public occasions)
> In celebration of
> 30 (or 31) years of doggedly devoted service!

Figure 5. The Long-Lasting, Loosely Lyrical
Legacy of Dr. Robert W. Fisher

teachers marking a grade-twelve writing assignment. The proverbial pennies fell off my eyes once and for all, and I realized that the text had to have been written by more than one author. I changed my major, and that set in motion a chain of events that changed my life."[308]

Some comments were gently teasing: "We were having a joint faculty meeting, and there were only three items on the agenda. I was overjoyed and was looking forward to a brief meeting since all three items were noncontroversial and easy of resolution. I was wrong! Item number one was 'how to order books for the library,' and, Bob, you managed almost single-handedly to sustain that issue for one hour and forty-five minutes. At the time, I would have supported your retirement . . . ! *In retrospect* it warms my heart; *then* it gave me heartburn. Have a marvelous retirement, my friend."[309]

For many it was a great relief to hear obvious, but minor, complaints uttered aloud in a good-hearted way.

People told stories or provided brief vignettes: "I didn't know the two men at the dinner table with me . . . , but that order gave me a glimpse of something so unmistakably Bob Fisher. Soft and mushy, the same qualities of his heart. It must have been his favorite dessert. I would guess that at the various departmental dinners . . . I saw him polish off at least a half a dozen, if not more. Before his bypass opera-

THE ORDER OF THE CELEBRATION

· Music ·

· Words of Appreciation,
Recollection,
& Bedevilment ·

· Presentation of Memorabilia ·

· The Oration ·

· Five (or fewer) Minutes (as promised) by Robert Fisher ·

· The Rite of Cutting the Cord ·

· The Commissioning ·

· Benediction for Bob ·

Figure 6. The Order of the Celebration

tion, I can't remember him ever ordering anything for desert except
crème brûlée. He gave it up, though. His heart must have said no
more, and the diet after his operation put a stop to that sort of mushi-
ness. So he gave it up. . . . Even after I got to know Bob better, that
first impression of a soft heart, a kind heart, has continued to ring
through. It shows up in little ways and big ones too, like the way he
thanked all of us at a recent department meeting. Tears and crème
brûlée. Thanks, Bob, for the kindnesses and strengths you've shared
with us."[310]

A retirement is an occasion that allows other retirees to greet, sympathize with, and cheer on one of their own. Bob heard from his seniors
as well as his juniors: "I first met Bob Fisher at a time so remote that
neither of us had as yet heard of . . . Wilfrid Laurier University. He was
a Ph.D. student at Union Theological Seminary. I was a very junior professor of Old Testament at Drew University. . . . My most vivid memory of that summer was commiserating with Bob on the iniquities of
the local muezzin, whose strident call to prayer at 4:00 A.M. woke the
roosters, who woke the dogs, who woke the donkeys. The resultant ca-
cophony made further sleep impossible."[311]

Myths plague and grace many faculty members, and rituals are likely
to evoke those myths. A persistent myth about Bob was recounted: "I
remember *you:* with your foot on the Bible, stomping bibliolatry out of
seminarians' minds."[312]

To demonstrate that the book itself *is not* sacred but rather that it *points to something sacred,* Bob tossed the holy book on the floor and stood on it while students gasped. Years later, the story was still being passed from student to student as well as harbored with suspicion among devout faculty of the seminary affiliated with the university.

Some of Bob's students "compiled, invented, and redacted" "The Fisher Glossary," which turned out to be much more than a glossary. It was a jocular account of his entire teaching style:

Words he can't spell
YAHWEH (spells it YAFWEH)
archaeology (because of the optional "a")
any Canadian word [Bob was an American immigrant]

Favorite words, phrases, and sayings
those wild and woolly Arameans
primordial mound
separation anxiety
For a paper to get an A, it has to make me want to get on the desk and dance a jig.
All we know about the ancient Near East is because of the accident of survival and the accident of discovery.
The Elamites were a thorn in the buttocks of the Babylonians.

Favorite Stories
Imdugud and the Fiery Bull of Heaven
Gilgamesh and Enkidu
Suffering Servant (in Isaiah)
rural Florida childhood stories
spiderweb in the orchard
anthill in the backyard

Pet Theories
Fisher's Formula: Political collapse occurs from the inside out.
Fisher's Paint Pot Theory: The Middle East is like a big pot of paint—all mixed up.
Fisher's Spiderweb Theory: There is always a ripple effect.

Topics labored in class
Migrations in the ancient Near East
Mythopoeic thought
Paper grading

Fisher's greatest disappointments
The Hebrew grammar that isn't published
He has tried three times, unsuccessfully, to get to Iraq.
Retirement

Mannerisms
He wipes his chalky hands on his butt and then walks around with hand marks on display.

When he's thinking hard, he reaches from over the back of his head and strokes the ten hairs on his forehead.

He speaks Hebrew with a south Florida accent.

"I don't want to spend time on this, *but . . . .*"

He goes off on tangent after tangent after tangent. Even though we think he's going nowhere, he always ends up somewhere.[313]

After the students finished their roast and appreciative caricatures, there followed a mock oration. The orator, himself retired from the department, began, "In addressing you on the subject of Dr. Robert Fisher, I want to say that while this is a phenomenon I have observed for some years, it has only been from afar; and it indeed falls outside my field—mumble, mumble—but I do want to ask a question. In fact, three questions. They are *Whence? Why?* and *Whither?*

"To begin, *Whence* that tumulus of paper and print, that mountain, that megamound of stuff that flows over, inundates, obliterates desk, table, chairs, walls, and floor of Dr. Fisher's office? Yes, Whence?

"Second, *Why?* Why this accumulation?

"And third, peering into the future, *Whither?* Yes, Whither this prodigious store?" [314]

The oration was a romp through Fisher's academic history as if we were excavating a mound. In the process of telling the mythic history of Dr. Bob, the Fisher myth reappears in yet another redaction: "Most perplexing to the investigators was a battered copy of the Bible, Revised Standard Version. Unable to account with certainty for the sorry state of this object, they resorted to the Tell el-Fisher Web site, where they learned that when Dr. Fisher was teaching Introduction to the Old Testament in the seminary in the 1970s, he one day threw an English Bible on the floor and exclaimed to the students, 'That's not the Word (word?) of God!'

"There is no record that he ever taught that course again."[315]

Since I had engineered "the rite of cutting the cord," it was my turn to speak: "We speak of the university as a community. Although such rhetoric may denote an aspiration more than an achievement, there is no mistaking the fact that there are ties that bind—for better, and for worse.

"As a faculty member, Bob, you are bound to administration and staff, bound to students, and bound to faculty colleagues. Thus, we enact the binding."

During the musical interlude Bob is bound by a set of ropes, first to an administrator, then to a student, and then to a faculty member.

"When I arrived at WLU, Bob was away, 'on leave,' they said. The child in me, which chatters incessantly even in middle age, heard their account as if they had said 'passed away.' The man was gone, but he was everywhere. I was blessed and cursed with having to occupy his office on Bricker Street, his books and files stacked in inimitable Fisher style—all around me. The office was a veritable cavern, and the stacks of paper were stalagmites growing from the floor. I was a mere supplicant in the mouth of a cave, and my mouth was stuffed with pious academic prayers: 'Please, let me stay, with tenure. . . . '

"The name 'Dr. Robert Fisher' was stamped everywhere—on boxes, on files, across the tops of yellowing envelopes. Here was a man who liked his title. . . . Dr. Fisher had authority. He had presence, but it was like that of God: largely known by a cloud-covered absence. In that year of absence, I became intimate with Dr. Fisher, perhaps even more intimate than he himself was. I had his files; all he had was just himself, and we all know the body is weak and the self, transient, if not nonexistent. So the man loomed. He was a Robert, not a Bob, a Dr., not a Mister. His books bespoke things ancient, dated, unintelligible, pondiferously impenetrable. And they smelled. The place reeked with odors Egyptian and tones Hebraic, if not seraphic. . . .

"Well, to make a long story short, Dr. Fisher returned. We are all shorter in presence than in absence (which is why I absent myself as often as I can). Bob, unlike God and Dr. Fisher, walked on the ground— at least when not professorially preoccupied. The Bob I came to know was mushy as a bog swamp, could pontificate with more persistence than the pope, would without much provocation wax and drone like a preacher at department meetings, wrote treatises only spirits can read, and was always present, never absent, when the Big Crunches came. . . .

"Now he stands in that ritually reputable place, the liminal zone, one leg on each side of the threshold. From that spot he, and we, must contemplate his absence yet again. We will miss him—that is truer than you'd guess from the ways he and we have sometimes butted heads. But we will be happy too. So will he. I asked him, and he said so.

"The time is ripe, so let there be dead silence, punctuated by howling and cheering with the cutting of each cord."

The three strands are cut with huge knives and with much bravado by a staff member, student, and faculty member. The loose ends are handed to Bob's family.

In conclusion several voices commissioned Bob. The president of the university announced: "We hereby declare you, Dr. Bob, on your way to joining the ranks of wise and retired scholars. We remind you of the August company of retired Religion and Culture members. . . . "

Another voice: "Dr. Robert W. Fisher, on behalf of the WLU community we hereby commission you to go forth, wrestle with, and master that great beast: *the ever-unfinished Hebrew grammar.* The world awaits it."

A concluding voice: "Bob, we release you into the arms of your family. May you walk away singing, and may they waltz you home, weeping only a tear or two."

There was supposed to be a benediction of sorts—in German, Hebrew, and English, but I forgot to make space for it. Such are the pitfalls of directing and performing in the same ceremony.

It was a risk to have enacted the rite the way we did. The core actions were unconventional and might incur the disdain of those who deemed conventionality the essence of formal occasions. There was also danger in the rite's frankness. Even though rites of passage are supposed to help people negotiate difficult moments, they more commonly disguise or minimize difficulty. Cutting someone loose who is having a hard time letting go would be the last thing one would perform publicly. For fear of offending a retiree or of exposing too much raw emotion, such a theme would more likely appear as a subtext, or it would be kept out of the rite altogether.

We chose instead to turn Bob's sense of connectedness into a hyperbole, staging it front and center. Tying him to community representatives acknowledged the power of social bonding but in a way that also exposed the foibles of community. Both during and after the knot tying, people joked, using phrases such "tying the knot," "getting entangled," "the endless web," "the knotty mess of human relationships." With ropes pulling in contradictory directions, it was obvious that community is not always harmonious, that it is hardly a warm and safe nest.

The greatest danger was in the act of cutting, since the gesture represented the essence of what Bob was resisting—at least on one level. On another, he did want to be set loose. If I had not been fairly certain of this fact, I would never have seized upon the metaphor. The stress of his job had already hospitalized him with a mild heart attack, so the dangers of staying on, had that been an option, were all too evident.

Someone observed that Bob got what he needed rather than what he wanted. Although there is truth in this way of summarizing the event, I would sum it up in a slightly different way: Bob needed and wanted a reaffirmation of his importance to the university. He also needed and wanted, though less consciously, a sharp, decisive severance. Having the cord cut would enable him to make the turn that was inevitable because of his health, the law, and customary practice.

As a consequence of the rite, Bob's retiring got far more attention than it would have otherwise, but it was attention of a different kind than he and many others had initially imagined. The risk Bob took was in letting his colleagues make him the object of their ritualizing, which was less genteel as well as more ironic and hyperbolic than he, left to his own devices, would have wanted. The rite, like Bob himself, is still remembered and talked about. It hasn't been emulated since.

Beyond Passage

By now readers should have a vocabulary with which to talk about passages and a keener sense of what rites, both traditional and reinvented, can and cannot do. Rites can make major transitions memorable and participants more humane, but they can also evoke anxiety or become occasions for abuse. By now it is obvious that rites of passage are valuable but imperfect ways of enacting meaning.

Passages, I hope, now seem not only surprisingly human, thus similar to one another, but also surprisingly local, thus different. If my argument has been convincing, readers should feel resistance to flattening cultural and religious differences and more willingness to celebrate them. If this book has achieved its aim, readers will experience more enthusiasm about ritualizing passages but also more skepticism concerning both rites and theories that too easily reduce the rich complexities of rites to simple patterns. We have become, I hope, less susceptible to ritual romanticism as well as more demanding of ritual structures, leaders, and theorists. Knowing some of the pitfalls that surround each passage, readers may be more courageous, able to ride the waves of passage with less need to become controlling in the face of their pounding rhythms.

It is time then to go beyond rites of passage, exposing their limitations and questioning the model upon which they are based. In the West the model for *all* rites of passage (not just initiations) has been largely initiatory, dependent upon the themes and activities of men's initiation: ordeals, secrecy, the promise of revelation, the hierarchy of elders and initiates, and so on. For this reason *rites of passage* is often used as a synonym for *initiation,* a usage that overlooks other moments of passage.

At best, the initiatory model should be regarded as one option among many. As the dominant model, it feeds a deeply ingrained prejudice rooted in an immature craving for adventure. If rites of passage are not built on foundations other than initiatory models, they will never succeed in creating a fully embodied ritual sensibility. Special ritual occasions are much less likely than sustained ritual routines to drive meaning into the bone. So it is necessary to consider ceremonies of the village green and of the kitchen so we do not overvalue initiations in the bush. Public and domestic places are also sacred spaces in which the human magnum opus is worked out.

Crying in the Night

Falling ill and being healed are not usually considered rites of passage, even though in some societies they are widely ritualized events. Healing rites are usually repetitious rather than once-and-for-all, like rites of passage are supposed to be. The other reason that healing rites are not considered rites of passage is that illness is not confined to a particular phase of human life.

However, studies of the human life course demonstrate that acute illnesses can become major spiritual passages.[316] There is little doubt that chronic illness has ritualistic qualities about it—if nothing else, it is repetitious. But acute illness is literally life transforming in the way a rite of passage is said to be. A serious illness creates a "before" and "after" that differ markedly from each other.

The Milan Group in Italy pioneered the use of ritual in family therapy. There are now American therapists who use ritual and are influenced by the Italians. Upon first meeting with clients, "ritual therapists" inquire about family rites and holidays, since stories about them may compress the whole family "scene" into a few hours or days, exposing the fault lines and habitual conflicts.

It is not only the lesbian wedding or the funeral for a gay AIDS patient that precipitates trouble in one's family of origin. Christmases and Hanukkahs of "normal" families are fraught with alignments and collusions that promise trouble. Joan Laird paints a scene that many of us readily recognize:

My mother began preparations for Christmas months in advance, shopping for and wrapping gifts, making new decorations for the house, and addressing cards. . . . Since she worked full-time as an administrative assistant, as Christmas approached she often stayed up late at night wrapping gifts, getting my father to sign the tags for the gifts she had purchased for his parents, siblings and other family members. . . .

My father, of course, assumed the role of Santa and presided over the distribution of gifts until he grew bored, at which point we would all share that role. Mother would rush in and out of the living room, trying not to miss anything while cleaning up the breakfast dishes, stuffing the turkey, and getting the rest of the dinner ready in time for the arrival of other family members. . . .

For as long as I can remember, there has been a sort of painful argument at dinner. . . . Someone usually gets a migraine headache, and my mother ends up in tears at least once during the day, making all of us feel guilty and irritated, because she is overburdened and we know it. On the other hand, it seems a source of pride to her to "do it all" and she often refuses help.

After dinner the males retreat, some to play cards or watch more television and some to nap, while the women and older female children begin the long and tedious business of cleaning up. . . .

I try to carry on most of the same traditions, even though I have a very demanding job. It just doesn't seem like Christmas if anything is skipped. My husband, who helps some and who tells me he doesn't want a "traditional" wife nevertheless seems to, like me, want a "traditional" life! It is difficult to understand why this special day, looked forward to all year long, usually leaves me exhausted, depleted, experiencing a sense of relief, of loss, but already thinking about next year.[317]

Rites are windows into the complications of family dynamics and thus useful as diagnostic instruments. Rites and holidays are sometimes photographed, often remembered, and likely to exhibit all the pathologies of family behavior but in a more focused way. Family ritualizing signals as much to the trained eye as a patient's heartbeat tells a doctor's ear—not everything, maybe, but very significant things.

In the family referred to above, a seasonal celebration is not only joyful but also a trap passed from generation to generation. The conundrum resists good intentions to revise the division of labor. So this story is less about passage than it is about stagnation. Ritualization hardens the family arrangement by evoking anxiety when ceremonial acts are not carried out in the same way from year to year.

Family therapists not only use ritual narratives as diagnostic tools, they also prescribe ritualized activities for therapeutic purposes. Family dynamics can be extraordinarily complicated, so as an illustration I have chosen a simple example of a prescribed family ritual.

Philip, an only child, is six. Even though he plays well alone and with other children, he cries over small things like peanut butter sandwiches or seeing the lace of his teacher's slip. Before school, his head is full of what-ifs: What if I trip? What if I run in the hall? He wants to be a good boy and cries, worrying that he won't, or can't. His family is caring and hides no great traumas. Schooling too is normal. So what should the parents do?

The therapist asked the father and son to list exhaustively in writing all the things that Philip could worry about. Philip was told that he needed to cry at night because in the morning there was not enough time to do his worrying justice while getting ready for school, whereas in the evening his father could give him his full attention. If he needed to cry and worry, father would be willing to sit with him. If Philip did not need all that time to cry and worry, his father and he could do other things like play catch, watch a movie, or play a game. But the men could only do this if Philip had done enough crying that night. . . .

Philip was also told that the more he talked to his father about feelings men had, and whatever worries he had, the more relaxed he would be and that he would worry and cry much less. The therapist asked father to give Philip a coin from his pocket. The therapist told Philip this was a special coin of his father's and that he could use the coin to help him not worry. Philip was told that, in school or when his father was not around, he could take this coin and squeeze it. The more he squeezed it, the more he could notice that he was worrying less and less, and when he let go of the coin, his worry would be gone. The therapist embellished this injunction, repeated it several times, and ended the session.[318]

The therapist's interpersonal tactic is obvious. It is to get the father and son to spend time together so that, in effect, the boy can be weaned off worrying, a debilitating activity, and onto a good thing, being with an attentive dad. Whether one calls the therapist's other ploys homework or ritual matters less than whether they worked. In this instance they did, quickly and effectively. Soon Philip preferred fun with dad over crying, which soon felt like a waste of time.

Some would not call these events ritual because they were not institutionalized and repeated, but then rites of passage are not supposed to be repeated either. There are several ritual-like features in the therapist's assignment. Philip is given a special time, evening; another time, mornings before school, is forbidden. Father and son create a ritual-like text, a complete list of things to worry about; the vaguely forbidden now becomes not only okay but obligatory and worthwhile. The previously shameful actions, worrying and crying, are now authorized. In addition there is a magical coin, a sacred object that, like his father, can actively absorb the boy's worries. The magic is sympathetic, the coin somehow participating in the power of the one who gave it. There is also the magic of the therapist's repeated verbal authorizations and empowering suggestions: The coin *will*, in fact, work.

The child is addressed in an idiom and logic appropriate to his age. Ritualizing works because the child believes, or, at least, he does not disbelieve.

Do such practices work with adults who are more skeptical, not so easily fooled by magical coins? The research and clinical practice seem to indicate that they can and that literal belief is not a requirement. Seriously playing along, serious make-believe, can be sufficient. On some level even the most rationalistic adult is affected by the power of special words, special objects, special places, and special actions.

Boiling Energy

Contrary to popular opinion, healing rites are not necessarily precipitated by a mental or physical illness. The Ju!'hoansi (Bushmen), who live in the Kalahari Desert of Namibia and Botswana, practice rites that are all-night, community-healing, trance dances.[319] These are not special-event rites but staple performances held four or five times a month. Sometimes Ju!'hoansi ceremonies are occasioned by an illness, but often they are not. Thus, they can be preventive as well as curative and collective as well as individual.

The Ju!'hoansi dance strenuously to "boil" spiritual energy, which they call *n/om*. It rises from the belly, coursing through the spine to the fingertips, where it can then be focused on pain in order to heal it. To heal, one must enter an extraordinary state of consciousness, and dance is both the means and occasion for its emergence.

Although the Ju!'hoansi use herbal medicine, the healing dance is brought to bear on almost every kind of illness. If the need arises, healers focus *n/om* on a single individual or small group. The larger, framing liturgy is enacted not only to heal but also because it is the community's way, the source of its life and identity. The rite does not merely symbolize their togetherness, it also effects a collective attunement that enables the people to survive in a harsh physical and social environment.

Though sacred, the trance dance is an occasion for great laughter and happiness but also of great pain. *N/om* hurts, burns as it courses through a healer's body. It requires "death," which, though not literal or total, is quite bodily. Healers in whom *n/om* reaches the boiling point scream and howl as they extract sickness from a person. Both healing and being healed hurt. There is great danger, thus great fear, surrounding the interaction. Healers must be able to see the sickness, yank it out, and argue with the gods over the fates of people whose illnesses threaten to take them. The health and illness of individuals are interpreted as expressions of the state of the entire community and the land it traverses.

The healing dance implicates not only what we Westerners conceive of as external (a community) or natural (the land) but also much that we imagine as either internal or supernatural:

Just yesterday, giraffe came and took me again. God came and took me and said, "Why is it that people are singing, yet you're not dancing?" When he spoke, he took me with him and we left this place. We traveled until we came to a wide body of water. It was a river. He took me to the river. The two halves of the river lay to either side of us, one to the left and one to the right.

God made the waters climb, and I laid my body in the direction they were flowing. My feet were behind, and my head was in front. That's how I lay. Then I entered the stream and began to move forward. I entered it and my body began to do like this. (Kxao Oah waved his hands dreamily to show how his body traveled forward, undulating in the water.) I traveled like this. My sides were pressed by pieces of metal. Metal things fastened my sides. And in this way I traveled forward. That's how I was stretched out in the water. And the spirits were singing.

The spirits were having a dance. I began to dance it too, hopping around like this. I joined the dance and I danced with them, but God said to me, "Don't come here and start to dance like that; now you just lie down and watch. This is how you should dance."[320]

This story is not about a rite, or, if it is, we cannot observe its performance. The account is, rather, a story or vision containing ritual instructions. Even though the account is about things invisible to the ordinary eye, it has visible, ritualistic consequences. It authorizes a particular way of dancing. Although the story narrates the origin of Kxao Oah's own style, it is also conventional, recognizable as constructed of a Ju!'hoansi idiom.

Just as there are stories about coming into one's own dancing-healing power, there are also accounts of particular healing events. Often they take the form of journey narratives like the one Oma Djo tells:

Oma !/Homg!ausi and I began to climb the threads to God's village. We traveled together, looking for that sick girl's soul. We climbed together, helping each other along the way. And we arrived in God's village, and were able to do our work. We were able to rescue that little girl's soul. And we knew she would be better.

As we began climbing back down the threads, we met Tshao Matze and !Kaece on the way. They were also trying to go to God's village to help save that little girl. We told them not to worry, that we already had done the work. We told them they could go back down now. And we all traveled back together.[321]

Westerners are apt to expect, or at least wish for, results from healing rites; so do the Ju!'hoansi. Performances of healing stories and rites occur so frequently that they are not really rites of passage. For Ju!'hoansi healers, they are, one might say, "rites of the routine." But for the little girl who recovers, this occasion is a passage.

The Western predilection is to label rites that aspire to verifiable results as magic. We like to say the work of a rite of passage is psychological and social, while the work of magic is physical and tangible. But Westerners, on the whole, do not believe in magic. We consider it fake, a delusion, or merely symbolic. In this washed-out view, symbols can mean but cannot effect. We tolerate notions like God's village, invisible threads, and soul loss by *demythologizing*, transposing them into forces our culture has taught us to invest our faith in: personal feelings, social attitudes, cultural values, and political realities. These, we believe, are what such stories are *really* about.

However we choose to explain Ju!'hoansi healing rites, they do heal. Like Western medicine, they work some of the time, not all the time. They work more effectively in some situations than others. Our empirical methods may produce better results than theirs with tuberculosis, but their ritualistic methods are more effective than ours in treating depression.

Medical sociologists distinguish illness from sickness. Sickness is the biological reality; illness is the social reality. Sickness happens, but illness is socially imagined and constructed. Illness is what patients, families, and doctors make of sickness; illness is how we frame and imagine sickness. Cancer is a sickness, but insofar as it is imagined as an "enemy" whom we "fight," it is also an illness. Healing rites deal more effectively with illness than with sickness.

The literature also distinguishes curing from healing. Cured, your illness goes away. Healed, your illness may or may not lift, but you have a different attitude toward it. Cured, you are fixed; healed, you are reconnected. Rites heal more effectively than they cure. Like the Ju!'hoansi, Tibetan Buddhists, Navajos, and Vodun practitioners perform healing rites when no one in particular is ill. "Things" get out of harmony, and they need reharmonizing or rebalancing. Not only can there be healing rites with no patient, but rites can also be performed without a precipitating event, an illness. One might think of such actions as the ritualistic equivalent of preventive medicine.

Metaphors and labels, especially when enacted, can make us sick or make us well; we *somatize* them, transforming words and images into flesh and bone, heart and gut. Metaphors not only sicken, they have a healing effect. One way to define ritual is as the enactment of a metaphor. Even though this definition is too broad, it points to a common characteristic of ritualistic activity: the serious use of metaphor. Ju!'hoansi "boil" the energy it takes to cure.

Because of its great dependence on metaphor, illness understood as an attack—for example, a heart "attack"—is akin to ritualizing. In the West two of the most common metaphors for illness are industrial and military. Some "thing" in a body or mind is "broken" or "defective," so medical personnel "fix" it. The body is a "machine"; physicians and psychiatrists are skilled "technicians" or highly paid "mechanics." Sick people are under "attack"; medicines and medical procedures are "weapons" to help them "fight back." There are "wars" on cancer and drugs just as there are wars with other countries. The idea that a sick person needs to fight back or fight off something is so ingrained that we hardly notice its metaphoric status.

Many of the same observations that anthropologist Robbie Davis-Floyd makes about hospital birth apply to hospital and doctors' office visits. The interactions are decisively symbolic. The doctor wears a uniform or other symbol of authority such as a stethoscope. The doctor speaks to you familiarly, addressing you by your first name, but you express deference by saying "Doctor so-and-so." The physician scribbles mysterious documents to which you, a mere patient, have no access. Patients submit to a doctor's authority and superior knowledge with little or no questioning, just as they would in approaching a priest in a shrine. Though not a rite like an indigenous healer might perform, the interaction between patient and doctor is heavily ritualized.

By considering illness and healing as passage, we have already begun to veer away from the classical rites-of-passage model, which centers on once-and-for-all events. !Kung healing rites are highly repetitive, the ritual staple of a culture. Even though a community healing rite *may* become a passage for an individual, it is daily, or rather weekly, bread for most. For the !Kung, as for many peoples, enacting rites is a way of cultivating a sensibility; thus, it is regular not merely occasional.

'Babette's Feast'

Ritual knowledge is nothing if not sensual. A rite is an activity that engages the hand and pricks the ear; it catches the eye and lifts the heart. Every ritual system cultivates a ritual sensibility, a way of being in the world that is at once ideological and sensory. Although rites may be taught by way of a book or learned as a formula, the aim is to create a repository of knowledge at the sensory level. Most of us know people who cook by taste, garden by instinct, or play music by ear. They proceed by sense rather than by recipe or guidebook. However awkwardly they may explain what they do, they accomplish their task with alacrity. Why? Because they have a sense for it. "How much baking powder?" I would ask my grandmother. Her reply was tossed off predictably, "You know, just enough."

If we have a tactile or kinesthetic sense for something, we do not need to depend on a book. Even in the so-called religions of the book, people learn what is in the book so that they can forget it, which is to say, embody it. Deep ritual knowledge, like inspired musical or choreographic knowledge, feels like the most natural thing in the world, even though it is not natural. Ritual is profoundly cultural; it is practiced, maintained by tradition, and deliberately cultivated. Like music and dance, ritual becomes deadening if inspiration, the breath of spontaneity, does not blow through the ritual structure itself.

In the film *Babette's Feast*, a chef from France is displaced by dire political circumstances. She arrives in Jutland, a northern, starkly Protestant area of Denmark beset with petty grievances and perpetual backbiting.[322] Taken in by two elderly sisters, Martine and Fillipa, daughters of the deceased local religious leader, Babette cooks their simple, tasteless food in the manner to which they have been accustomed.

After years of service in this austere household, Babette comes into money. The sisters fear she will use it to return to France. Instead, Babette wants to express her gratitude to the sisters for taking her in. She proposes to spend the money on a feast for them and their community.

For weeks Babette sweats and labors in the kitchen. The curiosity of the townspeople is peaked by the strange fare she begins importing: a live sea turtle, bottles and boxes and crates of things unknown or half revealed.

Babette has a sense for food that the sisters and villagers lack. The brethren and sisters are pure, free of contamination by alcohol (though not by gossip), but they are bereft of culinary art. A complicated set of circumstances leads them to agree that they will suffer through an ordeal of French food—just this once. Refusing such generosity of spirit would be a greater sin than letting the horrid stuff touch their lips, lips that surely, by the grace of God, relish the words of prayer more than fine French wine.

Then comes the night of the meal. As course after exotic course passes from palette to gut, the saints proceed from bafflement and barely concealed disgust to sheer delight bordering on religious ecstasy. They ingest the exquisite French fare and sacrifice themselves to fine wine. They argue, confess, and finally, sated and mellowed, forgive one another long-standing grudges.

By the end of Babette's feast, we begin to notice the beauty of the weather-beaten faces who have gathered around the table. As the people leave, weaving their way down the street, they revel in the fullness of the night sky that watches them wend their way home. Their sense of the world, spare to the point of being shrunken and ingrown, is now nourished by another sensibility, which is tastefully elegant without being self-serving.

The film reveals nothing new, only that which has not been truly seen or really tasted before. Even though no book of ceremonies prescribes it, the meal eventuates in a revelation of old things as if they were new. The meal scene evokes in many viewers a ritual sense. The film depicts what ritual is supposed to be—what it *really* is, not what it *ordinarily* is. The feast is special in such a way that the ordinary is transformed by it.

This special ordinariness is visually conveyed by the camera. It contemplates, meditatively, perhaps even lovingly, details of the food, setting, and interaction. We see the deep satisfaction of attending to what one is eating. We watch one whose skills are as no-nonsense as those of a plumber and whose sensibility is as finely tuned as that of a diviner. Babbette's attentiveness, along with the film's revelation of character and cosmos, gives it a ritualistic aura even though there is no formal rite in the film. *Babette's Feast* displaces ritual as routine in favor of ritual as attentive action.

Ordinary, or domestic, ritualizing spells the end of passage. The "end" of something can be either its demise or its goal. Rites of passage end when the special moment subsides in a way that renews one's ability to embrace the ordinary. The goal of ritual is to spice up daily existence with flavors so exquisite that we are unable to forget the banquet. Ordinary acts, when extraordinarily practiced, break open, transforming human conventions and revealing what is most deeply desirable, most cosmically orienting, and most fully human.

1. More on the topic of ritual invention can be found in Grimes, "Reinventing Ritual."

2. It is unnecessarily confusing to speak of every passage, birth and divorce, for instance, as a rite of passage, as does Ambert in *Divorce in Canada*, 130.

3. By *soul* I mean the self at its very root, the self in its most complete sense.

4. The distinction between transformation and transportation is made by Schechner, *Essays in Performance Theory.*

5. See, for example, Humphrey and Laidlaw, *Archetypal Actions of Ritual*, 95–100.

6. Two other scholars construct a story-ritual connection similar to the one I am presenting here; see Anderson and Foley, *Mighty Stories, Dangerous Rituals.*

7. An example of ritualizing on the plumber's model is that of Welfare State International. See Coult and Kershaw, *Engineers of the Imagination.*

8. An example of ritualizing on the mystical model is that of Jerzy Grotowski. See Wolford and Schechner, *The Grotowski Sourcebook.*

9. Rappaport, *Ecology, Meaning, and Religion;* d'Aquili and Laughlin, "Neurobiology of Myth and Ritual."

10. Eykamp, "Born and Born Again," 58. The phrase she quotes is from Fischer, "Ritual as Communication," 176.

11. See Klassen, "Blessed Events."

12. Davis-Floyd, *Birth as an American Rite of Passage,* 229–34.

13. See Wall, *Callisto Myth.*

14. As early as 1988, Karen and Jeffery Paige, using Jack Goody's definition of ritual, were claiming that delivery practices are ritual, but they did not develop or illustrate the argument. See Majumdar, *Age of Imperial Unity,* 268.

15. Davis-Floyd, *Birth as an American Rite of Passage,* 40.

16. Carolina Echeverria, Montreal, Canada, personal communication.

17. Laderman, *Wives and Midwives,* 173.

18. Davis-Floyd and Sargent, *Childbirth and Authoritative Knowledge,* 11. At the turn of the century the hospital birth rate was only 5 percent; by World War II, 50 percent; see Paige and Paige, *Politics of Reproductive Ritual,* 268.

19. Davis-Floyd, *Birth as an American Rite of Passage,* 8.

20. For more on my view of ritual in hospital settings see Grimes, "Illness, Embodiment."

21. Miner, "Body Ritual," 10–11.

22. Part of the following discussion draws on Grimes, *Ritual Criticism,* 9 ff.

23. A rite may be part of some larger whole, a *ritual system* or *ritual tradition* that includes other rites as well. *Ritual* is a more general, less specific term than *rite*. Ritual is what one defines in formal definitions and characterizations; rites are what people enact. Strictly speaking then, I do not say "a ritual" or "rituals" but "ritual," on the one hand, and "a rite" or "rites," on the other. Those who enact rites I call *ritualists*. People who observe and study ritual are *ritologists* or *ritual studies scholars*.

24. My description is based on Laderman, *Wives and Midwives*.

25. Laderman, *Wives and Midwives*, 86 ff.

26. Laderman, *Wives and Midwives*, 124.

27. Laderman, *Wives and Midwives*, 130.

28. Laderman, *Wives and Midwives*, 142.

29. Laderman, *Wives and Midwives*, 173.

30. For a view of magic that makes it a credible, contemporary category see Driver, *Liberating Rites*.

31. Laderman, *Wives and Midwives*, 210.

32. As reported by Mahdi, "Vision Quest," 356.

33. Mary Crow Dog, "Birth Giving," 157–59, 161–63.

34. Fried and Fried, *Transitions*, 28–32.

35. Shostak, *Nisa*, 177–99.

36. Firth, "Ceremonies for Children," 56–57.

37. Geertz, *Religion of Java*, 38–50.

38. Drewal, *Yoruba Ritual*, 56.

39. Brant, *Childbirth for Men*, 51.

40. Hall and Dawson, *Broodmales*, 25, 9–10.

41. Hall and Dawson, *Broodmales*, 28.

42. For more on the topic of imaginal ritual, see Noel, *Soul of Shamanism*.

43. Fock, *Waiwai*.

44. Paige and Paige, *Politics of Reproductive Ritual*, 50.

45. Paige and Paige, *Politics of Reproductive Ritual*, 48.

46. Much of the following discussion of baptism draws on Kavanagh, *Shape of Baptism*.

47. See, for instance, Roberts, Jr., *Initiation to Adulthood*.

48. The following account is largely dependent on Cressy, *Birth, Marriage, and Death*.

49. Cressy, *Birth, Marriage, and Death*, 136.

50. Cressy, *Birth, Marriage, and Death*, 160.

51. Cressy, *Birth, Marriage, and Death*, 121.

52. Shahar, "A Child Is Born," 36.

53. Cressy, *Birth, Marriage, and Death*, 223.

54. See United States Catholic Conference, *Catholic Household Blessings & Prayers*; Anonymous, *Book of Blessings*.

55. Anderson and Foley, "Birth of a Story," 57.

56. Anderson and Foley, "Birth of a Story," 51.

57. Anderson and Foley, "Birth of a Story," 55.

58. Kaplan, "Look Who's Talking Indeed," 126.

59. For comparative statistics see Jordan, *Birth in Four Cultures*.

60. Susan Scott, personal communication. Susan is a writer, editor, and spiritual director. She works with faith communities, artists, scholars, and those who are disabled or marginalized, facilitating stories that would otherwise remain hidden or lost.

61. Rabuzzi, *Mother with Child*. On the sacred dimensions of birth see Balin, "Sacred Dimensions of Pregnancy and Birth."

62. Readers may find it revealing to compare my account of the same birth: Grimes, *Marrying & Burying*.

63. Among the books now breaking this taboo is Martens and Harms, *In Her Own Voice*.

64. Priya, *Birth Traditions*, 86; Balin, "Sacred Dimensions of Pregnancy and Birth."

65. See www.islandnet.com/~browns/homebirth/stories.htm, as well as Klassen, "Blessed Events."

66. This definition of religion is proposed and discussed by Ferré, *Basic Modern Philosophy of Religion*.

67. Usually uttered when one does something for the first time.

68. Doug Abrams Arava, letter to Jesse, December 12, 1994. Doug is an editor for HarperSanFrancisco.

69. Doug Abrams Arava, personal communication, November 12, 1997.

70. See, for example, chapter 16 in Grimes, *Marrying & Burying*.

71. Erikson, "Development of Ritualization."

72. Coult and Kershaw, *Engineers of the Imagination*; Gill and Fox, *Dead Good Funerals Book*.

73. Coult and Kershaw, *Engineers of the Imagination*, 145–51.

74. Kylie Stark, personal correspondence, October 10, 1998.

75. Produced by the Union of International Associations in Brussels and accessible on the Internet at www.uia.org/uiapubs/pubency.htm.

76. Gloria Naylor, *The Women of Brewster Place* (1982), quoted in Hill, *Coming of Age*, 61–62.

77. This is the case, for example, on Manam Island, off the northeast coast of Papua New Guinea. See Lutkehaus, "Gender Metaphors," 198 ff.

78. Shorter, "Traditional Pattern," 276.

79. Roth, "Conversion of the Jews," 218–19.

80. Vivian Hansen, "One Flesh" (unpublished manuscript). Vivian lives in Calgary, Alberta, with her daughter, Alexis. Vivian has served as president of the Calgary Women's Writing Project, which facilitates the writing of women of color in *Forum* magazine.

81. Crapanzano, "Rite of Return," 28–29. Pp. 30–31 include a first-person account.

82. Schlegel and Barry, *Adolescence*, 35.

83. Eliade, *Rites and Symbols of Initiation*, 118, 130, 135.

84. An exposition and critique of the Jungian initiatory legacy can be found in Noel, *Soul of Shamanism*.

85. Bennett, "Islam," 98.

86. For instance, this is the case for the Daulo of Papua New Guinea. See Sexton, "Marriage as the Model," 208.

87. Herdt, *The Sambia.*
88. We might also add *rites of middle age,* which follow adult initiation, and *eldering* rites marking entry into old age or elevation to the status of elder.
89. Occasionally, the transition zone is called a *margin,* in which case *incorporation* is correspondingly named *aggregation.* These latter terms are closer to van Gennep's original French: *rites de séparation, rites de marge, rites d'agrégation.*
90. Van Gennep, *Rites of Passage,* 11.
91. Bynum, "Women's Stories, Women's Symbols."
92. Lincoln, *Emerging from the Chrysalis,* 101.
93. Sullwold, "Rites of Passage," 288–89. For a scheme that uses eight rather than ten elements see Sanyika, "Gang Rites," 117–20.
94. My summary depends largely on three sources: Young, *Initiation Ceremonies;* Schlegel and Barry, "Adolescent Initiation Ceremonies"; Schlegel and Barry, *Adolescence.*
95. Schlegel and Barry, *Adolescence,* 34.
96. Young, *Initiation Ceremonies.*
97. Strathern, *Reproducing the Future,* 66.
98. Whiting et al., "Male Initiation Ceremonies," 370.
99. A critique of the study conducted by Whiting and his coauthors can be found in Norbeck et al., "Puberty Rites."
100. This conclusion is implied by Schlegel and Barry, "Adolescent Initiation Ceremonies."
101. Quoted in Roloff, "Yes, We Carry On," 332–33.
102. Ritual sacrifice, perhaps, runs a close second, since, like initiation, sacrifice has been made the key to theories of religion and the subject matter of artistic creativity. No one is claiming that Western society should reinstate public sacrificial rites. However, many are urging us to reclaim or reinvent initiations for young people.
103. There is an important counterargument to be considered, namely, that initiation strengthens male solidarity and thus increases the likelihood that men will behave abusively toward women.
104. Moore and Gillette, "Masculine Ritual Process," 44.
105. Fried and Fried, *Transitions,* 23.
106. These are described in Peay, "Singing Sword."
107. Oldfield, "Journey of the Adolescent Soul," 219, 222, 218, 230.
108. For example, see Christopher, "Service as a Rite of Passage," 126–27. For Christopher, ritual needs are apparently identical with mythic ones.
109. For example, Kratz, *Affecting Performance.*
110. The account that follows is based on Carnes, *Secret Ritual.*
111. An especially good film on the topic is the National Film Board of Canada's *If Only I Were an Indian.*
112. Carnes, *Secret Ritual,* 99.
113. Carnes, *Secret Ritual,* 95.
114. Carnes, *Secret Ritual,* 99–101.
115. Carnes, *Secret Ritual,* 103.
116. Harwood, "Secret Societies in America."

117. Few Catholics joined because various edicts of the church prohibited membership in such organizations.

118. Carnes, *Secret Ritual*, 2–3.

119. Carnes, *Secret Ritual*, 14, 125–26.

120. Carnes, *Secret Ritual*, 155.

121. Turner, *Forest of Symbols*, 93.

122. Eventually, Turner stopped using the term *archetype*, since he came to reject Jung's idea of the collective unconscious.

123. Turner, *Forest of Symbols*, 106–8.

124. Turner, *Forest of Symbols*, 106.

125. Some of them are described in Wolford and Schechner, *Grotowski Sourcebook*. At around the same time Victor Turner, Edith Turner, Richard Schechner, and Erving Goffman were experimenting with theater and ritual.

126. Brown, " 'Plenty Confidence in Myself.' "

127. See, for instance, Kratz, *Affecting Performance;* Herdt, *Sambia;* Beidelman, *Cool Knife.*

128. Carnes, *Secret Ritual;* Kavanagh, *Shape of Baptism.*

129. This account is based on Roscoe, "In the Shadow of the Tambaran." There are many variations in the rite. My account is generic and ignores many of them.

130. Roscoe, "In the Shadow of the Tambaran."

131. Much of the following account is indebted to Cantú, "Quinceañera."

132. Cantú, "Quinceañera." Norma received her B.S. and M.S. from Texas A & I University in Laredo and Kingsville, respectively. She earned her Ph.D. in English from the University of Nebraska, Lincoln. Her scholarly interests include folklore, Chicana literature, and borderlands studies. Her most recent work, forthcoming from the Texas A & M University Press, is a study of the Matachines de la Santa Cruz, a religious dance tradition in Laredo. Her novel *Canícula: Snapshots of a Girlhood en la frontera* received the Premio Aztlán in 1996. She is completing a second novel, *Hair Matters.* She teaches at Texas A & M International and has served as acting director of the Center for Chicano Studies at the University of California, Santa Barbara.

133. Marcus, *Rituals of Childhood*, 1.

134. Early Christianity's scheduling of baptism to coincide with the Easter vigil employs a similar strategy.

135. Marcus, *Rituals of Childhood*, 114.

136. For a detailed study of this kind of educational ritual see McLaren, *Schooling as Ritual Performance.*

137. I owe this way of putting it to my brother Terry Grimes.

138. Miriam Ashkin Stanton, personal communication, August 1996. Miriam, who was thirteen when she wrote this account, is the only Jewish girl living in Portola, a largely Baptist town of two thousand inhabitants in the mountains of northern California. She regularly gives talks on Jewish holidays and the Holocaust. Her rabbi is Myra Soifer; their synagogue is in Reno, Nevada.

139. Eliade, *Rites and Symbols of Initiation*, 3.

140. Sekaquaptewa, *Me and Mine*, 23–29.

141. For a fuller discussion, see Gill, "Disenchantment."

142. The following account is based on Ortiz, "Pueblo Sacred Clown."
143. Ortiz, "Pueblo Sacred Clown," 9.
144. Ortiz, "Pueblo Sacred Clown," 10–11.
145. Ortiz, "Pueblo Sacred Clown," 15.
146. Myerhoff, "Death in Due Time," 152.
147. Churchill, *Fantasies of the Master Race,* 223–28.
148. Mesteth et al., "Lakota Spirituality."
149. For more on the topic see Grimes, "This May Be a Feud."
150. The institute's Web site is found at www.ritesofpassage.org.
151. Hill acknowledges the formative influence of several individuals who have shaped his African-centered thinking. Among them are John Mbiti, Kofi Opuku Asare, Peter Sarpong, Maulana Karenga, and Anthony Mensah.
152. Hill, "Back to the Future," 57.
153. See Hill, *Journey.*
154. For example, Piney Woods Country Life School in Piney Woods, Mississippi, has a rites of passage program. See their materials at www.pineywoods.org/savemale.htm#anchor825804.
155. Hill, "Rites of Passage Ceremony."
156. Hill, *Coming of Age,* 62.
157. Hill, "Africentric Rites of Passage," 9.
158. Hill, "Back to the Future," 47–48. Compare Hill, *Coming of Age,* 64–65.
159. Hill, "Back to the Future." Also available in *African American Male Research* 3.1 (September–October 1998).
160. Jones, "Rites 101."
161. Otnes, " 'Friend of the Bride,' " 229. See also Pleck, "Celebrating the Family," 69.
162. Pleck, "Celebrating the Family," 69.
163. Pleck, "Celebrating the Family," 38.
164. Epstein, *Rise and Fall of Diamonds.*
165. Otnes and Scott, "Something Old, Something New."
166. I am indebted to Shaun Douglas Poisson-Fast for the story.
167. McGrath and English, "Intergenerational Gift-Giving," 129–30.
168. Greenblat and Cottle, *Getting Married,* 198–99.
169. Kitahara, "Function of Marriage Ceremony," 171.
170. Lowrey and Otnes, "Meaningful Wedding," 168–69.
171. This historical sketch is indebted to Pleck, "Celebrating the Family."
172. Boswell, *Marriage of Likeness,* 11.
173. Judge, *Unveiled.*
174. One is left wondering whether the filmmaker moved the reception scene to the end (after, rather than before, the thank-you card scene) in order to provide a happier ending. If so, the daughter's presentation speech was not really generous but hollow, in which case the rite, rather than revealing the truth about love and family relationships, covers up their true nature.
175. Shaun Douglas Poisson-Fast, personal communication, April 20, 1998. Shaun was twenty-six and a Canadian student of religious studies when he wrote this piece. His religious background is Mennonite.

176. Dillingham and Isaac, "Defining Marriage Cross-Culturally," 60–61.

177. Laake, *Secret Ceremonies*, 72–73, 78, 87–88, 90.

178. Tanner and Tanner, "Temple Ritual Altered."

179. Laake, *Secret Ceremonies*, 97.

180. Schlegel and Barry, *Adolescence*, 93.

181. Singh, "Religious Life," 78–83.

182. Gillis, *For Better, for Worse*, 5.

183. Edwards, *Modern Japan*, 45.

184. Goldstein-Gidoni, *Packaged Japaneseness*, 14–15.

185. Goldstein-Gidoni, *Packaged Japaneseness*, 1.

186. Edwards, *Modern Japan*, 48–51.

187. Edwards, *Modern Japan*, 25. The following account is based on Edwards's book as well as Goldstein-Gidoni, *Packaged Japaneseness*.

188. Edwards, *Modern Japan*, 23.

189. Edwards, *Modern Japan*, 56.

190. Kapadia, "Hindu Marriage a Sacrament," 168.

191. Fruzzetti, *Gift of a Virgin*, 13.

192. The Widow Remarriage Act was passed in 1856, but it did not obliterate the popular view that widows are inauspicious.

193. Based on an interview with Dr. K. Janardhana Iyengar on June 9, 1998, in Montreal, Quebec. In 1979, at age thirty-five, Jan emigrated from India to Canada. After teaching and conducting research at the University of Windsor, Ontario, he moved to Atomic Energy of Canada in Mississauga. At the time of this interview, he was a structural engineer at Pratt & Whitney, Canada, and his wife, Vijaya, was employed at the Royal Bank of Canada. At the time of the interview, their twenty-two-year-old daughter, Pratibha, was in the final year of her M.D. at McGill University.

194. Cooper and Nanthapa, *Culture Shock!*, 171.

195. Richard Breedon is an experimental high energy particle physicist at the University of California, Davis; he is also a teacher of hatha yoga.

196. The account of Greek weddings is based on Garland, *Greek Way of Life*, and Oakley and Sinos, *Wedding in Ancient Athens*.

197. Quoted in Garland, *The Greek Way of Life*, 222.

198. Cited in Oakley and Sinos, *Wedding in Ancient Athens*, 22.

199. Oakley and Sinos, *Wedding in Ancient Athens*, 22.

200. Some scholars read the story of Demeter and Persephone as an allegory, thus not about weddings so much as about the change of seasons. There is no evidence that this myth was used in Greek weddings, but the abduction of a wife connects the myth with the ritual, so it is impossible to rule out a matrimonial reading in favor of the agricultural one.

201. Garland, *Greek Way of Life*, 227.

202. This account of Roman weddings is based on Johnston, *Roman Life*.

203. Johnston, *Roman Life*, 134.

204. For a provocative documentary on contemporary Jewish divorce see Coalition of Jewish Women for the GET, *Untying the Bonds*.

205. Hoffman, "Jewish Wedding Ceremony," 138.

206. Hoffman, "Jewish Wedding Ceremony," 143.

207. Boswell, *Marriage of Likeness*, 111.

208. Boswell, *Marriage of Likeness*, 178 ff.

209. Searle and Stevenson, *Documents of the Marriage Liturgy*, 239–51.

210. Ross-Macdonald, *Alternative Weddings*, v–vi.

211. See the materials posted at www.weddingcircle.com/ethnic.

212. *Sposa: The Magazine for the Discerning Bride* (spring/summer 1998).

213. Lalli and Dahl, "Ethnic Customs." See also McGrath and English, "Intergenerational Gift-Giving."

214. See Anderson and Foley, *Mighty Stories, Dangerous Rituals;* Anderson and Foley, "Wedding of Stories."

215. Butler, *Ceremonies of the Heart*, 55–69.

216. Crissman, *Death and Dying*, 84.

217. See the materials posted at vbiweb.champlain.edu/famsa/.

218. Langness, "Hysterical Psychosis."

219. The term was popularized in 1491 by William Caxton of Westminster; he published a little treatise called *Ars Moriendi, That Is to Say the Craft for to Die for the Health of Man's Soul.*

220. Blackman, *Graceful Exits*, 148.

221. In some strains of the Western theistic traditions (Judaism, Christianity, Islam), worship occasionally sounds a similar preparatory note.

222. Blackman, *Graceful Exits*, 42.

223. Nuland, *How We Die*, 244.

224. Nuland, *How We Die*, 257.

225. William H. Myers, personal communication, August 1997. Bill is a Baptist and a professor of New Testament and Black Church Studies.

226. Victor Hori, personal communication, August 1997. Born in Canada in 1944, Victor earned a Ph.D. in philosophy at Stanford University in 1976. From 1977 to 1990 he was a Rinzai Zen monk. Currently, he is a member of the Faculty of Religious Studies at McGill University in Montreal.

227. Lewis, *Death in the Sanchez Family*, x. The son was novelist Martin Nexo of Copenhagen.

228. The account that follows is based on Scheper-Hughes, *Death Without Weeping.*

229. Scheper-Hughes, *Death Without Weeping*, 253.

230. Scheper-Hughes, *Death Without Weeping*, 255–58.

231. The following account is based on Rawski, "Chinese Death Ritual," 26.

232. For the full text prescribing Chinese funerals, see Ebrey, *Chu Hsi's Family Rituals.*

233. This summary is based on Watson, "Chinese Funerary Rites."

234. Watson, *Mo Tzu*, 68.

235. Watson, *Mo Tzu*, 75.

236. Danforth, *Death Ritual*, 11–12.

237. Pseudonym for a village in Greek Macedonia. The names of all the participants are also pseudonymous.

238. Danforth, *Death Ritual*, 101–2.

239. Danforth, *Death Ritual*, 19–21.

240. This connection between the treatment of remains and the state of the soul is articulated in a theory developed by Hertz, *Death and the Right Hand.*

241. Danforth, *Death Ritual,* 129.

242. Danforth, *Death Ritual,* 129, 101. The kerchief is a strip of cloth used to tie up the lower jaw of a corpse.

243. Danforth, *Death Ritual,* 127.

244. Danforth, *Death Ritual,* 143.

245. Reginald A. Ray is a faculty member at Naropa Institute in Boulder, Colorado. He teaches Buddhist studies, specializing in the Buddhism of Tibet and India, and he is the author of the award-winning book *Buddhist Saints in India* (Oxford University Press, 1994).

246. Fort Worth Art Museum, *El Día de los Muertos,* 11.

247. Quoted in Monsivais, " 'Look Death, Don't Be Inhuman.' " Monsivais wryly complains that Octavio Paz codified a "vision of the internal and external tourism" that is "subject to the intensities of Kodak."

248. Lewis, *Death in the Sanchez Family,* 35–36.

249. Kastenbaum, *Death, Society, and Human Experience,* 59.

250. Kastenbaum, *Death, Society, and Human Experience,* 353.

251. In a personal communication of October 3, 1998, Kastenbaum wrote, "Students in my death classes and others who come by to see me almost never bring up the core death rites. Most often they do not feel a close connection with these rites and have responses to the entire funeral process that are more psychological than anything else. I don't think 'death educators' discourage discussion of funeral rites; other concerns and experiences seem to come up more often and more forcefully."

252. Huntington and Metcalf, *Celebrations of Death,* 186.

253. Huntington and Metcalf, *Celebrations of Death.* Notice the discrepancy between the two different summaries of the pattern. On page 187 the pattern is fourfold; on page 198 it is threefold.

254. Huntington and Metcalf, *Celebrations of Death,* 209.

255. Huntington and Metcalf, *Celebrations of Death,* 187.

256. Huntington and Metcalf, *Celebrations of Death,* 210.

257. Huntington and Metcalf, *Celebrations of Death,* 203.

258. Huntington and Metcalf, *Celebrations of Death,* 209.

259. Laderman, *Sacred Remains,* 8. Laderman's perspective is the classic Americanist stance, one that views American history as emanating from New England and its environs. In this view the Puritan way of death becomes root and soul of the American way of death. From such a perspective, Boston, Philadelphia, and New York loom large on the map. Not only are Los Angeles and Santa Fe, Atlanta and New Orleans missing, so are Detroit, Cleveland, and Minneapolis, much of the upper midwestern north.

260. Much of the following account is based on Laderman, *Sacred Remains.*

261. Laderman, *Sacred Remains,* 55.

262. For this reason, we should be skeptical of all three-phased patterns that researchers "find" in rites of passage.

263. Maris Vinovskis, cited in Laderman, *Sacred Remains,* 97.

264. Laderman, *Sacred Remains,* 162.

265. Laderman, *Sacred Remains,* 153.

266. Although it is tempting to think of the two columns as representing types of "death cultures," for example, secular and sacred or technological and traditional, it is dangerous to do so without issuing several caveats.

267. Prothero, "To Bury or to Burn?" 14.

268. White, "People's Republic of China," 304.

269. Feinstein and Mayo, *Mortal Acts.*

270. Feinstein and Mayo, *Mortal Acts,* 38–39.

271. Feinstein and Mayo, *Mortal Acts,* 103.

272. Available at www.cemetery.org.

273. Danforth, *Death Ritual of Rural Greece,* 129, 101.

274. Sheehy, *New Passages,* 5.

275. See, for instance, the section on "Celebratory Centenarians" in Sheehy, *New Passages,* 427.

276. I served as its content adviser.

277. Feinstein and Mayo, *Mortal Acts,* 5–6.

278. Herdt, *Sambia,* 141–44.

279. For a fuller discussion of the topic see Grimes, *Ritual Criticism.*

280. Kratz, *Affecting Performance,* 114, 121, 125.

281. Kratz, *Affecting Performance,* 347.

282. See especially Hoffman, *Covenant of Blood.*

283. Much of the following discussion of sati depends on Sharma, *Sati.*

284. Majumdar, *Age of Imperial Unity,* 567–68.

285. The full account is available at www.religioustolerance.org.

286. The estimate is proffered by Ross, *Satanic Ritual Abuse,* 71.

287. See the data gathered by the Ontario Consultants on Religious Tolerance and posted at www.religioustolerance.org/sra.htm.

288. Ross, *Satanic Ritual Abuse,* 99.

289. Ross, *Satanic Ritual Abuse,* 20–123.

290. For example, see Milloy, *National Crime.*

291. Ross, *Satanic Ritual Abuse,* 145.

292. Materials on her practice may be found at weddingcircle.com/gioia. All subsequent quotations concerning Joyce Gioia are from this Web site.

293. See their materials at www.ozemail.com.au/~jimbos/.

294. Devereux, *Abortion in Primitive Societies.*

295. Hardacre, *Marketing,* 251.

296. Hardacre, *Marketing,* 248.

297. Hardacre, *Marketing,* 158–59.

298. LaFleur, *Liquid Life,* 6–9.

299. LaFleur, *Liquid Life,* 155.

300. Hardacre, *Marketing,* 251.

301. Hardacre, *Marketing.*

302. Hardacre, *Marketing,* 26.

303. See also Smith, "Buddhism and Abortion."

304. Kluger-Bell, *Unspeakable Losses.*

305. Marie Snyder, thirty-three, is a single mother of two young children, a high school teacher, and an ecofeminist with no religious affiliation.

306. Ted Tollefson is a Unitarian Universalist minister who lives with his wife, Kristen, at a research and retreat center in Frontenac, Minnesota. He is director and cofounder of Mythos Institute (freenet.msp.mn.us/org/mythos/mythos.www/mythome.html), a nonprofit organization devoted to the study of mythology, dream work, and creative ritual. He teaches at Metro State University and United Theological Seminary near Minneapolis, MN.

307. One can see the rite enacted in Littman, *In Her Own Time.*

308. Sandra Woolfrey.

309. Oscar Cole-Arnal.

310. Kay Koppedrayer.

311. Larry Toombs.

312. Delton Glebe.

313. Jen Alboim, O. J. Poulsen, and Dax Thomas.

314. Harold Remus.

315. Harold Remus.

316. Kleinman, *The Illness Narratives.*

317. Laird, "Women and Ritual in Family Therapy," 342–45.

318. O'Connor and Hoorwitz, "Imitative and Contagious Magic," 152–54.

319. The following account is based largely on Richard Katz et al., *Healing Makes Our Hearts Happy.*

320. Katz et al., *Healing Makes Our Hearts Happy,* 107.

321. Katz et al., *Healing Makes Our Hearts Happy,* 113.

322. Axel, *Babette's Feast.*

Ambert, Annie-Marie. *Divorce in Canada*. Don Mills, ON: Academic, 1980.

Anderson, Herbert, and Edward Foley. "A Wedding of Stories." *New Theology Review* 3.2 (1990): 51–64.

———. "The Birth of a Story: Infant Baptism in a Pastoral Perspective." *New Theology Review* 4.4 (1991): 46–62.

———. *Mighty Stories, Dangerous Rituals: Weaving the Human and Divine*. San Francisco: Jossey-Bass, 1997.

Anonymous. *Book of Blessings*. New York: Catholic Book, 1989.

Axel, Gabriel, writer and director. *Babette's Feast*. 102 minutes. Color film based on a story by Isak Dinesen. N.p., 1987.

Balin, Jane. "The Sacred Dimensions of Pregnancy and Birth." *Qualitative Sociology* 11.4 (1988): 275–301.

Beidelman, T. O. *The Cool Knife: Imagery of Gender, Sexuality, and Moral Education in Kaguru Initiation Ritual*. Washington, DC: Smithsonian, 1997.

Bennett, Clinton. "Islam." In *Rites of Passage*, ed. Jean Holm and John Bowker, 90–112. London: Pinter, 1994.

Bettelheim, Bruno. *Symbolic Wounds: Puberty Rites and the Envious Male*, rev. ed. New York: Collier, 1962.

Blackman, Sushila, ed. *Graceful Exits: How Great Beings Die*. New York: Weatherhill, 1997.

Boswell, John. *Marriage of Likeness: Same Sex Unions in Pre-Modern Europe*. New York: HarperCollins, 1994.

Brant, Herbert A. *Childbirth for Men*. New York: Oxford University Press, 1985.

Brown, Karen McCarthy. " 'Plenty Confidence in Myself': The Initiation of a White Woman Scholar into Haitian Vodou." *Journal of Feminist Studies in Religion* 3.1 (1987): 67–76.

Butler, Becky, ed. *Ceremonies of the Heart: Celebrating Lesbian Unions*. Seattle: Seale, 1990.

Bynum, Caroline Walker. "Women's Stories, Women's Symbols: A Critique of Victor Turner's Theory of Liminality." In *Anthropology and the Study of Religion*, ed. Robert L. Moore and Frank E. Reynolds, 105–25. Chicago: Center for the Scientific Study of Religion, 1984.

Cantú, Norma E. "La Quinceañera: Towards an Ethnographic Analysis of a Life-Cycle Ritual." Available at www.tamiu.edu/~necantu/quincean.htm. Laredo, TX, 1996.

Carnes, Mark C. *Secret Ritual and Manhood in Victorian America.* New Haven: Yale University Press, 1989.

Christopher, Nancy Geyer. "Service as a Rite of Passage." In *Crossroads: The Quest for Contemporary Rites of Passage,* ed. Louise Carus Mahdi et al., 125–32. Chicago: Open Court, 1996.

Churchill, Ward. *Fantasies of the Master Race: Literature, Cinema and the Colonization of American Indians.* Monroe, ME: Common Courage, 1992.

Coalition of Jewish Women for the GET. *Untying the Bonds . . . : Jewish Divorce.* 44 minutes. Cote Ste. Luc, Quebec, Canada: Coalition of Jewish Women for the GET, 1997. Videocassette.

Cooper, Robert, and Nanthapa. *Culture Shock! Thailand.* Singapore: Times Books International, 1982.

Coult, Tony, and Baz Kershaw, eds. *Engineers of the Imagination: The Welfare State Handbook.* London: Methuen, 1983.

Crapanzano, Vincent. "Rite of Return: Circumcision in Morocco." In *The Psychoanalytic Study of Society,* ed. Werner Muensterberger, 9: 15–36. New Haven: Yale University Press, 1980.

Cressy, David. *Birth, Marriage, and Death: Ritual, Religion and the Life-Cycle in Tudor and Stuart England.* Oxford, England: Oxford University Press, 1997.

Crissman, James K. *Death and Dying in Central Appalachia: Changing Attitudes and Practices.* Urbana: University of Illinois Press, 1994.

Crow Dog, Mary. "Birth Giving." In *Lakota Woman,* 156–69. New York: HarperCollins, 1991.

Danforth, Loring M. *The Death Ritual of Rural Greece.* Princeton, NJ: Princeton University Press, 1982.

d'Aquili, Eugene, and Charles D. Laughlin. "The Neurobiology of Myth and Ritual." In *The Spectrum of Ritual: A Biogenetic Structural Analysis,* 152–82. New York: Columbia University Press, 1979.

Davis-Floyd, Robbie, and Carolyn F. Sargent, eds. *Childbirth and Authoritative Knowledge.* Berkeley and Los Angeles: University of California Press, 1997.

Davis-Floyd, Robbie E. *Birth As an American Rite of Passage.* Berkeley and Los Angeles: University of California Press, 1992.

Devereux, George. *A Study of Abortion in Primitive Societies: A Typological, Distributional, and Dynamic Analysis of the Prevention of Birth in 400 Preindustrial Societies.* Rev. ed. New York: International Universities, 1955.

Dillingham, Beth W., and Barry L. Isaac. "Defining Marriage Cross-Culturally." In *Being Female: Reproduction, Power, and Change,* 55–63. The Hague, Netherlands: Mouton, 1975.

Drewal, Margaret Thompson. *Yoruba Ritual: Performers, Play, Agency.* Bloomington: Indiana University Press, 1992.

Driver, Tom F. *Liberating Rites: Understanding the Transformative Power of Ritual.* Boulder, CO: Westview, 1998.

Ebrey, Patricia Buckley, trans. *Chu Hsi's Family Rituals: A Twelfth-Century Chinese Manual for the Performance of Cappings, Weddings, Funerals, and Ancestral Rites.* Princeton, NJ: Princeton University Press, 1991.

Edwards, Walter. *Modern Japan Through Its Weddings: Gender, Person, and Society in Ritual Portrayal.* Stanford, CA: Stanford University Press, 1989.

Eliade, Mircea. *Rites and Symbols of Initiation: The Mysteries of Birth and Rebirth.* Trans. Willard R. Trask. New York: Harper & Row, 1958.

Epstein, Jay. *The Rise and Fall of Diamonds.* New York: Simon & Schuster, 1982.

Erikson, Erik H. "The Development of Ritualization." In *Readings in Ritual Studies,* ed. Ronald L. Grimes, 201–11. Upper Saddle River, NJ: Prentice-Hall, 1996.

Eykamp, Myriel. "Born and Born Again: Childbirth Rituals from a Mother's Perspective." In *Sacred Dimensions of Women's Experience,* ed. Elizabeth Dodson Gray, 58–64. Wellesley, MA: Roundtable, 1988.

Feinstein, David, and Peg Elliott Mayo. *Mortal Acts: Eighteen Empowering Rituals for Confronting Death.* San Francisco: HarperSanFrancisco, 1993.

Ferré, Frederick. *Basic Modern Philosophy of Religion.* New York: Scribners, 1967.

Firth, Raymond. "Ceremonies for Children." In *Tikopia Ritual and Belief,* 31–78. Boston: Beacon, 1967.

Fischer, Edward. "Ritual as Communication." In *Roots of Ritual,* ed. James D. Shaughnessy, 161–84. Grand Rapids, MI: Eerdmans, 1973.

Fock, Niels. *Waiwai: Religion and Society of an Amazonian Tribe.* Ethnographical Series, no. 8. Copenhagen: National Museum of Denmark, 1963.

Fort Worth Art Museum. *El Día de los Muertos: The Life of the Dead in Mexican Folk Art.* Fort Worth: Fort Worth Art Museum, 1987.

Fried, Martha Nemes, and Morton Fried. *Transitions: Four Rituals in Eight Cultures.* New York: Norton, 1980.

Fruzzetti, Lina. *The Gift of a Virgin: Women, Marriage, and Ritual in a Bengali Society.* New Brunswick, NJ: Rutgers University Press, 1982.

Garland, Robert. *The Greek Way of Life from Conception to Old Age.* Ithaca, NY: Cornell University Press, 1990.

Geertz, Clifford. *The Religion of Java.* Glencoe, IL: Free Press, 1960.

Gill, Sam D. "Disenchantment: A Religious Abduction." In *Native American Religious Action: A Performance Approach to Religion,* 58–75. Columbia: University of South Carolina Press, 1977.

Gill, Sue, and John Fox. *The Dead Good Funerals Book.* Ulverston, England: Welfare State International, 1996.

Gillis, John. *For Better, for Worse: British Marriages, 1600 to the Present.* New York: Oxford University Press, 1985.

Goldstein-Gidoni, Ofra. *Packaged Japaneseness: Weddingness, Business, and Brides.* Honolulu: University of Hawaii, 1997.

Greenblat, Cathy S., and Thomas J. Cottle. *Getting Married.* New York: McGraw-Hill, 1980.

Grimes, Ronald L. "Illness, Embodiment, and Ritual Criticism." In *Ritual Criticism: Case Studies in Its Practice, Essays on Its Theory,* 145–57. Columbia: University of South Carolina Press, 1990.

———. *Marrying & Burying: Rites of Passage in a Man's Life.* Boulder, CO: Westview, 1995.

———. "Reinventing Ritual." *Soundings* 75.1 (1992): 21–41.

———. *Ritual Criticism: Case Studies in Its Practice, Essays on Its Theory.* Columbia: University of South Carolina Press, 1990.

———. "This May Be a Feud, But It Is Not a War: An Electronic, Interdisciplinary Dialogue on Teaching Native Religions." *American Indian Quarterly* 20.3 (1996): 433–50.

Hall, Nor, and Warren R. Dawson. *Broodmales.* Dallas: Spring, 1989.

Hardacre, Helen. *Marketing the Menacing Fetus in Japan.* Berkeley and Los Angeles: University of California Press, 1997.

Harwood, W. S. "Secret Societies in America." *North American Review* 164 (1897): 620–23.

Herdt, Gilbert H. *The Sambia: Ritual and Gender in New Guinea.* New York: Holt, Rinehart and Winston, 1987.

Hertz, R. *Death and the Right Hand.* New York: Free, 1960.

Hill, Paul, Jr. "Africentric Rites of Passage: Nurturing the Next Generation." *Reaching Today's Youth: The Community Circle of Caring Journal of the National Educational Service* 3.1 (1998): 9–13.

———. "Back to the Future." *Journal of African American Men* 1.1 (1995): 41–61.

———. *Coming of Age: African American Male Rites-of-Passage.* Chicago: African American Images, 1992.

———. *The Journey (Adolescent Rites of Passage): Organizational Manual.* Cleveland: National Rites of Passage Institute, 1998.

———. "Rites of Passage Ceremony." Unpublished typescript. Cleveland: National Rites of Passage Institute, n.d.

Hoffman, Lawrence A. *Covenant of Blood: Circumcision and Gender in Rabbinic Judaism.* Chicago: University of Chicago Press, 1996.

———. "The Jewish Wedding Ceremony." In *Life Cycles in Jewish and Christian Worship,* ed. Paul F. Bradshaw and Lawrence A. Hoffman, 129–53. Notre Dame, IN: University of Notre Dame Press, 1996.

Humphrey, Caroline, and James Laidlaw. *The Archetypal Actions of Ritual.* Oxford, England: Oxford University Press, 1994.

Huntington, Richard, and Peter Metcalf. *Celebrations of Death: The Anthropology of Mortuary Rituals.* New York: Cambridge University Press, 1979.

Johnston, Mary. *Roman Life.* Chicago: Scott, Foresman, 1957.

Jones, Jefferson. "Rites 101." www.ritesofpassage.org/drum2.htm.

Jordan, Brigitte. *Birth in Four Cultures.* Montreal: Eden, 1983.

Judge, Maureen, dir. *Unveiled: The Mother-Daughter Relationship.* Color film, 55 minutes. N.p.: Makin' Movies and the National Film Board of Canada, 1997.

Kapadia, K. M. "Hindu Marriage a Sacrament." In *Marriage and Family in India,* 167–97. London: Oxford University Press, 1966.

Kaplan, E. Ann. "Look Who's Talking Indeed: Fetal Images in Recent North American Visual Culture." In *Mothering: Ideology, Experience, and Agency,* ed. Evelyn Nakano Glenn et al., 121–37. New York: Routledge, 1994.

Kastenbaum, Robert J. *Death, Society, and Human Experience.* 6th ed. Boston: Allyn and Bacon, 1998.

Katz, Richard, et al. *Healing Makes Our Hearts Happy*. Rochester, VT: Inner Traditions, 1997.

Kavanagh, Aidan. *The Shape of Baptism: The Rite of Christian Initiation*. Collegeville, MN: Liturgical, 1991.

Kitahara, Michio. "A Function of Marriage Ceremony." *Anthropologica* 16.2 (1974): 163–75.

Klassen, Pamela E. "Blessed Events: Religion and Gender in the Practice of Home Birth." Ph.D. diss., Drew University, 1997.

Kleinman, Arthur. *The Illness Narratives*. New York: Basic, 1988.

Kluger-Bell, Kim. *Unspeakable Losses*. New York: W. W. Norton, 1998.

Kratz, Corrine A. *Affecting Performance: Meaning, Movement, and Experience in Okiek Women's Initiation*. Washington, DC: Smithsonian Institution, 1994.

Kvaerne, Per. *Tibet Bon Religion: A Death Ritual of the Tibetan Bonpos*. Leiden: E. J. Brill, 1985.

Laake, Deborah. *Secret Ceremonies: A Mormon Woman's Intimate Diary of Marriage and Beyond*. New York: William Morrow, 1993.

Laderman, Carol. *Wives and Midwives: Childbirth and Nutrition in Rural Malaysia*. Berkeley and Los Angeles: University of California Press, 1983.

Laderman, Gary. *The Sacred Remains: American Attitudes Toward Death, 1799–1883*. New Haven, CT: Yale University Press, 1996.

LaFleur, William. *Liquid Life: Abortion and Buddhism in Japan*. Princeton, NJ: Princeton University Press, 1992.

Laird, Joan. "Women and Ritual in Family Therapy." In *Rituals in Families and Family Therapy*, ed. Evan Imber-Black et al. New York: W. W. Norton, 1988.

Lalli, Cele G., and Stephanie H. Dahl. "How to Bring Ethnic Customs to Your Wedding." *Modern Bride* (February/March 1994), 558–64.

Langness, L. L. "Hysterical Psychosis in the New Guinea Highlands: A Bena Bena Example." *Psychiatry* 28 (1965): 259–77.

Lewis, Oscar. *A Death in the Sanchez Family*. New York: Random House, 1969.

Lincoln, Bruce. *Emerging from the Chrysalis: Studies in Rituals of Women's Initiation*. Cambridge, MA: Harvard University Press, 1981.

Littman, Lynne, director. *In Her Own Time*. 60 minutes. U.S.A.: Direct Cinema, 1986. Videocassette.

Lowrey, Tina M., and Cele Otnes. "Construction of a Meaningful Wedding: Differences in the Priorities of Brides and Grooms." In *Gender Issues and Consumer Behavior*, ed. Janeen Arnold Costa, 164–83. Thousand Oaks, CA: Sage, 1994.

Lutkehaus, Nancy C. "Gender Metaphors: Female Rituals as Cultural Models in Manam." In *Gender Rituals: Female Initiation in Melanesia*, 183–204. New York: Routledge, 1995.

Mahdi, Louise Carus. "A Note on the Vision Quest." In *Crossroads: The Quest for Contemporary Rites of Passage*, ed. Louise Carus Mahdi et al., 355–57. Chicago: Open Court, 1996.

Majumdar, R. C., editor. *The Age of Imperial Unity*. Bombay: Bharatiya Vidya Bhavan, 1953.

Marcus, Ivan G. *Rituals of Childhood: Jewish Acculturation in Medieval Europe.* New Haven, CT: Yale University Press, 1984.

Martens, Katherine, and Heidi Harms, eds. and trans. *In Her Own Voice: Childbirth Stories from Mennonite Women.* Winnipeg, Canada: University of Manitoba Press, 1977.

McGrath, Mary Ann, and Basil English. "Intergenerational Gift-Giving in Subcultural Wedding Celebrations: The Ritual Audience as Cash Cow." In *Gift-Giving: A Research Anthology,* ed. Cele Otnes and Richard F. Beltramini, 123–41. Bowling Green, OH: Popular, 1996.

McLaren, Peter. *Schooling as Ritual Performance: Towards a Political Economy of Educational Symbols and Gestures.* 2d ed. London: Routledge, 1993.

Mesteth, Wilmer Stampede, and others. "Declaration of War against Exploiters of Lakota Spirituality." Available at maple.lemoyne.edu/~bucko/war.html.

Milloy, John. *A National Crime: The Canadian Government and the Residential School System, 1879 to 1986.* Winnipeg: University of Manitoba Press, 1999.

Miner, Horace. "Body Ritual Among the Nacirema." In *Culture, Curers, and Contagion,* ed. Norman Klein, 9–14. Novato, CA: Chandler & Sharp, 1979.

Monsivais, Carlos. " 'Look Death, Don't Be Inhuman': Notes on a Traditional and Industrial Myth." In *El Dia de los Muertos: The Life of the Dead in Mexican Folk Art,* ed. Fort Worth Art Museum, 11–16. Fort Worth, TX: Fort Worth Art Museum, 1987.

Moore, Robert, and Doug Gillette. "The Crisis in Masculine Ritual Process." In *To Be a Man,* ed. Keith Thompson, 43–46. New York: Tarcher/Putnam, 1991.

Myerhoff, Barbara G. "A Death in Due Time: Construction of Self and Culture in Ritual Drama." In *Rite, Drama, Festival, Spectacle: Rehearsals Toward a Theory of Cultural Performance,* ed. John J. MacAloon, 149–78. Philadelphia: Institute for the Study of Human Issues, 1984.

Noel, Daniel C. *The Soul of Shamanism: Western Fantasies, Imaginal Realities.* New York: Continuum, 1997.

Norbeck, Edward, et al. "The Interpretation of Data: Puberty Rites." *American Anthropologist* 64 (1962): 463–85.

Nuland, Sherwin B. *How We Die: Reflections on Life's Final Chapter.* New York: Knopf, 1994.

Oakley, John H., and Rebecca H. Sinos. *The Wedding in Ancient Athens.* Madison: University of Wisconsin Press, 1993.

O'Connor, John J., and Aaron Noah Hoorwitz. "Imitative and Contagious Magic in the Therapeutic Use of Rituals with Children." In *Rituals in Families and Family Therapy,* ed. Evan Imber-Black, Janine Roberts, and Richard Whiting, 135–57. New York: Norton, 1988.

Oldfield, David. "The Journey of the Adolescent Soul." In *Nourishing the Soul,* ed. Anne Simpkinson et al., 217–30. San Francisco: HarperSanFrancisco, 1995.

Ortiz, Alfonso. "On Becoming a Pueblo Sacred Clown." Unpublished paper. N.p., 1977.

Otnes, Cele. " 'Friend of the Bride'—and Then Some: Roles of the Bridal Salon During Wedding Planning." In *Servicescapes,* ed. John F. Sherry, 229–57. Lincolnwood, IL: NTC, 1998.

Otnes, Cele, and Linda M. Scott. "Something Old, Something New: Exploring the Interaction between Ritual and Advertising." *Journal of Advertising* 25.1 (1996): 33–50.

Paige, Karen Ericksen, and Jeffrey M. Paige. *The Politics of Reproductive Ritual.* Berkeley and Los Angeles: University of California Press, 1981.

Peay, Pythia. "The Singing Sword: Images Guide Adolescents' Journeys." *Common Boundary* (January–February 1990), 1–3.

Pleck, Elizabeth. "Celebrating the Family: Gender, Ethnicity and Consumer Culture in American Domestic Rituals." Unpublished manuscript. University of Illinois, 1997.

Priya, Jacqueline Vincent. *Birth Traditions & Modern Pregnancy Care.* Rockport, MA: Element, 1992.

Prothero, Stephen. "To Bury or to Burn? Cremation in American Culture, 1874 to the Present." Unpublished manuscript. Berkeley and Los Angeles: University of California, 1998.

Rabuzzi, Kathryn Allen. *Mother with Child: Transformations through Childbirth.* Bloomington: Indiana University Press, 1994.

———. *Motherself: A Mythic Analysis of Motherhood.* Bloomington: Indiana University Press, 1988.

Rappaport, Roy A. *Ecology, Meaning, and Religion.* Berkeley, CA: North Atlantic, 1979.

Rawski, Evelyn S. "A Historian's Approach to Chinese Death Ritual." In *Death Ritual in Late Imperial and Modern China,* ed. James L. Watson and Evelyn S. Rawski, 20–34. Berkeley and Los Angeles: University of California Press, 1988.

Roberts, William O., Jr. *Initiation to Adulthood: An Ancient Rite of Passage in Contemporary Form.* New York: Pilgrim, 1982.

Roloff, Leland. "Yes, We Carry On." In *Crossroads: The Quest for Contemporary Rites of Passage,* ed. Louise Carus Mahdi et al., 331–33. Chicago: Open Court, 1996.

Roscoe, Paul B. "In the Shadow of the Tambaran: Female Initiation Among the Ndu of the Sepik Basis." In *Gender Rituals: Female Initiation in Melanesia,* 55–82. New York: Routledge, 1995.

Ross, Colin A. *Satanic Ritual Abuse: Principles of Treatment.* Toronto: University of Toronto Press, 1995.

Ross-Macdonald, Jane. *Alternative Weddings.* London: Thorsons, 1996.

Roth, Philip. "The Conversion of the Jews." In *The Rite of Becoming: Stories and Studies of Adolescence,* ed. Arthur Waldhorn and Hilda Waldhorn, 212–27. New York: New American Library, 1966.

Sanyika, Dadisi. "Gang Rites and Rituals of Initiation." In *Crossroads: The Quest for Contemporary Rites of Passage,* ed. Louise Carus Mahdi et al., 115–24. Chicago: Open Court, 1996.

Schechner, Richard. *Essays in Performance Theory, 1970–1976.* New York: Drama Book, 1977.

Scheper-Hughes, Nancy. *Death Without Weeping: The Violence of Everyday Life in Brazil.* Berkeley and Los Angeles: University of California Press, 1992.

Schlegel, Alice, and Herbert Barry III. *Adolescence: An Anthropological Inquiry.* New York: Free Press, 1991.

———. "The Evolutionary Significance of Adolescent Initiation Ceremonies." *American Ethnologist* 7.4 (1980): 696–715.

Searle, Mark, and Kenneth Stevenson. *Documents of the Marriage Liturgy.* Collegeville, MN: Pueblo, 1992.

Sekaquaptewa, Helen. *Me and Mine: The Life Story of Helen Sekaquaptewa as Told to Louise Udall.* Tucson: University of Arizona Press, 1969.

Sexton, Lorraine. "Marriage as the Model for a New Initiation Ritual." In *Gender Rituals: Female Initiation in Melanesia,* ed. Nancy C. Lutkehause and Paul B. Roscoe, 205–16. New York: Routledge, 1995.

Shahar, Shulamith. "A Child Is Born." In *Childhood in the Middle Ages,* 32–52. London: Routledge, 1990.

Sharma, Aravind. *Sati: Historical and Phenomenological Essays.* Delhi: Motilal Banarsidass, 1988.

Sheehy, Gail. *New Passages: Mapping Your Life Across Time.* New York: Random House, 1995.

Shorter, Edward. "The Traditional Pattern: Family and Community in Birth, Marriage, and Death." In *The Making of the Modern Family,* 213–34. New York: Basic, 1975.

Shostak, Marjorie. *Nisa: The Life and Words of a !Kung Woman.* New York: Vintage, 1981.

Singh, Nikky-Guninder Kaur. "Religious Life and Rites of Passage." In *Sikhism,* 64–85. New York: Facts on File, 1993.

Smith, Bardwell. "Buddhism and Abortion in Contemporary Japan." In *Readings in Ritual Studies,* ed. Ronald L. Grimes, 458–73. Upper Saddle River, NJ: Prentice-Hall, 1996.

Smith, J. *The Creative Wedding.* Holbrook, MA: Bob Adams, 1994.

Strathern, Marilyn. *Reproducing the Future: Anthropology, Kinship and the New Reproductive Technologies.* New York: Routledge, 1992.

Sullwold, Edith. "Rites of Passage at the End of the Millennium." In *Crossroads: The Quest for Contemporary Rites of Passage,* ed. Louise Carus Mahdi et al., 287–90. Chicago: Open Court, 1996.

Tanner, Jerald, and Susan Tanner. "Temple Ritual Altered: Mormon Leaders Delete Some of the Most Sacred Parts of the Ceremony." *Salt Lake City Messenger,* no. 75 (1990). Available at www.xmission.com/~country/reason/temple1.htm.

Turner, Victor. *The Forest of Symbols: Aspects of Ndembu Ritual.* Ithaca, NY: Cornell University Press, 1967.

United States Catholic Conference. *Catholic Household Blessings & Prayers.* Washington, DC: United States Catholic Conference, 1988.

Van Gennep, Arnold. *The Rites of Passage.* Trans. Monika B. Vizedom and Gabrielle L. Caffee. Chicago: University of Chicago Press, 1960.

Wall, Kathleen. *The Callisto Myth from Ovid to Atwood: Initiation and Rape in Literature.* Kingston and Montreal: McGill-Queen's University Press, 1988.

Watson, Burton, trans. *Basic Writings of Mo Tzu, Hsun Tzu, and Han Fei Tzu.* New York: Columbia University Press, 1963.

Watson, James. "The Structure of Chinese Funerary Rites." In *Death Ritual in Late Imperial and Modern China,* ed. James L. Watson and Evelyn S. Rawski, 3–19. Berkeley and Los Angeles: University of California Press, 1988.

White, Mark. "Death in the People's Republic of China." In *Death Ritual in Late Imperial and Modern China,* ed. James L. Watson and Evelyn S. Rawski, 289–316. Berkeley and Los Angeles: University of California Press, 1988.

Whiting, John W. M., et al. "The Function of Male Initiation Ceremonies at Puberty." In *Readings in Social Psychology,* ed. Eleanor E. Maccoby et al., 359–70. New York: Holt, Rinehart, and Winston, 1958.

Wolford, Lisa, and Richard Schechner, eds. *The Grotowski Sourcebook.* London: Routledge, 1997.

Young, Frank W. *Initiation Ceremonies: A Cross-Cultural Study of Status Dramatization.* Indianapolis: Bobbs-Merrill, 1965.

weddings (*continued*)
cultural elements in, 209; cultural variation in, 192; customized, 308; in daylight, 203; determining omens for, 196;
as distinct from marriages, 156; do-it-
yourself, 206; eclecticism of, 208; elements of, 171, 195; ethnic, 206; European and Japanese, 172; European-
American, 192; "event," 207; and
farces, 189; features of traditional, 206;
and fidelity, 163; front- and backstage,
158; gowns for, burial in, 244; Greek, as
religious events, 195; guarding chamber
door at, 195; as "her" day, 167; and
happy endings, 152, 189; Hindu, 177,
181, 192; history of, summarized, 203;
in homes and churches, 202; hymns,
194; images for, 154; immediately after
initiation, 295; interfaith, 207; Japanese,
170, 172, 210; Jewish, 200; joking in,
175; kinds of, 205; kinds of Roman,
197; lack of structural integrity in, 210;
lesbian, 211, 214; in liturgies, 204; manuals for, 154; Mormon, 164; as most
conspicuous public occasion, 193; as
mystically bonding, 169; mythic, 211; as
North American rites of passage, 152; as
objects of fantasy, 154; pagan, 207; parlors for, 173–74; "perfect," 11; as performances, 163; performed in commercial
establishments, 174; phases of, 199; and
photography, 163; planners of, 307; polarized feelings about, 191; preparation
for, 157; as prerequisites for sex, 161; as
public performance of romantic love,
162; purposes of, 210; reasons for, 162;
as religious events, 205; rings for, 196;
Roman, 196, 198; royal Thai, 186; as
sacraments of fidelity, 191; sacred and
civic, 191; same-sex, 207; saving money
for, 173; seventh century Christian, 201;
Sikh, 170; sites for, 205; and stereotypes,
163; and story of Demeter and Persephone, 353n200; tasks of, 171; term
wedding, 213; Thai, 186, 189, 190; tradition and innovation in, 208; traditional, 154; and transferring of females,
196; two phases of, 202; undoing, 320;
vows in, 156; and Welfare State Interna-

tional, 77; and Westernization, 173;
what they should do, 211; white, 155,
171, 205; in worship services, 202
Welfare State International, 76, 83; and
ritualizing, 347n7
Western Attitudes toward Death, 222
Westminster Cathedral, 277–79
White Crane Palace, 173
widow-burning, 299–302
Widow Remarriage Act, 353n192
widowers, 249
widows, 220, 247, 249–50, 299, 300;
burning in Bengal, 299–302; and property, 301; shunning, 299
Wilfrid Laurier University, 327
Williamson, Cris, 322
Willis, Luana Lynette, 211–14
wills, 220–21
wine, 52, 199, 200, 202, 211, 248, 323,
324, 345
winkte, 38
witchcraft, and baptism, 52
witnesses, 54, 82, 163, 170, 203; to
death, 225; for divorce rites, 323; in
Greek weddings, 193; in weddings,
197–98, 202
Witts, Katherine Bronia and Thomas
Christopher Llewellyn, 79
wives, 46, 47, 83, 168, 169, 195, 249,
295
womanhood, 93, 109, 155; and giving
birth, 314
women: and death, 249; and Japanese
abortion rites, 311; Lakota, 37; Malay,
23
Women of Brewster Place, The, 91
Women as Mothers, 20
wonder, as ritual attitude, 132
World Wide Cemetery, 274–75
worship, 2, 7, 28, 44, 49–50, 70, 81, 182,
202, 204, 250, 294, 304, 325
Wounded Knee, 38–40

Yangoru, the, 126–27
Yoruba, the, 43–44, 145, 308

Zaire, 218
Zunz, Leopold, 73

Design: Nola Burger
Text: 10/13 Sabon
Display: Sabon
Composition: Binghamton Valley Composition
Printing and binding: IBT